LIVING ABROAD

Costa Rica

FIRST EDITION

Erin Van Rheenen

© Ruben Piña

AVALON
TRAVEL

CONTENTS

PRIME LIVING LOCATIONS 267

RESOURCES 381

About the Author

© Nancy Romaine

Erin Van Rheenen began her career as a serial relocatee at the age of five, when her parents moved the family from Oregon to Nigeria. Most of her adopted locales, however, would turn out to be in Latin America, and included Ecuador, Guatemala, and Mexico.

In 2002 she arrived in Costa Rica, thinking she had it made. Her Spanish was good, she had a degree in Latin American literature, and she'd already adapted to many new countries. What more did she need?

Plenty, it turned out. Knowing all the conjugations of the verb "jump," for instance, won't help when the locals tell you that you need a *chapulín* (grasshopper) to pull your rented 4x4 out of the river. And having read dozens of Latin American novels doesn't make it any easier to decipher Costa Rica's labyrinthine medical system.

Erin now knows that a *chapulín* can be more than a hopping insect, and that medical care in Costa Rica, once translated, rivals that available in the United States. As for discovering the lush variety of this tiny country, that's a lesson Erin is happy to keep on learning.

Erin has been writing since she can remember, and in 1998 won the Pirate's Alley Faulkner Society prize for best new novel. More recently she has published essays and articles in venues including *Passionfruit: A Women's Travel Journal* and *The Sun.* She has also taught writing at City College of New York and at the San Francisco County Jail. She is a member of Bay Area Travel Writers.

Erin can be reached through her website, www.livingabroadincosta rica.com.

Preface

I made the final decision to move to Costa Rica in mid-August, just as my garden was in late summer bloom. I touched down in San José less than three months later, in October, the end of the rainy season, when tropical rains come down hard every afternoon, transforming the landscape into a riot of lush green that needs no tending to thrive.

During those brief months between the seed of the idea and the fruition of the dream, I scrambled to prepare for the big move. First, a host of questions needed to be answered. Would I rent or sell my house? What would I do about health insurance, bank accounts, credit cards, and my reliance on email and the Internet? In short, I was confronted with the basic questions that accompany any big life change: What would I take with me, and what would I leave behind?

Though I don't recommend such a compressed time line to anyone thinking of making such a move, sometimes you need to seize the opportunity. When it dawned on me that every question I had, every other person moving to the "Switzerland of Central America" would also have, I went about my research with newfound energy and desire to explore every angle.

Since I planned to work full-time up until two weeks before my departure, I had to take care of everything in the margins of my old life. But as often happens when you decide on a new path, you begin to see your intended destination in everything around you. Costa Rica was everywhere! I called AAA to ask if my membership had any benefits that extended abroad; the woman on the phone had just returned from Costa Rica. The beaches, she sighed. The forests. The cute little monkeys! It turned out that a colleague's brother went down regularly for month-long surfing stints. It's like no place else, he said. Everything there is so alive. A friend had a friend who with her husband had bought a bakery in a small town three hours from San José; would I like her email address? What began as peripheral to my everyday life started to push itself in to the very center.

Which is as it should be: You need to let the country take you, at least a little bit. To open up a space where the idea of living there can grow. But you're in luck—you've chosen to consider life in one of the most fertile places on earth. If it can't grow in Costa Rica, it can't grow anywhere. This book will help you determine whether this particular deep-green dream corresponds to what you've been longing for. And if it is, this book will help you make that dream a reality.

—Erin Van Rheenen

Introduction

© Erin Van Rheenen

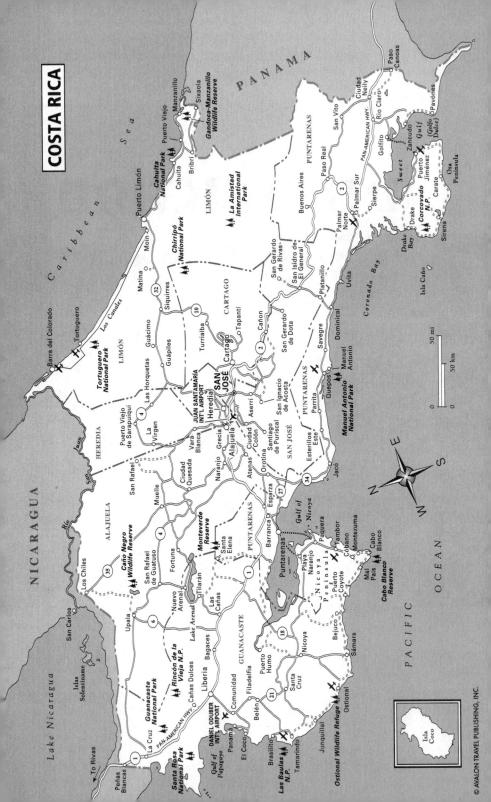

Welcome to Costa Rica

Are you ready for a change? Is it time to trade your old life for one that's a little more *livable?*

Picture a place so green you'll need new words to describe all of the different shades. A place with a thousand kinds of butterflies and half again as many types of orchids. A land where staying healthy is less a matter of doctors' visits and medication than of living simply in healthful surroundings.

Imagine a stable democracy where foreign business is encouraged even as the environment is protected. A country with near-universal health care and one of the highest literacy rates in the Western Hemisphere. A place where you can get away from it all without leaving behind your creature comforts, where you have both birdsong in the morning and the chirp of a modem making contact with the rest of the world.

The small but fertile nation of Costa Rica has been called many things: the Green Republic, the Switzerland of Central America, a Central American success story. Since 1889, only two brief periods

---

What I Love About Costa Rica

- Waiters and shopgirls call me *mi amor* (my love) or *mi reina* (my queen)

- Fathers here are so affectionate with their kids

- You can buy single cigarettes at kiosks and *pulperías,* thereby pretending that you're not really a smoker

- Roses and hibiscus, palm trees and pine, all grow in the same Central Valley backyard

- Good seats at a play in a venerable old theater cost around US$6

- Even on crowded city sidewalks, Ticos manage not to run into each other or poke each other with dripping umbrellas

- Fresh-squeezed orange juice costs about US$.35 from a streetside cart

- You'll never catch this country declaring war

---

of violence have interrupted its democratic development. Its economy has a solid agricultural base, and has expanded to include vibrant technology and tourism sectors. The standard of living is high and the cost of living moderate.

While many neighboring countries contend with war, death squads, and military dictatorships, Ticos (Costa Ricans) visit the polls to vote in multi-party elections. Since 1948, the country has had no army. The funds that would have gone to tanks and rocket launchers are invested in education and health care. And while many Latin American countries have a wealth of natural beauty, Costa Rica squeezes 5 to 6 percent of all known plant and animal species onto less than .03 percent of the world's land mass. Since the national park system began in the 1970s, the country has set aside a full quarter of its territory for the preservation of this living heritage.

Of course the nation is no utopia. Costa Rica is by no means undiscovered, and in fact may be a victim of its own popularity. Tourism has mushroomed into an industry sometimes at odds with environmental protection. The influx of foreign visitors and residents can strain basic infrastructure. Estimates are that at least 200,000 foreign residents live in the Central Valley alone. "We weren't ready for all of you," laughs Anabelle Furtado, a Costa Rica native who works for the Association of Residents of Costa Rica (ARCR; see Contacts in the Resources section). Economic hard times have meant cuts in previously flush social services, and locals complain that foreigners, with their easy spending habits, drive up prices on everything from pineapples to a four-bedroom house. And as in most countries of the world, crime and other social ills are on the rise.

Still, the benefits outweigh the problems. Costa Rica has an immensely appealing combination of the exotic and the familiar—primordial rain forests and modern urban centers, jaguars in the jungle and house cats in the suburbs. It's a far-off land less than three hours by air from Miami, an international destination with a decidedly local feel, a sophisticated place where life is still fueled by basic human warmth.

Tell anyone you're on your way to Costa Rica and they'll sigh with envy. If they haven't been here, it's high on their list. If they've already visited, they feel they've discovered gold and want to hurry back to mine that vein. Those ready to take the next step—to morph from visitor to resident—will discover a more complex alloy, as real life is always richer than fantasy.

Why People Come to Costa Rica

More and more North Americans are looking for a place to start a new life—whether it's for retirement, a career change, or plying one's current profession in a new market. Millions are choosing to live abroad, with many drawn to the physical beauty and lower prices of places like Costa Rica.

Many North American workers have been "made redundant" by on-going corporate efforts to reduce operating costs. A June 2003 article in *The New York Times* explored what it termed the "sink-or-swim" U.S. economy. As writer Harris Collingwood pointed out, "The big picture shows the economy tracing a gentle, rather lazy slope—a few tenths of a percentage point up or down, nothing too drastic. Closer to ground level, meanwhile, the action is nonstop and frenetic"—100,000 people lost their jobs in December 2003 alone.

Other workers retain jobs that they feel are sucking the life out of them, and dream of a time when they can get back in touch with themselves and with simple pleasures. Many fantasize about a place where the living is cheaper and the pace more humane. Parents of young children may long for an environment where kids can be immersed in another language and culture, one that emphasizes basic human values over relentless accomplishment and acquisition.

And for those approaching retirement age (or already there), places like Costa Rica are looking better and better. Persons over 65 make up one of the fastest-growing segments of the U.S. population. The availability of public services has already declined, and nursing homes have been reducing the number of Medicaid admissions. In 2003, 79 percent of U.S. citizens retiring had total assets of less than US$45,000 and yearly incomes—including pension and Social Security—of less than US$15,000. That's very little money to live on, at least in the United States. But US$15,000 a year goes a lot further in a place like Costa Rica.

Across the Atlantic, some of the same forces are at play. The United Nations estimates that by the year 2050, 29 percent of Europeans will be over the age of 65, with the continent's current low fertility rate—1.4 births per woman—a contributing factor. Europe, like the United States, will face the challenge of providing for older citizens even as the percentage of working adults decreases. A recent poll in Germany, for example, found that 55 percent of Germans believe that their pension system, long considered a crucial part of the country's generous social programs, is in trouble.

I WAS CALLED HERE

Beyond economic factors, and even beyond the longing for a better quality of life, there are more mysterious reasons why people come to Costa Rica.

There's a phrase in Spanish that speaks of fate and destiny: *está escrito*, or *it is written*. Ticos—on average more passive and superstitious (more accepting and spiritual?) than North Americans—use the phrase often. What's surprising is how often that same sentiment comes from foreign residents as they try to explain what brought them to Costa Rica.

I've spoken with an unexpected number of expats who talk of being "called" here. It comes in different language depending on the slant of the speaker, but I've heard "I came here in trust," "I followed my heart/gut/dreams," and "God/Spirit/the Turtles told me to come." We're not just talking evangelists or eco-activists or folks who tune into alien radio with their fillings. These are average North Americans, which is to say logical, restless, and driven. It's just that they've chosen to pay attention to the signals we all get but usually ignore—the messages to slow down, to open up, and to get yourself to a place where life slows down enough to let you jump on board.

So while all sorts of people end up in Costa Rica, there's a definite contingent of individuals who feel that in coming here they've answered a call. I'm not sure why at this point in world history Costa Rica seems to have a certain draw for a certain kind of people, but again and again I meet people who speak in these exalted terms. It can be inspiring, it can get on your nerves, and sometimes—like with the Canadian man who came to Manuel Antonio to chase the devil out of Costa Rica's favorite national park—it can make you shake your head in wonder.

What's an Expat?

Expat is short for expatriate, which doesn't have anything to do with patriotism, though the words are often confused because of their similarity. An expatriate (expat) is anyone who lives outside of his or her country, temporarily or permanently.

Some come here to save the world, others just to save themselves—from a lifetime of all work and no play if nothing else. Whatever their project, the people who come to Costa Rica often have a lot of heart and not a little nerve. Many hope to live in harmony with nature and to learn from the slower, less driven culture. These efforts meet with varying degrees of success, but at least most people have good intentions, which makes for a positive expat environment.

The bottom line is, if a voice is telling you to come to Costa Rica, why not listen? However crazily you come to it, it may be the sanest choice you ever make.

POLITICAL AND ECONOMIC STABILITY

Costa Rica boasts one of the most stable democratic governments in all of Latin America, and an economy that has long attracted foreign investors. Multinational corporations with branches in Costa Rica include Intel, Johnson & Johnson, Colgate-Palmolive, Monsanto, and Pfizer. All the baseballs used in the Major Leagues are sewn by hand in one small Costa Rican town called Turrialba, and even Wonderbras are assembled here. The United States is Costa Rica's most important trade partner, and the government here offers generous incentives to foreign businesses, including tax breaks and exemptions from some export tariffs. Big and small companies come to Costa Rica because of the solid telecommunications network, a very educated workforce, and a high standard of living.

It's easy for a foreigner to start a business here—you can do it even if you only have a tourist visa. Many expats work successfully in the burgeoning tourist sector, starting restaurants, hotels, and tour companies. Many say that although there are of course regulations to learn about and follow, in general there exist fewer constraints on businesses here than in their home countries.

AWARD-WINNING FRIENDLINESS

It's long been agreed that Costa Ricans are exceptionally friendly, but in 2003 science confirmed that impression. A study published in *American Scientist* revealed that, of 23 cities worldwide, San José ranked number two in Latin America in terms of friendliness (Rio de Janeiro came in first). The six-year study measured "simple acts of kindness," ranging from whether passersby returned a dropped pen to whether a blind man got help crossing a street. The Costa Rican capital received consistently high marks in every category. Robert Levine, the head of the study, commented that the cities with the friendliest inhabitants were ones where the pace of life was slower, and where the culture emphasized the value of social harmony.

And if San José qualifies as one of the friendliest cities in the world, then outside of the urban area, where life is slower, people are even friendlier. In small towns, everyone greets everyone else on the street, and citizens pitch in when their neighbors need help. Need to get to a bigger town? Start walking and you'll almost certainly get offered a ride. Need someone to look after your kids? Small-town folks routinely and casually trade child-care duties. If your car gets stuck in the mud, before you know it you'll have half a dozen people there to help you push it out. And the more generous you are, the more it comes back to you. Social scientists would call it reciprocity. Whatever you call it, it makes Costa Rica a very nice place to live.

UNIVERSAL HEALTH CARE

In 2004 more than 42 million U.S. citizens were without health insurance, and the number seems to be increasing every year. Costa Rica has made a commitment to provide health care to all of its residents, and even visitors can take advantage of the high-quality, low-cost care. For a small monthly fee (about US$60), residents can be a part of the public system that includes everything from drugs to dentistry, as well as care in public clinics and hospitals. For a little more each month, anyone (not just residents) can sign on with the INS, the state insurance provider—this route lets you choose your own doctor. International policies like Blue Cross/Blue Shield are accepted at the excellent private hospitals and clinics. If you have no insurance and don't want to join up with the public system, you can pay out-of-pocket and still spend a third less than you would in the United States.

And if you're cringing, thinking of third-world hospitals with poor hygiene and badly trained staff, think again. The University of Costa Rica has one of the most respected medical schools in all of Central America and the Caribbean, and many doctors do further study in Europe, Canada, or the United States. The private hospitals in particular have up-to-date equipment, like Hospital CIMA's open MRI, the only one in Central America. Confidence in the system is expressed by the number of people who come to Costa Rica just to have surgery, whether a facelift or a triple bypass.

An Overview of Costa Rica

At an outdoor café in downtown San José, the capital of Costa Rica, a gringo tourist is talking about his travel plans. "I want to get out of the city," he says. "See the rest of the island."

With the ease of air travel and North American ignorance of world geography, maybe it's not surprising to find a man sitting in San José who thinks he's in, say, San Juan, Puerto Rico. Many North Americans lump all south-of-the-border steamy vacation spots into a pleasant stew of palm trees, beach bunnies, and cute little monkeys.

And though this country has all that and more, Costa Rica is not an island. Sure, it lucked out with a disproportionate amount of coastline for such a small nation, but you won't find it on any map of the Caribbean. Look instead to the bent elbow of land that connects North and South America. Costa Rica rests in the crook of that arm, at the northern edge of

© Erin Van Rheenen

Banana and palm trees near Quepos, on the central Pacific coast

What's a Tico?

Costa Ricans love nicknames; they even have one that covers the entire population of their country. They call themselves Ticos, after the local habit of adding the diminutive to as many words as possible. While other Spanish speakers are likely to add "ito" to make a word like *chico* (small) even smaller *(chiquito)*, Costa Ricans would say *chiquitico*. *"Ya voy en un minutico,"* is Tico for "I'll be there in a tiny little minute." Of course, another Tico habit is lateness, so that tiny little minute may be closer to a big fat hour.

where North America funnels down into a narrow isthmus separating the Pacific and the Caribbean.

Talk about centrally located. Costa Rica lies at the hub of two continents, and at the crux of two geographic plates—the Cocos and the Caribbean. In millennia past, the isthmus served as a land bridge, allowing flora and fauna to come up from the south and trickle down from the north. The resulting diversity of plant and animal life is staggering. Imagine 1,400 species of orchids and more than 100 kinds of bats and you get a taste of the huge feast spread on this small table of a country.

THE LAY OF THE LAND

At 50,000 square kilometers (19,305 square mi.), Costa Rica is the second-smallest country in Central America, after El Salvador. Its Caribbean coastline is a mere 160 kilometers (99.4 mi.) long, while the Pacific coast, with more bays and peninsulas, measures 480 kilometers (298 mi.) from the Nicaraguan border to Panama. At its widest—280 kilometers (174 mi.)—Costa Rica is still a narrow country that can be traversed in a few hours.

The country doesn't feel so small when you're clanking along a rutted back road at 15 kph, wondering when you'll hit the next gas station, but it feels very intimate in terms of people. Sometimes the whole country feels like a small town. When I first arrived in San José, I met a North American named Jay who worked as a builder in the northern province of Guanacaste. He said he'd be happy to talk to me about his profession and his adopted country. When later I traveled to Gaunacaste, I had, of course, left Jay's number in my San José apartment. But when I looked up a friend of a San Francisco friend, it turned out he was working construction, and his boss was . . . Jay. Guanacaste, let me add, is not a small town. At around 10,000 square kilometers (3,861 square mi.), it's Costa Rica's second-largest province, with a population of about 280,000.

This wasn't an isolated case. The Italian woman I bummed a cigarette

On Caño Island, off the north side of the Osa Peninsula

from in a San José café? A month later I walked into a yoga class in the Pacific beach town of Nosara, and there she was. Even in the capital city I would often run into friends and acquaintances. And if you live in a small town (most of Costa Rica seems to be made up of small towns), you'll see people you know about seven times a day. "After a while," one local admits, "you just smile and nod. How many times can you ask after someone's kids, their mate, or their health?" But the fact that people do ask after your family and your health, and that they do smile and nod, makes Costa Rica a very friendly place indeed.

Country Divisions
Costa Rica is divided into seven provinces: San José, Heredia, Alajuela, Cartago, Puntarenas, Guanacaste, and Limón. In every province except Guanacaste, the province and its capital share the same name (Guanacaste's provincial capital is Liberia). San José, with nearly two million inhabitants, is by far the most populous province, while Puntarenas, which accounts for most of the country's Pacific coastline, is the largest. The provinces of San José, Cartago, Heredia, and Alajuela fan out from the Central Valley; the latter two stretch north all the way to the Nicaraguan border.

Each province is divided into counties, of which the country has 81. Counties are divided into districts; there are 449 districts in Costa Rica.

Locals also divide the country into "zones," which have less precise boundaries. There's the *Zona Norte* (Northern Zone), composed of the northern parts of Heredia and Alajuela, along with some of inland Guanacaste. From misty mountain towns to fiery Arenal Volcano to Caño Negro's flocks of roseate spoonbills and snowy egrets, the *Zona Norte* is nothing if not varied.

The *Zona Sur* (Southern Zone) is best known for spectacular Corcovado National Park, Costa Rica's Amazon, which takes up much of the Osa Peninsula. But the zone also includes inland marvels like Cerro Chirripó, at 3,820 meters (12,530 feet) the highest peak in the country, as well as cool and verdant towns like San Vito, not far from the Panamanian border. The large and placid Golfo Dulce (Sweet Gulf) is part of the *Zona Sur*, as are the fabled beaches along that gulf's eastern edge: Playa Zancudo and Pavones are the best-known of the seemingly endless number.

The *Zona Caribe* (Caribbean Zone) is almost, but not quite, synonymous with Limón province—the zone is mainly the Caribbean coast, while the province extends inland into mountain ranges like the mighty Talamanca. Many tourists know of the sea turtle migrations at Tortuguero National Park, some have heard of the famed *Salsa Brava* wave at Puerto Viejo, but only a select few have visited the indigenous reserves and the vast unexplored wilds inland from Costa Rica's lesser-known coast.

The Central Valley, sometimes called the *Meseta Central* or Central Mesa, is the heart of the country. Measuring about 80 by 40 kilometers (50 by 25 mi.), the area is ringed by a series of steep-sloped volcanoes, some of them still active. The capital city of San José lies at the center of the Central Valley, and at 1,150 meters (3,772 feet) enjoys year-round temperatures between 21°C and 26°C (70°F and 80°F).

Great Weather

Climate is one of the country's big draws. Those who've had it up to their wool turtlenecks with cold and snow find relief in Costa Rica's tropical sun and balmy breezes. The northern province of Guanacaste in particular is a sun-worshiper's dream, with hardly a drop of rain falling between December and May. The green season brings more rain, but even then showers are usually confined to afternoon and evening hours, with mornings as glorious as ever.

But if you've never been a beach person, don't worry. Even those who prefer cooler climes will thrive here. Temperature in Costa Rica is less a function of season than altitude, and you can fine-tune your weather

Just How Hot Is It?

If you're among that minority of world citizens who thinks 32 degrees means you better bundle up, it's time to learn about Celsius. Thirty-two-degree weather in Costa Rica means you better break out your bathing suit—it's almost 90°Farenheit.

To go from Celsius to Farenheit, multiply by 1.8, then add 32. To go the other way (Farenheit to Celsius), subtract 32, then divide by 1.8.

Below are the average temperatures in major Costa Rican cities on a day in late March.

City	Celsius	Farenheit
Alahuela	25	77
Golfito	29	84
Liberia	29	84
Limón	26	79
Puntarenas	28	82
Quepos	29	84
San José	23	73

by going up or down a few hundred meters. If you like an occasional bite in the air, just look for an emerald-green lot on the side of one of the (inactive) volcanoes, where the sun shines brightly at midday but where dawn and dusk bring cooling mists. At higher elevations you'll see pine trees alongside vine-draped tropical hardwoods.

The variety of climates means that the natural world is one of the most varied you'll ever see. Of course it helps that Costa Rica has set aside a quarter of its territory in parks and reserves where rare animals still roam freely. Jaguars, tapirs, sloths, and monkeys call this country's rain forests home, and get ready for a stunning variety of birds, including 50 species of hummingbird, various toucans and parrots, and the dazzling scarlet macaw.

Earthquakes and Volcanoes

Costa Rica is the child of a volatile but enduring relationship between sections of the earth's crust that both want to have—or rather *go*—their own way. The Caribbean and Coco plates come together just off Costa Rica's coast, and the resulting clash produces pent-up geological energy that finds release in earthquakes and volcanic eruptions. Of the county's 12 volcanoes, five are still active. Watching truck-sized hot rocks tumble down Arenal Volcano's perfect cone is a sight not soon forgotten, but even the wisps of smoke issuing from Rincon de la Vieja Volcano are impressive reminders that the earth's surface is still very much a work in progress.

Earthquakes have also played their part in teaching Ticos to respect the "fire down below." The colonial capital of Cartago was destroyed by quakes in 1841 and again in 1910. More recently, in 1991 a 7.5 earthquake rocked the Caribbean and South-Central zones, destroying the San

José–Limón railroad and countless roads and bridges. More gentle quakes are common, and geologists say the frequent tremors serve as relief valves to postpone the next really big one.

Volcanic peaks help make up the country's four major mountain ranges. In the north, the Cordillera de Guanacaste rises up in a series of peaks that includes Rincon de la Vieja, 1,895 meters (6,217 ft.) high and the centerpiece of a national park of the same name. The Cordillera de Tilarán is dominated by Arenal Volcano, one of the most active in the world. Hemming in the Central Valley to the east is the Cordillera Central, which includes Poás, Irazú, Barva, and Turrialba Volcanoes. To the south of the valley surges the Cordillera Talamanca.

A Green Republic

The varied terrain makes for an amazing number of microclimates, each with its own complicated ecosystem. Incredibly, only 18 percent of this biodiversity has been scientifically identified, making it all the more important to preserve the land until scientists can catch up with nature. Who knows if a cure for Alzheimer's or a solution to world hunger lies in the depths of the disappearing rain forest? The National Institute of Biodiversity (INBio), a joint public/private venture, is working hard to find out.

Costa Rica is one of the countries in the world most devoted to protecting its own environment—nearly 25 percent of national territory is set aside in parks and reserves. Still, there are serious challenges. The country doesn't have the money or human resources to enforce laws or patrol preserves. Poachers and lumber companies continue to chip away at the land ringing the protected areas, even making forays into national parks when they think they can get away with it. Another problem has been the government's inability to pay landowners for the territories expropriated for national parks. Sometimes these uncompensated landowners return to their land and continue farming, mining, or logging it.

Still, with all its problems, Costa Rica is teeming with life, and the country knows that it's this life that draws tourists. And since tourism is a huge business, there's yet another incentive to pass—and enforce—laws that protect the environment.

It's not only the land that boasts so many species; Costa Rica has ten times as much territory underwater as it does on land, and is working hard to protect everything from its giant sea turtles to its shark populations, recently threatened by the practice of finning—removing fins for the Asian markets in which they are a delicacy, while leaving the rest of the mutilated shark to a watery grave.

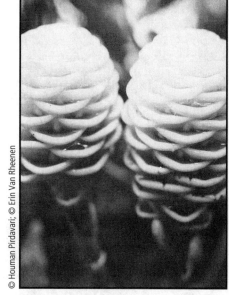

Flowers in rainy San Vito   Poison dart frog

On a happier note, the Tourism Institute has created a *Bandera Azul* (Blue Flag) program to recognize beach towns that commit to cleaning up their act. Program assessors look at not only whether there's trash on the beach, but also judge waste disposal, security issues, and environmental education efforts. More and more beaches, on both the Pacific and Caribbean coasts, are working to be green enough to fly the blue flag.

Local newspapers are filled with accounts of struggles to balance industries like fishing, mining, large-scale agriculture, and oil exploration with protection of the land. Some call Costa Rica hypocritical for billing itself a "green republic" while still allowing some exploitation of its natural resources, but it seems inevitable that there will be conflict and compromise along the road to balancing all the country's needs. Those who lament the sometimes slow progress and backsliding often take matters into their own hands, joining forces with national and international conservation organizations or even buying up land so developers won't be able to get their hands on it.

National Parks

The strength and importance of the National Conservation Area System (SINAC) is all the more impressive when you realize it began very recently—in the 1970s. And Costa Rica's 33 national parks are just the tip of

Entrance to Tortuguero National Park

the iceberg; there are also dozens of reserves and refuges that seek to protect varied habitats and ecosystems for both present and future generations.

By far the most popular park is Manuel Antonio on the central Pacific coast, with its beaches bordered by wildlife-rich rain forest and its location only a few hours from San José. Also popular and even closer to the capital are Braulio Carrillo, a teeming, dripping forest that you can see via aerial tram if you'd rather not get your shoes muddy; and stunning Irazú Volcano, from which on a clear day you can see both coastlines. More effort is required to get to two other popular parks: the Caribbean coast's Tortuguero, with its canals, crocs, turtles, and teeming bird population; and Corcovado, on the lushly wild Osa Peninsula. After you've visited the big guns of the system, it's a pleasure to start exploring the lesser-known and less-visited reserves, where you might see no one on the path for hours or even days.

One exciting development in the park system is the founding of international reserves. Parque Nacional la Amistad (Friendship Park) is a 622,000-hectare (1,537,000-acre) tract of remote forest that straddles the Costa Rica–Panama border. Up north, Sí-a-Paz (Yes to Peace) Park seeks to protect one of the last great stands of rain forest, shared by Costa Rica and Nicaragua. Extending even farther and involving more nations, the

MesoAmerican Biological Corridor aims to create a protected passage-way from Mexico all the way to Columbia. The isthmus once served as a land bridge for migrating species; the hope is that soon it will be able to serve that function once again.

Getting Around

With all the wild and rugged corners of this country, you might imagine that to get anywhere you'd need several weeks and a pair of seven-league boots. Not so. Costa Rica is small enough that you can snorkel the Caribbean in the morning and surf the Pacific in the afternoon. And if you choose to fly instead of drive, puddle jumpers will speed you to places that used to require a full day's (or two) journey. A 40-minute flight from San José puts you in Golfito (an eight-hour drive) for a day of sportfishing, then you can hop back up for a gourmet dinner in San José.

Those on a budget will appreciate the extensive network of buses that take you anywhere in the country for no more than US$12. Buses run often, they run on time, and most are at least as comfortable as the Grey-hounds you've ridden back home.

Renting a car is another option. A 4x4 will be your best bet, so that you

© Erin Van Rheenen

Carate airstrip

won't be denied if a highway suddenly peters out into rutted track. It's exhilarating to stop at nothing—not even a river—to get where you want to go. For those accustomed to glassy-smooth interstates, Costa Rica's roads will come as a shock, but soon enough you'll be four-wheeling with the best of them. Getting back on an easy track even starts to be somewhat of a disappointment, like eating a hot dog after you've been chewing on a char-grilled steak.

Oh, and getting to Costa Rica is easy. You don't need a visa—just a valid passport. Airfares from the United States and Canada are quite reasonable (typically US$400–700, depending on your departure city), and sometimes downright cheap. At the airport you'll get a stamp on your passport saying you have up to 90 days in the country. And if you have no interest in San José, international flights now speed you to Liberia, only half an hour from some of the best beaches in Guanacaste.

STANDARD OF LIVING

Newcomers to Costa Rica are often surprised that the country doesn't have that third-world, shanty-town look that they were expecting of a Central American "banana republic." Indeed, Costa Rica is a relatively well-off nation that takes care of its own much better than many more developed countries. Everyone here has access to decent health care and education, which makes for infant mortality rates up there with Canada and the United States, and literacy rates that rival those of Europe. People look healthy, and even those with little money take care to dress in clean, new-looking clothes. If you see someone with holes in his jeans, he's almost certainly a tourist, affecting a down-and-out look while no doubt having more money in his pocket than the smartly dressed locals.

Life here is not dirt cheap, but it's a lot less expensive than living in the United States or Canada—from 30 to 50 percent cheaper, depending on your lifestyle. A couple can live frugally but not without a few frills for US$1,500 a month. Travel within this small but wondrously varied country could be one of those frills, since buses are a bargain, and there are plenty of reasonably priced beachfront or mountaintop hotels.

Real estate is affordable, much more so if you stay away from the hottest markets, like well-known beach towns or upscale suburbs of San José. Many of the local financial institutions that were paying out astronomical interest rates to expats have recently gone belly up, bad news for investors but good news for those looking for a reasonably priced house or lot. The dollar is strong here and continues to grow stronger; just holding money in dollars is a form of investing here.

Schoolkids in San José

SOCIAL CLIMATE

"Stay a week and you think you know a country," goes the old adage. "Stay a year and you know you never will." When you first arrive in Costa Rica, you may be struck by how similar it is to the United States, especially in and around the capital city of San José. You'll see the same fast-food franchises, like McDonald's and KFC; the same stores, from Foot Locker to Office Max; and the same products in U.S.-style supermarkets, even Häagen-Dazs ice cream and Celestial Seasonings teas. Food labels are almost always in Spanish and English, and at ATMs you can opt for instructions in English.

When there's a problem here, people dial 911, just like in the States. On TV, many programs and even commercials are in English. In U.S.-style multiplex theaters in U.S.-style malls, you'll see trailers for the latest Hollywood movies as you munch on overpriced hot dogs and popcorn. And just like back home, you can drink the water—probably one of the most profound differences between Costa Rica and its Latin American neighbors. Somehow that small fact looms large, and is one of the many reasons North Americans feel comfortable here.

Stay a little longer and you start to notice the differences. "The idea that we're all the same is a myth," opines Joy Rothke, a freelance writer who moved to La Fortuna in 2002. "Sure, there may be superficial commonalities, but deep down, Costa Rican culture is very, very different from U.S. culture." This is doubly true for cities and towns outside the Central Valley.

An Unfinished Country

North Americans, especially when we travel to Europe, are used to feeling like the kids of the world—very young in comparison to much of world culture. But if the United States and Canada are cultural adolescents, Latin America is, in some ways, still in its infancy. Costa Rica, for example, is shaped by a constitution drafted in 1949, and nearly a third of the population is under the age of 14.

It's a country in progress, where the gap between law and law enforcement, between intention and actuality, is as wide as the crown of a Guanacaste tree. There is a rawness here that can be both liberating and exasperating. Laxity of law enforcement allows a certain freedom, but it also means that petty theft is a fact of life that individuals must deal with themselves by putting bars on windows and hiring security guards.

There are lots of laws, and at least as many ways around them. Building codes exist, for example, and you're supposed to apply for permits before you start work. But it can take years (literally) for permits to be issued, so some take the risk of doing without. One hotel owner relates that he built an addition to his hotel without bothering to apply for any of the necessary permits. After the addition was completed, he was fined a small amount for not going through the proper channels, but the fine was a fraction of what he would have had to pay to do it all legally.

Despite the frustration of inconsistently enforced laws, many people breathe a sigh of relief to be in a place where not everything is regulated. Along hiking trails you'll see no signs warning you away from cliffs—it's taken for granted that people look out where they're walking and have a vested interest in taking care of themselves. For that matter, you'll see no warnings along the highway that up ahead is a rain-filled pothole so big you'll need to hire a boat to get across.

If you want to sleepwalk through your days, don't come here. Being alert is the price you pay (or the reward) for not being told, at every turn, what to do. For those who adapt well to it, Costa Rica is the ideal place to live a rich, independent life, and a great place to make a fresh start. I hear story after story of troubles left behind in the home country, and a new life and sometimes new identity being forged successfully in this country where you can put a stick in the ground and watch it grow.

Life on a Human Scale

The independent spirit here coexists with a level of human warmth that has all but disappeared from many more-developed nations. Expats who stay here for a while and then go north for a visit are shocked all over again by the fact that "nobody talks to anyone else up there." It's a commonplace that is nonetheless true: In the United States, people live to work; in Costa Rica, they work to live.

Human interaction is far and away the most important thing here, and people take their time to say hello to neighbors or to make small talk with clerks and taxi drivers. This is true even in the relatively fast-paced capital city, but it is much more pronounced in small towns. I heard the story of some gringos in a rented 4x4 stopping on a dirt road to ask an old man for directions. "I'll be happy to tell you the best way there," replied the man. "But first: It's a pleasure to meet you." When you slow down enough to enjoy it, it will be a pleasure for you to meet the entire country.

History, Government, and Economy

History

Tens of thousands of years ago, early settlers in what is now Costa Rica hunted mastodon and giant sloth, tracking their prey through dripping tropical forests. Between 8000 and 4000 B.C., these nomadic bands learned to domesticate plants, and around the start of the Christian era, they made the transition to farming. Sedentary life brought on a more complex social hierarchy and division of labor. Instead of making only tools for hunting, like stone spearheads and knives, people began creating farming implements and vessels to cook and store their food.

Located on an isthmus between two great continents, Costa Rica was a meeting place for cultures from the south and the north. From South America came yucca, sweet potatoes, coca leaves for chewing, and Andean gold-working techniques. Tribes from the southern forests and Caribbean coast of Costa Rica traded with the peoples of Panama, Colombia, and

Guayabo National Monument

Guayabo Tombs

© Erin Van Rheenen

Ecuador. Other parts of the country—especially the Gran Nicoya, located in what is now Guanacaste—were more influenced by Mesoamerican cultures to the north. From Mesoamerica came corn, beans, jade, hieroglyphic books, the practice of filing teeth to points, and certain pottery styles still in use today.

There were cultural and linguistic differences among the many indigenous groups, but the tribes also had a lot in common. Most were matrilineal, and some—including the Chibchas and the Diquis—are said to have been matriarchal. Religious beliefs pivoted on the conviction that not only animals and plants were alive but that even natural phenomena like rivers and stones were animate and possessed their own spirit. Funeral rites implied a belief in an afterlife—ritual objects and even slaves were buried with the bodies of powerful women and men.

Tribes congregated in large and small settlements, and the village was, according to Molina and Palmer in *The History of Costa Rica,* "the axis of everyday life, which was taken up by agriculture, crafts, commerce, and war." Tribes and villages banded together to form *cacigazcos* (chiefdoms), and *cacigazcos* might unify into larger political and military alliances called *señoríos.*

In the Pacific Northwest of what's now Costa Rica, the *cacigazcos* of the

Gran Nicoya, influenced by Maya, Aztec, and Olmec culture, practiced human sacrifice and cannibalism. Three times a year, on dates coinciding with the corn harvest, the nobility dressed in their finery, drank *chicha* (corn liquor), and presided over the ritual murder of five or six pre-selected women and men. These chosen few had their hearts cut out, their heads chopped off, and their bodies rolled down the side of the temple—to later be eaten as the most sacred of food.

War was widespread and was waged for a variety of reasons: to expand or defend territory, to gain access to trade routes, or to take prisoners for slave labor or, in the case of women of childbearing age, to serve as breeders. In some areas, like the Diqui region in southern Costa Rica, both men and women went into battle together.

Remnants of the Past

The Museo Central estimates that in Costa Rica today, there are at least 2,000 archaeological sites, most of which are still buried in deep forest or under mounds of earth. The region that was the Gran Nicoya, now in Guanacaste, has the most sites, but the most accessible and fully excavated site is Guayabo, now a national monument. Located on the southern flank of Turrialba Volcano in the Central Valley, Guayabo shows us the remains of a settlement at its height between 1000 B.C. and A.D. 1400, when an estimated 10,000 people lived in its conical structures and walked its cobblestoned streets. An aqueduct system built more than 2,000 years ago still functions today.

Other sites take more effort to find and visit. Until Costa Rica can devote time and expertise to more excavations, locals will probably continue to stumble upon old stone roads and pre-Columbian artifacts half-buried in cattle pastures or strewn along centuries-old jungle paths.

One type of relic that is *puro Tico* (purely Costa Rican), is the *bola*, stone spheres found mostly in the southern part of the country near the Valley of Diquis. Researchers still can't say for sure how they were made or what their function was, but some of these strangely moving sculptures measure as much as 1.5 meters (4.9 ft.) across and weigh several tons. There are a few at the Museo Nacional, which may whet your appetite to see others in their original context, like the ones on Caño Island off the Osa Peninsula. Since the spheres are found nowhere else in the world, they have become a symbol for Costa Rica, and you'll see the *bola* motif worked into the architecture of government buildings and upscale homes.

Indigenous Culture Today

For years it was thought that as few as 30,000 people were living in Costa

White People Are Leaf-Cutter Ants

In the book *Taking Care of Sibö's Gifts*, coauthor Gloria Mayorga, of the Kéköldi Indigenous Reserve on Costa Rica's Caribbean coast, writes of the mythic origin of white people:

> The origin of white people is the King of Leaf-Cutter Ants. Just look at the leaf-cutter ants, how they all work together cleaning and clearing the land around their nests. Where the leaf-cutter ants live, all the vegetation is gone because they cut every last leaf and take them back to their big nests. That's how the white man is. He works very hard, but he destroys nature. He chops down all the trees to make his cities, and where he lives all the vegetation is gone. There is nothing there. The white man cuts down everything that is green, and where he lives there are no trees, no rivers, no animals. He destroys everything in his path.

Rica when the Spaniards arrived. This figure supported the myth that the country has little indigenous heritage, but more recent scholarship puts the number at between 400,000 and 500,000.

The half-million people here when Columbus landed in 1502 were reduced to 120,000 by 1569 and whittled down to 10,000 by 1611, mostly due to infectious diseases brought by the Spaniards. The 2000 census counted 63,876 indigenous persons, but one of the few books on indigenous Costa Rican culture by indigenous authors, *Taking Care of Sibö's Gifts*, by Paula Palmer, Juanita Sánchez, and Gloria Mayorga, says that fewer than 25,000 people here "retain a cultural identity as indigenous people." Whatever the true figure, native peoples make up only about 1 percent of the national population. Many live on one of 22 reserves, which collectively make up about 6 percent of national territory.

Quite a decline, to be sure. But some aspects of indigenous culture have survived since the arrival of Europeans, and other features are being revived. The largest tribes are the Cabécares and the BriBrí, concentrated on the Caribbean coast and in the Talamanca mountains. Both groups actively work to maintain and revive their language and customs, as well as adapt tourism to their own needs, allowing a few visitors onto their reserves for cultural and natural history tours. When I took a tour of the Kéköldi Reserve (within which Cabécares and BriBrí live), a native guide walked us through mud and heavy brush to a spectacular waterfall deep within the reserve, stopping along the way to point out trees and vines traditionally used for medicinal purposes.

In the 1970s, legislatures passed the Ley Indígena (the Indigenous Law), establishing autonomous governing structures within the existing indigenous reserves. During the same period, CONAI (the National Commission for Indian Affairs) was established, but indigenous people felt it did not represent them and so created their own organization in 1981, the Pablo Preserve Indigenous Association. Members of both organizations work to forge alliances between various indigenous groups within Costa Rica and to reach out to similar groups throughout the Americas. They also try to maintain the reserves, which are threatened on all sides: by mining and lumber companies, hydroelectric projects, tourism, and non-indigenous peasants who want land to farm. The government still holds deed to all reserves, and has been known to cut deals with outside companies at the expense of indigenous land and autonomy.

Besides trying to revive their customs, indigenous groups are also looking to their economic future. In 1995, for example, the Cabécares and BriBrí created their own bank, the Banco Indígena de Talamanca, which they say is "neither a private nor state bank. It is a bank of and for Indians."

THE COLONIAL ERA
On his fourth and final trip to the New World, Cristobal Colón (Christopher Columbus to English speakers) landed in September 1502 at what is now Puerto Limón on Costa Rica's Caribbean coast. His four ships had been damaged by storms, and his crew of 135—a third of whom were young men between 13 and 18—badly needed a break.

The indigenous people of the area welcomed the new arrivals, swimming out to the ships with gifts of finely woven cloth and pendants made of tumbago, an alloy of copper and gold. These necklaces, among other finds, convinced arriving Europeans that the area was rich in mineral deposits, and later the region was christened Costa Rica, or Rich Coast.

In fact, Costa Rica turned out to be one of Spain's poorest colonies, and this lack of wealth made it a backwater of the empire for the next several hundred years. Thick forests, impassable mountains, and raging rivers didn't help matters. Settlers had a rough time of it, and often lived like the "savages" they had come to conquer, dressing in clothing made of pounded bark, employing native farming methods, and using cacao beans as money when the paper bills and metal coins ran out.

Early Settlements
It was sixty years after Columbus's arrival that Juan de Cavallón founded what was to become the first permanent settlement in Costa Rica, christened Garcimuñoz in 1561 and located in what is now the Río Oro de Santa Ana region of the Central Valley. Towns had been founded earlier on both coasts, but most didn't last long, as settlers battled harsh conditions, lack of supplies, infighting among the townspeople, and attacks from

pirates and what were then called *indios bravos* (wild Indians). Garcimuñoz was moved and renamed several times, until it ended as Cartago, which would become the colonial capital.

In *The Ticos*, coauthors Mavis, Richard, and Karen Biesanz characterize Spanish Costa Rica as "the Cinderella of Spanish colonies, [which was] taxed, scolded, ignored, and kept miserably poor. An isolated and neglected province of the captaincy general of Guatemala, it was unable to raise enough revenue to pay its own administrative expenses. Its clergy was subordinate to the bishop of León in Nicaragua, who rarely visited."

> *Many historians believe that Costa Rica's poverty during the colonial era, when everyone struggled just to survive, actually helped to lay the foundation for a democratic nation of equals.*

In addition, the colonial practice of *encomienda*, in which European invaders were granted land that didn't belong to them and allowed to extract labor or tribute from the true owners (indigenous people), never really took hold in Costa Rica, in part because the indigenous peoples either died from disease, headed for the hills, or offered up armed resistance to the idea that they should become slaves on their own land.

So instead of the vast *encomiendas* found elsewhere in Central American, in Costa Rica small, family-owned farms were more the norm, and even governors were said to work their own land. This was less true in Guanacaste, where enormous cattle ranches were worked by not only indigenous but also black slaves. Guanacaste was part of the richer colony of Nicaragua until just after both countries declared independence from Spain, when it chose to ally itself with poor but peaceful Costa Rica over wealthy but war-torn Nicaragua.

Many historians believe that Costa Rica's poverty during the colonial era actually helped to lay the foundation for a democratic nation of equals, where all struggled just to survive and where class differences were not as pronounced as elsewhere.

INDEPENDENCE AND EARLY NATIONHOOD

When in September 1821 the captaincy general of Guatemala declared independence from Spain, Costa Rica didn't receive word until a month later. The news sparked confusion in a land that was less a nation than a loose collection of rival city-states. Some Costa Ricans wanted to become part of the powerful Mexican Empire, while others wanted to help create a federation of newly free Central American states. Still others suggested that Costa Rica become part of Colombia, which then included present-day Panama and was ruled by the "Great Liberator," Simón Bolívar.

William Walker and Juan Santamaría

An egomaniacal mercenary from Nashville, Tennessee, ended up playing an unexpectedly large role in the formation of Costa Rican national identity. The man's name was William Walker, and he dreamed of ruling over a Central American empire that would be a fresh source of slaves for the United States.

As crazy as the idea sounds, Walker had an army and the backing of several U.S. industrials, and he had some success, first taking Nicaragua and then invading Costa Rica. The year was 1856, not far into the first decades of a fledgling nation in which people still felt more identified with their city or region than their country. Cutting across these regional iden-

tities, President Juan Rafael Mora called together a ragtag army to drive Walker's forces from the northern province of Guanacaste.

The Costa Rican army, some of them armed with little more than farming tools, chased Walker into Nicaragua, where, at the town of Rivas, a young soldier, Juan Santamaría, set fire to Walker's barracks before collapsing under a hail of bullets. Costa Rica thus reclaimed its territory and also got its first national hero, who now has his own holiday, celebrated most fervently in Santamaría's hometown of Alajuela. Santamaría's nickname was *El Erizo,* the hedgehog, for his thick hair that stood straight up.

The four most powerful Costa Rican cities—San José, Cartago, Alajuela, and Heredia—all had different plans for newly liberated Costa Rica, and they backed up their ideas with guns. A side issue was which of the cities should be the capital; for a while the honor was rotated among the cities, and then a battle decided the issue in San José's favor.

Those who wanted Costa Rica to become a state in the Central American Federation won out, but a few decades later, when it was obvious the experiment had failed, the country became its own republic in 1848.

The first head of state after independence was Juan Mora Fernándes, who founded the country's first newspaper, expanded public education, and established a judicial system. Braulio Carrillo, remembered as a heavy-handed dictator who nonetheless fostered national unity, ruled from 1835 to 1842; he presided over Costa Rica's withdrawal from the federation of Central American states and its emergence as an independent country. Carrillo is also known for planting the seeds of the nation's coffee economy—he offered free land to those who would reap and sow the glossy-leafed crop.

The 1880s brought a succession of liberal governments that made far-reaching and lasting changes, most involving the separation of church and state. Presidents during this period secularized schools, making primary and secondary education free and obligatory, shut down the church-run

University of Santo Tomás, and expelled the Jesuits and one Catholic bishop. They also allowed for civil marriage and divorce, secularized the cemeteries, and abolished the death penalty.

A PIVOTAL DECADE

During the volatile 1940s, two larger-than-life political figures fought each other for power, war was declared on Nazi Germany, and Costa Rica suffered through its own 40-day civil war. The constitution drafted after that battle shook the country to its roots and provided the basis for what was seen at the time as a new nation.

The decade began with the election of Rafael Angel Calderón Guardia, who gave workers' rights a huge boost with reforms such as a guaranteed minimum wage, unemployment compensation, and paid vacations. Calderón's administration was responsible for the Labor Code of 1943, a lengthy series of constitutional amendments that is still in effect today.

During Calderón's tenure the country declared war on Nazi Germany, just one day before the United States did the same. Germans in Costa Rica lost their property and were sent to internment camps, many located in the United States.

When Calderón lost the 1948 elections, his government cried fraud; the resulting conflict erupted into a battle that killed 2,000 people, most of them civilians. Jose María ("Don Pepe") Figueres Ferrer and his National Liberation Party emerged victorious, and Don Pepe became head of the Founding Junta of the Second Republic of Costa Rica, pushing through reforms such as nationalizing banks and insurance companies, abolishing the army, and finally giving blacks and women full citizenship, including the right to vote.

THE MODERN ERA

Don Pepe's National Liberation Party (Partido de Liberación Nacional, or PLN) ruled Costa Rica from the late 1940s to the late 1970s, consolidating the reforms of its early days and building an even larger bureaucracy to promote social justice through a welfare state. A growing middle class began to undercut the power of the traditional elite, such as coffee barons, even as the government worked to attract foreign capital to help industrialize the country.

In the late 1970s and the early 1980s, the bill for big government came due, and at a time of worldwide economic crisis. In 1981 Costa Rica was forced to suspend debt payment to its creditors, and had to ask for help from lenders like the World Bank and the International Monetary Fund

Costa Rican Presidents

Year Elected	President
1953	José Figueres Ferrer
1958	Mario Echandi Jiménez
1962	Francisco J. Orlich Bolmarich
1966	José Joaquín Trejos Fernández
1970	José Figueres Ferrer
1974	Daniel Oduber Quirós
1978	Rodrigo Carazo Odio
1982	Luis Alberto Monge Alvarez
1986	Oscar Arias Sánchez
1990	Rafael Angel Calderón Fournier
1994	José María Figueres Olsen
1998	Miguel Angel Rodríguez Echeverría
2002	Abel Pacheco

(IMF). Costa Rica got its loans, but at a price: The country had to promise to cut government spending and begin to privatize its economy.

This puzzle—of how to maintain the best parts of the welfare state while still cutting costs and moving toward privatization—is still being pieced together today.

Government

The Costa Rican constitution of 1949 guarantees a host of rights for residents and foreigners alike. These rights include freedom of speech, press, and assembly, all of which are exercised on a daily basis and underline Costa Rica's enviable place among its neighbors. Unlike many other Latin American nations, Costa Rica has no standing army, no guerrillas, and no political prisoners. For more than half a century, power has changed hands peacefully and voter turnout has been high.

The country is a democratic republic that elects a new president every four years. Though the presidency is a powerful position, the constitution guards against concentration of power in any one of the three branches of government: executive, legislative, and judicial.

EXECUTIVE BRANCH

The president coordinates government programs, commands the police, and directs national and international policy. He or she exerts

San José residents watch CNN coverage of the 2003 invasion of Iraq.

considerable power through ties to all manner of ministries, but must also answer to the party that sponsored his or her candidacy, to labor unions, and to public opinion. Presidents had been limited to one four-year term, but this restriction was overturned in 2003. Many former presidents had been waiting for just such a development, and in 2004 Nobel Peace Prize winner and former president Oscar Arias announced that he will run again in 2006.

LEGISLATURE

Fifty-seven elected *diputados* (deputies) serve four-year terms; they can seek reelection after a term spent out of office. The legislature makes, amends, and repeals laws, and imposes taxes. It also has some say on budget issues, including foreign loans negotiated by the president, which it must ratify by a two-thirds majority.

For the 2002–2006 term, of the 57 deputies in the country's Legislative Assembly, 20 are women.

JUDICIAL SYSTEM

The legislature chooses the Supreme Court's 22 magistrates, who serve for six years and then, usually, renew their term. The Supreme Court in turn appoints judges for civil and penal courts. In 1998 there were about 200 judges in Costa Rica.

The Supreme Electoral Tribunal

This special branch of the judicial system oversees electoral issues, from the functioning of political parties to the actual counting of votes. A recent poll showed that Ticos, more and more cynical about politicians, still hold this body in high regard.

BIG GOVERNMENT

There's no denying that Costa Rica has opted for big government. Besides the three branches discussed above, autonomous institutions like ICE, the state electricity and telecommunications monopoly, exert influence over national policy and everyday life. Along with ICE, the Caja (Social Security) and RECOPE, the state oil agency, are important players on this field.

In 1996, one out of seven employed Ticos was a public employee. Government not only controls utilities and health care, it also has monopolies on liquor production and health insurance and majority interests in banking and tourism. Ticos and foreign residents alike complain of the inefficiency of the bureaucracy. Often an agency's budget goes almost entirely to salaries and operating expenses rather than to the purpose—say, alleviating poverty—for which the agency was created.

Sometimes it's all but impossible to know which institution does what, and people who enter the system (to obtain residency, for example) can be

> Unlike many other Latin American nations, Costa Rica has no standing army, no guerrillas, and no political prisoners. For more than half a century, power has changed hands peacefully and voter turnout has been high.

shunted from one office to the next. The coauthors of *The Ticos* acknowledge that "the public sector includes such a bewildering maze of agencies that it is often difficult to know who is responsible for making what decisions—and who actually does make them. And therefore, it is easier to understand why some decisions are slow to be made and why many others are made only symbolically, if at all."

POLITICAL PARTIES

The largest and most powerful two political parties are the National Liberation Party (Partido de Liberación Nacional, or PLN) and the Social Christian Unity Party (Partido de Social Cristiana, or PUSC).

The PLN was founded in the middle of the last century by "Don Pepe"

State workers on strike

Figueres; a coalition of parties opposing the PLN has been around for a long time and became the PUSC in the 1980s. The PLN is known for "welfare state liberalism," while the PUSC has traditionally had more conservative policies.

Economy

COFFEE, BANANAS, AND BEEF CATTLE

Costa Rica will forever be associated in the world's imagination with both the *grano de oro* (golden grain) that wakes up half the world every morning, and the yellow fruit that became synonymous with Central American backwaters ("banana republics"). Historically the country's primary exports have been agricultural, principally coffee—so well-suited to the rich volcanic soil and mild climate of the Central Valley—and bananas, which thrive in the wet coastal lowlands. Of the two crops, coffee is perhaps most tied up with the national identity, but bananas are more lucrative. After Ecuador, Costa Rica is the second-largest banana exporter in the world.

Though farming is still vitally important, the country's economy is now much more diversified. Cattle ranching began in the early colonial period, and in the 1960s many more Ticos invested in beef cattle. By 1975, there were almost as many cows as people in Costa Rica. These "locusts with hooves" have not been kind to the environment nor the economy. Demand for beef waned in the 1980s—fast-food chains up north were ordering less as North Americans became more health conscious. Forest converted to pasture causes drought in many regions (like Guanacaste), and ranching puts people out of work—it takes fewer people to work a herd then to work fields planted in crops. But, as Mavis, Richard, and Karen Biesanz report in *The Ticos,* "Ticos still see cattle as a profitable and prestigious investment. Over two-thirds of agricultural land (and 40 percent of the national territory) was pasture in 1994; only 7 percent was devoted to crops."

NEW INDUSTRY

Starting in the 1990s, electronic components, furniture, and pharmaceuticals (among many others) became important exports. Multinational pharmaceutical companies—such as Abbot Labs, Bristol-Myers Squibb, Johnson & Johnson, Colgate-Palmolive, Monsanto, and Pfizer—have branches here. The textile industry has also grown by leaps and bounds, from 14,000 workers in 1986 to 43,000 in 1996. In some years textiles bring more foreign exchange than the all-important banana.

Tourism, the "industry without smokestacks," also exploded in the 1990s, with the number of foreign tourists doubling in a single decade (376,000 in 1989, more than a million in 1999). Tourism has now surpassed all other moneymakers and is the number-one source of income for Costa Rica. Fifteen percent of employed Ticos work at jobs connected to tourism.

In more recent years, tourism has not lived up to the very high expectations generated in the boom of the late 1990s. A worldwide economic slump, coupled with war and terrorist activity, convinced many travelers to stay home. Some tourist areas here were overbuilt, and many hotels stand empty. Still, the industry is strong, and Costa Ricans and foreign investors hope that it will become even stronger.

Another recent and dramatic change to the economy came when Intel, based in Santa Clara, California, began to build assembly plants here in 1997. The big daddy of foreign investors, Intel has three sprawling plants in Costa Rica, which churn out a third of its worldwide production of computer chips and provide thousands of jobs. In 1998, the company's exports accounted for 8 percent of the country's GDP (gross domestic product; in Spanish, PIB, for *producto interno bruto*). In 1999, Intel exports represented nearly 40 percent of the country's total exports. Thanks to a world slump in computer sales, these figures have gone down a bit in recent years, but Intel still plays an important role in Costa Rica's economy.

U.S. INFLUENCE

The United States is by far Costa Rica's most important trading partner, buying up 53 percent of its exports in 2002. Next were Holland, at 5.9 percent, and Guatemala, at 4.5 percent. In terms of foreign investment, the United States also leads the way by leaps and bounds. Of all foreign investment in Costa Rica in 2001, U.S. companies accounted for some 58.9 percent (US$264 million), followed by Canada at 11.6 percent (US$52 million), and Mexico with 6 percent or US$27 million.

Thus the United States plays a disproportionately large role in the Costa Rican economy. Almost every day, the local press reports on the ins and outs of this crucial relationship, like when CEOs of U.S.-based companies with branches in Costa Rica threaten to take their business elsewhere unless the government agrees to give them more tax breaks. Articles on the state of the U.S. economy also appear daily, since a downturn up north can have a dramatic effect on countries like Costa Rica who are so closely tied to the world's biggest economic engine.

McDonald's in Escazú

© Erin Van Rheenen

THE PRICE OF A LOAN

The United States exerts its influence in other ways as well. In the 1960s and 1970s, Costa Rica borrowed large sums of money—mostly to improve infrastructure and social services—from international lending institutions, many of them based in the United States. When the country had trouble repaying the loans, the lenders—USAID, the International Monetary Fund (IMF), the World Bank, and the Inter-American Development Bank—offered up easier repayment terms in exchange for what in essence became their greater control of the Costa Rican economy. Other developing countries were in similar positions, and similar deals were struck around the world, as the lending institutions saw their "opportunity to convert the world's many state-managed and protectionist economies into free-market systems," as coauthors Mavis, Richard, and Karen Biesanz explain in *The Ticos*.

In 1985 Costa Rica signed the first of many structural adjustment pacts (PAEs) with these lenders. The PAEs require increased imports, reduced external tariffs, and the privatization of some state agencies. That last requirement is especially onerous to Costa Rica, whose national identity is largely based on its strong state-run agencies. Some industries, like banking, have already been at least partially privatized, but there are many others, like the health system (the Caja), the state electricity utility (ICE), and the national oil company (RECOPE), which politicians and the public alike vow will remain state-run and strong.

GOVERNMENT MONOPOLIES AND FREE TRADE

Alan Weeks, financial advisor and columnist for the *Tico Times,* says that as of 2003 Costa Rica had the second-most government-regulated economy (after Cuba) in Latin America and the Caribbean; many industries (such as insurance, utilities, and health care) were government monopolies and thus closed to private investment.

But in 2004, Costa Rica signed the Central American Free Trade Agreement (CAFTA, this region's NAFTA) with the United States. Other Central American and Caribbean nations are also party to the agreement, though each country has thus far negotiated separately with the United States. Costa Rica, for instance, pledged to open up parts of its state-run telecommunications sector by 2007; starting then, private investors will have a crack at broadband internet service, cell phone service, and private data networks. The country also agreed to open up its state-run insurance sector by 2011.

There is much debate here about whether CAFTA will be good for Costa Rica. Proponents say it will allow Central America to "speak with one voice," to band together to negotiate better trade opportunities with North American markets. Others say that Costa Rica cannot compete with the United States and will come out the loser in any battle. "It's like a fight between a wild tiger and a tied-up mule," says one critic of the plan.

GAMBLING

Some commercial sectors in Costa Rica are much more open than they are in other countries. Gambling, for instance, is legal in Costa Rica, and is big business. There are dozens of casinos operating in the San José area alone, and many sportsbooks, or betting services, have moved operations here. In 2003 the largest in Costa Rica (and perhaps the world—it also operates in Ireland and Great Britain) was BetonSports.com, with 1,300 employees occupying seven floors of a large San José office building. Row upon row of workers sit at their computer terminals, speaking into telephone headsets, taking calls from all over the world and arranging bets in 13 languages. Callers to the sportsbooks bet on sports, of course, but they also bet on elections and even on the romantic lives of movie stars.

Asked in 2003 by reporters from *La Nación* why his company came to Costa Rica, BetonSports.com's owner, Brooklyn-born Gary Kaplan, cited solid infrastructure, educated workers, and good telecommunications. He said the company moved much of its business from Antigua because such incentives were lacking. According to Kaplan, the company is 20 times larger than it was in Antigua, but its phone bills here in Costa Rica are the same as what they had been in Antigua.

Studies have shown that sportsbooks contribute US$100 million a year to the Costa Rican economy in salaries, taxes, and rent. In 2003, approximately 6,500 Ticos, most of them college students, worked at the 125 betting and gambling firms operating here.

Sportsbooks may be attracted to Costa Rica in part because there are fewer regulations to comply with here, and those that exist are often not enforced. There's more than a whiff of underworld in this business; a few sportsbooks have been linked with mob activity in New York. It's also unclear how long their commitment to Costa Rica will last—probably until the government starts imposing more taxes on gambling proceeds.

STABILITY

On balance, Costa Rica is still a good place to live and do business. It has one of the most stable economies in all of Latin America, a fact that draws many foreign companies here, further anchoring the economy. The top five foreign investors are Intel, with more than US$400 million invested; Baxter Healthcare with US$125 million; Hanes Underwear with

US$117 million; Pindeco (which grows and exports pineapples) with US$96 million; financial services group Banex with US$79 million; and Kimberly-Clark (paper products) with US$72 million (figures from 2002).

In 2001, Costa Rica's GDP was US$31.9 billion. Panama to the south weighed in the same year with a GDP of US$16.9 billion, and Nicaragua to the north clocked US$12.3 billion. Unemployment in Costa Rica in 2000 was 5.2 percent, about the same as the United States (the rate in Nicaragua for the same year was 23 percent).

Sure, there are problems. Devaluation of the *colón* is as sure as afternoon rain in the green season, and averages about 10 percent per year. The country is battling a large foreign debt, trying to impose IMF-mandated austerity measures while continuing to provide the social services its people have come to expect. Free education and health care are priorities for Costa Rica, and they don't come cheap. But for the moment, at least, Costa Rica is still erring on the side of maintaining a high level of health and education services, while offering incentives to foreign businesses so that they might come here and provide jobs for Ticos.

People and Culture

Though the Tico national identity is as hard to pin down as any other, one current that runs through the culture is the belief that Costa Rica is unique. Ticos define themselves against their neighbors, in ways that range from the "whiteness" of their racial makeup to the pacifism that does indeed distinguish this country from others in the region. Since 1948 Costa Rican leaders have come to power not through violence or fraud but via more or less honest elections. Ticos are proud of this democratic heritage, and many see theirs as an egalitarian society relatively free of class and racial distinctions. Costa Ricans are also justifiably proud of the fact that 25 percent of their national territory has been set aside in parks and reserves, and that the country has a commitment to preserving its natural heritage even as it encourages economic development.

Of course there's always a gulf between a culture's defining myths—what it wants to believe about itself—and the society's day-to-day reality. But there's no argument that Costa Rica has its heart in the right place, and is hard at work negotiating the contradictions of its character.

41

Ethnicity and Class

WHO IS *PURA TICA*?

As recently as the early 1990s, a Costa Rican president (Rafael Calderón, on a visit to Spain) was claiming publicly that there had been no Indians in his country when Columbus arrived. Of course there had been—perhaps as many as 500,000—but only lately have Ticos begun to assimilate that truth into their national consciousness. And until very recently, tourist literature mentioned the overwhelmingly "European" blood of the country's inhabitants as one more plus for prospective visitors.

Whiteness has been, and still is to some extent, a national preoccupation. This is not so very different from some other nations on the American continent, where Indian and African influences are not much celebrated, and where darker-skinned peoples tend to be overly represented in the lower socioeconomic strata. But because there's a kernel of truth in the Tico myth of whiteness—Costa Ricans *do* tend to be lighter-skinned than, say, Nicaraguans or Mexicans—the country seems slower than most to embrace the mixture of ethnicities present in even the lightest-skinned Tico.

In 1995, and utilizing five decades' worth of research, UCR geneticists Ramiro Barantes and Bernal Morera declared that almost all Costa Ricans are mestizos (mixed bloods) with varying combinations of the general population's gene pool: 40–60 percent white, 15–35 Indian, and 10–20 percent black. The census tells a different story (see the sidebar "Ethnic Makeup of Costa Rica"), in part because "race" here, as elsewhere, is often less a matter of ancestry than of culture. A Guanacasteco with a fair share of African blood, for instance, may or may not think of himself as black, depending on his cultural affiliations. And though

Ethnic Makeup of Costa Rica

Ethnic Group	Percent of Population	Number
Indigenous	1.68 percent	63,876
Black	1.91 percent	72,784
Chinese	0.21 percent	7,873
Other (mestizo)	93.66 percent	3,568,471
Unknown	2.55 percent	97,175

—*from 2000 census*

there is pride among minority ethnicities, there are also plenty of incentives to assimilate into the mainstream.

After all, the word *indio* here is still usually an insult, and many "white" Ticos think blacks aren't "real" Costa Ricans. During the 19th century, the elite boasted of their pure European stock and slandered their rivals with racial epithets. Presidential portraits often showed the men as lighter-skinned than they actually were. And when in the 1930s the United Fruit Company moved its banana plantations from the Caribbean to the Pacific coast, President Ricardo Jiménez forbade the transfer of "colored" employees, saying the move would "upset racial balance" and cause "civil commotion" in Costa Rica. The decree was repealed in 1949. In recent decades, the influx of an estimated 1 to 2 million Nicaraguan immigrants has rekindled Tico resentment against darker-skinned outsiders. Ask any taxi driver why violent crime is on the rise in Costa Rica, and he will have an easy answer: It's the Nicaraguans, so accustomed (goes the prejudice) to bloodshed.

Chinese, Jews, and members of other immigrant groups are often not considered *pura Tica,* even if their families have been here for generations. Twice—in 1862 and again in 1896—the government prohibited immigration of "Orientals," claiming that "race is hurtful to the progress of the Republic." The laws were quickly repealed when cheap labor was needed, as when in 1873, 600 Chinese were allowed to immigrate, and then, paid one-fifth of the going wage to help build the Atlantic railway.

Despite the fact that the country is populated almost entirely by mestizos (a word you almost never hear in Costa Rica), to this day the nation is dominated by a handful of families who trace their ancestry back to the Spanish *hidalgos* (aristocrats) who arrived during the colonial period. No matter that many of the Spaniards were poor and had to work their own land, or that because most settlers were men they coupled with non-Spaniards, setting into motion the genetic mixing of Spanish, Indian, and African blood that has made Ticos who they are. But even today, the perception of "European" blood seems stronger in Costa Rica than the mestizo reality.

Still, Costa Rica has done much to combat racism. The 1949 constitution declared that anyone born in Costa Rica has the full rights of citizenship, which meant that blacks, women, and members of other marginalized groups finally had the right to vote. In 1992, President Calderón (the same man who had claimed his country had no Indians) signed the United Nations Treaty on Indigenous Populations and Tribes, which puts Indian sovereignty above national law, and guarantees them bilingual education and health care. Academics study indigenous language and culture, and encourage "average Ticos" to value their indigenous heritage rather than separate themselves from it by calling it "pre-Columbian culture." And while past tourism campaigns showcased the country's whiteness, now you'll often see indigenous and black people pictured in ads.

Increasingly, there are cultural festivals that celebrate black and indigenous culture. A recent Festival of the African Diaspora drew well-known dancers and musicians from Brazil, Cuba, and the United States. At a 2003 exhibition of paintings by a group called Divas Afrolatinas, academics from the University of Costa Rica announced the formation of a group that would study *cultura afrocostarricense* (Afro–Costa Rican culture). In his enthusiasm for the project, President Abel Pacheco told the assembled guests, "There is a kind of black, one that wants to sing with more feeling—that is the black we all carry inside of us." Although to North American ears Pacheco's comments may sound a little off, they nevertheless suggest that Ticos—all the way up to the president—are making efforts to embrace their multicultural heritage.

A SHRINKING MIDDLE CLASS

While racial and ethnic biases may be on the wane, economic inequities seem to be on the rise. One of Costa Rica's claims to fame has been its large middle class, the group thought to stabilize a country economically and politically. Historically, Costa Rica was a poor Spanish colony, less a society of land barons and peons than surrounding states. When in the 1880s coffee began dominating the national economy, the tradition of small independent landowners persisted in a core of small coffee growers that made up a significant middle class. And although economic frustrations led to the 1948 civil war, for three decades after the war far more Ticos climbed up the class ladder than slid down it.

Beginning in 1979, worldwide recession and a sharp devaluation of the *colón* had a chilling effect on the economy. Between 1980 and 1983, the number of poor families doubled, and buying power was so severely reduced that even nominally middle-class families began to feel poor.

Taxes also played their part in widening the gap between rich and poor. In the 1980s, revenue from direct taxes (such as income and corporate taxes) fell from 44 to 19 percent. Revenue from indirect taxes (such as those on goods and services) shot up from 47 to 71 percent, putting a greater burden on those who could least afford it.

The Costa Rican economy has recovered from the hardest hits of the last few decades, but there is still a sense that the middle class—not to mention the working class—is hurting. The increasing availability of credit and the pressures of consumerism don't help matters. An influx of relatively well-off foreign residents has also driven prices up, especially in real estate, making it harder for Ticos to buy property.

Still, a newcomer to Costa Rica who has traveled in other Central American countries will see far less evidence of dire poverty here than elsewhere. However humble, most homes are in good repair, with healthy children playing in well-tended yards.

Customs and Etiquette

More than one observer has noted the similarities between Asian and Latin American cultures: Both emphasize social harmony and saving face. To North Americans, who often value honesty above harmony, the Costa Rican method of preserving accord and personal honor can sometimes look a lot like lying. Ticos don't much like our version of honesty, however, thinking it clumsy and rude.

What you see here is not what you get. Ticos are known as "icebergs" because often only a fraction of their true selves is visible; it's easy to crash into the 95 percent hidden beneath the surface. The smiling exterior of a Tico acquaintance may conceal many things, including that you just offended her deeply. Attempts to get things straight—to speak perhaps uncomfortable truths for the good of the relationship—don't find much favor in this culture.

Things do get communicated, but to the uninitiated, the language in use might as well be code. In the rare instances I manage—with the help of locals—to gain insight into problematic situations, from giving the wrong

Culture Shock Can Liberate You

In the excellent *Survival Kit for Overseas Living,* L. Robert Kohls offers these wise words on the value of culture shock.

"Be ready for the lesson culture shock teaches. Culture is a survival mechanism which tells its members not only that their ways of doing things are right but also that they are superior. Culture shock stems from an in-depth encounter with another culture in which you learn that there are different ways of doing things that are neither wrong nor inferior.

"It teaches a lesson that cannot be learned by any other means: that one's culture does not possess the single right way, best way, or even uniformly better way of providing for human needs and enjoyments. Believing it does is a kind of imprisonment—from which the experience of culture shock, as painful as it may be, can liberate you."

gift at a child's birthday party to the proper way to issue dinner invitations, I hear comments like, "I thought you knew," or "But wasn't it obvious?"

No, it wasn't obvious. When you're new to a culture, what's obvious to natives is not obvious to you. One consolation is that you're expanding your awareness of your own assumptions, as well as opening your eyes to the fact that there are dozens of ways in this world to solve the same problem. Keen observation, good will, and a boundless sense of the absurd will serve you well as you adapt to your new environment. The process brings unexpected gifts of self-knowledge, as you discover what parts of yourself you're willing and able to change, and which are more bedrock aspects of your character. If all else fails, remember the old saying: What doesn't kill you makes you stronger.

PERSONAL SPACE

You're on a crowded bus, and you've been lucky enough to get a seat. In the press of bodies, the señora in the aisle has her behind smashed up against your arm, the kid in the seat behind you is playing with your hair, and a man leans over, a few inches from your face, to pull the cable that signals the driver to stop. No one says *perdón*, no one even glances your way to acknowledge that they are—by North American standards at least—making serious incursions into your personal space.

Whether you think this normal, charmingly different, or downright rude will depend on your culture and upbringing. It's one of my pet peeves, in part because my response to it is so very physical. I can explain away other cultural differences, but this one makes me feel like a dog with her hackles up. A local told me to think of it as a sort of compliment—a collective hug, welcoming me to the extended family.

This reduced margin can also be seen in the way Ticos drive. They pull out into traffic that would give others pause, pass even if a truck is bearing down from the other direction, and cut off cars so closely you're amazed that there aren't even more accidents.

EARLY (AND NOISY) RISERS

Most Ticos are up before six in the morning, and they aren't tip-toeing around, trying not to wake the gringos who sleep till eight. Señoras bang pots, kids squeal, and the buses that pick up the kids honk at every door. Construction crews hammer away, leaf blowers are turned on high, and even the birds get up early to contribute to the racket.

If you can't fight them (and you can't), you may as well join them. You will be much, much happier if you adjust to Tico hours, which means getting up with the sun and going to bed as early as 9 or 10 o'clock. Out in the country there's little to do at night, and even in cities things are usually quiet by midnight. After the adjustment period you may even find that you really like being up for the sunrise.

The Family

In Costa Rican society, it's all in the family, with the law backing up generations of tradition. Slights of honor against family members—even long-dead ones—are punishable by law. A person who murders a relative may get a longer jail sentence than one who kills a stranger. Adults are legally responsible for not only their spouses and children but also other family members in need, such as a sibling with disabilities.

Relatives who live outside the city may come to live with urban relations in order to find better work or attend school. Children are more likely to play with their siblings or cousins than "outsiders." Many adults count their siblings among their best friends, and spend most of their social time with family members. Families go into business together, and government officials hand out prime jobs to family members.

What does this mean to the newcomer? Many North Americans leave home at an early age, perhaps settling far from their family of origin. They create a new sort of family out of good friends and community. That happens much less in Costa Rica, where people tend to stay put and are more insular and clannish.

It can be hard to break into these clans, and although Ticos are known as polite and welcoming, the welcome often stops at the front door—literally. Especially in the country, visitors are not often asked to come inside, though you may be invited to sit on the front porch and have a lemonade. Long-term expats joke that if you're lucky enough to

Household Help

Having servants is more common in Costa Rica than in North America, and many expats of even relatively modest means hire a cook, a gardener, or a housekeeper. Nannies, often from Nicaragua, are common in both expat and Tico households, especially those in which both parents work. Wages for household help are low, but are strictly regulated by the government. As with any employee, employers are required to provide holiday and vacation pay for household help. For more information, see the Labor Laws section of the Employment chapter.

What's in a Name?

Let's say your new friend introduces herself as María José Mora Pacheco de Vargas. Before you roll your eyes in exasperation and wonder why anyone would need five names, let's dissect her monikers and see what we can find out.

María—first name
José—second name; like our middle name (middle names can go against gender)
Mora—first surname; comes from María's father
Pacheco—second surname; comes from María's mother
de Vargas—married name; comes from María's husband

Confused yet? Okay, let's take a step back. First of all, like other Latin Americans, Costa Ricans trace descent through both their mother and father. The father's last name is the child's *primer apellido* (first surname); the mother's last name is the child's *segundo apellido,* or second surname.

María's father's name is Wilbur Álvaro Mora Espinoza; his first surname becomes his daughter's first surname (as for the "Wilbur," English names are popular in Costa Rica). María's mother's name is Soledad Berta Pacheco Molina; her first surname becomes María's second surname. María's husband's name is Victor Hernán Vargas Salas; his first surname is sometimes appended to María's parade of names, preceded by "de" (of) to denote that she is married to him. But for most purposes, including legal documents and medical files, María will not use the "de Vargas."

If she wants to be quick, María may write her name María J. Mora P., spelling out the most important names (first name, first surname), while abbreviating the less important names (second name, second surname). If she works with North Americans, she might call herself María Mora, knowing that non-natives sometimes get confused by the Costa Rican carnival of names. Poor gringos, she might be thinking, with so few names.

If you meet someone with two identical *apellidos* (surnames), like Julio Ricardo García García, either both Julio's parents had the same *primer apellido* (first surname), or his father is "unknown," and they repeated his mother's surname twice on the birth certificate.

For official records, which are set up to require two surnames, clerks may try to solve the inconvenience of a one-surname foreigner by repeating her surname twice. Thus I became Erin Kathleen Van Rheenen Van Rheenen for Social Security purposes. My documents are sometimes filed under *V,* sometimes under *R,* and often not filed at all because no one can figure out why the gringa has not two surnames but four.

have a Tico invite you to his house, he won't tell you how to get there. Ticos may also be wary of people who they think will be here today and gone tomorrow.

It's not impossible to make Costa Rican friends, but it takes time and effort. Start by being as polite as you know how, and try not to take offense if your friendly overtures are not reciprocated as you would like. If you have children, you're one step ahead—you'll have a door in to Tico families with kids the same age as yours. If you work with locals, that's another way in. And remember, there are plenty of other foreign residents who are in the same boat, and more than happy to commiserate about it. Enduring friendships have been based on less.

Gender Roles

Officially speaking, women and men in Costa Rica enjoy absolute equality. The 1949 constitution says as much, and the 1974 family code stipulates that husbands and wives share equal rights and responsibilities, and that a woman can do everything from inherit property to form a corporation on

Husbands for Rent—We Do Everything

her own. There are laws on the books against sexual harassment and gender discrimination. The 1990 Law for Promotion of the Social Equality of Women forbids schools to use materials that promote antiquated notions of gender identity, like books that state: "Mother kneads the dough while Father reads the paper."

Sound like a feminist utopia? Not exactly. Traditions die hard, and Costa Rica is still a *machista* society, where little girls are taught to serve their brothers at table. In hiring, men are more likely to get high-level positions; on the other hand, if a woman is well trained, she is more likely than her peers in more developed societies to get a good job, since well-trained workers are less common here. In 1997, one in every three workers was female, and in 1992, women accounted for 46 percent of all professionals. There are more women than men currently enrolled in most of the country's universities, though it is still common for women to give up their studies or careers once they marry.

But how do all the statistics translate into day-to-day life? Let's start on the street. Women—even grandmothers—dress more provocatively here than in North America. Pants are almost comically tight, heels high, and blouses revealing. The attitude seems to be, if you have it, flaunt it, and if you don't have it, flaunt that too. Women, especially ones showing a lot of skin, get plenty of attention on the street, with men hissing and murmuring sweet (and not-so-sweet) nothings under their breath. Men are expected, to a certain extent, to proposition every eligible woman they meet, and there's still a strong double standard when it comes to fidelity. A man who strays expects to be forgiven by his long-suffering partner; a woman better not expect the same indulgence.

Most Ticos are married by the age of 25, though those who are studying for advanced degrees tend to wait longer. Increasingly, both husband and wife work, and often a nanny or female relative spends more time with the children than their parents do. In 1992, the fertility rate was about three children per woman, with rates varying depending on everything from place of

Out-of-Wedlock Kids

It's a Catholic country, but 53 percent of children born in Costa Rica in the year 2000 were born out of wedlock. Of those, 59 percent had no father declared on their birth certificate. Also, 21 percent of all children were born to mothers under 20 years of age.

—from 2000 census

residence to education level. Out-of-wedlock births have grown common; the law deals with this trend by insisting that both parents, whether the couple is married or not, are responsible for their children. But when a deadbeat dad skips town, there are no official resources to track him down.

A 1994 study showed that 70 percent of women in active sexual relationships used contraceptives, at least some of the time. Abortion is illegal (except when the mother's life is at stake), though it is widely available in private clinics for those with money, and in back alleys for those without.

LOOKING FOR LOVE

Many couples relocate together, and are not looking to branch out. Expats who come down solo, however, may be actively seeking a mate or at least open to the possibility of meeting one. Some North American men, often quite advanced in years, come to Costa Rica expressly to meet and sometimes marry a Tica, often half or a third their age. These couples frequently have little in common—they don't even speak each other's language—and the liaisons can be short-lived. Other expat men marry Ticas closer to their age and educational level, settle down and have kids, and fully integrate into Costa Rican society.

Women seeking adventure will most likely find it, as Tico men are often on the lookout for new conquests. Those hoping for something more lasting may find that Costa Rican men can be less egalitarian and faithful than North American women are accustomed to. Many of the single expat women I meet go out with fellow expats, not necessarily from their own country.

Those looking for a same-sex partner will find their pool of applicants even further reduced. But many a great love are based on exceptions to all sorts of rules, so never say never.

GAYS AND LESBIANS

San José is known as a gay-friendly city. There are at least three openly gay bars in town, lots of gay-friendly restaurants and guesthouses, and in 2003 the city organized its first "Pride" festival, which attracted more than 2,000 people. One speaker at the festival joyfully proclaimed that Costa Rica had come out of the closet, but it's clear that most Tico gays still live a fairly closeted life, especially if they are in positions of power. Guides to gay Costa Rica stress that the country is a fairly tolerant place as long as you're not "openly affectionate" in public. Gay men, by the way, are far more visible than gay women, and there is a big transvestite community, with cross-dressing sex workers much in evidence along some downtown streets.

Legally speaking, homosexual activity is not a crime between consenting adults (over 18). There have also been court rulings prohibiting police raids and harassment at gay locales.

There are many resources for learning more—in Costa Rica, look for a copy of the magazine *Gente 10* (www.gente10.com), search for gay-owned and gay-friendly lodging, restaurants, or tour agencies at www.purpleroofs.com/centralamerica/costarica, or go to the largest site, www.gaycostarica.com, which has everything from news to personal ads.

Religion

CATHOLICISM

Costa Rica is a visibly Catholic country and the great majority of Ticos call themselves Catholic. Churches are everywhere, and shrines to the Virgin can be seen in parks, public buildings, and even taxicabs. Most Ticos are baptized and married in the church, and everyday speech is full of religious phrases. Ask a Tica how she is, and most likely she'll reply, *"Muy bien, gracias a Dios"* (Very well, thank God). A fair number of peo-

Cartago Basilica

© Erin Van Rheenen

ple cross themselves when passing a church or beginning a journey. Religious festivals are often national holidays: The country all but shuts down during Easter week, and on August 2, hundreds of thousands of Ticos make the pilgrimage to the Cartago cathedral that houses the Virgin of Los Angeles, Costa Rica's patron saint. (See the sidebar "La Negrita's Gifts" in the Central Valley and Beyond chapter.)

Even so, Costa Ricans are not necessarily devout. Catholic influence here seems almost more cultural than religious, with people observing the outward rituals but lukewarm to the Catholic precepts that don't fit with their individual philosophy. Premarital and extramarital sexual activity is common, out-of-wedlock births are on the rise, and contraception is promoted by the government and embraced by the people. Holidays, whether secular or religious, often seem to be an excuse to drink and carouse.

> *Costa Ricans are not necessarily devout. Catholic influence here seems almost more cultural than religious, with people observing the outward rituals but lukewarm to the Catholic precepts that don't fit with their individual philosophy.*

This lukewarm faith is nothing new. In 1711, the bishop in charge of Costa Rica was so appalled by low church attendance and nonpayment of church fees that he ordered chapels built in every town and mandated that fees be paid before any marriage or funeral could be performed. His decree had little effect.

The country's first constitution specified Catholicism as the state religion, but in 1853 a visiting German Catholic noted that Ticos "attend church more from hereditary custom than from individual impulse . . . . Above all, they do not want to give much money to the church." Although Ticos have historically been less than pious, neither have they been anticlerical, perhaps because the church was never powerful enough to thwart secular desires. Still, the church is the strongest nongovernmental organization, and Roman Catholicism remains the official religion.

OTHER FAITHS

Just over 10 percent of Costa Ricans identify themselves as Protestants, and most belong to one of the approximately 100 small evangelical sects active here. Most of the country's blacks arrived in this country as Protestants and remain so today.

Denominations include Baptists, Methodists, Mormons, Seventh Day Adventists, and Jehovah's Witnesses. As elsewhere in Latin America, Protestant fundamentalism is on the rise, in part because converts feel a greater sense of community in their small sects than in the often-impersonal state-sanctioned Catholic church. Many Protestants belong to missionary orders, and sometimes you'll see the faithful going door-to-door or performing concerts or plays in local parks. At my local park there are occasional Christian rap concerts, with Christ-centered lyrics and heavy bass booming through our quiet suburban streets.

Two synagogues in San José serve the city's Jewish community of just under 3,000. Some Jews are new arrivals, mostly from North America; others are descended from families that came from Europe in the early 20th century. Many Jewish children attend the Weizman Institute in San José, a trilingual school with classes in English, Spanish, and Hebrew.

Many Ticos of Chinese descent have converted to Catholicism, though some still practice Buddhism or Confucianism. There is a small Quaker community, mostly living in the northern mountain town of Monteverde. As in the United States, many Ticos study yoga, Zen, or Asian martial arts, and they may shoehorn a bit of Eastern spirituality into their mostly Catholic or secular worldview.

Expats will have a wide choice of services to attend, some in English. The weekly *Tico Times* lists the various options. There is also plenty of new age spirituality on offer, from indigenous-inspired rites to a Course in Miracles.

The Arts

For such a small country, Costa Rica gives a lot of support to its arts. The Ministry of Culture, Youth, and Sports sponsors music and dance performances in towns throughout the country, workshops for kids, and an annual international arts festival. The government subsidizes the House of the Artist, founded in 1951 and offering free painting and sculpture lessons—many Tico artists began their careers here. Musicians and dancers have the Conservatorio Castella (started in 1953), and the state-subsidized Editorial Costa Rica (founded in 1959) publishes local writers and sponsors yearly writing awards.

There is also the National Symphony Orchestra, until the early 1970s a small ensemble playing a few poorly attended concerts each year. President Pepe Figueres sparked the revitalization of the orchestra, asking "Why should we have tractors if we lack violins?" Now the orchestra is first-rate, featuring famous international soloists but still staying true to its roots, playing not only in the elegant National Theater but also in small-town plazas throughout the country. When musicians are hired (often from outside the country), they know they must not only play but also teach: The "second orchestra" is one of the few state-sponsored youth orchestras in the world.

The National Dance Company is also on the upswing, as are all sorts of theater groups, including expat troupes that perform works in English. During one recent week in San José, arts lovers could choose among flamenco dance, Tibetan music, a monologue about Nicaraguan immigrants, many broad comedies in Spanish, *You're a Good Man, Charlie Brown* put on by an expat theater group, and all sorts of popular music and dance concerts. Tickets are usually very reasonably priced (often under US$5). Check listings in the English weekly *Tico Times* or the Spanish daily *La Nación*.

Private financing of the arts is also on the rise, with some of the larger multinational corporations supporting mostly music and theater, and *La Nación* sponsoring yearly writing awards.

Film here is pretty much a Hollywood import, with blockbusters shown at multiplexes not unlike the ones back home. In San José, there is the occasional foreign film festival, and two venues—Sala Garbo and the Teatro Laurence Olivier, right next door to each other near Paseo Colón—regularly show foreign and independent films. There is a Centro de Cine that sometimes organizes film series, like a recent series of Cuban films. The Costa Rican film industry is in its infancy, though business forces are trying hard to sell the country as a beautiful and economical movie location.

> *One craft that is* pura Tica *is the kaleidoscope-bright painting of wooden oxcarts. Even in the mid-20th century, oxcarts were in daily use, and farmers would decorate their carts in patterns resembling Tibetan mandelas or Pennsylvania Dutch motifs.*

Almost all of the cinemas in the country are in San José. Outside of the capital, the cultural pickings in general can be slim, though you could always start your own theater group, film club, or chamber orchestra.

CRAFTS

Tourists looking for crafts are disappointed to find that many of the "souvenirs" in this country are made in Indonesia—beach towns in particular offer up a glut of batiked sarongs and colorful bikinis from halfway across the world. You'll also see street vendors—often itinerant South Americans—selling handmade jewelry and head-shop paraphernalia. Costa Rica lacks the rich tradition of native crafts enjoyed by nearby countries whose African and indigenous arts have been preserved and/or absorbed into a hybrid of old- and new-world forms.

But increased tourist demand has led to the revival of some traditions, and now you may see reproductions of pre-Columbian stone statues, wooden masks, and pottery that resuscitates ancient techniques and designs.

One craft that is *pura Tica* is the kaleidoscope-bright painting of wooden

Oxcart

oxcarts, based in the Central Valley town of Sarchí. Even in the mid-20th century, oxcarts were still used daily to transport coffee and other crops. Farmers would decorate their carts in patterns resembling Tibetan mandelas or Pennsylvania Dutch motifs. You'll still see the occasional cart in use today, though mostly they've been taken out of circulation and put in people's front yards, as North Americans might have flamingos or garden gnomes. Miniature painted carts are now popular in tourist shops.

Costa Rican craftspeople also make full use of the tropical hardwoods found here. Some of the objects—from bowls to chairs to keychain figurines—are crudely carved by hopeful amateurs, while other items are true works of art.

LITERATURE

Despite the high literacy rate here, Costa Rica is not a country of readers. The lack of public libraries attests to this, and, apart from newspaper journalists and advertising copywriters, Costa Rican authors might win prizes but are unlikely to make a living at their craft.

Even so, there are plenty of Tico writers who have made their mark on popular culture. (All works mentioned here have been translated into English unless otherwise noted.) Carmen Lyra is known for her 1920 collection of folkloric short tales, *Los cuentos de mi Tía Panchita (My Aunt Panchita's Stories)*, still read today. Carmen Naranjo is a writer, visual artist, activist, and stateswoman. She was the first woman appointed to a cabinet post (in the Ministry of Culture, Youth, and Sports, in 1974), was ambassador to Israel, and has published dozens of novels, plays, essays, and books of poetry. Her best-known works are the novel *Diario de una multitude (Diary of a Crowd*, 1974), a book of short stories titled *Ondina* (1983), and *Mujer y cultura (Women and Culture*, 1989), essays that take on cultural myths relating to gender. Carlos Luís Fallas is known for *Mamita Yunai* (1976), a lively novel about banana workers in the early 20th century. Quince Duncan, a descendent of English-speaking West Indian blacks, is known for his two novels, *Los cuatro espejos (The Four Mirrors*, 1973) and *La paz del pueblo (The People's Peace*, 1978). Eulalia Bernard also explores the black Costa Rican experience with her books of poetry, including *My Black King*, written in a medley of Spanish, standard English, and Jamaican English. Anacristina Rossi takes on the environmental destruction wrought by foreign investment and tourism in her novel *La loca de Gandoca (The Crazy Lady from Gandoca*, 1992). *El expediente* (not translated, 1989) by Linda Berrón shows the comeuppance of a compulsive womanizer. Jaime Fernández Leandro writes of the life of petty bureaucrats in *Aquel fue un largo verano* (not translated, 1993).

Playwright Alberto Cañas has been enormously influential, both through works like *En agosoto hizo dos años (Two Years Ago in August*, 1966) and through his work as Secretary of the Ministry of Culture, Youth, and Sports, where he did much to bring the arts to a wider audience.

PAINTING AND SCULPTURE

The best-known Costa Rican artist is probably the sculptor Francisco Zúñiga (1912–1998), whom many people mistakenly believe to be Mexican because he lived much of his life in that country. Zúñiga left his homeland in anger after critics said that his *Maternity* sculpture, placed outside a San José hospital, looked more like a cow than a woman. As is often the case in the art world, the artist had to go into exile before his work began to be appreciated at home. Now Ticos claim Zúñiga as a native son, and his work can be seen in many public spaces.

Sculpture has a long tradition in Costa Rica, both in stone and, especially, in wood, as artists take advantage of the gorgeous tropical hardwoods their native land has to offer.

In painting, Tico artists looked to Europe for their inspiration until around 1920, when a homegrown movement called *costumbrista* was launched. Up north in Mexico something similar was happening, as

Spraypaint artist in downtown San José

artists like Diego Rivera, David Alfaro Siquieros, and Frida Kahlo rejected European models and embraced their national roots. Here in Costa Rica, artists painted scenes from daily life—farmers in their fields and tile-roofed rural houses were favorite subjects. In the 1950s, Tico artists moved toward the abstract, rejecting as corny the *casitas* (little houses) favored by their predecessors. More recently, Costa Rican artists have followed the international trend of exploring new media, from film to performance art to holographic sculptures.

Museums and Theaters

Most of the country's museums are in San José. They include the National Museum, housed in a pleasant colonial-style building with breezy tiled verandas and a good view of downtown. The museum's small but interesting collection of archaeological artifacts refutes the notion that this country has little pre-Columbian history. So, too, the Gold Museum houses a remarkable collection of pre-Columbian gold pieces, while the Jade Museum has this hemisphere's largest collection of jade sculptures.

Smaller museums include the Insect Museum, on the UCR campus, Barrio Amon's Museum of Contemporary Art and Design, and the Costa Rican Art Museum, located at the eastern end of Sabana Park.

There are many theaters in San José; the most architecturally interesting of the bunch are the splendid National Theater, in the heart of downtown, and the nearby Melico Salazar. Both host highbrow music, theater, and dance performances, and both have lovely cafés in their lobbies.

See the Resources section for contact information of museums and theaters.

POPULAR MUSIC AND DANCE

San José in particular has a hot dance and music scene, but Ticos wanting to shake a leg or be moved to tears by a ballad will not be denied anywhere across the country. Whether it's reggae in Puerto Limón, a traditional love song in Guanacaste, or deep house in the capital city, there's no shortage of music in Costa Rica. Ticos are great dancers, and a party isn't a party until the first couple takes the floor. Ticos also like to sing, and get-togethers are likely to include sing-alongs of popular songs, accompanied by someone's cousin on the guitar.

Sports and Recreation

SPORTS

To understand sports in Costa Rica, you only need to know three words: *fútbol, fútbol,* and *fútbol.* You might know it as soccer, but this sport has a stranglehold on the nation, with little boys taught to play before they're potty-trained, and almost half of all front-page newspaper photos pertaining to recent matches. In taxi cabs you'll be treated to games broadcast at full volume, the familiar *gooooooooal!* eliciting cheers and the honking of horns from half the drivers on the road, the waving of banners, and, in some cases, drunken revelry and mayhem. The streets often empty out during important matches.

No, it's not on the level of countries where spectators pull guns on rival fans, but it's still a very big deal. In fact, soccer seems to excite more passion in Ticos than anything else, including love and politics. A columnist in *La Nación* called it "a functional alternative to the violence of more militaristic peoples."

Boys kick the ball around in the streets, fishermen play impromptu matches on the beach as they wait for the tide to turn, and bus drivers play a little game before their shifts. Towns and neighborhoods organize their own teams, and most villages have at least one scheduled weekly *mejenga* (match), not to mention countless pickup games.

It used to be that soccer was the province of young men, but now

The surfer's dream: to disappear into a barrel. Costa Rica makes it more than likely.

there are leagues for girls, women, and older men. Ticos, in fact, are much more active than they were just a decade or two ago, and if you get up early enough (while it's still cool), you'll see men and women of all ages jogging at the nearby *polideportiva* (sports center), or walking briskly along city streets, dressed in sneakers and sweats.

Basketball, baseball, and volleyball all have their fans here, and bicycling is surprisingly popular, given the state of the country's roads and the plumes of car exhaust riders must inhale. Tennis and golf are played mostly at private clubs, with golf courses multiplying as well-heeled tourists and foreign residents arrive wanting to wield their clubs. There's one polo field (at Los Reyes, a gated community near San José), with another being built on the central Pacific coast.

RECREATION

Don't have the stable of horses you need for polo, and can't kick a soccer ball to save your life? Not to worry. There are so many recreational opportunities in this country that you could spend years sampling them all. In fact, most visitors to Costa Rica come with outdoor fun in mind, from surfing world-renowned waves to rafting tumultuous rivers.

Surfing is first-rate on both coasts, with especially potent waves at places like Puerto Viejo on the Caribbean and Pavones on the Pacific. As soon as you've met a few planes at the San José airport, and seen how many travelers arrive lugging board bags, you'll realize that Costa Rica is an internationally known surf spot. One plus is that the tourist low season (the rainy season, May–October) also happens to be the best time to find good waves.

Fishing is also a huge draw, especially in Quepos, Golfito, and out of northern Guanacaste beaches like Flamingo and Tamarindo. Head out into the Pacific for sailfish, wahoo, or the hard-fighting blue marlin. Inland you'll find *trucha* (trout), *machaca* (a kind of shad), and *mojarra* (a bluegill with teeth), among many others. The Caribbean side has excellent tarpon and snook action. Fishing lodges abound, and it's easy to find a captain willing to take you out at a moment's notice.

White-water rafting devotees have dozens of put-ins to choose from, with the Reventazón and Pacuare Rivers the most popular choices. Tour companies big and small offer trips that take rafters through Alpine-like territory at higher elevations and through steamy rain forests closer to sea level.

Windsurfers can try Bahía Salinas, on the northernmost Pacific coast, or head inland to Lake Arenal, considered one of the best freshwater wind-surfing spots in the world.

Scuba diving and snorkeling are good on the Caribbean coast when big waves aren't churning things up, and excellent at places like Caño Island off the Osa Peninsula. Dive boats take the truly dedicated on ten-day excursions to Cocos Island, 500 kilometers (311 mi.) off Costa Rica's Pacific coast and one of the world's best dive spots. There you'll share the water with huge populations of white-tipped and hammerhead sharks, manta rays, and whales.

For those in search of more land-bound pleasures, there's hiking, from the challenging ascent of Chirripo (at 3,820 meters/12,532 feet, the highest mountain in the country) to strolls through easy but gorgeous territory like Manuel Antonio National Park.

Serious bird-watchers have to make a pilgrimage to Costa Rica at least once in their lives, to check off some of the fifty species of hummingbirds here, or to catch a glimpse of the resplendent quetzal, with its three-foot iridescent green tail feathers. There are nearly as many bird species here as there are in all of North America.

Planning Your Fact-Finding Trip

The only way to know if Costa Rica is the place for you is to come here, as many times as possible, for as long as your life will allow. But there's always a first time, or the first time you visit with the possibility of living here lurking in the back of your tourist brain.

A trip in which you're window-shopping for a new life will be different from one in which you just want to see volcanoes erupt and hear monkeys howl. That doesn't mean you can't take in some of the best-loved sights and have a little fun—in fact, it would be a shame not to take full advantage of what Costa Rica has to offer, even as you assess the country for its longer-term potential.

The trick will be to strike a balance between hurrying around and seeing every area, and staying long enough in each place to get a sense of more than the airport or bus station. Below I've outlined two possibilities: a ten-day whirlwind tour, and a more leisurely three-week excursion. Both are designed to give you a glimpse of as many different areas of the country as possible without running you ragged. Remember not to overbook in the activities department—a day hanging out and talking to locals is at least as valuable for your purposes as one spent whizzing above the treetops on a zipline. Hotel and restaurant owners—often expats themselves—are excellent sources of information, and life is slow enough that you needn't worry about "wasting" people's time. Talk is what people do here instead of going to the movies, since in most parts of the country there are no cinemas.

And when you find the place that speaks to you—that murmurs *you could be happy here*—well, it's never too soon to book your next trip.

Preparing to Leave

LEARN A LITTLE SPANISH

Of the many things you can do to enhance your trip to Costa Rica, the most important is to study Spanish, even if you learn just a few basic phrases. The country will open up to you in direct proportion to how open you yourself are to it, and making an effort to communicate with locals just shows basic respect. Learning a language well is a lifetime endeavor, but even small efforts will yield great rewards.

How to begin? A class—perhaps at a nearby university or community college—is a good investment, but don't stop there. Rent movies in Spanish, watch Spanish-language TV, and listen to Spanish radio stations. At first it may all sound like gibberish, but without even realizing it you'll be absorbing the tone and rhythm of the language. In many parts of the United States, there are large communities of Spanish-speaking residents. Perhaps a recent arrival from Central America would like to meet regularly to practice English. You could converse half the time in Spanish, half in English, and you'd both be learning a great deal. Or look for children's books in Spanish—the basic vocabulary is about the right speed for beginners, and the illustrations will help fix the vocabulary in your mind.

READ UP

You'll also want to read about Costa Rica, from guidebooks to short stories (see Suggested Reading in the Resources section). Internet resources are extensive, including online discussion groups like Yahoo's GalloPinto and CostaRicaLiving, the bulletin board at www.discoverypress.com, or more general sites like Lonely Planet's Thorn Tree (http://thorntree.lonely-planet.com). Wondering if there's a good vet in Dominical or a fun bar in Nuevo Arenal? Post your question and you'll get a variety of replies, often from foreigners living in Costa Rica.

Poás Crater

STUDY MAPS

Some people are map lovers and others aren't, but even if you don't know true from magnetic north and your refolded maps look like origami swans, get a map of Costa Rica and put it on your wall. As you read about the country, try to find the places mentioned. Soon you'll know by heart that Guanacaste is up north and Osa down south, and that the oft-mentioned town of Escazú is just west of San José. You'll know that the volcanoes closest to the capital are Poás and Irazú (not to be confused with Escazú!), and that the Caribbean coastline is much shorter and straighter than the Pacific coast.

Such basic geographical knowledge will be a great satisfaction when you touch down at Juan Santamaría airport. If a customs officer asks where you're heading, you can reply, "Twenty-two kilometers southeast to Cartago, the oldest colonial city in the country, which, as I'm sure you know, was destroyed by a volcanic eruption in 1723." If you say this in English some of the effect will be lost, which is why it is so important to study Spanish.

ASK AROUND

Hit up friends, relatives, and colleagues for their experiences in Costa Rica or for the names of people they know who have visited—or have made the move. Most people will be happy to talk about their vacation or

Going Back

If you stay in Costa Rica for a while and then go home for a visit or to stay, you may find that reverse culture shock can be even more jarring than culture shock. In a new culture, you expect to feel out of place, but you don't expect to feel that sense of dislocation in what used to be home.

Brenda Burnside went home to Las Vegas for a three-week visit after a year and a half of living in the Pacific coast town of Nosara. "I was miserable," she said. "People there don't know how to live. You say hi to them and they look at you like, 'What do you want?' My friends had all the best new electronic equipment, flat-screen TVs, and killer stereos—all in these dinky little apartments. They work all the time to be able to afford the stuff.

I went to see a friend and she didn't even have time to talk to me—she was too busy showing off her new TV.

"I'd rather have nothing, but have time to sit around and talk to my friends."

Gina Hyams, who returned to Oakland after four years in the Mexican state of Michoacan, has some interesting things to say about going home. In her essay, "Before and After Mexico," in the book *Expat: Women's True Tales of Life Abroad,* she writes: "Perhaps we've become permanent expatriates—neither fish nor fowl, forever lost no matter our location. But the fluidity also means that we're now like mermaids and centaurs—magic creatures who always know there's another way."

to share their knowledge of living here. That said, don't expect folks you don't know to write a ten-page treatise for you on the country's politics or to offer their house for your upcoming visit. Costa Rica is a real place, not just a vacation destination, and people here (even foreigners) lead real lives.

CHECK YOUR DOCUMENTS

Citizens of the United States or Canada don't need visas to enter Costa Rica, but they do need a passport, valid for at least the amount of time they plan to be in Costa Rica. Remember that visitors have been known to ignore their ticket home and to stay on longer than planned.

WHAT TO TAKE

Besides your passport, your plane ticket, and money in a variety of forms, pack as light as possible. You may be taking buses or flying in small planes with luggage restrictions. Even with a car, you'll be happier if you don't have to pack up four large suitcases every time you change hotels.

It's never really cold here, so don't worry about heavy sweaters or jackets, though a light, breathable raincoat will come in handy. Take beachwear, of course (two or three swimsuits may seem excessive, but you'll be happy to not have to put on a wet suit). Remember that in bigger towns beachwear will mark you as a clueless tourist—adult Ticos just don't wear shorts in the capital, for example, no matter how hot it is. Take at least one lightweight but citified outfit for nice dinners out and to feel at home in bigger towns. Even if you're not a beach lover, take gear to protect you from the sun:

- sunscreen
- sunglasses
- hat
- long-sleeved, lightweight shirt

Other items to consider:

- camera and lots of film
- insect repellent (I have hardly ever needed it, but when I did, I was very glad to have it)
- sturdy shoes if you plan to hike, though lightweight running shoes will be fine for most purposes
- sturdy flip-flops
- a travel alarm clock so you won't miss that early-morning flight
- your own washcloth and soap (especially if you're staying in bare-bones hotels, but even some nicer lodging options won't necessarily provide washcloths)
- a clothesline and clothespins (things get wet here, and take a while to dry)
- extra medication (and your prescription, so that customs officers won't think you're transporting illegal drugs)
- extra contact lenses or an extra pair of glasses
- flashlight and extra batteries
- Ziploc plastic bags of various sizes
- duct tape

You may balk at that last item, but you won't after you've used it to fix a window screen or a snorkel, hold your backpack together, and even do emergency repair on your shoes.

Currency

Gone are the days when travelers carried all their money in travelers checks. Nowadays, diversification is the name of the game. A thin packet of travelers checks is still a good idea, if only for backup, but credit and debit cards will be your best bet. Credit cards are widely accepted, especially in tourist areas, and debit cards will allow you to get money out of ATMs, which are abundant, especially in larger towns. You can also get an advance of cash on the credit card, of course. Before you go, make sure you

have PINs for both your credit and debit cards, so that you can use both in ATMs. I also like to bring some cash with me, maybe a few hundred dollars in twenties. If there's a problem with the banks or ATMs nearby, you won't be left high and dry. U.S. dollars are accepted in the more touristed areas, and you can usually pay for a taxi in San José with dollars.

And speaking of diversification, it's a good idea to keep your money in a variety of locations—pockets, purse, backpack, and suitcase—so that if one stash gets lost or ripped off, you'll still have the others.

WHEN TO GO

Costa Rica's tourist high season runs from early December through the end of April. This is the country's dry season—or summer, if you like—though temperatures remain fairly constant year-round, with variations more a function of altitude than season. In the Central Valley, for instance, temperatures usually stay around 21°C–26°C (70°F–80°F) throughout the year, while beachside temperatures are most often in the 20s Celsius (80s Fahrenheit). The difference between Costa Rica's "winter" and "summer" is rainfall, and most rain falls between May and November, with the fiercest storms often in September or October. November and May are good times to come—they are relatively untouristed months in which the rains are either just beginning or just tapering off.

There are regional variations, of course. In Guanacaste and on the Nicoya Peninsula, the dry season is bone-dry—hardly a drop falls between December and April. On the Caribbean coast (a different world, climatically speaking), you may find rain at any time of the year, with somewhat drier times to be had in February, March, September, and October.

Rain here can feel like one of the seven wonders of the world, with

National Holidays

Official holidays in Costa Rica are listed below, but these are just the beginning of the revelry. Ticos also celebrate with fairs, festivals, and carnivals, not to mention the *festejo* that each town has to honor its patron saint.

January 1: New Year's Day
April 11: Juan Santamaría Day
May 1: International Day of the Worker
July 25: Annexation of Guanacaste
August 2: Virgen de Los Angeles (Costa Rica's patron saint)
August 12: Mothers' Day
September 15: Independence Day
October 12: Day of the Cultures (Columbus Day)
December 25: Christmas

Easter: The week before Easter Sunday is an unofficial vacation time. Much of the country shuts down. On Thursday and Friday of this week, only essential services function; even many of the public bus routes cease operation.

aguaceros (downpours) no umbrella can stand up to. But even when the rains are at their heaviest, it's rare that they will come down all day long. Each microclimate has its patterns, to which you quickly adjust. During the Central Valley's rainy season, for example, the mornings are glorious, the rain comes after lunch (just in time for siesta), and most often the evenings are clear again.

The winter, or wet season, has been dubbed the "green season" by tourist promoters, and it can be a great time to come to Costa Rica. Sometimes there are deals on airfare or hotels during that time, though most hoteliers I spoke with said that they really have two high seasons—December through April and again in June and July, the Northern hemisphere's summer, when kids are out of school and families take their vacations.

I've traveled during each and every month, and I've never had a bad trip. One caution: If you're heading to remote areas, the rains may turn unpaved roads into impassable stews of mud and streams into raging rivers that no sane person would attempt to ford. In the more developed areas, however, the rain doesn't have to slow you down. One Oregonian who'd relocated to lush Lake Arenal put it this way as we sprinted for cover: "You're not made of sugar—you're not going to melt!"

Arriving in Costa Rica

CUSTOMS AND IMMIGRATION

As mentioned earlier in this chapter, U.S. and Canadian citizens don't need visas to travel to Costa Rica, but they do need a valid passport. Children traveling with one parent are required to provide official permission from the other parent. You won't always be asked for it, but it's a good idea to have a notarized letter on hand.

Going through customs is usually fast and painless. At the San José airport, you'll be asked to push a button. If the light turns green, you're on your way without a hitch. If you get the red light, your bags will be searched. More people come up green than red.

If you know you'll be here for a while, bringing possessions in as regular luggage is the fastest and easiest way, even if you have to pay for the extra weight. For details on bringing children, pets, or possessions into the country, see the Making the Move chapter.

Can You Bring Me . . .

Visiting Costa Rica, and want to get on the good side of an expat living down here? Ask what you can bring when you fly in, and don't flinch when the list includes the new Nicholson Baker novel, the first Orishas CD, and five boxes of o.b. tampons.

Books and CDs cost about the same here as they do up north, but the selection (especially for English-language books) is much reduced. Music stores are everywhere, but it's hard to find non-mainstream recordings, and even for well-known groups, stock is usually limited to their latest release. A limited selection of vitamins are available in Costa Rica, but they're a lot more expensive than the generic stuff you can pick up in any stateside Longs Drugs. As for appliances, selection is poor, and prices—due to duties of up to 100 percent—can be high. It's usually not worth shipping large appliances, but small electronics—phones, answering machines, boom boxes, even small TVs—are best brought in with your or a friend's luggage. As for tampons, they're more readily available in Costa Rica than in some other Latin American countries, but Kotex seems to have a monopoly down here.

Another group of items that's best bought outside Costa Rica is any sort of recreational equipment, whether for hiking, kayaking, surfing, or biking. There are a few stores in San José that deal in such equipment, but selection is poor and prices high. Stock up before you come on boots, boards, sleeping bags, or any high-tech or specialized clothing.

Your suitcase is by far the easiest way to bring what you need into Costa Rica. Shipping is problematic—claiming your box at customs can be a lengthy and expensive proposition. For more details, see What to Bring in the Making the Move chapter.

TRANSPORTATION

Taxis are easy to come by and relatively cheap. There's a taxi stand at the San José airport; you can even pay with dollars. A cab to the center of town will cost around US$12.

Buses are one of Costa Rica's great bargains, and they go just about everywhere. Renting a car isn't cheap but can be an excellent investment, especially if you want to explore off the beaten track. Small planes fly throughout the country and are a good bet if you have more money than time. A one-way flight from San José to the Guanacaste beach town of Tamarindo, for instance, will cost about US$60 on Sansa (Costa Rica's national domestic airline), more on other carriers. You'll get there in 40 minutes, be treated to spectacular views, and save yourself a five- or six-hour road trip.

Although Costa Rica is a small country, getting where you need to go can take a while. All roads lead to San José, and often it's quicker to return to the capital and venture out again, rather than try to get from one out-lying area to the next.

You'd think, for instance, that going from the southern Pacific coast to the southern Caribbean coast would be easy. In practice, it's all but impossible. There are no roads, and small planes don't usually make the trip. Your best bet is to return to San José, by air or overland, and then either fly or take the well-traveled highway from the capital to the Caribbean coast.

For more detailed information on transportation to and within Costa Rica, see the Travel and Transportation chapter.

TIPPING AND TAXES

Since a 10 percent service charge is included on all restaurant bills, most Ticos leave no tip. If service has been exceptional, you might want to leave another 5 percent, but it's not required or expected. There will also be a sales tax—13 percent—added to restaurant bills, making the final bill 23 percent more than you were expecting.

That 13 percent sales tax applies to all goods and services except fees to independent professionals like doctors and lawyers. The sales tax on airline tickets is 5 percent. The sales tax on hotel rooms is the usual 13 percent but with an additional tourist tax of 3.9 percent, for a total of 16.9 percent.

Taxi drivers are not tipped, while bellboys, hotel maids, and tour guides are.

For more information, see the Finance chapter.

SAFETY PRECAUTIONS

Costa Rica has less violent crime than the United States and is safer than most of its Central American neighbors. Still, visitors need to be alert.

Petty theft is common, and tourists are easy targets. Keep your bags close, your money in deep pockets or tucked into a money belt, and your wits about you. Make photocopies of important documents—passport, plane tickets, drug prescriptions, address book—and keep the copies separate from the originals. If you're traveling by bus, try to make sure that your luggage stays in sight (all the more reason to travel light, with one or two small bags). If you're driving, don't leave anything in your car, and make sure you find a safe place to park it overnight. Keep your doors locked while driving.

For more on safety, see the Health chapter.

Sample Itineraries

You can find more about each day's itinerary in the Prime Living Locations section; the appropriate chapter is listed with each area. *¡Buen viaje!*

TEN-DAY ITINERARY

Days 1 and 2: San José and Environs
First day, explore western neighborhoods (Los Yoses, San Pedro) and western suburbs (Escazú, Santa Ana, Ciudad Colón). Second day, explore cities to the north of San José, like Heredia, Alajuela, and the small towns surrounding them. (See the Central Valley and Beyond chapter.)

Day 3: Zona Norte
North to Arenal Volcano and town of La Fortuna. (See the Central Valley and Beyond chapter.)

Days 4 and 5: Guanacaste Beaches
Playas del Coco and/or Tamarindo area. (See the Guanacaste and the Nicoya Peninsula chapter.)

Day 6: The Nicoya Peninsula
Choose either Nosara/Playa Samara area or Montezuma/Malpaís area. (See the Guanacaste and the Nicoya Peninsula chapter.)

Day 7: Central Pacific
Jacó/Quepos/Manuel Antonio National Park. (See the Central and South Pacific Coast chapter.)

Finding Your Way

Whether you're driving on a dirt road deep in the jungle or walking along a crowded city street, finding your way in Costa Rica can be a real challenge. Roads—even major highways—are often not signed at all, and even main streets will have no indication of what they're called. Most buildings have no numbers, and a mailing address (and directions to the place) may look like this:

de la Farmacia San Francisco
100 e, 200 n, 75 e.
Casa izquierda, rosada, dos pisos
La Pacifica, San Francisco de Dos Ríos
San José, CR

Translation, please.

Your starting point is the pharmacy in the San Francisco section of the city of San Jose. From there you go 100 meters (109 yds.) to the east, then 200 (218 yds.) to the north, then 75 (82 yds.) to the east. One hundred meters is a block, so the above would mean 1 block east, 2 blocks north, and 3/4 of a block east: "Casa izquierda, rosada, dos pisos," means "house on the left, pink, two floors." La Pacifica is a section of San Francisco de Dos Ríos, which in turn is a neighborhood in San José.

If you think that's confusing, consider that many "addresses" aren't even that specific. Some use landmarks that you probably won't know; some of the landmarks used to be there but aren't any more. Addresses and directions in Costa Rica are definitely geared towards long-term locals—who would know that "Coca Cola" means where the Coca Cola bottling plant used to be 20 years ago. Some addresses take as their reference point a tree (god help you if it's been cut down), or the big house where the doctor killed himself. I'm not kidding.

But people here are friendly, and anxious to help. Asking for directions may not come easily to some people, but you'll need to learn to do it, again and again, if you want to get where you're going in Costa Rica.

Day 8: Dominical Area
See the Central and South Pacific Coast chapter.

Days 9 and 10: Caribbean Coast
Tortuguero, Cahuita, Puerto Viejo. (See the Caribbean Coast chapter.)

THREE-WEEK ITINERARY

Days 1–3: San José and Environs
Visit the towns mentioned in the ten-day itinerary; see the Central Valley and Beyond chapter to decide which other neighborhoods and towns you'd like to explore.

Days 4 and 5: Zona Norte
Arenal Volcano, La Fortuna, Lake Arenal, Nuevo Arenal, Tilarán, Monteverde. (See the Central Valley and Beyond chapter.)

Days 6–10: Guanacaste and the Nicoya Peninsula
From this part of the trip through Day 19, a car is all but essential. Start north (Playas del Coco area) and drive down the coast to the southern tip (Malpaís), exploring towns along the way. The unpredictable roads are best tackled during dry season (December–April), and there's a stretch—from Playa Samara south—where you'll need to leave the coast and take inland roads. (See the Guanacaste and the Nicoya Peninsula chapter.)

Days 11–13: Central Pacific
Take the car ferry from Paquera or Playa Naranjo (on southern Nicoya Peninsula) to Puntarenas, then head south to Jacó. Quepos and Manuel Antonio are an hour or so from Jacó. Dominical is an hour and a half (on a gravel road) from Quepos. (See the Central and South Pacific Coast chapter.)

Days 14–17: Southern Pacific
Head south for the Osa Peninsula and beyond. Choose a few but not all of the following: Drake Bay, Corcovado National Park, Puerto Jimenez, Golfito, Playa Zancudo, Pavones. (See the Central and South Pacific Coast chapter.)

Day 18: Inland
To San Vito and San Isidro de General, then back to San José. (See the Central Valley and Beyond chapter.)

Days 19–21: Caribbean Coast
I recommend flying by light plane from San José to Tortuguero (staying at a lodge on the river or in a *cabina* in the town itself), then taking a boat from Tortuguero to Puerto Limón. From Puerto Limón you can either rent a car or bus it to southern Caribbean towns like Cahuita and Puerto Viejo. Distances on this coast are shorter than on the Pacific coast. The bus from Puerto Limón to Cahuita, for example, takes less than an hour. From Cahuita back to San José is about three and a half hours by bus; remember that you'll need to come back to the capital for your flight home. (See the Caribbean Coast chapter.)

Practicalities

Note: A *soda* in Costa Rica is somewhere between a café and a full-fledged restaurant. *Sodas* usually serve economical, Tico-style meals, including the omnipresent *casado*, a cheap lunch or dinner plate that includes meat, rice, salad, and sometimes a drink and dessert.

SAN JOSÉ AREA

Accommodations

Hotel Grano de Oro

This hotel in the Paseo Colón area of San José is one of the most charming lodging options in the city; a rambling old house has been converted into 35 rooms, ranging from US$85 for a small but elegant double to US$240 for the deluxe Vista de Oro suite, with its own private staircase and stunning views of the city. There are two rooftop whirlpool tubs and an excellent restaurant in the lobby.

Calle 30, between Avenidas 2 and 4, 150 meters (164 yds.) south of Paseo Colón

tel. 506/255-3322

fax 506/221-2782

www.hotelgranodeoro.com

Hotel Aranjuez

A popular budget option in Barrio Aranjuez, within walking distance of downtown San José, this hotel is made up of five contiguous houses in a quiet and historic neighborhood. Rooms are basic but satisfactory, with TV, safe, and fan. Great common areas, including an open-air dining room set in lush gardens and offering a big breakfast that's included in the nightly rate. Free parking and Internet access. About US$35/night.

Calle 19, between Avenidas 11 and 13

U.S. tel. 877/898-8663, Costa Rica tel. 506/256-1825

fax 506/223-3528

www.hotelaranjuez.com

Hotel Bougainvillea

If you'd like to be based north of San José, a good choice is the Bougainvillea in Heredia, a midpriced hotel set amid extensive and well-designed grounds. For what it offers—great views across the valley, easy airport access, tennis courts, whirlpool tub and sauna, pool, restaurant, plus a free shuttle to downtown San José—the rates (US$80–100 double) are quite reasonable. In Santo Tomás de Heredia, 100 meters (109 yds.) west of the Escuela de Santo Tomás.

tel. 506/244-1414

fax 506/244-1313

www.bougainvillea.co.cr

Hotel Alta

Some of the rooms in this boutique hotel in Escazú, an upscale suburb of San José, have sweeping views of the Central Valley from private balconies; others have garden views.

The hotel's eclectic La Luz restaurant is a destination in and of itself. From about US$105 for a low-season double to US$865 for the top-floor, three-bedroom penthouse. On the old road to Santa Ana. U.S. tel. 888/388-2582 Costa Rica tel. 506/282-4160 fax 506/282-4162 www.altatravelplanners.com

CasaElena Hotel and Spa

An hour and a half from San José, on the road to the coastal town of Puntarenas, CasaElena is a great place to hole up for a few days of healthful pampering. It's above the town of San Ramon, and at 1,000 meters (3,280 ft.) has sweeping views all the way to the coast. All your typical spa treatments and activities are available, from yoga and a sauna to facials and collagen injections. Vegetarian and vegan cuisine is available, and all sorts of excursions can easily be arranged. Adults only. US$72 per person double occupancy, in one of the spacious guest rooms with private bath—price includes breakfast and use of all facilities. Check website for specials. tel. 506/445-0004 or 506/381-1032 casaelena@racsa.co.cr www.costaricarelax.com

Food and Drink

Machu Picchu

Great ceviche and Pisco sours at this reasonably priced Peruvian restaurant in the Paseo Colón area of San José. Open Mon.–Sat. 11 A.M.–3 P.M. and 6–10 P.M. Calle 32, between Avenidas 1 and 3; 150 meters (164 yds.) north of KFC (Pollo Frito Kentucky) on Paseo Colón tel. 506/222-7384 There's another Machu Picchu in San Pedro, 150 meters (164 yds.) south of Mas x Menos. tel. 506/283-3679

Lubnan

Good Lebanese food, cool bar that stays open until 1 A.M. Closed Sunday and Monday. Inexpensive. Paseo Colón, between Calles 22 and 24 tel. 506/257-6071

Tin Jo

Places that try to do too much usually get into trouble. But Tin Jo in downtown San José takes on a full range of Asian cuisines, from Japanese tempura to Indian curry, and is the delicious exception to the rule. Moderate prices, creative cocktails, vegetarian-friendly, and real cloth napkins! Open Mon.–Sat. 11:30 A.M.–3 P.M. and 5:30–10 P.M.; Fri. and Sat. same hours but until 11 P.M.; Sun. 11:30 A.M.–10 P.M. Calle 11, between Avenidas 6 and 8, in front of Teatro Lucho Barahona tel. 506/221-7605

L'Île de France

Intimate French restaurant inside the Hotel Le Bergerac has very good food and excellent service. Garden terrace. Expensive. The hotel has nice rooms, too, that go for US$68–95 double.
Hotel Le Bergerac, Calle 35, 50 meters (55 yds.) south of the first entrance to Los Yoses off the Avenida Central (coming from downtown San José)
tel. 506/283-5812
www.bergerachotel.com

Vishnu

A chain of eight vegetarian restaurants; try the one on Avenida 1 between Calles 1 and 3, a few blocks east of the big downtown post office. Vishnu serves fruit plates, filling *platos del dia* (soup, salad, entrée, and dessert) for about US$3, and excellent smoothies. At the front counter you can get good whole-grain bread. Inexpensive.
Locations all over San José
downtown tel. 506/256-6063

Café Mundo

Eclectic international cuisine served in a former colonial mansion in a historical district. Pasta, pizza, and Asian-inspired dishes abound. The slightly bohemian crowd belies the prices, which are moderate to expensive. Open Mon.–Thurs. 11 A.M.–11 P.M.; Fri. 11 A.M.–midnight; Sat. 5 P.M.–midnight.
Avenida 9 at Calle 15, or 200 meters (219 yds.) east and 100 meters (109 yds.) north of the INS building in downtown San José
tel. 506/222-6045

Café Britt del Teatro Nacional

A lovely high-ceilinged café tucked inside the architecturally stunning National Theater. Espresso drinks, desserts, and light meals. Open Mon.–Sat. 10 A.M.–6 P.M.
Teatro Nacional, Avenida 2 at Calle 3
tel. 506/221-3262

Calle de la Amargura

A short street near UCR (University of Costa Rica) that's lined with bars and packed on weekends with a university crowd. Tell the taxi driver the name of the street and then take your pick of loud or louder places to eat and drink. One of the nicer places, in an old house, is La Villa (tel. 506/280-9541).

Jazz Café

A more sophisticated alternative to nearby Calle de la Amargura, and a great place to hear live music. The place is on the main San Pedro drag and doesn't usually get hopping until after 10 P.M. Dinner available.
tel. 506/253-8933

Restaurant and Pub Olio

In the Los Yoses area of San José, a low-key but hip place for drinks and tapas. From Bagelemen's on main drag, go 300 meters (328 yds.) north, then 20 meters (22 yds.) east.
tel. 506/281-0541

El Bolinche
Popular gay-friendly hangout in downtown San José.
Calle 11 between Avenidas 10 and 12
tel. 506/221-0500

Café Loft
Downtown spot with a cool crowd and comfortable sofas; gay-friendly. DJs spin low-key techno, some patrons venture to dance. Closed Sundays.
Avenida 3 at Calle 3
tel. 506/221-2302

Shops and Activities
Costa Rica Expeditions
Based in the capital but operating throughout the country, this venerable tour agency is the one to beat. Great packages to its Corcovado Tent Camp or Tortuga Lodge on the Caribbean coast, wonderful guides, and high safety standards. Its San José office is on Calle Central at Avenida 3, a few blocks from the main post office.
tel. 506/257-0766
fax 506/257-1665
www.costaricaexpeditions.com

North American Cultural Center
An attractive complex of classrooms, galleries, the Mark Twain library (books, magazines, and newspapers in English and Spanish), and the Eugene O'Neill Theater (with plays in English). Definitely worth a look, and one of the

city's few bowling alleys is right across the street! In Barrio Dent.
tel. 506/207-7500
fax 506/224-1480
mercadeo@cccncr.com
www.cccncr.com

Biesanz Woodworks
Exquisite (and expensive) wooden bowls and boxes made of tropical hardwood. In Escazú, and not easy to find; call ahead for directions.
tel. 506/289-4337
fax 506/228-6184
woodworks@biesanz.com
www.biesanz.com

Museo de Insectos
A small and rather odd museum, but fascinating if you like bugs. Even the location is unlikely—it's in the basement of the music building on the UCR campus, in the San Pedro area. Closed weekends; call ahead to make sure of the hours.
tel. 506/207-5318

ZONA NORTE

Accommodations
Hotel La Mansion Inn, Marina, and Club (Lake Arenal; 8 km/5 mi. east of Nuevo Arenal)
With a name that leaves no stone unturned, this hotel also covers all the bases in terms of peace, luxury, and absolutely stunning views of Lake Arenal. Splurge for a night or two in one of Belgian-born Peggy Ponteur's 14 *cabinas,* equipped with king-sized bed, hand-painted

stucco walls, lounge area, mini-fridge, and private patio. Take a dip in the horizon-edge pool, or make use of the Inn's three canoes or 20 horses, free of charge. US$125–220/night.
tel./fax 506/384-6533
marinha@skynet.be

Arenal Observatory Lodge
(near Arenal Volcano)
Imagine lying in bed in front of a big picture window, watching as lava pours down the side of a volcano. The best rooms in this well-run lodge allow you that privilege, and Arenal Volcano obliges by going off just about every night. Built as a vulcanology research station, the lodge is now considerably more posh, with a pool, comfortable rooms, and paths and hanging bridges through the landscaped grounds. Rates vary considerably—from US$52 to US$170—depending on room and time of year.
reservations tel. 506/290-7011
lodge tel. 506/695-5033
fax 506/290-8427
info@arenal-observatory.co.cr
www.arenal-observatory.co.cr

Food
La Choza de Laurel (La Fortuna)
Great *tipico* food in a rustic, open-air setting a few blocks west of the town square. Try the chicken, roasted to perfection in a brick oven. Inexpensive.
tel. 506/479-9231
chlaurel@sol.racsa.co.cr

Soda El Río (La Fortuna)
Of all the inexpensive *sodas* in town, this is my favorite. Good basic fare (*casados, arroz con pollo,* and the rest), low prices, riverside location. They also rent out a couple of budget *cabinas.*
tel. 506/479-9341

Tom's Pan (Nuevo Arenal)
Excellent German bakery that also serves enormous lunches. Enjoy strong coffee and delicious pastries on the funky terrace.
tel. 506/694-4547

Shops and Activities
La Fortuna Waterfall
(La Fortuna)
About five kilometers (3.1 mi.) south of town lies a stunning waterfall that plummets into a steep ravine. You can walk or drive from town, then (after paying a small entrance fee) make your way down a slippery trail (use the handrail!) to the falls. The pool at the base of the falls is lovely, but it's best not to go for a dip in the churning waters; swimming is safer a little ways down the river (follow the path). If you're going to walk all the way, it's best to start relatively early in the morning, thus avoiding the midday heat.

Tabacón Hot Springs
(near La Fortuna, at the base of Arenal Volcano)
For soothing tired muscles or just taking in the exquisite tropical

gardens, nothing beats Tabacón Hot Springs, 13 kilometers (8 mi.) west of La Fortuna. A naturally warm river has been guided into pools and even trained over a small falls, which will drum the tension right out of your shoulders and neck. Entrance is not cheap (it's up to almost US$20), but you shouldn't miss this Shangri La experience. There's also a big pool with a slide for the kids and a swim-up bar for adults, a well-regarded restaurant, massage and spa treatments, and a hotel up the hill. If you stay at the hotel (42 rooms, expensive), entrance to the springs is free. Visit at night for the full effect, when you can sometimes see lava tumbling down the flanks of nearby (*very* nearby) Arenal Volcano. The springs are open 10 A.M.–10 P.M.
tel. 506/256-1500
fax 506/221-3075
sales@tabacon.com
www.tabacon.com

ZONA SUR

Accommodations
Wilson Botanical Garden
(San Vito)
Stay in rustic luxury amid extensive and varied gardens, and eat family-style with students, researchers, and other nature-loving tourists. Book through the Organization for Tropical Studies, which oversees the garden. US$70 s/US$125 d, meals included.

tel. 506/240-6696
fax 506/240-6783
reserves@ots.ac.cr
www.ots.ac.cr

Food
Strapless Kafe
(San Isidro de General)
Strange name, superior coffee, along with good Tico breakfasts and light lunches. Betty Boop, Jackie O, and Princess Di dolls peer out of a locked case as you sip your iced cappuccino and watch the expats come and go. A block north of the main square on Calle 0.
no phone

Taquería México Lindo
(San Isidro de General)
Real Mexican food made by real Mexican cooks. After a few dozen *casados,* you'll be more than ready for some tacos or a spicy *mole.* On the west side of the main square, in a little mall that also has a good Internet café. Open Monday–Saturday 11 A.M.–8 P.M.
tel. 506/771-8222

Pizzería Liliana (San Vito)
Partake of San Vito's Italian heritage with Liliana's great pasta and pizza. Decent red wine is available by the glass. Just up the hill from the tiny main square (actually, it's more of a triangle).
tel. 506/773-3080

GUANACASTE AND NICOYA PENINSULA

Accommodations

Listed from north to south:
Hotel Villa Casa Blanca
(Playa Ocotal)
An intimate bed-and-breakfast a short walk from peaceful Playa Ocotal. Fifteen rooms (US$60–95), some with views, others with kitchenettes. Breakfast is on the plant-draped patio—there's a view not only of the beach but of the resident parrots.
tel. 506/670-0518
fax 506/670-0448
www.costa-rica-hotels-travel.com

Sueño del Mar (Tamarindo)
Vermont transplants Nancy Money and Paul Thabault run this intimate B&B right on Playa Langosta, a few kilometers south of Tamarindo. Lounge by the pool, relax in a rocking chair on the breezy porch, or go straight to your room, where eclectic furnishings and a private outdoor shower await. Over a delicious breakfast Nancy and Paul will chat with you about the area, refer you to a real estate agent, or arrange a turtle tour for later in the evening. From US$115 in low season to US$220 for the honeymoon suite during high season. From Tamarindo, take the Playa Langosta road, and watch for the Sueño del Mar signs.
tel. 506/653-0284
suenodem@racsa.co.cr
www.tamarindo.com/sdmar

Luna Llena (Tamarindo)
A stylish spread with bungalows set around a pool and linked by stone pathways through lush foliage. The two-story bungalows have kitchenettes and spacious bathrooms with lovely tile work. There are also standard rooms, and breakfast is served in a poolside cabaña each morning. Moderate rates, breakfast included.
tel. 506/653-0082
fax 506/653-0120
lunalle@sol.racsa.co.cr

Café de Paris (Nosara)
Not just a popular bakery (expats congregate here) but a good hotel as well, with pleasant, high-ceilinged rooms, some with kitchenettes, all with a/c. Tables set out under thatched lean-tos invite a game of outdoor chess, while the hammocks beckon at siesta time. US$40–70, includes breakfast. Pool, game room, restaurant, and bar. On the main road into Nosara, just where you turn for Playa Guiones.
tel. 506/682-0087
fax 506/682-0089

Cabinas Don Jaime
(Playa Samara)
Basic but comfortable *cabinas* just south of town and right on the beach, rented out by Don Jaime, an erudite Tico artist who lived for years in the San Francisco Bay Area. Inexpensive.
tel. 506/656-0284

Luz de Mono (Montezuma)
A lovely spread on the edge of town, with 12 standard rooms and six private casitas, with ocean views and fully equipped kitchens. There's occasional live music, an open-air restaurant, and local art exhibits. A troop of howler monkeys comes by almost every morning. Moderate to expensive.
tel. 506/642-0090
fax 506/642-0010
luzdmomo@racsa.co.cr

Flor Blanca (Santa Teresa)
A big-time splurge (US$250–550), but worth it if you can swing it. Ten truly luxurious *cabinas* set just off a sweeping white-sand beach at the western tip of the Nicoya Peninsula. The best restaurant for miles, great surfing, and a loving attention to detail not often found hereabouts.
tel. 506/640-0232
fax 506/640-0226
florblanca@expressmail.net
www.florblanca.com

Food
Listed from north to south:
Lazy Wave (Tamarindo)
One of the most popular restaurants in Tamarindo (arrive early or be ready to wait), the Lazy Wave specializes in seafood dishes like Thai seared tuna, but also usually has something on its blackboard for meat-eaters, like fried rabbit or the ever-popular surf and turf. Entrées about

US$10. Located just before the Hotel Pasatiempos.
tel. 506/653-0737

Sano Banano (Montezuma)
Banana pancakes, vegetarian stir-fries, and great coffee. What more could you ask for? How about a movie screened every night, free to those who buy US$5 or more worth of the Sano Banano's delicious vegetarian fare. Open daily 7 A.M.–9:30 P.M., on Montezuma's main street—you can't miss it, and you won't want to.
tel. 506/642-0638

Shops and Activities
Chica Surf
(Tamarindo)
U.S. transplant Heather Ellis teaches girls and women to surf. Look for her sign on the Playa Langosta road.

Jesse's Gym and Surf School
(Playa Samara)
Surf lessons and board rentals by U.S. expat Jesse. Right next door to Cabinas Don Jaime.
tel. 506/656-0055
whiteeagle@racsa.co.cr

Topsy Bookstore
(Montezuma and Santa Teresa)
A cozy little place where you can not only buy but rent "wicked good books."
tel. 506/642-0576 (Montezuma)
tel. 506/640-0316 (Santa Teresa)

CENTRAL AND SOUTH PACIFIC COAST

Accommodations

Listed from north to south:

Best Western Jacó (Jacó)
Especially if you have kids, this sprawling complex of U.S.-style rooms, swimming pools, and restaurants could be just what you're looking for. It's right on the beach and a short walk to town. Moderate prices.
tel. 506/643-1000
fax 506/643-3246
www.bestwesterncostarica.com/
 locations_jaco_amen.html.

Ola Bonita
(Playa Hermosa, just south of Jacó)

Modest rooms right on the beach are a good choice if you want a kitchen and good a/c. There's also a pool where the two resident iguanas like to hang out. US$50–80. Owner Freddy is Italian and his co-owner wife, Joanna, is a Tica who also deals in real estate.
tel./fax 506/643-3990
www.olabonita.com

Casitas Eclipse (Manuel Antonio)
The white-walled, red-roofed bungalows here cascade down a verdant hill. Rooms are simple but elegant, with tile floors and spacious bathrooms. Paths lead to not one but three swimming pools, one with stunning views of the

© Erin Van Rheenen

Ola Bonita, Playa Hermosa

coastline below. The hotel's Gato Negro restaurant serves Italian food. Located about midway between Quepos and Manuel Antonio. Prices vary depending on season and size of room, from US$90 for a low-season double up to US$275 for a high-season two-bedroom casita.
tel. 506/777-0408
fax 506/777-1738
www.casitaseclipse.com

Pacific Edge
(4 km/2.5 mi. south of Dominical)
A kilometer or two up a steep gravel road just south of Dominical, these rustic *cabinas* have absolutely gorgeous views, along with kitchenettes and front porches perfect for lounging and bird-watching. Moderate prices.
tel. 506/381-4369
pacificedge@pocketmail.com

Villas Gaia
(Playa Tortuga, about 30 km/18.5 mi. south of Dominical)
Eleven charming and spacious bungalows (US$60) well-placed amid densely landscaped grounds, as well as a two-bedroom house that runs US$110. Awe-inspiring views from the hilltop swimming pool, and a very good international restaurant, which offers everything from Greek salad to Thai curry.
tel./fax 506/244-0316 or 506/382-8240
info@villasgaia.com
www.villasgaia.com

Villas El Bosque
(Playa Tortuga, about 30 km/18.5 mi. south of Dominical)
Immaculately maintained rooms and *cabinas* with high beamed ceilings, fans in every room, and abundant hot water. *Cabinas* have fully equipped kitchens and private decks great for lounging and bird-watching. Lighted paths wind through lush foliage and vine-draped trees. There's a pleasant small pool, and it's a short walk to Playa Tortuga (Turtle Beach). Presided over by a helpful French-Canadian named Michel Benoit and his dog, Bosco, who will happily accompany you on your walk to the beach. Prices range US$30–75, with discounts during low season and for longer stays.
cell: 506/398-2112
international fax 801/218-7936
Costa Rica fax 506/786-6358
villaselbosque@yahoo.com
www.villaselbosque.com

La Paloma Lodge
(Drake Bay, Osa Peninsula)
A very popular lodge where you'll meet your fellow guests at mealtime in an open-air dining room with long communal tables. Potted palms, ceiling fans, and cloth napkins make you think you're back in the British raj, but the stunning views of Drake Bay and beyond are *pura Tica*. Spacious bungalows dot the hillside and share in the view; some are big enough to accommodate whole families. Bungalows 1

© Erin Van Rheenen

Corcovado Tent Camp

and 3 are especially nice. The lodge arranges all manner of tours—to Corcovado National Park and Caño Island, among others—and its guides are excellent—ours knew just where to look for the giant sea turtles, manta rays, and sharks that scared us halfway out of our snorkels. US$140–170 per person, meals included; also look into the packages, which include tours.
tel. 506/239-2801
fax 506/239-0954
www.lapalomalodge.com

Casa Corcovado Jungle Lodge
(Drake Bay, Osa Peninsula)
If you're tired of running around and want some pampering, this is the place. Right on the edge of Cor-

covado National Park and a short boat ride to the excellent diving at Caño Island, this lodge is remote but not at all rustic. Orchids on your pillow, fine dining, and very attentive service. All-inclusive packages mean you don't have to worry about details but are free to enjoy the extensive grounds (including spring-fed pool and private beach) and luxurious bungalows. Most people come on package tours. Two- and three-night packages run from US$700 to US$900, and include airfare from San José and two tours. Check website for other packages.
tel. 506/256-3181
fax 506/256-7409
corcovdo@racsa.co.cr
www.casacorcovado.com

Corcovado Tent Camp
(Carate, on Osa Peninsula)
Fly by light plane to Carate, then walk along the shoreline for half an hour to get to this seriously relaxing spread on a long, beautiful beach. Don't let the word "tent" throw you—these tents are basically raised cabins with flexible walls, with beds and tables and little front porches. Good access to Corcovado National Park. Meals are family-style, bathrooms are shared (but kept scrupulously clean), and there are guided hikes and horseback rides. About US$50 per person per day, meals included.
tel. 506/257-0766
fax 506/257-1665
www.costaricaexpeditions.com

Playa Zancudo Beach Club
(Playa Zancudo)
First on the road into town and a good option for laid-back elegance. The raised wooden *cabinas* have comfortable queen-sized beds, table and chairs, spacious bathrooms, and nice front porches from which to watch the waves break. The club also rents out a brand-new condo with beach view. Either way, you're only a few steps from the excellent open-air bar and restaurant, which serves up specialties like brick-oven pizza and grilled ribs with Jack Daniels sauce. Owners Gary and Debbie Walsh are friendly and knowledgeable about the area; surfing, fishing, or horseback riding tours can be arranged. Gary also deals in real estate. US$42–75, with discounts during low season and for longer stays.
tel. 506/776-0087
zbc@costarica.net
www.zancudobeachclub.com

Casa Siempre Domingo
Bed & Breakfast (Pavones)
Share the lofty hilltop home of Greg and Heidi Norris and their young son, Winston. With soaring hardwood ceilings and cool tiled floors, the immaculately maintained rooms have at least two comfortably firm beds, private baths, and ceiling fans. The common area, where guests are served breakfast, has one of the most amazing views I've seen, with the Golfo Dulce to the right and a sweep of open ocean to the left. Check out the spiraling outdoor shower, studded with mosaic tiles and shells. A bargain at US$25 per person.
tel./fax 506/775-0631

Food
Listed from north to south:
Café Milagro
(locations in Quepos and Manuel Antonio)
Excellent espresso drinks, hot and iced, along with homemade muffins and sandwiches. Open daily 6 A.M.–10 P.M.
tel. 506/777-1707
fax 506/777-2272
info@cafemilagro.com
www.cafemilagro.com

Balcon de Uvita
(Uvita, 15 km/9.3 mi.
south of Dominical)
You'll need four-wheel drive to get to this lofty retreat in the woods above the coastal town of Uvita, but the trip is worth it. Owners Bart ten Kate and Gabriella van Ijsseldijk, both from Holland and she of Indonesian heritage, have created an unlikely destination restaurant. Amazing views, excellent food, and the added pleasure of incongruity—what's a delicious Indonesian rice platter, with all the trimmings, doing in Costa Rica? Exotic food from across the globe fits surprisingly well with this hemisphere's tropics. When I visited, it was open only Thursday, Friday, and Saturday evenings—call ahead. You can also rent *cabinas* here. From in front of the gas station one kilometer (.6 mi.) north of Uvita, follow the gravel road to the east.
tel. 506/743-8034
info@balcondeuvita.com
www.balcondeuvita.com

Exo-Tica
(Ojachal, 35 km/21.7 mi.
south of Dominical)
Down an unlit dirt road is this gem of a French restaurant, one of the best in the country. Lucy from Quebec makes the luscious desserts, while the Belgian Marcela works her magic with the entrées, from classics like beef bourguignon to innovative curries full of locally caught fish. Funky, open-air elegance, with candles lining the path

to the dining area. Open Mon.–Sat. 11 A.M.–9:30 P.M.
no phone

La Manta Club (Pavones)
Good Mediterranean food—hummus, falafel, fresh fish kabobs—served in an open-air, thatch-roofed restaurant. Every evening, footage of the day's surf action is projected hugely on a white wall. Wall-dwelling geckoes seem to be part of the picture, riding the waves or perching on an unsuspecting surfer's shoulder. BYOB. Open Monday–Saturday 11 A.M.–9:30 P.M.
no phone

Shops and Activities
Tree of Life Tours (Dominical)
A tour company with a decidedly spiritual bent, but even hardened cynics will see god(s) in the spray of the 26-meter (85-ft.) waterfall along which you rappel.
tel. 506/787-0184
cell: 506/355-8215
info@treeoflifetours.com
www.treeoflifetours.com

Drake Bay Guide
Javier Mora grew up in the tiny town of Agujitas, his father was a park ranger, and he knows the area like the back of his hand. Javier specializes in hiking, bird-watching, and snorkeling.
tel. 506/824-1151
aguijitasdrake_mora@hotmail.com, or ask for him at La Paloma Lodge

Shooting Star Yoga Studio
(Pavones)

Amy Khoo presides over this thatch-roofed, open-air studio with a view of the beach, leading classes in bikram, ashtanga, and "yoga for surfers." She also hopes to host yoga workshops soon.

tel. 506/393-6982
info@shootingstarstudio.org
www.shootingstarstudio.org

CARIBBEAN COAST

Accommodations

Listed from north to south:

Tortuga Lodge (Tortuguero)

You won't regret booking a day or two at this lovely riverside lodge right next to Tortuguero National Park. Run by well-respected Costa Rica Expeditions, the lodge is a class act, with rustically elegant rooms and excellent food. It employs some of the best guides, who will show you the boas, caimans, crocodiles, and turtles that call the area home. Birds abound, and if you're really lucky, you may see a manatee. US$115, with many package deals available. Book through Costa Rica Expeditions.

tel. 506/257-0766
fax 506/257-1665
www.costaricaexpeditions.com

Laguna Lodge (Tortuguero)

Not quite as deluxe as Tortuga Lodge but still very nice, Laguna Lodge is set on a wedge of land between river and beach. This Tico-owned lodge has 5.7 hectares (14 acres) of attractive grounds, where you're likely to see innumerable birds and bright green and blue frogs that fit in your cupped palm. Some of the newer buildings are architecturally ambitious, like the reception area in the shape of a spiraling shell. Nearby Mawamba Lodge is similar, and in fact is owned by the brother of the Laguna Lodge owner. Rates are moderate to expensive.

tel. 506/225-3740
fax 506/283-8031
laguna@sol.racsa.co.cr
www.lagunalodgetortuguero.com

Magellan Inn (Cahuita)

An elegant option about 135 meters (148 yds.) north of Playa Negra. Six well-appointed rooms overlook a lush garden—ylang-ylang blossoms perfume the air, and ripe guavas fall from the trees. There's an excellent restaurant, and owners Terri Newman and Slavko "Topo" Topolovsek are multilingual and can tell you all about the area. Rates US$69–89, including continental breakfast. Topo also deals in real estate.

tel./fax 506/755-0035
magellaninn@racsa.co.cr
http://magellaninn.topos
    realestate.org

Centro Turistico Brigitte
(Cahuita)

Fifty meters (55 yds.) inland from

the Playa Negra road, Swiss-born Brigitte Abegglen runs a small but pleasant complex with three *cabinas* (US$15 s/US$25 d), a small restaurant, and a few computers with Internet access. Horseback riding and bicycle rentals are also available.
tel./fax 506/755-0053
brigittecahuita@hotmail.com
www.brigittecahuita.com

Cabinas Casa Verde
(Puerto Viejo)
Good in-town choice. Well-maintained rooms are set among front and back gardens with hammocks and lush gardens. Doubles from US$34–52.
tel. 506/750-0015
fax 506/750-0047
www.cabinascasaverde.com

Food
Listed from north to south:
La Casona (Tortuguero)
San José–born Jenny Madden, her son Andrés, and his young son Michael make this cozy restaurant a family affair. Jenny offers up "alternatives to the usual rice and beans," and the traveler weary of that sacred combo can feast on pasta, fish, or delicious banana pancakes. Eat inside or out on the patio, where beach finds like weathered paddles and turtle shells hang helter skelter on the walls. Right next to the town soccer field.
no phone

Sobre las Olas (Cahuita)
On the Playa Negra road (a short walk north of town), and right on the beach, this Italian-run place lets you dine alfresco on creative cuisine. Lots of fish, of course, but also non-Tico treats like bruschetta. Closed Tuesdays.
tel. 506/755-0109

Cha Cha Cha (Cahuita)
Delicious international cuisine—from hummus to grilled shrimp—a block west of the main plaza. Open noon–10 P.M.
tel. 506/394-4153

Red Stripe Inn (Puerto Viejo)
Eclectic, mostly Asian-influenced fare served by young San Francisco transplants. A few streetside tables overlook the beach. Homemade ice cream and a shelf of books to trade complete the homey picture. Near the bus station.
no phone

Café Rico (Puerto Viejo)
The best (and strongest) cup of coffee in town. Nice garden setting, friendly Brit manager. They also serve breakfast and sandwiches.
no phone

Miss Sam's (Puerto Viejo)
Always full, and for good reason. Afro-Caribbean specialties at very reasonable prices. Sometimes Miss Sam runs out of the excellent rice and beans cooked in coconut milk—arrive early, and BYOB if you

want to drink with your meal (there's a liquor store down the street). Closed Sunday. Hours flexible, but usually open for dinner. tel. 506/750-0108

La Pecora Nera
(near Puerto Viejo)
Excellent Italian food on the road between Playa Cocles and Playa Chiquita. Closed Sunday. Hours flexible; call ahead to make sure they're open.
tel. 506/750-0490

Shops and Activities
John H. Phipps Biological Field Station (Tortuguero)
The Caribbean Conservation Corporation (CCC) runs this one-room but very informative museum featuring fascinating displays on the sea turtles that give the area its name (*tortuguero* means turtle hunter). To get there you walk north on an overgrown path from the town center. Open daily 10 A.M.–noon and 2–6 P.M. Learn more about the CCC at www.cccturtle.org.
tel. 506/710-0545

Daryl Loth, Guide (Tortuguero)
Canadian-born naturalist guide has a vast knowledge of the area. Daryl has a few boats for river touring; he and his wife also rent out four clean and pleasant rooms by the riverside, each with private

Nosara Beach, on the Nicoya Peninsula

© Erin Van Rheenen

bath, for US$25 s/US$35 d, breakfast included.
tel. 506/711-0673
cell: 506/392-3201
safari@racsa.co.cr

Barbara Hartung, Guide
(Tortuguero)
Barbara is a German-born biologist
and guide who has lived in Tortuguero for many years.
tel. 506/842-6561
tinamon@racsa.co.cr
www.tinamontours.de

Paraíso Tropical (Tortuguero)
Fifty meters (55 yds.) north from
the main dock, this gift shop has
a large selection for such a small
town. Lots of batiked sarongs,
along with jewelry, posters, knick-
knacks, and books. Owners Enrique
and Jessica Obando also rent out
modest apartments in town, short-
or long-term.
tel. 506/710-0323

ATEC (Puerto Viejo)
The Talamanca Association for Ecotourism and Conservation is a
grassroots group working hard to

promote responsible tourism. Its
Puerto Viejo office is a community
center of sorts, offering Internet access and tour information and
booking.
tel./fax 506/750-0191
atecmail@sol.racsa.co.cr
www.greencoast.com/atec.htm

Florentino (Tino)
Grenald, Guide (Manzanillo)
A long-time resident of Manzanillo,
Tino helped plan and administer
the Gandoca-Manzanillo reserve.
early in the reserve's history. He
grew up here and knows the reserve
and surrounding areas like few others. To list all the flora and fauna
Tino pointed out on our walk
through the lowland jungle would
take pages, but here's a small sampling: cacao trees, wild turmeric, a
sloth, a spectacled owl, toads, tree
crabs, bats, and three eyelash vipers.
tel. 506/759-0619 or ask for
him at the ATEC office in
Puerto Viejo

Daily Life

© Erin Van Rheenen

Making the Move

Visas and Immigration

Immigration policy in Costa Rica is a moving target, but the good news is that North Americans are for the most part given a warm welcome. A Nicaraguan day laborer will be treated differently from, say, a retired couple from Vermont who just invested in a seaside bed-and-breakfast. North American and European visitors, in most cases, have a fairly easy time of it immigration-wise; the most that a law-abiding visitor will have to deal with are bureaucratic headaches.

The agency that enforces immigration law is the Department of Immigration (Dirección General de Migración y Extranjería), which in turn is under the jurisdiction of the Ministry of Public Security (Ministerio de Seguridad Pública). There is also a National Immigration Council (Consejo Nacional de Migración y Extranjería), charged with review of residency petitions.

Though the processes may seem arbitrary, there are official policies in place, replete with stamps, seals, and much waiting in line. Still, even seasoned expat organizations like the ARCR (Association of Residents of Costa Rica) warn that immigration laws are hard to fathom and even harder to keep up with. But one thing is for sure: In August 2002, the Department of Immigration issued a statement saying residency applications should be made in the applicant's country of origin rather than here in Costa Rica (the full text of the statement, in Spanish, can be seen at www.msp.go.cr/residencia.htm). It is much easier, with these new regulations, to begin the residency process in your home country. It's not *impossible* to do it from Costa Rica, but you would need to confer power of attorney on someone back home and have him or her act on your behalf. It's much easier to start before you move here.

Still, policy is anything but crystal clear. Regulations and laws are one thing; enforcement (especially consistent enforcement) is quite another. Students of Costa Rican policy will find many contradictory statutes; it's often up to the individual official to play judge and jury, choosing which of the many laws he or she will enforce on any given day. An editorial in the February 2003 *Tico Times,* entitled "Fix the Immigration Mess," takes on the government's first attempt since the 1980s to overhaul immigration policy. "The current system," writes the editor, "in which processes are at the whim of the transitory official holding positions of power, needs to be reformed to one in which, from the start, applicants know what the requirements are and when they need to comply with them."

Lest you dismiss the situation as hopelessly third world, remember that at least two U.S. agencies—the IRS (Internal Revenue Service) and the INS (Immigration and Naturalization Service)—have been shown to operate in a similarly heavy-handed and arbitrary fashion. Big government means lots of laws; some are bound to contradict others. And then, "public servants" around the world are often anything but, wielding their tiny swords with surprisingly lethal effect. When confronted with such officials, make nice. Count to ten, then grit your teeth into a smile. For the moment, they have the power and you don't. Save your rage and dreams of revenge for later, over a drink with friends. Then order another round.

But I digress. Costa Rica is making a real effort to streamline its immigration process, and everyone agrees it's high time for a change. Even with all the flux, the categories of residency are fairly straightforward, and not apt to change significantly anytime soon. What may change is where you apply for residency and how quickly your papers are processed. The ARCR is a good source of up-to-date information.

One more thing you should know is that if you gain any type of residency or even citizenship in Costa Rica, your U.S. or Canadian citizenship is not affected. And there's no problem on the Costa Rican end of things, either. Since 1996 this country has recognized dual citizenship. The change in policy came about when Dr. Franklin Chang, Costa Rican–born scientist and NASA astronaut, became a U.S. citizen and was consequently stripped of his Costa Rican citizenship. There was a public outcry—the country didn't want to lose such an illustrious Tico to the United States—and in response the policy was changed.

TOURIST VISAS

No paperwork, no job, no muss, no fuss—nice work if you can get it. And it can be that easy, though recent crackdowns have put the fear of expulsion in the hearts of long-term expats who've never bothered about renewing visas or getting residency. A side note: It used to be that people from Canada, the United States, and Panama could enter and exit Costa Rica without a passport, though they did need some form of identification, like a driver's license. As of April 30, 2003, however, all visitors to Costa Rica must travel with valid passports.

Here's how the perpetual-tourist thing works. Visitors from Canada, the United States, and most of Europe don't need to apply for visas in their home countries but instead receive, upon arrival in Costa Rica, a stamp on their passport authorizing a 90-day stay. When that 90 days is almost up, you leave the country for at least 72 hours—maybe you've always wanted to visit the colonial city of Granada in southern Nicaragua, or snorkel at one of the Bocas del Toro islands in northern Panama. After your three-day vacation, you cross back into Costa Rica and get another 90-day stamp on your passport. This category of visa is called the B1, or tourist visa.

Some people do this for years, but it's not an ideal solution. Although not strictly illegal (you're not overstaying your visa), the practice is considered a little shady by Costa Rican officials—a way of getting around the law. What you're doing and how often is visible in full color—soon your passport will be a riot of blue, red, and purple stamps and seals that mark you as a come-and-goer. And who knows when the government will decide to crack down on this category of tourist?

If you have anything to lose in Costa Rica—a house, a business, a family—this gray-area existence is apt to make you a little bit anxious. Not to mention that leaving the country every three months gets to be tiresome and expensive. There are shady ways to skip the trip, but they are truly back-alley and indisputably illegal. A guy knows a guy who can take care of it—and suddenly your money and passport are long gone. On the open market, U.S. and Canadian passports are said to fetch around US$5,000.

Expat Profile: Mary Ann Jackson

Born in Kentucky in the mid-20th century, Mary Ann Jackson thought her name suited her fine until one day just past the turn of the millennium. She was working at Family Court in Brooklyn, New York, and her client that day was a stunning black woman in a bright yellow print native dress and headwrap. Elegant and imposing, the woman had a presence so powerful that all eyes in the room were drawn to her. When she spoke, her voice was equally impressive—a deep and rich sound that boomed through the cramped institutional rooms.

"It's a place where we don't get to laugh a lot," says Mary Ann of her job. "My boss likens it to a jurisprudence MASH unit. Sometimes it feels like the misery has seeped into the walls." Mary Ann had never seen a woman so fully in possession of herself and her mature beauty. It turned out the woman's name was Ruby. A jewel of a name for a jewel of a woman. Mary Ann told Ruby how much she loved her name. Ruby looked at Mary Ann for a long moment, seeming to take in Mary Ann's entire life in one glance. "It's yours," she pronounced regally. "I give it to you. It will make you smile."

Mary Ann did not take such a gift lightly. She recognized it for what it was: a chance to remake herself, to try on a new identity, or circle back to one she'd lost sight of. Mary Ann had been feeling for a long time that she needed a change, something that would take her out of Brooklyn and release her from the persona that she'd settled into over the years. And so tentatively at first, and then with more confidence, she began to embrace her new name, which was all about confidence and daring. She told new friends she'd been born Mary Ann but had recently been rechristened Ruby, which felt like a part of her that had always been there but had never before been named.

The new name coincided with the working out of a new plan: to take early retirement and move abroad. She didn't want to wait until she turned 65 to get a reprieve; she knew that her new life hinged on having the courage to make big changes, and soon.

Though not born in Brooklyn, Mary Ann has a big Brooklyn personality: feisty and fearless. She's had a full life, with lots of work, travel, men, and a gaggle of nieces and nephews who adore her. She has a streak of giddy spontaneity that means she's pretty much up for anything, anytime. But she's also a practical girl, and has a mania for doing her homework and plotting her course. Not one but two people—a psychic and a man who gave her a battery of psychological tests in the course of a job interview—have told her that she would have made an excellent general.

And it's the combination of those two character traits—throwing caution to the wind while making sure she knows exactly which way that wind is blowing—that makes her the perfect candidate for relocation to an exotic locale.

Costa Rica wasn't first on her list. "First I worked my way down the East Coast," she says. "Both coasts of Florida, into Louisiana—New Orleans almost had me except for the mosquitoes and heat. Texas, then Ireland, which isn't cheap anymore. I checked out Belize but the infrastructure and medical care sucked; I have no intention of being flown to Miami for an emergency operation.

"Then a friend went to Costa Rica, and when she told me about it, bingo! It was close enough, had great medical care, decent infrastructure, lots of Americans and Canadians, cheap living."

When she got to Costa Rica she wasn't disappointed. The country was not only gorgeous but it *worked.* Each of the four times she's visited, Mary Ann has explored more of the Central Valley (she wants a temperate climate) and worked out more logistical details, from visas to real estate possibilities. The ARCR (Association of Residents of Costa Rica) has been an enormous help, says Mary Ann, as has her lawyer back in Brooklyn, who convinced her that the move was do-able on a financial level. She owns and lives in an apartment building in Brooklyn—the rent from the other apartments make her mortgage, and the rent from her own apartment (along with her pension) will provide the income she needs to live well in Costa Rica. Even more important than the financial details, for Mary Ann there's something special about this country, something hard to put into words but that makes her excited as hell about the upcoming move.

"What's funny," she says, "is that I ran around telling everybody I was retiring to Costa Rica before I even went there. I just knew."

When she goes down for good, she'll study language, staying with a Costa Rican family until she finds the ideal place of her own. She jokes about opening Ruby's Shame and Scandal Saloon, but is pretty sure she doesn't even want a part-time job, at least in the beginning. She's worked enough for a lifetime, maybe two. After her last day at Brooklyn Family Court and upon arrival in Costa Rica, she'll be Ruby full time, living in a place where a Ruby can thrive.

Even if you don't have anything to lose in Costa Rica, there are reasons to apply for residency. "I'm not sure why I was so into getting those papers," says Peggy Windle, who in 2002 took early retirement from her teaching job in Arizona and moved to Costa Rica. "I want to belong somewhere, I guess. To not be 100 percent vagabond."

If you're not planning to stay more than four months in Costa Rica, there are a few ways to legally extend your 90-day visa that don't involve a trip out of the country. You must be sure, however, to start these processes well before your visa has expired. These solutions only give you 30 additional days, are often more trouble than they're worth, and probably will not work more than once. One way is to apply at the immigration office (Migración) opposite Hospital Mexico in the La Uruca section of San José. The office is open 8:30 A.M.–3:30 P.M. You may also be asked to obtain an affidavit, in which you swear that you have no dependents in Costa Rica, from the Justice Tribunal (Calle 17, Avenidas 6/8, tel. 506/223-7555, ext. 240 or 276, fax 506/221-2066). The results of a blood test to see whether you have AIDS or HIV may also be required. To apply for the extension you'll need three passport-sized photos, a plane ticket out of the country, and funds judged sufficient to see you through your proposed stay. This procedure also involves multiple forms, stamps, line waiting, and fees. Another possibility is to see if a travel agent can get you an extension. This way is usually easier but is not something you can keep doing every 30 days.

What happens if you skulk around Costa Rica with an expired 90-day visa? It depends just how expired it is. If you're a few days or weeks in arrears, you'll probably get off with some smooth talking and the payment of a fine. If you arrived in 1985 and haven't thought about visas since, you're still okay—until someone checks your passport. Then you'll most likely get a free trip home, a.k.a. deportation. If you're deported, you can't legally return to Costa Rica for ten years.

One more thing—when you enter Costa Rica (each time), you could be asked to prove that you have sufficient funds to support yourself for the time you intend to be here. They may also ask you to show a return or onward plane or bus ticket. In practice, this rarely happens.

Types of Residency

There are countless types of residency, from refugee to diplomatic status, but for the purposes of the average North American or European, four of these will be of interest: permanent resident, *pensionado* (pensioner or retiree), *rentista* (loosely translated as "small investor"), and *inversionista* (large investor). In the shorthand of immigration agencies, the permanent resident visa is an A1 visa; *pensionados* and *rentistas* are subcategories of the A2 visa, and *inversionistas* have A3 visas.

PERMANENT RESIDENCY

After two years, *pensionados, rentistas,* and *inversionistas* can apply for permanent residency, which gives you all the rights a Costa Rican citizen enjoys, save voting. Other ways of obtaining permanent residency include being a citizen of another Central American country or of Spain and having lived in Costa Rica for five years; marrying a Costa Rican citizen; or having a child in Costa Rica. I know an unmarried couple whose decision to have kids was helped along by the fact that their Costa Rican–born child automatically conferred permanent residency upon both (foreign-born) parents.

Applicants for permanent residency must demonstrate that they will make a positive contribution to the country. Benefits of permanent residency include being able to work (rather than just own a business, as is allowed under temporary residencies), reduced fares on air travel within Costa Rica, and much-reduced admission to national parks and reserves. Permanent residency also offers up the same sort of safeguards extended to citizens, such as protection against extradition (except in high-profile cases, like when drug lords or big-time financial scamsters try to hide out in the wilds of Costa Rica). As a permanent resident, you don't need to worry about remaining in the country for four months (to maintain *pensionado* or *rentista* status) or six months (to maintain *inversionista* status) out of each year. Your only obligation as a permanent resident is to visit Costa Rica at least once a year.

PENSIONADO (PENSIONER)

Most retired people opt for this category, which requires you to prove at least US$600 a month in pension income. The income can come from a public source, like the U.S. government, or a private source, like the brokerage house that administers your IRA account. You must document that you will be receiving at least US$7,200 a year, and arrange to have the checks deposited to a Costa Rican account in *colones,* not dollars. For a married couple, the spouse with less (or no) retirement income is considered a dependent, and a dependent need show no proof of income—they ride free on their partner's US$600. Children under 18 (or a child between 18 and 25 enrolled in university) can also be claimed as dependents, and receive the same immigration status as their parents.

The downside is that two people's incomes cannot be combined to make up the required US$600 a month, though the combined income sources of one person will do the trick. If the pensioner is a little short of the US$600 a month, the balance can be made up by depositing five years' worth of the difference in a Costa Rican bank. So if your pension is US$545/month, you could make up the extra US$55 a month (for five years) by depositing US$3,300 in the bank.

Pensionados need to spend at least four months in the country a year, though the time need not be contiguous—you could spend January, February, October, and November here, for instance. You can't work as an employee, but you can own and receive income from a business.

When the Costa Rican government created the *pensionado* and *rentista* immigration categories in 1971, the idea was to attract foreign capital, and certain tax breaks were given to holders of these temporary residency visas. *Pensionados* and *rentistas* were allowed to bring in all their household goods, appliances, and one car duty-free, which with Costa Rica's high import duties was a very nice perk. But in 1992, in need of greater tax revenue, the government abolished the tax benefits associated with *pensionado* and *rentista* status. For more on what it will cost you to bring your household goods to Costa Rica, see the What to Bring section later in this chapter.

RENTISTA (SMALL INVESTOR)

For those who have not yet reached retirement age but have managed to make investments that bring in regular income, the *rentista* option is an attractive one. You'll need to prove a monthly income of US$1,000 (usually a CD or annuity), guaranteed by a banking institution. Another option is to deposit US$60,000 (US$1,000 a month for five years) in a Costa Rican bank, which will authorize you to withdraw US$1,000 of your money each month. If, after two years of *rentista* status, you apply for and receive permanent residency, you can withdraw all the money out of the account.

Other details of the *rentista* visa are similar to those of a *pensionado:* You can own a business but not work as an employee; you need to be in the country for at least four noncontiguous months each year, and dependents, whether spouse or child, enjoy the same immigration status as is awarded to the applicant.

INVERSIONISTA (LARGE INVESTOR)

Although you can legally own and operate any sort of business in Costa Rica even if you only have a tourist visa, an investment of at least US$50,000 in a sector the government deems a priority will get you *in-*

versionista temporary resident status. Costa Rican officials have declared as priority businesses related to tourism, forestry, and low-income housing. Non-priority reforestation projects will require US$100,000 in order to qualify you for *inversionista* status, and any other business ventures will call for US$200,000 or more. *Inversionistas* must stay in Costa Rica six months out of every year, though as with other categories of temporary residency, the time need not be contiguous.

For any investment, please exercise extreme caution—many people who come to Costa Rica seem to leave their common sense at home. Perhaps lulled by the tropical climate and the friendliness of the people, they trust too easily and don't do their due diligence—checking out every facet of the project before putting any money down. While living in the tropics is relatively easy, making a business profitable here is perhaps even more challenging than it would be at home.

OTHER TEMPORARY RESIDENCE

Other types of temporary residency usually require a sponsor, and may be the way to go for:

- Anyone who renders special services to governmental, international, or educational institutions in Costa Rica.
- Highly specialized technical or professional workers granted prior authority by the Ministry of Labor. Managers and executives of multinational corporations with branches in Costa Rica often fall into this category. The company that sponsors these workers must meet certain qualifications, such as having at least 50 million *colones* in real capital investment and employing a labor force that is made up of at least 90 percent Costa Rican citizens. Companies that routinely sponsor their workers are likely to be already registered with the Department of Immigration.
- Students at public or private schools or universities recognized by the government.
- Domestic servants.

Sometimes the company that employs you, the institution you are rendering services to, or the school you attend will take care of the paperwork. Make sure that is the case, and/or contact your Costa Rican Consulate or Embassy for the latest on the above categories of temporary residency.

The Application Process

You can file the paperwork on your own, you can hire a lawyer to do it for you, or you can fill out the forms and gather the necessary documents yourself, then pay a *tramitador* to stand in line for you. The whole process will be much easier if you start it in your home country, working with the nearest Costa Rican consulate.

PAPERWORK FOR RESIDENCY

Whether you're applying for permanent or temporary residency, much of the process is the same. You'll need:

1. An application that is filled out and filed with the Costa Rican consulate in your country of origin, or directly with the Department of Immigration in Costa Rica if you're in the country. (There is some question as to whether it will continue to be possible to apply for residency while in Costa Rica; right now people are still doing it, but the situation may change.)

2. If not within Costa Rica at the time of the application, you must appoint a representative and grant special authority to this representative *(apoderado)*. You'll need to provide a San José address where the representative will receive mail pertaining to your residency application.

3. Birth certificate, marriage license if you're married (if you've divorced and remarried, no divorce papers are required), copies of academic or professional degrees (if you plan to practice your profession in Costa Rica), and a police certificate of good conduct from the last place you've lived for at least two years. The police certificate should be obtained last, as it is only good for six months and may expire while you wait for your other documentation to come through.

Note: All of the documents in Item 3 must be translated into Spanish (by the office of the Costa Rican consulate), then submitted to and authenticated by the Costa Rican consulate officer in the country where the documents are issued. Having your documents authenticated by a Costa Rican consulate is not the same as having them notarized. Documents that are not "public documents" must be certified by a notary public of the state where the documents were issued. Public documents (those issued by a governmental institution) do not need to be notarized.

Authorization means that the consulate makes sure the documents are valid and belong to you; the consulate will also make sure the notary who notarized your documents is fully certified. There is, of course, a fee for each document authorized, at present about US$40 per document.

You can begin to see how it might be easier to apply for residency in your country of origin. Ask a good lawyer, the ARCR, or other expats what they would recommend for your particular case.

4. An authenticated copy of your passport (every page).

5. Authenticated copies of dependents' birth certificates (spouse and/or

Becoming "Legal": Two Cautionary Tales

Immigration policy is hard to keep up with, and much of the information you come by is anecdotal. Here, with names withheld to protect the outraged, are two such stories.

Control Yourself

"One time my husband was trying to renew his *pensionado* status. He got frustrated and lost his temper with someone who worked at the Ministry of Tourism, where he had to go and renew his residency every two years. In Costa Rica, you should never, ever raise your voice—they consider that worse than slapping them.

And so they 'lost' five years of his file. They wouldn't renew his residency because they said he hadn't changed enough money—you have to change so much every month, and give them the receipts—but there was no proof that he'd changed money because they'd lost the file with the receipts in it. We said, 'You renewed his residency last year, and there were plenty of receipts.' But now that they didn't have the file, there was no proof. My advice: Control your temper, no matter what."

Good Faith Isn't Always Enough

"I applied for residency through my lawyer, but the law changed while my case was being considered. Actually, the law changed three times between September 2002 and May 2003, with no grandfather clause that would take care of those of us already in line. The new law says that for residency, you need to go back to your country of origin to apply.

So now, though I've done everything right and in good faith, I think I'm an illegal alien. I'm afraid to leave the country, or to even travel. There's a permanent visa checkpoint near where I like to go on the Caribbean side, and I think there's one near Jacó, too. What is my lawyer doing to try to fix the mess? He's wining and dining the immigration officials. It's all about personal contacts."

children) if they are to be included in the residency application. You'll also need police certificates of good conduct for dependents over 18 that you're including in your application.

6. Four passport-sized photos.
7. Your fingerprints—the Ministry of Public Security will run them through Interpol, who will do an international background check on you.
8. You may be asked to provide proof of a doctor's exam. There are laws on the books allowing Costa Rican officials to refuse entry into the country to people with AIDS, although I've never heard of that happening.
9. Proof of income. This is the most important part of your application. The more income, the better; the government wants to be sure you have enough money to support yourself while in Costa Rica.

If you're going for *pensionado* or *rentista* status, you'll need a letter from your financial institution saying that you will be receiving at least US$600 a month (for *pensionados*) or US$1,000 a month (for *rentistas*). The financial institution must be an "internationally recognized entity," listed in Polk's International Banking Directory. If your income is from a brokerage or insurance company, you'll need to submit a copy of its annual report along with your residency application. The letter issued by your financial institution is supposed to say that your income is "permanent and irrevocable" for at least the next five years. Since it is the client who ultimately controls the investments, some financial institutions balk at using the phrase "permanent and irrevocable." The usual way around this is to have them add in their letter a line that states, "in the event the funds invested or on deposit are reduced in any manner, the bank shall notify the Costa Rican Tourism Institute," which, along with the Department of Immigration, has a say in residency issues.

For *inversionista* applications, you'll be submitting business rather than personal financial records. If you invest in an already existing business, you'll need to provide balance sheets and profit-and-loss information along with your residency application. For a new business, especially if you're hoping your enterprise will qualify as "priority" and thus allow you to invest US$50,000 rather than the usually required US$200,000, the forms and documents needed are beyond the scope of this book. A good accountant and a lawyer familiar with the Costa Rican business world will be your best resources. Starting a business in Costa Rica need not be bound up with a residency application. Many people start businesses with far less than US$50,000, and do so while here on a 90-day tourist visa. This is perfectly legal.

Whatever category of residency you're after, the application and supporting documentation are submitted to the Department of Immigration (when you apply from your country of origin, you apply at the consulate, which sends your documents to the Department of Immigration in San José). The Department of Immigration issues a receipt of filing to the applicant. If all is in order and the application is complete, it is forwarded to the Immigration Council, where it may languish for months or even years. While they consider your application (or let it sit on someone's desk), you are legally allowed to remain in the country.

For permanent residency, the applicant (or her lawyer) will eventually receive a resolution (resolución) detailing the finding of the Immigration Council. If the resolution is approved, authorities will issue a residency card (cédula de residencia). Before the applicant can pick up this card, she must pay the government US$300 for its trouble. Residency must be renewed each year, but is usually a matter of going into an office and getting a new stamp.

Check the website www.costarica-embassy.org for information on current visa requirements.

GETTING HELP

You can hire a reputable lawyer, or go through the ARCR (Association of Residents of Costa Rica), which has a very good reputation and has helped many an expat through the residency maze. Right now it charges US$735 for processing *pensionado* or *rentista* applications, and US$1,000 to process an *inversionista* application. If you're applying with dependents, spouses will cost an additional US$365, and each child will be US$155.

Moving with Children

Costa Ricans love children, and the society as a whole is more kid-friendly than the United States. Even unplanned children are cherished, and motherhood is still seen here as a woman's highest calling. Many family decisions—like where to live—are heavily influenced by what would be best for the children.

Ticos are indulgent parents, and kids are often given a lot of freedom, their misdeeds ignored. An interesting historical explanation of this phenomenon is offered up in *The Ticos:* "Until half a century ago, many children died very young, and parents let small children enjoy what might be a brief stay on earth. Infants and toddlers are still allowed much free rein."

If you move here with kids, you'll be in the majority—almost all Costa Rican couples have children—and you will have an edge in making friends with locals. An expat mother in San José told me that her social life consisted mostly of children's birthday parties, where the kids would go outside and play and the mothers would stay inside, gossip, and eat cake.

Schooling will of course be a concern if you're moving with kids; see the Language and Education chapter for information on education in Costa Rica and a list of public and private schools.

ENTERING AND EXITING

Non–Costa Rican Children

In an effort to foil traffic in human beings (child prostitution rings often operate internationally) and to prevent international child abduction, many governments have special rules for minors entering and exiting their countries. For children traveling with one parent, Costa Rica officially requires evidence of relationship and permission for the child's travel from the parent or legal guardian not present.

Parents must take this very seriously if they don't want to be refused entry or exit; they might miss their plane while scaring up the necessary forms and signatures. To be on the safe side, parents should carry the child's birth certificate, along with a notarized copy of a letter that says both parents agree to this particular trip.

For more information and for downloadable forms, visit www.family-travelforum.com.

Costa Rican Children

If your child was born in Costa Rica, or if one or both parents is a Costa Rican citizen, the child will automatically be a Costa Rican citizen. So even if your child travels on, say, a U.S. passport, if she or he qualifies as a Costa Rican citizen, in effect the child has dual citizenship and will need to comply with entry and exit requirements applicable to Costa Rican children. To exit Costa Rica, she or he will need an exit permit issued by the Costa Rican immigration office. This office may be closed for several weeks during holiday periods.

It is also imperative that if a Costa Rican–born child is visiting Costa Rica with only one parent (even if the child lives full-time in another country, and his or her parents are not Costa Rican), the child must have the permission of the absent parent (signed in the presence of a Costa Rican consulate) to leave Costa Rica.

The rules are complicated, inflexible, and they change often—a bad combination. Parents of kids born in Costa Rica are advised to consult with the Costa Rican embassy or consulate in the United States about entry and exit requirements *before* travel to Costa Rica. Also check the Costa Rican embassy website for more information: www.costarica-embassy.org.

Moving with Pets

Jerry Ledin arrived in San José in 1998 with six black duffel bags and Piper, his Scottish terrier. "It was crazy to think I could bring my dog along," admits Jerry. "But I never considered not bringing him." It was easier than Jerry imagined. Unlike in other countries, there is no quarantine period; Jerry could take Piper with him right from the airport. "Everything turned out just fine," he says, "and Piper adjusted faster than I did—he's converted to Catholicism and now speaks fluent Spanish."

Even if your pet is not good with languages, bringing cats and dogs into Costa Rica is a fairly simply procedure. Bringing cows, horses, and other livestock is a bit more complicated, and if you want your snake or parrot to accompany you, you'll have to jump through some hoops, especially if your scaled or feathered friend is on any endangered species list.

DOGS AND CATS

For dogs and cats and other small pets, you'll need to prove to both the airlines and Costa Rican customs officers that your animal is healthy. Schedule an exam with your local veterinarian a week or two before your departure date—the vet should fill out a health certificate stating that the animal is disease-free and has been vaccinated against distemper, hepatitis, leptospirosis, parvovirus, and rabies. The rabies vaccination is supposed to be more than 30 days but less than a year old, and is necessary only for animals 4 months or older. The health certificate should then be endorsed by a Veterinary Service (VS) veterinarian, but need not be notarized. The Costa Rican consulate says the examination for the certificate must be conducted within the two weeks prior to travel to Costa Rica, though anecdotal evidence suggests that a certificate up to 30 days old will do the trick.

Pet owners also need to get authorization from the Costa Rican Health Ministry; go through your nearest Costa Rica consulate or embassy to obtain this permission.

When you arrive in Costa Rica, the customs officer will do a visual inspection of your pet (for which you will be charged US$1), and look over the health certificate and the authorization from the Costa Rican Health Ministry. If all is in order, you're through, and can find a pet-friendly taxi (not an easy task) and stuff your Irish wolfhound in the backseat. Some people traveling with pets report that they weren't even asked for their documents, but you can't count on encountering such relaxed attitudes yourself.

If you're missing any documents or the officer decides your pet looks ill and might transmit disease, the animal will either be temporarily released to your care (kind of like being out on bail) or (if the official decides there's a real health risk) kept in a state kennel for up to 30 days, until you work out what to do next—arrange for the necessary paperwork, or contact a local vet if your animal needs care.

HOLSTEINS, THOROUGHBREDS, VIPERS, AND MACAWS

Livestock will need permission from Costa Rica's Agriculture Ministry's Animal Sanitation Department to enter the country. Ask your Costa Rican consulate or embassy how to go about getting this authorization, or, if you speak Spanish, call the San José office at 506/253-5605. More exotic animals, like lizards, will be allowed in if they have a clean bill of health from a vet—you'll need to check what diseases might affect your particular creature to know what vaccinations will be required. If your pet is on the endangered species list, the paperwork will be more complicated (from both the Costa Rican end and from your country of origin, which may have even stricter regulations); required information may include the animal's country of origin and permission to take it out of that original country. Such regulations aim to protect against illegal traffic in endangered animals. Again, the Costa Rican consulate in your country of origin is your best source of information for up-to-date specifics.

FLYING WITH PETS

Most likely you'll bring your pet with you on the plane. Most airlines allow seeing-eye dogs in the cabin, and some allow small pets to accompany you in your seat. I know a few women who always carry their little dogs with them in big purses; sometimes the flight crew doesn't even realize the animals are along for the ride. I never asked these women what they do about letting the animals relieve themselves on long flights. Bigger animals (or all animals, on some airlines) will need to ride in the cargo hold or even on a separate cargo flight. Some airlines will not accept pets as checked baggage May 15–September 15, since the cargo hold is not air-conditioned. Depending on the animal's weight and size, airlines usually charge between US$70 and US$100 one-way.

Animals checked as baggage need to travel in leak-proof cages that have handles, so baggage handlers will be able to easily lift and carry the cage. The cage should be just large enough for the animal to turn around. Vets say animals should fast for six hours prior to the flight in order to reduce nausea. If the flight is longer than four hours, the animal should eat a few hours before takeoff.

The bottom line is that each airline has a different policy regarding pet transport, and those policies often change. Set aside some time before your departure to research which airlines offer the best deal for your needs.

PETS IN COSTA RICA

Most buses and taxis will not welcome animals, though they must, by law, accept seeing-eye dogs. Some hotels accept pets—check ahead of time. There are plenty of vets in Costa Rica, especially in the Central Valley area. Vets in more rural areas will probably specialize in livestock. Vets will often board pets for around US$10 a day; animals stay in cages but are supposed to be exercised daily. Check out the K9 Country Club in Ciudad Colón, 20 minutes outside of San José (tel. 506/249-3539, K9CountryClub@expressmail.net). Also try the newish Villa Felina (for cats only), also in Ciudad Colón. Owners Yadira Jiménez and Claudio Pujol have converted their house into cat heaven, where boarding felines have the run of the couple's home. Call 506/249-0228 or email them at villafelina@costarricense.cr.

Pet food is easy to come by in Costa Rica, even upscale brands like Iams and Eukanuba.

> *Although Costa Ricans love their pets, they think of them differently than do most North Americans. Dogs are valued for their ability to protect people and property, and are often not let into the house.*

Costa Rican Attitudes Toward Pets

Although Costa Ricans love their pets, they think of them differently than do most North Americans. Dogs are valued for their ability to protect people and property, and are often not let into the house. The U.S. practice of letting dogs sleep on the sofa or even the bed would be considered in Costa Rica hopelessly *cochino* (which literally means piggy, and is used as a synonym for dirty).

You won't see many cats out and about in Costa Rica, maybe because the street dogs would consider them tasty morsels. Walk down any street or along any beach with your dog at your side, and a motley crew of other canines will rush out to see who dares to invade their territory. In the dog world there is a complicated pecking order that is given freer reign here than in other countries; you better not stand in the way as the dogs work out for themselves who's on top. Each block has its neighborhood bully dog, so if you're going to let your beagle roam free, she or he better be street-wise. There aren't as many mangy street dogs in Costa Rica as you see in other developing countries, but they do exist, and it's best to give them a wide berth—they've had to adapt to a life of people kicking them and throwing rocks at them, so they're not likely to be too friendly.

That said, there are many good things about bringing your pet to Costa Rica. Especially if you move here with children, your dog or cat could be that living, breathing piece of home that helps its human owners adjust to their new environment. And there's nothing like a big dog—however sweet-tempered—to discourage burglars and other scoundrels. Dogs also have such keen senses of smell and direction that if you get lost in the jungle that is your new backyard, your dog will almost certainly know the way home.

LEAVING WITH PETS

Animals leaving Costa Rica require exit permits. You'll need a local vet to fill out a health certificate; often she or he will accept the original health certificate from your country of origin as proof that the animal is in good health. For a fee, the vet can take care of all the paperwork, or you could check in with the Department of Zoonosis at the Ministry of Health, located in San José (tel. 506/223-0333, ext. 331).

What is likely to be more of a hassle is getting the animal back into your country of origin, which may have stricter regulations about animals entering their territory. England, for instance, has a mandatory six-month quarantine for most dogs; owners have to pay their pet's boarding fees, of course, and there are special visiting hours where you can come and play with your incarcerated pal. It's best to check out your country's regulations even before you leave for Costa Rica.

What to Take

Most people—even adventurous souls who decide to pick up and move to another country—have a lot of stuff that they've accumulated over the years. Even if you consider yourself non-materialistic and have made an effort to keep your possessions to a minimum, chances are that what you own is more than you could check as baggage on a flight to Costa Rica.

> *Bringing your personal belongings with you as checked baggage is your best option. Check as much luggage as possible, as this is the only way to import your belongings without duties and customs hassles.*

And this method—bringing in your possessions as checked baggage—is by far the cheapest and easiest option. As long as you can convince customs officials that everything you bring is portable, for your own personal use, and necessary for your enjoyment or for the practice of your profession while in Costa Rica, you will pay no duties (taxes on imported goods) and there will be no bureaucracy save filling out the usual customs form that flight attendants hand out just before the plane lands.

The second-easiest option is to send a small shipment as air cargo (not as luggage accompanying you on your flight)—at least some of the shipment will be taxed, and there will be forms to fill out and lines to stand in.

The third option is to ship your possessions by boat; the container will arrive at a port on either the east or west coast of Costa Rica. In terms of customs, hassles, and duties, this is the most time- and money-intensive option, but it's the way to go if you really want to bring your entire household with you: books, CDs, stereo, sofa, bed, stove, and refrigerator—even your car can go in the shipboard container.

But why lug your old life with you to a new country, especially when you have to pay so dearly for the privilege? If you've lived in one place for more than a few years, I'll bet that you've been meaning to purge your belongings—to have a garage sale or take a few trips to the Salvation Army drop-off station. It feels good to pare down, and a lot of people who move to Costa Rica do so in part because they want to simplify their lives. You can start simplifying even before you get here, by thinking carefully about what possessions you can't live without, then selling or giving away the rest. "I thought about selling all my favorite things, all the great stuff I've collected over the years, and I just couldn't do it," says Mary Ann Jackson, who planned to move to Costa Rica in 2004. "But I wasn't going to lug it all with me, either. So I gave it all away to friends. Now I can visit my stuff in their houses."

You may be tempted to bring your appliances, but I would advise against it. You will pay high duties on these items (sometimes more than 50 percent of the item's value), and it's easy to buy appliances here. You'll probably pay about what you'd pay in the United States, though the selection isn't as good down here. The best deals are in the Pacific coast port of Golfito, near the border with Panama. There Ticos and tourists alike can buy up to US$500 in duty-free goods every six months. Many people hang around the area, selling off their buying rights to the highest bidder. Golfito is near the legendary surf spot of Pavones, and close to the Osa Peninsula, home to magnificent Corcovado National Park. You could do worse than head south for a week of surfing, tapir-watching, and appliance-shopping.

Furniture is another thing that it's easy to come by in Costa Rica. In fact, many newcomers have pieces custom-made for not much more than they'd pay for ready-made items in the United States or Canada. Costa Rica is known for its gorgeous tropical hardwoods and for its tradition of woodworking. Even if you don't want to spring for a custom-made dining room table or a hand-carved headboard, there are plenty of ready-made items that show the local materials and skills to good advantage. The Central Valley town of Sarchí, for example, is known for its lovely wood-and-leather rocking chairs, which are very comfortable and will look great on your tiled front porch with volcano view.

Things that *are* hard to come by in Costa Rica:
- good books in English (they exist, but the selection is small)
- non-mainstream videotapes, DVDs, and CDs
- high-quality hand tools
- low-priced or highly specialized vitamins and nutritional supplements

- good chocolate (something bad happens to chocolate in the tropics, and even high-end brands here often have turned partially white)
- the latest technology, like the newest laptops and their accessories (you can often get these in Panama, however).

ON THE PLANE

As discussed above, bringing used goods and personal belongings with you as checked baggage is your first and best option. Some airlines allow you to pay extra and bring a little more than the usual two-bag, 66-pound limit. It's worth checking as much luggage as possible, as this is the only way to import your belongings without duties and customs hassles. Everything you bring must be for your own personal use (not intended for resale), be portable, and be a reasonable quantity for the duration of your stay. Most people, even those who plan to stay years, first come in on a 90-day tourist visa, so what you bring in as luggage should look like a reasonable amount of goods for that amount of time.

On the other hand, consider the case of Brenda Burnside, a former professional boxer who moved to the Pacific coast town of Nosara. When she saw the reduced circumstances of the local public school, she wanted to help. Enlisting the help of eight members of her church back home in Nevada, she offered them a free place to stay in sunny Costa Rica if they would fill their luggage with books, school supplies, and sports equipment. When Brenda lugged the precious cargo to the school, the teacher cried in gratitude—she couldn't believe such generosity. Now, a persnickety customs official at the airport could have challenged the travelers' need for so many pens, notebooks, geography textbooks, and soccer balls for a stay of just a few weeks. As luck would have it, all of the do-gooders got the green light at the airport. That's how customs decides whose bags to check at the San José airport: You push a button, and if the light comes up red, they search your bags. If it comes up green, you're on your way without even a glance inside your luggage.

What you're allowed to bring in as luggage includes:

- Clothing, jewelry, purses, umbrellas
- Medicine and medical equipment if necessary for personal use (such as a wheelchair or oxygen tank)
- Sporting equipment, including surfboards, kayaks, golf clubs, fishing poles, etc.
- One video camera, one still camera, one portable tape recorder, one portable computer, one portable telescope
- One portable television, one portable radio
- One portable typewriter, one calculator, one portable printer

- Paint and canvases
- Tools, supplies, and manual instruments pertinent to the trade of the traveler, as long as these do not constitute a complete set for an office or laboratory
- Portable musical instruments and accessories (no pianos!)
- Books, tapes, photos, CDs, if for non-commercial use
- 500 grams (1.1 lbs.) tobacco, five liters (1.3 gallons) of wine or hard liquor (per adult traveler), two kilos (4.4 lbs.) of candy, baby food (an amount "sufficient for your proposed stay")
- Tent and other camping gear
- Up to four hunting or marksman rifles and 500 rounds of ammunition (subject to additional regulation by the Firearms and Explosives Department of the Ministry of Security).

If you arrive at the airport with items that don't qualify as luggage, don't despair. There's a duty-free exemption of up to US$500. So if you bring, say, two portable TVs instead of one, if the second one is worth less than US$500, you're still okay. Customs will stamp your passport, and you'll need to wait six months to take advantage of that US$500 exemption again.

If the US$500 exemption isn't enough, and you get slapped with some duties, you have two choices: Pay the bill right then and there if you think the amount is fair, or leave the goods in question at the airport (ask for a receipt), and return the following day to argue your case (bring along someone who speaks Spanish).

AIR CARGO
You can send up to 500 pounds as air cargo. Duties for items sent air cargo differ from those of items carried into the country as luggage, though personal clothes, shoes, purses, books, hand tools, and some sports equipment will still be duty-free. Everything else will be taxed—each item has its own duty, from paintings at 15 percent to pots and pans at 54 percent of declared value. You will even be taxed on the freight charges you pay, and on any insurance, which is why some customs brokers suggest you forgo insurance.

When your shipment arrives in Costa Rica, it will be sent to a bonded customs warehouse. To pick up your shipment, you will need:
- Your passport (copy the main page and the page with your last entry into Costa Rica, proving you've entered the country within the last 90 days)
- The Air Way Bill, which the freight handler you contract will have given you

- Packing inventory that includes declared value of contents.

Then you pay the duties assessed, the Terminal Handling Fee, and the bonded warehouse fee. You can do this on your own, hire a customs broker, or bring along a calm, savvy, Spanish-speaking friend who can help you out.

Very important: For claiming either an air cargo shipment or a surface (boat) shipment, you need to prove (by the stamp on your passport) that you have entered (or re-entered) Costa Rica within the last 90 days. If you've been here longer, your shipment will be considered a commercial one, and all hell will break loose. You'll have to pay duties on everything, even books and clothes, a health certificate will be required for used clothing, and you'll need invoices for everything shipped. And if you don't have the necessary invoices and certificates? Good luck trying to claim your stuff.

SHIPPING BY BOAT

If you have a lot you want to ship, you can pay for a quarter, half, or full ocean container, which is a steel box 20 by 40 feet. The box will be loaded onto a ship, which will eventually dock on either the Atlantic or Pacific coast of Costa Rica, depending on where it's coming from. You can fit a great deal in one of these containers—even a car—but every item needs to be numbered and inventoried, including the serial numbers of all appliances and electronic items. And you can't just dump it all in—you need to pack carefully, because it will need to withstand a lot of moving around and perhaps a lot of heat. Experienced movers recommend putting any heat-sensitive items in the middle of the load. Most people hire professional movers and so don't need to worry about packing the box themselves.

It's important that you ship only used items (more than six months old); otherwise you may end up paying duties on new items, which are much higher. The serial numbers on appliances and electronics allow customs agents to know exactly how old they are and what their average prices are.

If you choose to go it alone, you'll either meet the ship to pick up your possessions or ask that the container be trucked to a warehouse in San José. The documents needed to claim the shipment are:

- Your passport (copy of the main page and of your last entry into Costa Rica, showing you've entered the country within the last 90 days)
- Inventory list with declared value of container contents
- Original Ocean Bill of Lading.

DRIVING TO COSTA RICA

If you've got some time on your hands, are good at talking your way in and out of rough spots, and don't really mind if you lose some or all of your cargo en route, you might want to drive all the way from North America to Costa Rica. You could load your car or truck with all your worldly possessions, then hit the road and see what happens. You'll pass through some gorgeous country and will cross many borders, all of which will be enforcing different regulations concerning what you can and can't bring into their country. It's not for everyone, but it's not a trip you will soon forget. *¡Buen viaje, y buena suerte!*

For more information on bringing your car to Costa Rica, see the Travel and Transportation chapter.

© Erin Van Rheenen

Language and Education

Learning the Language

Spanish is the first language of the Americas, and learning it will serve any New Worlder well. Costa Rica is an excellent place to learn, with friendly people with whom to practice and a national tendency to not pronounce the *rr*, the rolling *r* that foils so many non-native speakers.

There are as many ways to study Spanish in Costa Rica as there are students who want to learn. Sign up for a 12-week intensive, with six hours a day of rigorous instruction, or arrange for a leisurely hour of private instruction each morning before heading for the beach. You could combine language study with volunteering, or enter a specialty program geared to your profession, like courses for Spanish teachers or classes that focus on medical terminology. The biggest leaps in learning often come when you least expect them, and if you take care to mix mostly with Spanish speakers, just going about your daily business will be a crash

Speaking Costa Rican

Sure, Ticos speak Spanish, and you'll find a portable Spanish-English dictionary worth its weight in gold if you plan to converse with anyone outside of gringo enclaves. But Ticos also speak Costa Rican, using terms that you'll never hear in Madrid or Mexico City. Here are a few to get you started.

adios: the word for "good-bye" can also (especially in rural areas) mean "hello"

chunche: 1) thingamajig, thingee 2) car or bus

con gusto: literally means "with pleasure;" the phrase is often used in response to "thank you," instead of *de nada,* (you're welcome)

estar de goma: literally, "to be gummed up;" means to have a hangover

maje: pal or buddy. Kind of like *dude* in the United States or Mexico's *güe, maje* is most often pronounced with the *j* (equivalent to the *h* sound in English) swallowed; the omnipresent term ends up sounding like the English *my*

la mamá de Tarzán: conceited; a know-it-all
Ex: *Él se cree la mamá de Tarzán.* (He thinks he's Tarzan's mom, or He thinks he's so great.)

un montón: literally, a mountain; often used to mean "a lot"
Ex: *Habia un montón de gente en la fiesta.* (There were a lot of people at the party.)

porfa: short for *por favor* (please)

tuanis: good or fine. Thought to derive from the phrase "too nice," from the English patois–speaking Caribbean coast.

upe: Anyone home? Called out at someone's door: ¡uuupeee!

If you ask ¿*Como esta?* (How are you?), they may say:

Muy bien, por dicha. Very well, fortunately.

or *Muy bien, gracias a Dios.* Very well, thank God.

or they may answer with the national phrase: ¡Pura Vida! Great!

course in the language. The best motivation for improving your skills is the genuine desire to communicate with someone who speaks only Spanish, so get out there and meet the locals.

However you choose to learn, working on your Spanish is the single most important investment you can make in adapting to Costa Rica. Think about how you feel when someone in your home country doesn't even try to learn your language. Seems like a lack of respect, doesn't it? The same holds true here. Sure, a lot of people in Costa Rica speak English (though not as many as you might think), ATM machines have instructions in English, and English-language TV and movies dominate the media. Still—at the risk of stating the obvious—Costa Rica is a Spanish-speaking country, and if you're going to make this your home, you need to speak the language, if only to greet people politely and thank them for their help. Learning a new language is not easy, but Ticos applaud all genuine efforts. And language is more than just words—it carries with it an entire civilization. Deny yourself the language and you'll never get more than ankle-deep in the culture.

Especially if you're a beginner, it's a good idea to sign up for a course, preferably one that meets every day for at least a few weeks. Language study benefits from daily reinforcement, and it's good to get a base of grammar and verb forms. After that, you can design your own course of study, which might include reading at least one article in the newspaper every day (dictionary at the ready), watching Spanish-language soap operas, or falling in love with someone who doesn't speak a word of English.

Most language schools are based in the capital city of San José, but there are also programs in beach towns and other tourist centers. You can find a list of schools at the end of this chapter, but note that it only scratches the surface of what is on offer. I've tried to cover some of the better-known and established places, but there are dozens more. And even if a school is listed, that doesn't mean it has my personal recommendation—call or visit the school's website to learn more details about programs offered. Competition has benefited the industry; be sure to shop around and ask about any special deals—for students, senior citizens, professionals, or off-season visitors, or for longer stays. Prices change often; make sure you obtain up-to-date prices from any schools you are considering.

Education

A strong commitment to education is one of the defining characteristics of Costa Rican culture. The 1949 decision to abolish the armed forces meant that Costa Rica could spend more on infrastructure, health care, and, perhaps most important for the country's future, education. For decades after that decision, education spending took up almost a third of the entire national budget. It still holds a place of prominence, though public schools have in recent years felt the effect of budget cuts imposed on all manner of social services.

PRIMARY AND SECONDARY EDUCATION

Grades 1–12 are free, and for kids aged 6–14 (the ninth year in school) attendance is compulsory. Consequently, Costa Rica has one of the highest literacy rates—94 percent—in Latin America, second only to Cuba, and a culture that values education as one of the pillars of national life. The first two heads of state were elementary school teachers. Costa Rica is the most stable and democratic society in the region, and its emphasis on education has a lot to do with that status. On Election Day, in fact, schoolchildren participate in mock elections in their classrooms, and the results are published in the national papers. This early introduction to participatory democracy may have something to do with the fact that voter turnout in Costa Rica is traditionally high—hovering around 80 percent for the last three decades. More recently, turnout rates have started to drop, as mistrust of politicians (always a part of the national culture) increases and as people lose faith in government effectiveness. During the 2002 elections graffiti on highway overpasses read *No Vote*—Don't Vote.

The country's commitment to education didn't begin in 1949. In 1821, the government, newly independent from Spain, established the University of Santo Tomás, and in 1825, a law was passed requiring every municipality to found a public school. Both sexes were guaranteed equal instruction in 1847, and education became free and compulsory (for primary grades) in 1869.

COSTA RICAN SCHOOLS

If you have school-age children and are considering relocating to Costa Rica, schools will be a major concern, and will probably determine, at least in part, where you choose to live. The Central Valley is rich in educational choices, while towns in outlying areas—if they have a school at all— may feature a one-room schoolhouse that offers instruction only through the ninth grade.

Public Schools

Costa Ricans value education highly, and have made sure that a good portion of the yearly national budget goes to schools. By law, 6 percent of the

GDP must be set aside for education, and often many times that amount is spent. Article 78 of the 1949 constitution states that "general education" (through grade 9) is free and obligatory for all Costa Ricans; in 1992 legislators went even further, asserting that education is not only the state's obligation but a fundamental human right.

The school year is usually divided into two terms, from February through July and from August through November or December. The longest break comes between November and January and used to be associated with the coffee harvest (so kids could help), but now is seen more as a lengthy Christmas holiday. There is usually a two- to three-week break in July as well. National standardized exams are administered during the third, sixth, ninth, and eleventh grades; students must pass them to advance to the next level. The above holds true for both public and private schools, as the Ministry of Education's policies apply to both types of education.

Public school begins with kindergarten and runs through what in the United States would be eleventh grade. From there some students go on to local universities; the University of Costa Rica (UCR) in San José is the largest (about 30,000 students) and the most respected. Primary school is kindergarten through sixth grade; secondary school (or *colegio*) consists of grades seven through eleven.

Unfortunately, public education in Costa Rica is in a time of crisis. In the past few decades, budget deficits have led to severe cuts in the funding of social services, and education has not been spared. Schools have had to make do with less money even as they try to educate a growing population. Salaries for the country's 27,000 teachers were never high, and now their pensions have been reduced, causing fewer qualified people to be attracted to the field. Private schools have rushed in to fill the gap.

Private Schools

Most expat families choose to send their children to private schools, as do many Costa Rican families who can afford to do so. Kirt Wackford, who teaches science at Saint Paul's College, says it's more common here than in the United States for families of modest means to send their kids to private school. Ana, Kirt's Tica wife, comes from a family of seven. Her father was a shopkeeper and her mother a housewife, and yet they made the sacrifices that would allow all seven kids to attend good private schools. Most of them went on to public higher education at the prestigious University of Costa Rica.

The San José area phone book lists almost 300 private elementary and secondary schools. There are Catholic schools, evangelical Christian schools, Jewish schools, German, French, and Japanese schools, and dozens of "bilingual" English/Spanish schools, with wildly varying ratios of which language is used more often. The list of private schools at the end of this chapter provides a good starting point.

"Private education here is top quality," another teacher told me. "From what I understand, if you compare a ninth grader here to a ninth grader in the States, the Costa Rican student will be way ahead; they could go into tenth grade in a U.S. school. If students are coming down here from the States, they'll probably have to do a bit more work to be up to speed. Spanish and science, especially, might be a challenge for them."

It's a good idea to start researching schools as soon as you know you'll be moving to Costa Rica. Ideally, both you and your children will make a scouting trip to visit campuses and talk to school administrators months in advance of your arrival. Parents agree that it's a good idea to arrive a few weeks before school starts, so kids can get used to a new house and area before having to adapt to a new school. Arriving too far in advance, however, may be a bad idea, since kids can begin to feel at loose ends when their days have little structure.

HIGHER EDUCATION

Higher education had to wait until the 1970s to get its share of attention. The prestigious University of Costa Rica (UCR, founded in 1940) was in full swing by then, and several important public institutions joined its ranks in the '70s: the National University in Heredia, Cartago's Institute of Technology, and The State University's Distance Learning Program. The government funds public universities, and tuition is on a sliding scale, with about one in every four students paying nothing at all. At the turn of the millennium, more than 70,000 students in Costa Rica were enrolled in institutions of higher learning, with 30,000 of them at UCR.

There's a sense that students who enjoy the benefits of Costa Rican public higher education should "give back," and indeed students must complete 150 hours of public service for their bachelor's degree and 300 hours for a master's.

UCR's main campus is in the San José suburb of San Pedro; there are branch campuses in Alajuela, Cartago, Turrialba, and Puntarenas. The National University, based in Heredia, also has regional centers in Liberia and Perez Zeledon. The State University's Distance Learning Program has 32 regional centers scattered around the country. People who live far from urban centers can hear lectures on the radio or on TV, or meet once a week with professors who make the rounds of the rural outposts.

There are also a growing number of private universities and colleges—the count was 42 in 1998. The first was the Autonomous Central

American University (UACA), founded by a group of UCR professors in 1976; by 1995, the university enrolled 5,000 students at its several campuses.

Private universities may have more relaxed entrance requirements, or offer programs similar to those at public institutions but at a more rapid pace and with greater flexibility in terms of when students attend classes. Some private institutions, like the tiny Universidad de Diseño (the University of Design), have excellent reputations, both nationally and internationally. Others seem to be run strictly as businesses, and are dismissed as degree mills. Concerned with the declining quality of instruction at some private universities, a number of professional guilds, like the Lawyers' Guild, now require prospective members to pass an exam rather than simply present their degree.

Many public universities offer not only courses but also seminars and talks that are free and open to the general public (and are advertised in local newspapers like *La Nación*). A sampling of recent offerings at the UCR-San Pedro campus includes a talk on the history of film in Costa Rica, a discussion of Latin American literature (in English, by a U.S. professor), a panel discussion on urban development in San José, and a vulcanology seminar. In short, there's a wealth of continuing education options, especially in the San José area, with events either free or very reasonably priced. Most are in Spanish, but what a great way to improve your language skills! You can find a list of public universities at the end of the listings that follow.

School Listings

SPANISH LANGUAGE SCHOOLS
Note: A "homestay" usually means a single room in a local family's home, and often includes two meals a day and laundry service. The nature of the housing and the neighborhood it's located in vary considerably; some schools even offer both "standard" and "deluxe" homestays.

Academia de Idiomas Escazú
Escazú, a suburb of San José
Small classes (about four people) use the total immersion method; the school also arranges volunteer positions at national parks, hospitals, or social agencies. Participants must stay for at least 15 days and have a command of basic Spanish. The Medical Spanish program involves four hours a day of language study and four hours of time in a medical facility. Prices range from two weeks of language study (without lodging) for US$280 all the way to 12 weeks of language study plus

Ways to Say Rain

Rain-soaked Costa Rica has more than a few terms for what makes this country so green. Here are a few terms to start with; you'll no doubt discover many more.

lluvia: plain old rain

pelo de gato: (cat's fur) a soft drizzle

garua: drizzle or sprinkle

aguacero: downpour

temporal: a storm that can last for days, most common in September and October, the wettest months

granizado: hail

llueve a cantaros: raining buckets

deluxe homestay (including two meals a day and laundry service) for US$3,060.
tel. 506/228-7736
spanish@crspanish.com
www.crspanish.com

Academia Tica
San Isidro de Coronado, 10 kilometers (6.2 mi.) northeast of San José Academia Tica offers two- to four-week programs. Most meet every weekday morning from 8 A.M. to noon; starting dates throughout the year. Prices are US$170–230 per week for small group classes, accommodations not included. Homestays can be arranged.
www.academiatica.com

Berlitz Language Center (Centro de Idiomas Berlitz)
Santa Ana, a suburb of San José
tel. 506/204-7555
fax 506/204-7444
and in San Pedro, a neighborhood of San José

tel. 506/253-9191
fax 506/253-1115
www.berlitz.com

Central American Institute for International Affairs (ICAI)
San José
tel. 506/233-8571
fax 506/221-5238
www.educaturs.com

Centro de Idiomas del Pacifico
Quepos/Manuel Antonio
tel. 506/777-0805
fax 506/777-0010
www.cipacifico.com

Centro Lingüístico Conversa
downtown San José and the nearby town of Santa Ana
Prices include instruction, meals, lodging, textbooks, and airport pickup, and range US$475–750 a week, depending on location and intensity of program. Family groups may receive discounts, and prices

drop for stays of more than four weeks. Classes are generally small, and you can choose Intensive (four hours per day) or Super-Intensive (5.5 hours per day) courses.

College credit is available through Miami-Dade Community College (Florida) and Truman State University (Missouri), and Conversa's Spanish programs are accredited by more than 100 universities and colleges in the United States by the College Consortium for International Studies (CCIS).
toll-free in U.S. and Canada: 800/354-5036
tel. 506/221-7649
fax 506/233-2418
www.conversa.co.cr

Centro Panamericano de Idiomas (CPI)
near San José, on Pacific coast, and in Monteverde
CPI has three campuses—in Heredia (near San José), in the mountain town of Monteverde, and near the Pacific coast beach of Playa Flamingo. Programs are from one to four weeks. Prices range from US$230 for a week of instruction (four hours a day, five days a week, without homestay), to US$1,290 for four weeks of instruction, including homestay.
toll-free in U.S.: 888/682-0054
tel. 506/265-6866
fax 506/265-6213
info@cpi-edu.com
www.cpi-edu.com

City Playa
Jacó (Pacific coast)
tel. 506/643-2123
fax 506/643-2122
www.cityplaya.com

Costa Rican Language Academy
Barrio Dent, San José
Courses are offered year-round, and class schedules are flexible. Prices are US$245–380/week, including homestay. Fees go down the longer you stay, and there are discounts during low season (March–April and October–November).
toll-free in U.S.: 866/230-6361
tel. 506/280-1685
fax 506/280-2548
crlang@racsa.co.cr
www.spanishandmore.com

Costa Rican Spanish Institute (COSI)
San José and Manuel Antonio
COSI offers classes in San José and near Manuel Antonio National Park on the Pacific coast. Prices are US$345–535 per week, including instruction and homestay, less for longer stays or if you arrange your own accommodations.
toll-free in U.S.: 800/771-5184
San José:
tel. 506/253-9272
fax 506/253-2117
Manuel Antonio:
tel. 506/777-0021
fax 506/777-3506
info@cosi.co.cr
www.cosi.co.cr

Escuela D'Amore
Manuel Antonio
tel./fax 506/777-1143
www.escueladamore.com

Escuela de Español Chirripó
San Gerardo de Rivás, near Chirripó,
the highest peak in the country
tel. 506/200-5125

Escuela de Español Dalfa
San José
A school "based on Christian principles." Four-week programs begin in early January, March, May, July, September, and November and cost US$400, not including homestay. Fifteen-week courses begin in early January, May, and September (US$790 excluding homestay). The school can help you arrange a homestay, or you can find your own lodging.
tel./fax 506/226-8584
dalfad@sol.racsa.co.cr
www.amerisol.com/costarica/ed/
  dalfa.html

Forester Institute
Los Yoses, San José
One- to four-week programs, with many different options, but in general prices run from US$650/week to US$1,500 for four weeks, covering instruction, room and partial board, and extras like dance classes and excursions. If you don't need a place to stay, you could study four hours a day, five days a week, at US$350 for one week, US$550 for two, and US$610 for

three weeks—the weekly price goes down the longer you study.
tel. 506/225-3155
fax 506/225-9236
forester@racsa.co.cr
www.fores.com

Horizontes de Montezuma
Montezuma Beach
tel./fax 506/642-0534
www.horizontes
  -montezuma.com

ICADS: Institute for Central American Development Studies
Curridabat, San José
Offering "study programs for progressive minds," ICADS allows you to earn college credit while learning Spanish and interning in the areas of public health, wildlife conservation, and women's issues.
tel. 506/234-1381
fax 506/234-1337
www.icadscr.com

ILISA Language Institute
San Pedro neighborhood of San José
Billing itself as a "school for professionals" that "does not cater to backpackers," ILISA offers a variety of programs, including small group classes Monday–Friday, 8 A.M.–noon, for around US$310 a week (with homestay, one week would be US$590, two weeks US$980, with the price going down the longer you study). Special programs for professionals—from nurses to

teachers—are also on offer. The school employs 12 full-time and as many part-time teachers, many of whom are graduate students at the nearby University of Costa Rica.

Biweekly cultural activities like lectures and dance classes are included in the price of classes, as is a happy hour on Tuesday evenings. ILISA prides itself on being gay-friendly, and will arrange for homestays with families who welcome gays. ILISA plans another campus at Playa Samara on the Guanacaste coast.
tel. 506/280-0700
fax 506/225-4665
spanish@ilisa.com
www.ilisa.com

Institute for Central American Studies
Sabanilla, San José
This organization puts out a monthly English-language newsletter covering Central American politics and also offers language study and internships.
tel. 506/253-3195
fax 506/234-7682
mesoamer@racsa.co.cr
www.mesoamericaonline.net

Instituto Britanico
Offering everything from two weeks of general Spanish (40 hours a week), at US$440, to a week (15 hours of instruction) of "Spanish Express," a crash course in basic Spanish. Homestays cost US$125/week.

Los Yoses, San José:
tel. 506/225-0256
fax 506/253-1894
Liberia, Guanacaste:
tel./fax 506/666-0141
info@institutobritanico.co.cr
www.institutobritanico.co.cr

Instituto Universal de Idiomas
Moravia, San José
From a three-day Survival Course (six hours of instruction per day; US$140, not including homestay) to a four-week "Economic Global Package" (three hours of instruction per day, homestay included; US$940).
tel. 506/223-9662
fax 506/223-9917
info@universal-edu.com
www.universal-edu.com

INTENSA: Intensive Learning Programs
Located in San Pedro, the University district of San José, INTENSA offers programs that last from one to four weeks. Four weeks costs US$730, excluding home-stay, which runs US$120/week. New programs start every Monday throughout the year

There are also special programs, like Intensive Spanish and Volunteer Work. Four weeks runs you US$1,360, which includes homestay, four hours a day and five days a week of Spanish instruction, plus placement in a volunteer position, which will require two or three days a week of your time, three to

four hours a day. Volunteer programs range from teaching art to young children to working with recovering addicts.
toll-free in U.S. and Canada: 866/277-1352
tel. 506/281-1818
fax 506/253-4337
www.intensa.com

Intercultura
Heredia, north of San José, and in Samara Beach
Intercultura has campuses just outside of San José (in Heredia) and in the Pacific coast beach town of Samara. Programs range from one to four weeks, and provide four hours of daily instruction, Monday–Friday. Prices for instruction with homestay run from US$350 for one week to US$1,125 for four weeks. Without homestay, prices run from US$250/week to US$725 for a four-week program. ARCR members get a 10 percent discount on fees.
toll-free in U.S.: 800/205-0642
tel. 506/260-8480
tel./fax 506/260-9243
info@interculturacostarica.com
www.interculturacostarica.com

IPEE Spanish Language School: Instituto Profesional de Español para Extranjeros
Curridabat, San José
Intensive one-week course (30 hours of instruction), with home-stay, US$540; eight-week course (four hours of instruction per day; 160 hours total), with homestay, US$2,470. There are specialty courses for Spanish teachers or to learn about Latin American literature.
tel. 506/283-7731
fax 506/225-7860
ipee@gate.net
www.ipee.com

Language and International Relations Institute (ILERI)
Escazú, a suburb of San José
tel. 506/289-4396
tel./fax 506/228-1687
www.ilerispanishschool.com

Las Osas Mayor y Menor Language Center
Puerto Jimenez, on the Osa Peninsula
Language study with an emphasis on nature (Puerto Jimenez is close to the spectacular Corcovado National Park); homestays also available.
tel. 506/735-5440
fax 506/735-5045
cocotero_tico@yahoo.com

New Dawn Center
near San Isidro de General
Spanish classes offered at an organic farm, along with seminars on natural health care and tropical medicinal plants. A one-month Spanish course (40 hours of classes, 100 hours of practice) costs US$400. Overnight accommodations available at the farmhouse for US$10/night; meals are US$5 each.
www.thenewdawncenter.org

Rey de Nosara
Nosara Beach, Guanacaste
tel. 506/682-0215
fax 506/682-0215
www.reydenosara.itgo.com

Spanish Abroad, Inc.
based in Phoenix, Arizona
A clearinghouse for many programs
in the Spanish-speaking world, it
links up with schools in many parts
of Costa Rica.
toll-free in U.S. and Canada:
888/722-7623
tel. 602/778-6791
fax 602/840-1545
info@spanishabroad.com
www.spanishabroad.com

UCR's Spanish as a Foreign Language Program
San Pedro, San José
UCR (University of Costa Rica), the
largest and most prestigious university in Costa Rica, has a Spanish
as a Foreign Language Program
that also gives participants access
to a vibrant community of more
than 30,000 students. Language
students (who need not be enrolled in the larger university) are
issued student cards, which allow
them to use campus libraries and
sports facilities.

Semester courses are offered
March–June and August–November.
These classes meet two hours a day,
Monday, Wednesday, and Friday.

One-month intensive courses are offered in January, February, and July,
four hours a day, Monday through
Friday. Six-week intensive courses are
offered in May and September, three
hours every evening, Monday–
Friday. Courses cost US$500, whether
for the semester course or the six-week intensive.

There are also two-month classes
on Latin American literature, advanced Spanish conversation, and
advanced Spanish literature, for
groups of at least six students.
Classes meet six hours a week (45
hours total), and cost approximately US$300.

Homestays can be arranged, and
run about US$350/month.
tel. 506/207-5634
fax 506/207-5089
espaucr@le.ucr.ac.cr
http://cariari.ucr.ac.cr/~filo/
   ingles.htm

WAYRA Instituto de Español
Playa Tamarindo, Guanacaste
A school in the cool beach town
of Tamarindo where a week of
classes (Monday–Friday, four hours
a day) will cost you US$200; double
that amount for private lessons.
Homestay prices are US$320–380
week. Class and homestay rates go
down the longer you stay.
tel./fax 506/653-0359
info@spanish-wayra.co.cr
www.spanish-wayra.co.cr

A Subjective Ranking of San José Area Private Schools

"First and foremost," advises a long-term expat who has taught at several San José area private schools, "parents must ask themselves what they want for their kids. They especially need to think about what sort of qualification the child will leave the school with. Tico-style private secondary schools may be very good, but they end at the 11th grade—fine if you want to go to university here in Costa Rica, insufficient if you want to go to college in the United States, Canada, or Europe. U.S.-style schools go through 12th grade, and European-style schools mostly offer the I.B., the International Baccalaureate, which will get the kids into European universities and can sometimes count as first-year university credit in the United States.

Another issue is language. Do you want your kid to speak mostly English, Spanish, German, or Japanese? Schools that call themselves bilingual are all over the map—make sure you know which language is emphasized."

When asked to rank some of the better-known private schools in the San José area, this expat at first demurred. "It's entirely subjective—it depends what you're looking for. Some are good for science, others for humanities. And there are dozens of schools with which I'm not familiar that may well be excellent." Even so, and with apologies for lapses of memory and quirks in taste, this seasoned teacher offered up a quick list, warning that the order of schools within the levels is not a further ranking, but just the order in which the schools came to mind. "There are a lot of good places here in the Central Valley," the teacher concluded. "Even the so-called 'third level' schools are high-quality institutions."

Top Level
British School (Escuela o Colegio Britannica)
Country Day School
Lincoln School

Second Level
St. Paul's
Panamerican School (Colegio Panamericano)
Marion Baker School
European School (Colegio Europeo) known especially for its primary school
Saint Francis
Methodist College (Colegio Methodista)

Third Level
Weizman Institute (Instituto Dr. Jaim Weizman)
Japanese School (Escuela Japonesa)
French School (Liceo Franco-Costarricense or Lycée Franco-Costaricien)
West College (Colegio del Oeste)
Blue Valley School

PRIVATE PRIMARY SCHOOLS

San José Area

American International School of Costa Rica (formerly the Costa Rica Academy)
Ciudad Cariari
Founded in 1970, AIS offers pre-K through grade 12, with a U.S.-style curriculum. The school year comprises two semesters, from mid-August to mid-December and from mid-January to mid-June. Classes are in English, and Advanced Placement (AP) programs are available. Total enrollment is around 250 students, with 32 teachers. AIS is accredited by the Southern Association of Colleges and Schools, and there are varsity athletics in soccer, volleyball, and basketball, as well as co-curricular offerings like studio art, music appreciation, band, and choir.
tel. 506/293-2567
fax 506/239-0625
aiscr@cra.ed.cr
www.cra.ed.cr
Mailing address:
Interlink 249, P.O. Box 02-5635
Miami, FL 33102

Anglo-American School (Centro Educativa Angloamericano)
Concepción de Tres Ríos (near Cartago)
Founded in 1949, pre-K through high school, classes in both English and Spanish. Day care is also available.
tel. 506/279-2626
fax 506/279-7894
angloam@racsa.co.cr
www.angloamericano.ed.cr

Blue Valley School
Escazú
Pre-K through high school.
tel. 506/215-2203
fax 506/215-2205
bvschool@racsa.co.cr

British School (Escuela o Colegio Britannica)
Santa Catalina
K-12, around 850 students total. Offers National, IB (International Baccalaureate), or other curricula. ECIS (European Council of International Schools) accredited. Art, music, drama, and interschool sports.
tel. 506/220-0719
fax 506/232-7833
britsch@racsa.co.cr
www.infoweb.co.cr/britsch

Canadian International School
Curridabat
Pre-K through 11th grade; 400 students.
tel. 506/272-7097
fax 506/272-6634

Calasanz School (Colegio Calasanz)
San Pedro
tel. 506/283-4730
fax 506/283-1890

Country Day School
Escazú
Founded in 1963 and modeled after prep schools in the United States, CDS has a total enrollment of around 700 students. It is one of the most prestigious schools in Costa Rica, and also has a branch in Guanacaste. Pre-K through 12; with classes in English and extras such as outdoor education, arts, and college counseling.
tel. 506/289-8406
fax 506/228-2076
www.cds.ed.cr

**European School
(Colegio Europeo)**
San Pablo de Heredia
Founded in 1989 by Anne Aronson, mother of five and the school's current director, the European School goes from pre-K through high school, and has 300 students from 20 countries. Key to the school's philosophy is the concept of integrated teaching. "From fourth to tenth grades," says the school's website, "a central theme unifies and interrelates academic work in literature, history, geography, and art, through the broader perspective of a given geographical area or historical period. The result is a global, cultural, and historical education that engages students in a way that few other schools do."
The school offers the IB (International Baccalaureate), and has its own calendar, from late July through late June, with short vacations every nine or 10 weeks.
tel. 506/261-0717
fax 506/237-4060
eurschool@cafebritt.com
www.europeanschool.com

French School (Liceo Franco-Costarricense or Lycée Franco-Costaricien)
Concepción de Tres Ríos
Pre-K through high school, about 800 students, most classes taught in French, but also English and Spanish. Tuition is very reasonable.
tel. 506/279-6616
fax 506/279-6615
lyfracos@sol.racsa.co.cr
www.lefranco.ac.cr

**Humboldt School
(Colegio Humboldt)**
Rohrmoser
K-12 classes taught in German, English, and Spanish; 750 students.
tel. 506/232-1455
fax 506/232-0093
www.infoweb.co.cr/Humboldt/

Institute of Holistic Psychopedagogy (Instituto de Psicopedagogia Integral)
Moravia
Founded in 1981 by psychologist Annie Blanco, IPI began as a school for "at-risk" kids but is now popular with all manner of students and parents. Primary and secondary education; about 500 students.
tel. 506/235-5362

Monthly Tuition at Some Private Secondary Schools

The following list of San José area schools appeared in the newspaper *La Republica* in October 2002. The figures were originally in *colones* (local currency), and were converted to dollars using the exchange rate at the time (380 *colones* to the dollar). What tuition includes varies from school to school—sometimes it covers just about everything, from books to extracurricular activities; sometimes it covers instruction only. Be sure to ask for details as you research schools for your child(ren).

School	Monthly Tuition
Oasis de Esperanza	US$129
Calasanz	US$151
Colegio Methodista	US$182
Saint Francis	US$188
San Judas Tadeo	US$195
Humboldt	US$228
San Pablo (St. Paul's)	US$240
Lincoln	US$303
British School	US$363
Panamerican	US$459

International Christian School

San Miguel, Santo Domingo de Heredia
Pre-K through 12th grade; around 600 students. Operates on U.S. academic calendar.
tel. 506/241-1445
fax 506/241-4944
intchris@racsa.co.cr

Japanese School (Escuela Japonesa)

Los Colegios, Moravia
Classes in Japanese, English, and Spanish.
tel. 506/236-3159

Kiwi Learning Center

Santa Ana
Day care and preschool; 35 students.
tel. 506/282-6512

fax 506/282-4319
www.edenia.com/kiwi

Lincoln School

Moravia
Offering classes from pre-K through 12th grade, Lincoln is one of the larger private schools in the San José area, with around 1,200 students and a faculty of 120. It offers either a U.S.-style college-prep curriculum or the IB (International Baccalaureate). Lincoln is considered a prestigious place to send your kid—it's where "the kids of big Costa Rica politicians go," according to one source. The school is outgrowing its Moravia campus, and is constructing a new campus in the San Isidro area.
tel. 506/247-0800
fax 506/247-0900
director@ns.lincoln.ed.cr
www.lincoln.ed.cr

Marian Baker School
San Ramón de Tres Ríos
Pre-K through 12th grade; 200 students. Operates on the U.S. academic calendar.
tel. 506/273-3426
fax 506/273-4609
mbschool@sol.racsa.co.cr
www.marianbakerschool.com

Methodist College (Colegio Metodista)
San Pedro and Sabanilla
Bilingual Christian school, pre-K through 12.
tel. 506/225-0655
administracion@metodista.ed.cr
www.metodista.ed.cr

Monterrey College (Colegio Monterrey)
San Pedro
Pre-K through 11th grade; 1,200 students.
tel. 506/224-0833
fax 506/244-3386
www.colegiomonterrey.ed.cr

Panamerican School (Colegio Panamericana)
San Antonio de Belen
Pre-K through 12th grade; 700 students.
tel. 506/298-5700
fax 506/293-7392
cpcrsa@racsa.co.cr

Saint Anthony School
Moravia
Pre-K through 6th grade; 500 students.

tel. 506/235-1017
fax 506/235-2325
santhony@racsa.co.cr

Saint Cecilia Bilingual College
San Francisco de Heredia
Pre-K through 11th grade; 680 students.
tel. 506/237-7733
fax 506/237-4557
colsupcr@racsa.co.cr

Saint Clare Educative System (Sistema Educativo Saint Clare)
San Vincente, Moravia
Grades 7 through 11; 650 students.
tel. 506/235-7244
fax 506/235-7271

Saint Francis College
Moravia
K through 11th grade; 1,200 students.
tel. 506/297-1704
or 506/240-8277
sfc@stfrancis.ed.cr

Saint Gregory School
Tres Ríos
Pre-K through 11th grade; 350 students.
tel. 506/279-4444
fax 506/279-9727
www.sgs.ed.cr

Saint John Bilingual College
Desamperados de Alajuela
Pre-K through 11th grade; 850 students.
tel./fax 506/440-8200
yebez@racsa.co.cr

Saint Mary's School
Guachipelín de Escazú
Pre-K through 10th grade; 530 students.
tel. 506/215-2135
fax 506/215-2132
cosama@racsa.co.cr

Saint Monica's School (Escuela Santa Mónica)
Guadalupe
Pre-K through sixth grade; 250 students.
tel. 506/235-4119
fax 506/240-2172
smonica@racsa.co.cr

Saint Paul College (Colegio Saint Paul)
San Rafael de Alajuela
Pre-K through 11th grade, bilingual English-Spanish; the majority of the 1,200 students are Costa Rican. "The idea behind this school is to offer a quality bilingual education to national students," says a teacher here.
tel. 506/438-1661
fax 506/438-2122
hsstpaul@racsa.co.cr
www.saintpaul.ed.cr

Saint Peter's School
Curridabat
Pre-K through 11th grade; 215 students.
tel./fax 506/272-2045
spetershigh@yahoo.com

San Judas Tadeo Bilingual School (Colegio Bilingue San Judas Tadeo)
Barrio Don Bosco
Pre-K through 12th grade.
tel. 506/257-8778
fax 506/233-3973
csanjudas@racsa.co.cr

Weizman Institute (Instituto Dr. Jaim Weizman)
Mata Redonda
Pre-K through 11th grade.
tel. 506/231-5566

West College (Colegio de Oeste)
Escazú
Pre-K through high school.
tel. 506/215-1016
fax 506/215-1384

The Central Valley and Beyond

Centro Educativa Jorge Debravo
Turrialba
tel. 506/556-0411
fax 506/556-1516

Creative Education Center (Centro de Educación Creativa)
Monteverde, Puntarenas
K through 9th grade; 180 students.
tel. 506/645-5161
tel./fax 506/645-5480
www.cloudforestschool.org

Escuela International CATIE
Turrialba
School associated with CATIE (Centro Agronómico Tropical de Investigación y Enseñanza/Center for Tropical Agriculture Investigation and Learning), one of the top tropical research stations in the world. Turrialba is about 65 kilometers (40 mi.) from San José.
tel. 506/556-7942
fax 506/556-1533

Monteverde Friends School (Escuela de Amigos)
Monteverde, Puntarenas
A small bilingual school run along Quaker principles, located in the mountain town that was forever changed by the 1951 arrival of a group of Quakers from Alabama. Pre-K through 12th grade; 80 students.
tel./fax 506/645-5302

Pindeco
Puntarenas
tel./fax 506/730-0097

Guanacaste and the Nicoya Peninsula
Academia Teocali
Liberia, Guanacaste
Pre-K through 11th grade; 290 students.
tel. 506/666-1914
fax 506/666-2953
ateocali@racas.co.cr

Country Day School of Guanacaste
Playa Brasilito, Guanacaste
Billed as "a serious school at the beach," this is a branch of the well-known institution based in Escazú. CDS Guanacaste offers classes from pre-K through 12th grade, and boarding for students in grades 8–12. About half of the approximately 80 students are children of U.S. expats, with the other half from Costa Rica, Mexico, France, Germany, Canada, Great Britain, Italy, Argentina, the Philippines, and the Netherlands. There's a nice campus, with gym, pool, playing fields, library, and computer lab.
tel. 506/654-5042
fax 506/654-5044
www.countrydayschool
guanacaste.org

Institute for Bilingual Schooling (Escuela Instituto Bilingue)
Playas del Coco, Guanacaste
Pre-K through sixth grade; 60 students.
tel. 506/670-0378
tedshirl@racsa.co.cr

Instituto Pedagógico EUPI
Guanacaste
tel. 506/686-6561
fax 506/686-4884

The Central and South Pacific Coast
Private School of Quepos (Escuela Privada de Quepos)
Quepos, Puntarenas
tel. 506/777-2211
fax 506/777-0164

The Caribbean Coast
Centro Educativa Caribe
Limón
tel. 506/798-0307
fax 506/798-1152

Escuela Complementaria de Cahuita
Cahuita, Limón Province
Current fees run about US$75/ month for kindergarten, US$80/ month for grades 1–6, and US$95/ month for the upper grades.
tel. 506/755-0075

PUBLIC UNIVERSITIES
University of Costa Rica (Universidad de Costa Rica)
Main campus in San José; branch campuses in Alajuela, Cartago, Turrialba, and Puntarenas.
tel. 506/207-5535
www.ucr.ac.cr

The National University (Universidad Nacional)
Based in Heredia, the National University also has regional centers in Liberia and Perez Zeledon.
tel. 506/277-3317
fax 506/277-3225
www.una.ac.cr

The State University's Distance Learning Program (Universidad Estatal a Distancia)
The main campus is in San José, with 32 regional centers scattered around the country.
tel. 506/253-2121
www.uned.ac.cr

Institute of Technology (Instituto de Tecnologia de Costa Rica)
The campus is in Cartago.
tel. 506/552-5333
www.itcr.ac.cr

Health

Costa Rica is an exceptionally healthy place, and a large number of people come here at least in part for their health. Some are suffering from stress- and work-related conditions that often clear up after a few months of this country's saner pace and salubrious environment. Others have no specific complaint but are drawn to the high-quality medical care, which is extremely cheap if, as a resident, you become part of the country's socialized medicine system, and is still quite a bargain if you opt to go the private route. In the United States, more than forty million people have no health insurance, and the government is dismantling the Medicaid system so that even fewer people will be covered. A place like Costa Rica, which considers health care a fundamental human right, looks very good to refugees from societies where even basic health care seems to have become a privilege.

Costa Rica spends a lot of money to keep its people healthy, and statistics reflect this commitment. Life expectancy is high at just under 77, infant mortality low at 10.6 per 1,000 births—figures that put most other

Latin American countries to shame, and compare favorably with first-world nations like Canada and the United States. According to the United Nations, an impressive 98 percent of Ticos have access to health care; as recently as the 1960s, the figure was 15 percent. Ninety-two percent of people here have access to clean water; in Guatemala the figure is 62 percent, and in El Salvador only 47 percent of the population has such access.

Medical Care

THE CAJA

More than fifty years ago, the Costa Rican government created a worker's health insurance program that has, over the years, grown to cover more than 90 percent of the population. Today a person can be insured as a worker or as part of the worker's family. Or, as a resident, you can insure yourself by paying *seguro voluntario,* or voluntary insurance. The big mama of an agency that makes this possible is the Caja Costarricense de Seguro Social, otherwise known as the Caja. Even if you self-insure, rates are reasonable, topping out at about US$60 a month.

The Caja system extends to every corner of the country, although the majority of well-regarded public hospitals—including San Juan de Dios, Calderon Guardia, and Hospital México—are in San José, and outlanders will routinely journey to the capital for specialized services.

Due to a general downturn in the economy that began in the 1980s, social services have suffered budget cuts, with the Caja taking its share. Though the system is overburdened, it still delivers an admirable level of care to people who could not otherwise afford it. And the Caja is expanding. From 2003 to 2007, the Central American Integration Bank (BCIF) will loan the Caja US$60 billion to modernize and expand Costa Rica's health care system. In the works are new hospitals in the Central Valley city of Heredia and in Ciudad Cortéz, just north of the Osa Peninsula. Also planned are three new Integral Health Attention Centers (CAIS)—in Siquirres, Cañas, and Puriscal—and 10 new Basic Attention Integral Healthcare Centers (EBAIS, the smaller neighborhood clinics) scattered throughout the country. The Caja says that with the new facilities in place, it will be able to attend to 410,000 additional patients.

Still, Ticos and resident foreigners who can afford to often chose to use the Caja as a backup to private care, which they pay for out of pocket or through international or national insurance. (See the sidebar "Kafka Would Love the Caja" for more information.)

THE INS

No, it's not the dreaded *migra* (the U.S. Immigration and Naturalization Service), but the Costa Rican Instituto Nacional de Seguros (INS) is equally omnipresent in its own way. This government agency is the only authorized dealer in health insurance in Costa Rica, though if implementation of CAFTA (the Central American Free Trade Agreement) goes as planned, the insurance industry will be open to private competition in 2011. Currently, INS rates depend on age, sex, and physical condition. INS policies are usually more expensive than the Caja, while still cheaper than international policies. Approximate annual premiums in 2003: Women up to age 59 around US$900; men up to age 59 approximately US$600. Women ages 60 to 75 about US$1,350; men in the same age group pay a few hundred dollars less. With INS insurance you can choose your own doctors and go to private clinics (which have better reputations than public hospitals), and the INS covers 70 percent of the bill.

MIXED MEDICINE

Most Ticos and resident foreigners use both public and private health care. I met a man in the waiting room at Calderon Guardia (a public hospital) who was fully covered under the Caja but had up until then paid for private care—he wasn't crazy about the Caja's bureaucracy and long waits. But now he needed an operation on his hand, and he couldn't afford to have that done by a private doctor in a private clinic. So he'd returned to the Caja fold and was trying to schedule his operation within the next decade. If he had the money for the operation, he said, he wouldn't be there.

Prices at the Three Top Private Clinics in San José

Prices go up and the exchange rate shifts, but these 2003 rates for a single hospital room and for one hour in the operating room will give you an idea of the prices at three of San José's best-known clinics.

Price for one night in a single room with adjustable bed, cable TV, phone, and a daybed for a companion (nursing care is also included):

Clínica Catolica	US$115
Clínica Biblica	US$175
CIMA Hospital	US$182

Price for one hour's use of operating room:

Clínica Catolica	US$166
Clínica Biblica	US$165
CIMA Hospital	US$217

Kafka Would Love the Caja

If you don't have international health insurance and don't want to pay all medical expenses out of pocket, you have two alternatives.

You can arrange for coverage through the INS (Instituto Nacional de Seguros, tel. 506/223-5800, www.ins-cr.com). INS costs less than the international companies, lets you choose your own doctors, and pays 70 percent of doctors' visits, medication, exams, and hospitalization. Unfortunately, it won't cover you if you have a preexisting condition, and dental work, eye exams, and preventive checkups are excluded. It also refuses to cover any "illnesses or disorders related to the female reproductive organs during the first 12 months of coverage, or the birth of a baby during the first 6 months of coverage."

Or, you can sign up with the Caja Costarricense de Seguro Social (a.k.a. the Caja, tel. 506/295-2000, www.ccss.sa.cr). They'll take anyone who is a resident of Costa Rica, no matter how old, infirm, or female. Sometimes they don't even ask to see proof of residency. Once you're a part of the Caja, everything is covered—doctors' visits, prescriptions, lab tests, dental care, eye care, and hospitalization. There's no deductible. The downside is you can't choose your own doctors and often have to wait weeks or months for an appointment. But the price is right—between $40 and $60 a month.

I choose the Caja. Here's what happens.

At the local police station, my papers are stamped and I'm assigned to a clinic several miles from my home. There, I wait in line to learn which line I should be waiting in. Two hours later, I find I'm at the wrong clinic. The *right* clinic is a few blocks from my house—a pleasant place where the nurses are polite and helpful, though exasperated when I don't understand their rapid-fire Spanish. The clerk issues me a Caja ID card and tells me to come back the next morning.

The next day, a doctor writes up a prescription, orders tests, and refers me to a specialist. I pick up my prescription (a few blocks away) and get my tests done (also nearby), and the following week see a specialist who tells me I'll need to see another specialist at a hospital downtown.

Downtown, I'm directed to a drab room staffed by a clerk who takes my referral and tells me to come back the next morning between 10 and 11 A.M. to schedule an appointment. Couldn't I make the appointment now? I ask. No, comes the reply. It's 11:05 A.M.

On my way out, I catch a glimpse of a patients' room. In a small space are wedged four narrow beds; in each lies a woman dressed in a rumpled green gown. There are no partitions or curtains between the beds, and there are no televisions, flowers, pictures on the walls, or telephones.

At 10:15 the next morning, I'm back, but no one knows where the clerk is—maybe she went for coffee, someone suggests. Twenty minutes later, another clerk comes in and says she'll help us, though it isn't her job. She stamps my referral and directs me to a window by the front door.

On my way there, I notice people staring at me, and am suddenly aware that I am the only foreigner in the place. I feel guilty, making use of their already overburdened socialized medical system.

© Erin Van Rheenen

At the window, a woman says I need an *asegurado* before I can make an appointment.

"The building in back," she gestures vaguely. I wander out, and a friendly guard asks me what I'm looking for. An *asegurado*, I tell him. "Look for a pink building," he says.

I find no pink building, but then notice some pink traces on a wall that has been painted white. Eureka!

Back at the first window, the woman smiles. "Now you're all right," she says, proud of me for not giving up. I tell her that my health situation is more serious than the referral would suggest—I've been told to exaggerate my problem so I won't have to wait months for an appointment. I get an appointment for a week later.

Next visit, after waiting two hours, I ask the nurse when my turn will come. She looks at my slip of paper and says, "We're not seeing anyone with morning appointments." I point out that when I arrived (on time) it was still morning. She shrugs—the national gesture of Costa Rica—and

tells me to make another appointment for another day.

After a few months of this, I think hard about whether private care would be a better option and decide that, damn it, I'm a middle-class American with a credit card; I can buy my way out of the Caja. I'm not proud of this response, but I can't deny it, either.

Though I defected to private care for this particular complaint, I still use the Caja for more routine matters, and my private doctor employs *medicina mixta* (mixed medicine) whenever she can—if I need tests, for instance, she'll send me to a Caja lab. But I pay her for appointments, and I spend a lot of time in her waiting room. Scheduling is not a Tico strong point—everyone is told to come at 10 A.M., then wait until the doctor is available. If you don't come at 10, you lose your place in line.

Bottom line: If your Spanish is decent, if you're persistent, and if you have a fondness for labyrinths, by all means, give the Caja a try. Just bring a book along to read while you wait, maybe Kafka's *The Trial*.

Other people will use the Caja for routine care—minor ailments, blood tests, and medication—but turn to private care when the going gets tough. One reason for this is that the sicker you are, the harder it is to navigate all the forms in triplicate you'll need to see Caja specialists, and the more taxing will be the hours of waiting you'll endure at every turn. Another reason to go private is to engage a respected specialist who doesn't work in the Caja (though many doctors have a private practice and also work for the Caja, and can schedule their private patients' surgeries there, thus eliminating hospital expenses but not the surgeon's fees).

If you need surgery, but it's not an absolute emergency, the Caja may assign a surgery date many months from diagnosis. And while some Caja delays are unavoidable, given the system's scant resources, other delays are the result of sheer incompetence, and may have lethal results. Take the case (in May 2003) in which 81 patients at San Juan de Dios Hospital in San José waited more than eight months for biopsies to ascertain whether or not they had prostate cancer. Orders for the necessary medical equipment were approved but then got lost on some bureaucrat's desk. No hospital official followed up on this incredible lapse until patients and journalists pressed for an investigation.

Such incompetence is the exception rather than the rule, and similar outrages have no doubt occurred in health facilities the world over. Still, there's no denying that public hospitals here, though the facilities are adequate and the doctors often very good, are not cheery places. Nurses are overworked and rooms are small and often shared with three or more other patients. You'll find no telephones, TVs, or privacy in these rooms. Some public hospitals lack basic supplies, like toilet paper.

An inquiry that began in June 2003 turned up many "irregularities" in the Caja system, from very long waits to charges that some doctors ask for money in exchange for putting patients higher on waiting lists for specialized treatments or operations. The investigation seems in earnest, and may yet weed the offenders out of the system.

PRIVATE CARE

Doctors in Costa Rica, whether they work for the Caja, in private practice, or a combination of the two, are in general very well trained. Many have studied in the United States, Canada, or Europe. They keep up with developments in their field and often have access to the latest technology. Some doctors who work privately are associated with private clinics; others are not. Either way they can send you to private clinics for tests, or operate on you there.

The best private clinics are in San José, and they are very good indeed (see the list at the end of this section). A note on nomenclature: A "clinic," which is sometimes the size of a large hospital, usually denotes a private institution, while a "hospital" is most often public. This is confused somewhat by the fact that smaller, neighborhood public health facilities are also often called clinics. And one of the best private clinics, CIMA, takes pains to call itself a hospital.

Clinic administrators agree that competition among the top clinics has benefited the consumer. Alfonso Chapa, vice president of hospital operations at CIMA, says that when his clinic opened, Clínica Biblica, a San José favorite, started renovating and expanding.

Prices at private clinics are often beyond the reach of the average Costa Rican, but resident foreigners—who tend to have greater financial resources and are accustomed to higher prices—find the fees refreshingly low. Open-heart surgery, with no complications, staying in the clinic for about a week, will run around US$15,000 (half of that for surgeon fees), a fraction of what one would pay in the United States. A hysterectomy will cost about US$3,000, surgeon fees included. Part of the reason prices are lower is that malpractice lawsuits are rare here; when damages are awarded, they're only enough to cover hospital bills and other expenses.

Clínica Biblica

Founded in 1929 by Christian missionaries from Britain, the Biblica (as it's known) takes up more than a city block in downtown San José; ground was broken for a new wing in July 2003. Right now the clinic has 41 beds, 16 examining rooms, five operating rooms, and modern ultrasonography, mammography, radiology, CAT scan, and MRI equipment. The clinic's cardiology and maternity units are well-known, and about 100 babies are delivered here each month.

The older wing of the clinic has sky-blue walls and tiled floors; the newer parts of the building are also pleasant, especially if you're fond of the color blue. Each of the 41 rooms has a private bath, cable TV, phone, safety deposit box(!), and electric beds. Rooms also have either a rocking chair or a recliner, along with a sofa bed so that a friend or family member can stay overnight. Other visitors are allowed from 9 A.M. to 9 P.M. On the clinic's second floor you'll find a small chapel, and there's a rack of religious tracts near the front desk.

The Biblica works with many international insurance providers. "Almost all U.S. health care insurers work with us," says Brad Cook, the clinic's insurance and claims administrator, who was born in Costa Rica of missionary parents. "The exceptions would be Kaiser and Cigna, though

Cigna International will work. Blue Cross/Blue Shield is great, but there are more than 200 others that will work just fine."

If you'll be paying out of pocket, ask for an estimate, but don't expect it to be accurate. I was quoted US$625 for a surgery that ended up costing me US$1,700, mostly because medications and surgical supplies were excluded from the estimate and ended up being the lion's share of my bill.

If you have questions about what your insurance would cover at the Biblica, you can call Brad Cook at 506/221-7717 or 506/257-5252, ext. 1120, fax 506/257-7307, or email him at claimsclinicabiblica@hotmail.com or bcook@clinicabiblica.com.

The Biblica is located on Calle Central, between Avenidas 14 and 16. The mailing address is Apartado 1307-1000, San José.

tel. 506/257-5252
fax 506/221-0645
clinicabiblica@hotmail.com
www.clinicabiblica.com

Clínica Católica

Católica is a clean, rather stark clinic run by Catholic nuns. Set in the quiet suburb of Guadalupe, just north of San Pedro and the University of Costa Rica, the clinic has 62 beds and is adding eight more. Most are in single rooms, but there are also a few shared rooms (which cost less) and several suites—large two-room spreads, with Monet prints on the walls and upholstered chairs for visitors.

Although well regarded, the Católica is not as geared toward foreign patients as CIMA and the Biblica are. Sister Ramirez, the general director of the clinic, says at least one person per shift speaks English, and that the clinic works with INS, the national health insurance, and with many international insurance companies, including "Blue Cheese" (I think she meant Blue Cross/Blue Shield). Still, it is clear that the Católica hasn't put its energy into wooing foreigners as much as in keeping costs down (it's the cheapest of the four major clinics). "Our mission isn't a commercial one," elaborates Sister Ramirez. "We're run by a Franciscan order; our mission is one of service. If we make any profit, we immediately reinvest it in equipment and infrastructure. And unlike CIMA and even Biblica, we don't have outside investors we have to answer to."

Sixty doctors maintain private consulting offices in the hospital's east wing, and many doctors not officially affiliated with the clinic use the facilities to treat their patients, since the clinic is known for its up-to-date equipment and quality care. Católica is affiliated with Our Lady of the Lake Regional Medical Center in Louisiana, and has ties with Global Medical

Management Inc., Group Hospitalization and Medical Services, Inc. (GHMSI; Blue Cross and Blue Shield), and is a part of the Administrative Network of Americas International Hospital Service Network.

The clinic is located in San Antonio de Guadalupe, a suburb of San José. tel. 506/283-6616
fax 506/283-6171
infoing@clinicacatolica.com
www.clinicacatolica.com

Clínica Santa Rita

Santa Rita is a small downtown clinic known for its ob/gyn and plastic-surgery departments. A bit down at the heels, the clinic may offer lower rates in some cases, and local doctors say it's a fine place to perform surgery. Santa Rita offers sonograms and mammograms, but for EKGs, CAT scans, or MRIs, patients are sent to Biblica or CIMA.

The clinic is located on the south side of Tribunales de Justicia, next door to the *Tico Times* office, Avenida 8, Calles 15 and 16.
tel. 506/221-6433
fax 506/255-1248
starita@racsa.co.cr

Hospital CIMA

Located just off one of Costa Rica's few stretches of superhighway, CIMA is nothing if not modern. The clinic opened in early 2000, near the upscale suburb of Escazú. Rumor has it that CIMA was built to work as a hotel if it failed as a hospital, and with its marble-floored foyer, glass-bricked administrative offices, and the white tablecloths in the cafeteria, CIMA does indeed resemble a tasteful, upscale chain hotel.

Downstairs, you'll find the emergency room, the outpatient clinic, and the big guns of medical technology: a cardiac cath lab, CAT scans, sonograms, x-rays, and the only open MRI in Central America.

Upstairs, the patient rooms and nurses' stations are spotless, with watercolors of flowers and landscapes decorating the walls. Rooms feature everything that most San José private clinics offer—cable TV, phone, adjustable bed, private bath, safety deposit box, and a daybed for overnight guests—but on a grander scale. Of 58 beds, four are equipped for neonatal care, six are in the Intensive Care Unit, and six are suites (all patient rooms are private).

CIMA stands for Centro Internacional de Medicina, and there are 10 CIMA hospitals in Latin America, including facilities in Mexico and Brazil. All are owned and managed by International Hospital Corp. in Texas.

CIMA Hospital

CIMA San José cost a great deal to build and equip, and has struggled with debt since it opened. But as of early 2003, says vice president of hospital operations Alfonso Chapa, the hospital has "a clean bill of economic health," which doesn't mean it's out of debt but does mean it will stay open.

CIMA is associated with Baylor University Medical Center in Dallas, which means, says Chapa, that CIMA "has an obligation to deliver the same standard of care as a quality U.S. hospital. We also use Baylor as an educational resource, to train medical staff. Baylor doctors will come here as well—most recently a cardiologist came down and gave a seminar for local doctors."

It's clear that the equipment here is up-to-the-minute, from the x-ray machines to the computers at the front desk. You can arrive unannounced with diagnosis in hand, speak with the admissions department about the surgery you require, and within five minutes have a written, signed estimate of how much your stay here would cost. CIMA works with all major international insurance companies, as well as with INS.

Depending on what services you require, care here will probably cost you more than it would elsewhere, though Chapa says CIMA tries to be within 5–10 percent of the prices offered at other private clinics in San

José. The higher prices are relative, of course, with totals still coming in far below what you'd pay in the United States. CIMA is a favorite among resident foreigners.

tel. 506/208-1000
fax 506/208-1001
cima@hospitalsanjose.net
www.hospitalsanjose.net

INTERNATIONAL MEDICAL COVERAGE

Before coming to Costa Rica, learn what medical services your current health insurance will cover outside your home country. If your policy provides international coverage, be sure to carry both your insurance identity card and a claim form or two (nowadays claim forms are usually available for download from company websites). Clarify whether your insurance will come through with payment while you're in Costa Rica, or if you have to save receipts and then file claims when you get home. If you know you'll be in Costa Rica for a while, it's a good idea to research the various forms of insurance that have international coverage. The best-known private clinics in San José make every effort to work with international insurers, and often have a separate claims department that will tell you what your particular company covers.

Medical care in Costa Rica is very good, and it's unlikely that you'll want to be flown back home for treatment. But if you do, it'll cost a small fortune (up to US$10,000), so you might consider a policy that covers medical evacuation back to your home country. If you have an American Express Platinum card or the Plus membership offered by AAA (Automobile Association of America), you are automatically covered for medical evacuation from abroad.

Kaiser will only cover emergency medical care while its clients are out of the United States, and even with that, you'll need to pay out of pocket, then submit the claim when you get home. Aetna and Blue Cross/Blue Shield international policies get good marks from both customers and health care providers, but there are dozens of other companies that offer similar coverage (see Contacts in the Resources section at the back of the book). Do your homework, and ask the hard questions. By law, Costa Rican hospitals and clinics must accept any and all patients who need emergency care. But if your problem doesn't qualify as an emergency but still needs attending to, you'll be much better off with good health insurance.

If your current insurance has no international coverage, and you plan to be in Costa Rica for just a short time, traveler's insurance may be the way to go. Such coverage often includes health and baggage insurance, along

Cesarean Sections, Now Just $600!

If you're paying out of pocket for surgery at a private clinic in Costa Rica (or even if insurance pays most of your stay), you'll probably be negotiating the cost of your care in ways that you're not used to. Get over the feeling that health care is not something you haggle over, because here, it is—the tests, the room, even the operation, are all just products. You need to be a good shopper and find the best value for your money. Competition among the major private clinics has benefited the consumer (a.k.a. the patient), in that clinics have been driven to buy new equipment and to lower their prices to draw people in. For common operations, clinics sometimes offer package deals. In mid-2003, for example, CIMA was advertising a deal on cesarean sections—"Were $695, now just $600!"

As a side note, cesareans in the United States aren't considered elective surgery, but in Latin America, many women choose to have them. In the United States, says Alfonso Chapa, vice president of hospital operations at CIMA, most deliveries are vaginal, while in Latin America, a greater percentage of babies are delivered by C-section. Why? I asked Chapa, who is a Texas native and has worked in hospital administration in the United States as well as in Costa Rica. One reason, he says, is that doctors get paid more for surgical procedures, so they push women to have C-sections. Another reason is that C-sections can be scheduled, so, unlike natural births, they "won't interfere with the doctor's lifestyle."

Many patients have a private doctor, who will often operate in whichever clinic the patient prefers. It's up to the patient to research the clinics and compare prices. You'll be paying a fee to your doctor (which will usually cover the assisting physician and the anesthesiologist; most doctors have teams that they always work with). The doctors' fees are completely separate from what you pay the clinic—what you pay for at the clinic is the hospital room, the use of the operating room, and any tests or medications needed while hospitalized. In the case of most special deals, like the advertised cesarean section, the price does not include doctors' fees.

Getting Estimates from Private Clinics

If your surgery is elective, you may have time to ask the various private clinics for cost estimates (*presupuesto* in Spanish) before you choose a clinic. In my experience, of the four major clinics, CIMA will come up with a written estimate very quickly; the other three clinics need to be prodded, and even then may not give it in writing (I received only verbal estimates from Clínica Catolica and Clínica Santa Rita).

· Clinics say they are reluctant to give estimates because there are so many variables, like what sort of medication your doctor prescribes. One dose of antibiotics can cost US$25, for instance, depending on the type and the brand. Imagine if you have three doses a day for a week—that's US$500 spent on antibiotics alone.

If some clinics balk at providing written estimates, and if written estimates themselves can be off, what can a prospective patient do? If a clinic will only give you a verbal estimate, at least write it down yourself, and ask the clinic to break it down, to tell you what elements are included in the total. Then go to your doctor with all the figures and details, and ask him or her what the estimates might be leaving out. A layperson probably won't know that electrocauterization of a wound will cost around US$33, a biopsy may cost close to US$200, and a dose of generic morphine will be less than a dollar. Your doctor will know what he or she will need for surgery, what kinds of medicine he or she will be prescribing, and (hopefully) approximately how much it will all cost.

If you don't want to get into this level of nitty-gritty, you could ask the clinics and/or your doctor for the final total bill of similar operations that have been performed recently. (You'd think this would be how they'd compile estimates, but apparently it is not.) You'll need to be persistent—it seems to really throw Ticos if you ask for something that is quite possible but isn't a part of the general routine. Be friendly and respectful, but don't take no for an answer.

A few more things to remember:

- All clinics require a pre-surgery deposit, anywhere from US$1,000 to US$10,000, depending on the estimated cost of surgery. This deposit can be put on your credit card.
- You will usually have to pay your entire bill upon release from the hospital. They don't mail the bill later—they want their money before you step out (or are rolled out) the door. One of the reasons for this is that it's easy—especially for foreigners who live elsewhere—to skip the country and leave the bill behind.
- If you're in the clinic for a while, they will probably ask you to pay a little on your bill every few days. It seems ghoulish to come to someone's hospital bed and ask them for money, but that's how it's done here. If your bill is more than you expected, you can usually work out a payment plan with the billing department.
- Most clinics will do their best to work with your insurance (arrange this ahead of time if you can), and most clinics accept credit cards.

with insurance against cancellation of a prepaid tour or flight. See Resources in the back of the book for the contact information of companies who provide this type of coverage.

SENIOR CITIZENS

U.S. citizens need to know that Medicare does not provide coverage for hospital or medical costs outside the United States. If you've bought other coverage to supplement Medicare, that policy may pay for up to 80 percent of your care abroad, as in the absence of Medicare it becomes your primary coverage. Among other organizations, AARP offers Medicare supplement plans that include foreign medical care coverage.

Nursing Homes

Of the 155 nursing homes in Costa Rica, 26 are privately run and the rest are funded (often inadequately) by the government. More than 4,000 senior citizens (known in Spanish as *personas de la tercera edad,* or people of the third age), make use of these facilities, either residing there or coming every day for meals and activities. An April 2003 article in *La Nación* noted that 75 percent of all nursing homes were not in compliance with federal regulations, most noncompliance relating to a shortage of qualified staff.

There are no figures available on how many foreign-born seniors make use of Costa Rica's nursing homes, but I would guess that it's not a high number. For many seniors, the language and the culture would be barriers to feeling at home.

High life expectancy and a decline in childbearing have made people over 60 the fastest-growing segment of the Costa Rican population. In 1995, one Tico in 12 was over age 60; by 2025 the figure is expected to be one in seven. And many foreign residents who live in Costa Rica come in their later years. Under pressure from foreign lenders to make budget cuts, the Costa Rican government stopped building public-funded nursing homes in 1992. Though only a small percentage of Tico seniors live in such centers, the existing facilities barely keep up with present demand, and certainly will not be sufficient in years to come.

Victoria Schwartz, who moved here from California in 2002 at the age of 52, wonders what her future holds. "What if, in twenty years, I need nursing care?" she asks. "Will I have to go back to the U.S., which by then will be a different country? People here have families—I don't. And soon, I think, the Tico family will change to more closely resemble the U.S. family, in that there won't be anyone willing to care for aging relatives."

She and other expats and Ticos I spoke with think the lack of nursing homes and extended care facilities are a gap in the social services net. Some see the lack as an opportunity, especially with the growing number of English-speaking resident foreigners who might need such services. "You could pay doctors and nurses here far more than what they'd normally earn, make sure everyone speaks English, ánd rent or buy a great facility. You'd still be able to provide quality care for much less than it would cost in the U.S. or Canada," says Barry Wilson, who runs a company that supplies surgical gowns and drapes to private clinics.

AT-HOME CARE
At-home care, for seniors or others in need of help, can be very reasonable compared to how much it would cost in the United States or Canada. A registered nurse makes US$300–500 a month working at a hospital, which would be a fair salary to pay an RN for a 48-hour week of at-home care. A caretaker with no official credentials would cost less.

Pharmacies and Prescriptions

Pharmacies in Costa Rica (called *farmacias* or *boticas*) are on every other corner, and most are well-stocked. If you bring a prescription from outside the country, make sure it is for generic rather than brand-name medication—generic names are common to all countries, while brand names are not. And unless you're looking for antibiotics, narcotics, or psychotropic drugs, you don't even need a prescription (even many antibiotics don't require a prescription). You can tell the pharmacist what you're looking for, or, if you're not sure what you need, the pharmacist will diagnose you and suggest appropriate medication—thus saving you the price of a doctor's consultation.

Pharmacists being able to diagnose is especially helpful when you're far from a doctor, but of course you shouldn't expect the pharmacist to have specialized knowledge of arcane ailments. For simple problems, however, it's a godsend that in this country pharmacists have more power than their counterparts back home. I've had skin problems, ear infections, and stomach ailments diagnosed and treated by pharmacists (in different parts of the country)—and every time, the medication prescribed cleared up the problem in short order. Most pharmacists will even give injections for a small fee.

Prices are usually reasonable, but do shop around, and know that prices will be higher in heavily touristed areas. In San José, for instance, the pharmacy at Clínica Biblica and the Fischel chain of pharmacies are known to be well-stocked but much more expensive than lesser-known shops.

MEDICAL RECORDS

If you have any preexisting medical problems, carry a letter from your doctor, describing the condition and any prescription medications you need, including the generic name of prescribed drugs. Better yet, request your medical records before you leave home, and carry them with you. Make sure any medication you bring is still in its original container, clearly labeled. You don't want customs inspectors to think you're trafficking in prescription drugs.

Preventive Measures

VACCINATIONS

Epidemic diseases have mostly been wiped out in Costa Rica, and the country requires no proof of vaccination upon entry. But travelers or potential residents planning to rough it, suggests Christopher Baker in *Moon Handbooks Costa Rica,* should consider vaccinations against tetanus, polio, typhoid, and infectious hepatitis, which is contracted through contaminated food or water. For the latest information on epidemics and vaccinations, contact the Centers for Disease Control and Prevention in Atlanta (tel. 800/311-2425, www.cdc.org).

ALTERNATIVE THERAPIES

Alternative medicine—such as acupuncture and homeopathy—is popular in Costa Rica, especially in the Central Valley and in touristed beach towns, where arrivals from other countries have brought with them their interest in all things holistic. You'll have no problem finding massage therapists, health-food stores, or yoga classes. The best way to find a reputable practitioner is word of mouth. Barring that, the following places are a good place to start your search.

Unity (tel. 506/228-6051, www.unitycostarica.org) is a nondenominational center that sponsors spiritual and holistic workshops and speakers. Try also the Harmony Center for Holistic Medicine (tel. 506/228-1623, centroharmony@hotmail.com), or Clínica de la Paz (tel. 506/225-2620, clinicalapaz@hotmail.com), a holistic center in Los Yoses (a neighborhood in San José) with its own resident homeopaths. Ciudad Coln–based Dr. Kim (tel. 506/249-1826, www.drkimcostarica.com) gets high marks for his work in acupuncture, nutritional counseling, and allergy elimination. Casa de la Cultura Alternativa Osiris (Osiris Alternative Culture Center, www.gruposiris.com) offers all sorts of activities, from vegetarian cooking classes to tai chi and astrology.

Especially on the Caribbean coast, you will hear about native healers—called bush doctors (usually of African heritage) or *sukias* (of indigenous heritage). The healers don't have web sites or phones—this is one place where you definitely need a personal recommendation. But if you're in a place for a while, you'll no doubt hear stories, some of them true.

"Alternative" birthing methods—using midwives, or giving birth at home with a trusted friend or relative—used to be the norm, but over the past half century hospital births became the only way to go, with cesarean sections promoted even when a vaginal birth would have presented no hazard to mother or baby. (See the sidebar "Cesarean Sections, Now Just $600!") Recently, there has been a renewed interest in midwives and natural birthing practices, although you'll have to look hard for this small but growing movement, especially because practitioners operate in a legal gray area and are not likely to advertise. In Costa Rica, one is a certified midwife only through a specialization after obstetrical nursing studies, and officially, midwives are allowed to attend births only in an emergency. Otherwise mothers must go to the hospital. But, there are ways around these restrictions.

According to Uva, a German-born birth assistant, the handful of midwives in Costa Rica are mostly foreign-born, with a strong sense of mission. Uva herself provides extensive preparation ("spiritual, emotional, and physical") for the expectant mother, then makes house calls every day for one week postpartum and three times the following week. Some midwives use a portable birthing pool or a birthing chair, depending on the expectant mother's wishes. For more information on alternative birthing possibilities in Costa Rica, contact Uva at 506/268-2127. Uva speaks six languages, including English.

Environmental Factors

DRINKING WATER

Water quality is, in fact, one of the biggest differences between Costa Rica and other Latin American nations. Often people don't believe it until they arrive, but it's true: You can drink the water! Something so basic has profound implications, not the least of which is that it feels like the natural world is working with rather than against you, offering up an abundant and untainted supply of the most essential of elements. Anyone who's lived in a place where they can't even wash vegetables or brush their teeth with what comes out of the tap knows what a blessing this is. Clean water also eliminates most water-borne diseases, such as cholera, typhoid fever, and dysentery. Also rare in Costa Rica are the less dangerous but still annoying intestinal upsets from tainted water so familiar to third-world travelers. The country has a few areas—like remote parts of the Talamanca Mountains and (ironically) the upscale San José suburb of Escazú—where the drinking water is suspect. Sometimes water quality worsens with heavy rains, as debris is washed into water supplies. Ask around, and if there's any question, stick with bottled water. Otherwise, turn on the tap, fill up your glass, and enjoy.

> *Water quality is, in fact, one of the biggest differences between Costa Rica and other Latin American nations. Often people don't believe it until they arrive, but it's true: You can drink the water!*

FOOD

You might get sick of all the rice and beans, but you won't get sick *from* the rice and beans. Food hygiene standards in Costa Rica are very high. Of course you'll want to take the usual precautions: Think twice about buying food from street vendors, and be careful about raw fish and shellfish (where cholera bugs like to hang out). That said, I wouldn't trade my ceviche (raw fish marinated in lime juice) for anything. I just make sure to go to established restaurants, which have a vested interest in keeping their customers healthy and happy. The usual third-world warnings—Wash it, boil it, peel it, or forget it—don't really apply in Costa Rica, at least not in the Central Valley or the more developed tourist destinations. I don't have an ironclad stomach, and yet I've eaten every salad served to me here, with no ill effects whatsoever. In fact, I wish I would encounter more salads—they're not easy to come by in this starch-loving nation. Most traditional meals will boast two, three, or even four starches—usually rice, potatoes, and fried plantain, with some yucca, chayote, or a few tortillas thrown in for good measure. You may also get a dollop of cole slaw or a few slices of tomato. Making up for the lack of good salads is the astonishing variety of fruits; you'll want to try them all, from the heart-shaped *anona* to the purple-fleshed *zapote*.

SMOKING

Costa Ricans on the whole smoke more than North Americans but not as much as Europeans. Smoking is usually prohibited on buses and in some restaurants, but bars often seem to be full of smoke. Cigarettes are for sale everywhere; singles are often sold at kiosks on the street, where a lighter attached by a string is often available.

Would you like fries with your rice? Starch is king in Costa Rica.

TRAFFIC

Without a doubt, the biggest threat to your safety here comes from cars and the way Ticos wield them like enormous machetes. The risk of motor vehicle–related death is generally many times higher in developing countries than in the United States (no haven of safety itself), and Costa Rica is no exception to this rule. Some observers suggest that the national character—which is one of avoiding conflict and smoothing things over at any cost—does a flip-flop when Ticos get behind the wheel, with drivers asserting every bit of the hostility they repress in other parts of their lives.

Automobile accidents are the leading cause of death here for people under the age of 50. In 2002, more Ticos died in auto accidents (365, one for each day of the year) than U.S. soldiers died in the Persian Gulf War (293). If you find that an odd comparison, thank *La Nación,* the country's biggest daily paper. The parallel shows two things: just how much influence the United States has here, and also that although Costa Rica has no army and does not enter into battle, war is waged daily on the country's streets and highways.

Michael Kaye, owner of Costa Rica Expeditions, has another theory: "Driving in Costa Rica is inspired by the ancient tradition of the bullfight. The driver who cuts you off is not insulting you. She's playing with you.

The best way for you to handle this is the same as for newcomers to all games. Play; but play by local rules, don't play too intensely, and expect to lose."

Be prepared to lose that game of chicken, but take care not to lose your life. Every day the newspapers report on the previous night's wrecks and on the pedestrians who've been *aplastados* (flattened, or run over). Most of the country's roads are atrocious, and as for walking—there's a public service announcement on TV that urges pedestrians to wear white, and to step off into the dirt whenever they see a car coming. No mention is made of the fact that the country could use a few more sidewalks, and that drivers should be on the lookout for "obstacles," especially in rural areas where cars share the road with horses, oxcarts, and whole families walking to weddings, baptisms, and funerals.

> Without a doubt, the biggest threat to your safety here comes from cars and the way Ticos wield them like enormous machetes. Automobile accidents are the leading cause of death here for people under the age of 50.

In Costa Rica, the car is the *patrón* and the pedestrian the *peón*. The culture here is that cars stop for nothing—not an old woman limping across the street, not a stalled car, not a group of schoolkids trying to get to class on time. In many cultures, people are taught to drive defensively. In Costa Rica, parents teach their kids to *walk* defensively. Ticos on foot know to treat cars as the unpredictable animals they are. Follow their lead and don't expect cars to stop just because there's a stop sign or a red light. And if you're wondering how you're ever going to cross that busy street, watch what the locals do. Shadow one of them; walk when they walk. And watch out for potholes—not just in the road but on the sidewalks.

If you can avoid driving at night, do so. Eighty percent of insurance claims come from nighttime accidents. In rural areas, be on the lookout for cows or dogs lying in the road, or for people who consider the bank of a highway a good place to hang out and socialize.

THE HAZARDS OF ADVENTURE TOURISM

Care to run a raging river, surf some nefarious waves, or whiz above the canopy on a zipline? It's all good fun, but be careful. Surfers should ask locals for tips and try to surf with a buddy. Rip tides are common here, as are sharks, crocodiles, and, at river mouths during the rainy season, human waste and agrochemical runoff. For group activities, try to hook up with an established tour company, one that has a reputation for doing things right. There are fewer safety regulations here, and any bozo can set up a zipline or a bungee jump. Try to get a personal recommendation before stepping off into the wild blue yonder.

Costa Rican Expeditions' Michael Kaye thinks safety is adventure tourism's Achilles' heel. "A lot of accidents don't get reported," he says. "Not long ago a seven-year-old girl lost her finger—it got caught in a line. It may take fatalities to get some of these people to clean up their act."

The bottom line is that you need to go with a reputable operator. Costa Rican Expeditions, for instance, employs a safety expert to check out any canopy tour it sends clients to. "We've lost customers because we say we can't recommend any canopy tour where they're going. But in good conscience we have to have checked them out ourselves."

THE NATURAL WORLD

Manmade threats—like cars and their drivers—are the most serious hazards; what comes at you from the natural world pales in comparison. Still, it's a good idea to know what kinds of creatures you'll find here, and how the environment might affect you.

Bugs

In and around the Central Valley, there are surprisingly few bugs. You hardly ever see houseflies, spiders are normal-sized and lead discreet lives, and even the ants are generally small and non-biting.

In lowland and more humid areas, you'll find more quantity and variety in the insect department. Some, like the enormous Hercules beetle or the bright blue morpho butterfly, are stunning but harmless. It's the more prosaic insects like mosquitoes that do greater harm, occasionally transmitting dengue fever and, more rarely, malaria—mostly in wet, lowland areas with poor sanitation. Malaria is rare enough in Costa Rica that few doctors suggest taking chloroquine pills along on your trip. But cases have been reported, and the best prevention (against both malaria and dengue fever) is to guard against mosquito bites. Wear long sleeves and long pants, use insect repellent containing DEET, and sleep under a mosquito net. Some suggest that spraying your clothes with the insecticide permethrin will guard against dengue fever.

Africanized bees have arrived in parts of Costa Rica, and are as aggressive here as they are elsewhere. Experts advise running in a zigzag pattern if they come after you, getting under a sheet, or submerging yourself in water if there's any available.

Some areas have scorpions. I heard of a woman who, when she washed her family's clothes, made sure to put them away inside out. That way, when they dressed, they'd have to turn everything right side out, and thus would be automatically checking for bugs that may have hidden in the armpit of a shirt or in the leg of a pair of jeans. Despite her precautions, one day her husband found a scorpion crawling out of his sleeve. Then he noticed the seams on his shirt—it was still inside out. In scorpion areas, make sure you shake out your clothing and shoes before getting dressed in the morning. This will help with snakes, too, which love nothing better than to curl up in a warm, odoriferous boot.

Snakes

Costa Rica has more than 100 kinds of snakes, including venomous ones such as the much-feared fer-de-lance, which accounts for 80 percent of all snake bites in the country, and the yellow-bellied, black-backed sea snake, which paddles along in the Pacific Ocean with its oar-like tail. Despite the variety of snakes here, death from snakebite is rare. Most bites occur when snakes are stepped on—watch where you're going!—or if you harass or try to handle a snake. Leave snakes alone and they'll return the favor. Be especially careful in long grass, and remember that many snakes are arboreal—the tree branch you grab onto for balance just may be alive. Snakes also like to hang out in bromeliads, so be careful when looking inside these tightly wound whorls of stiff leaves and brilliant flowers. If you are bitten, move as little as possible. If the bite is to a limb, apply a tight bandage (not a tourniquet) above the bite, and release it for a minute or two every fifteen minutes. Apply ice if available, and keep the bitten limb elevated while getting yourself to a hospital or clinic. Don't try that old remedy of cutting an X over the bite and sucking out the venom. Some snake venom contains anticoagulants, which will make any cut bleed like crazy.

Sun

What people come to Costa Rica for can also be their downfall. The sun can be like a molten hammer, especially around midday. Sunscreen, a wide-brimmed hat, sunglasses, and a long-sleeved, light-colored shirt may make you look like your typical gringo in the tropics, but that's a small price to pay for guarding against sunburn, skin cancer, and heatstroke. Don't forget to drink a lot of liquids, and I'm not talking beer, which goes right through you. Take it slow at first, especially in areas of high humidity. After you've been here for a while you'll adjust to your chosen area's weather. In the most sizzling areas, early mornings and late afternoons are the best times to be out and about. There's a reason hot countries invented the siesta, that midday break that gets you out of the sun and into a hammock. Do as the locals do, and spend the early afternoon swaying on the front porch, a cool drink within reach.

Safety

CRIME

You're probably safer anywhere in Costa Rica than in a similar-sized place in the United States, but you still need to be cautious. The U.S. State Department says that crime here is increasing, and tourists are frequent victims. It advises "the same level of caution that one would exercise in major cities or tourist areas throughout the world." The police have limited capabilities and are not up to U.S. standards, especially outside of San José. Some city blocks hire their own security guard, who sits in a little booth and occasionally patrols the street. Gated communities are popular in part because they offer better security.

Once you get a feel for the country and its people, you'll be able to recognize potentially dangerous situations and ease out of them gracefully. Until then, be wary. Petty theft is on the rise, especially in San José. Keep your bags close at all times, and don't be flashy with money, jewelry, or cameras. Make photocopies of important documents—passports, visas, and plane tickets—and keep the originals at home or in a hotel safe. Burglary is also common; that's why you'll see bars on so many windows and fierce dogs in people's yards. Cars are broken into on a regular basis—don't leave anything of value in your car, and if possible, park your car in a garage or a guarded lot.

Costa Rica is also the land of scammers, many of whom will look like you and speak your language. Scams range from low-tech—someone spilling a drink on you and, in "helping" you clean it off, relieving you of

Emergency Numbers

911: National emergency number for all of Costa Rica
118: Fire Brigade
128: Red Cross
800/376-4266: Drug Control Police
800/800-8000: To report traffic accidents
506/222-9330: Traffic Police
  See Contacts in the Resources section for hospital and private clinic contact information throughout Costa Rica.

your wallet—to more sophisticated schemes that ask for investments of tens of thousands of dollars. In late 2002, for instance, hundreds of expats and Ticos lost an estimated US$200 million when a financial entity known as Ofinter S.A. (a.k.a. "The Brothers") closed up their offices overnight and fled the country, taking investors' money with them. Clients had been lured by promises of 3.5 to 4 percent interest a month (that is, 42 to 48 percent a year), and the Brothers had indeed delivered on those promises for years, supporting many an expat in high style. But then the goose laying those golden eggs flew the coop, and investors were left in the feather-strewn mud.

There are many other such schemes still in operation—beware of investments that seem too good to be true. The maxim "If you wouldn't do it at home, don't do it here," isn't nearly strong enough, since there's less effective government oversight of financial dealings here than there is in North America or Europe.

DRUGS

The North American appetite for recreational drugs has helped make Central America a conduit for marijuana, heroin, and cocaine moving up from South America. Drug trafficking and money laundering is on the rise in all of the isthmus, including Costa Rica.

What that means to the average visitor or foreign resident is that Costa Rican police, assisted by the U.S. Drug Enforcement Agency (DEA), are on high alert. The DEA's Central American headquarters, in fact, is in San José. In late 2002, a high-speed cigarette boat loaded with cocaine was chased down near the Osa Peninsula by none other than the U.S. Coast Guard, and that is not an isolated case of U.S. involvement in the drug war here. The big guns are trained on this little republic, and anyone suspected of participating in international drug trafficking will be dealt with harshly. Jail terms for such offenses range from 8 to 20 years. The rise in drug trafficking has also contributed to increased theft and muggings.

If you tend toward addiction and have dabbled in recreational drugs, be especially careful in Costa Rica. Marijuana and cocaine (including crack) are easy to come by and a lot less expensive than they are back home. Many an expat has been brought low by the availability of cocaine, in particular. I've heard stories of gringos ending up broke and on the street.

Alcohol is another drug that expats may abuse when they move to Costa Rica. The stress of adapting to a new culture, coupled with feelings of isolation and boredom, drives many newcomers to drink. "If you have a drinking problem," advises Chris Simmonds of Remax Realty in Tamarindo, "don't come to Costa Rica—it'll just get worse." Costa Ricans also like their liquor, which is no good thing but has a silver lining: There are Alcoholics Anonymous meetings in almost every neighborhood and town in the country. Some meetings are in English, but don't worry if the meeting is in Spanish and you can barely say "Hola." The camaraderie of such gatherings transcends language.

PROSTITUTION

There are tens of thousands of prostitutes in Costa Rica, and the majority operate well within the law. Yes, prostitution is legal here, and working girls are supposed to have special ID cards *(carnets de salud)* proving that they are disease-free. Most prostitutes work independently, as the legal status of their occupation makes pimps redundant. There are brothels in most towns and scores of them in San José, as well as bars that are known as gathering places for prostitutes and potential clients. Sixteen is the age of consent in Costa Rica, but it is illegal for young people under 18 to work as prostitutes; anyone who engages the services of an underage prostitute is at serious legal risk.

In 2000, ABC's *20/20* broadcast a report that Costa Rica was second only to Thailand in underage sex tourism. Since then, there has been increased awareness of the issue and heightened police vigilance. The Costa Rican government formed the Commission Against the Sexual Exploitation of Children, and private organizations also lend a hand in rectifying the situation, offering job training for young people who might otherwise be drawn to the "easy" money of prostitution, or providing rehab and employment opportunities for those already in the life.

Beyond the straightforward sex-for-money world of prostitution lies a wide gray area of "arrangements." In this country, where women (as elsewhere in the world) are at an economic disadvantage, and where it is not uncommon for men to abandon their wives and children (desertion is called "the poor man's divorce"), some women actively seek out relationships with foreign men in the hopes of garnering support for themselves and their families. These women believe that most foreign men are well-off, and by Costa Rican standards, most are. Some Ticas also claim that foreign men are less likely to stray. Expat men looking for such arrangements should go in with their eyes wide open. Love *can* be found under such circumstances, but don't count on it. Think twice when a beautiful young woman claims that she truly prefers a man three times her age.

That said, marrying *por interés* (for money, or security) here is not uncommon, and is not limited to Tica women looking for foreign sugar daddies. In terms of world history, marrying for love is a relatively recent development, and in poorer countries marriage is still seen as an economic contract as much as a romantic one. There's nothing wrong with that, as long as you don't confuse a mutually beneficial arrangement with true love.

AIDS AND OTHER STDS

STDs and the AIDS virus are less prevalent in Costa Rica than in many other nations. According to the CIA Factbooks, the HIV/AIDS Adult Prevalence Rate (which estimates the percentage of adults 15–49 living with AIDS or HIV) was .54 percent in 1999 in Costa Rica. For purposes of comparison, the rate in the United States for the same year was .61 percent, and in Zimbabwe, over 25 percent of the adult population is now affected. Rates for Costa Rica's neighbors are .2 percent for Nicaragua and 1.54 percent for Panama.

Even though Costa Rica has done an admirable job with AIDS education, and the country's public health system cares for people living with the virus, it's still very important to be careful, especially if your plans here include casual sexual contact.

As explained in the previous section, prostitution is legal and prostitutes are supposed to be checked regularly for disease, but some prostitutes aren't registered, don't get checked, and are therefore at high risk of contracting AIDS and other STDs, and of passing them on to their clients. Even if your partner is non-professional, know that Costa Rican men usually prefer not to use condoms, and Costa Rican women don't tend to insist. You do the math. Practice safe sex, and use condoms, every time.

SAFETY NOTES FOR WOMEN

North American and European women may get a lot of attention in Costa Rica, especially if they're young and/or blonde. Some women appreciate the attention; many more do not. You may hear wolf whistles, hissing, or suggestive comments as you walk down the street. If you speak fluent Spanish and are one of those lucky people who always thinks of the right thing to say at the right moment, by all means, attempt a witty comeback. Most of us, however, would do well to ignore unwanted attention, and to walk on by with purpose and confidence.

Most guidebooks advise women to dress like the local women do, but if you did that in Costa Rica, you'd draw even more attention, since most Ticas favor skin-tight pants, plunging necklines, and high heels. If you dress conservatively, you'll get less attention, but not that much less. Costa Rican men seem to believe that North American and European women—whether in miniskirts or overalls—are easy conquests. This may have some basis in truth, as many visiting women enjoy brief beach flings or chose the optional night tour with their nature guide. There's nothing wrong with that if everyone's a consenting adult, but remember that you are in unknown waters here. Even supremely confident and experienced women probably don't know the ins and outs of dating etiquette in an unfamiliar place. For your own safety, it's best to lay low at first, taking it all in but not acting impulsively. And be sure to observe the same commonsense precautions you would in any new place: Don't walk alone in remote places, especially after dark. Grab a cab whenever you feel you've strayed into an iffy neighborhood (cabs are cheap). And don't hang out late at unfamiliar bars unless you have friends around who'll make sure you're OK.

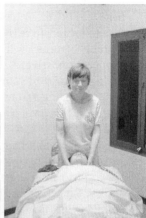

Employment

S elf-starters will do well in Costa Rica. It's actually easier to establish
your own business here than to get a decent job working for someone else. Compared to many other countries, which put up obstacles
to foreign-owned enterprise, Costa Rica welcomes foreign investment
with open arms, especially businesses that create jobs for Ticos. Tax
breaks are offered to new ventures related to tourism, reforestation, and
low-income housing; and specially designated free trade zones *(zonas
francas)* offer further tax breaks for businesses located within their boundaries. You don't even need residency to start that rafting business, flower
shop, or underwear production plant you've always dreamed of. Since
most businesses here are owned and operated by a corporation (in Costa
Rica called an S.A., or Sociedad Anónima), you can even start and run a
business on a tourist visa.

A few decades back, the average North American living in Costa Rica—
well past midlife, living off a pension or investments—wasn't looking to
work or start a business. More and more, however, those who move

169

here are still smack in the middle of their working years. Some have been laid off; other have cashed in or dropped out. They come to Costa Rica to escape, to reassess, and to start over. If they decide to stay, most of these sojourners will, sooner or later, need to think about how they will support themselves.

You *can* support yourself here, but it will take more than picking up coconuts, sticking a straw in them, and selling them to tourists—that job is taken. And it's not a place to come to get rich quick, or to get rich at all, for that matter. Those who do best simply want to live here and do what it takes to make that happen. Lance Byron, co-owner with Adrienne Pellizzari of the ever-expanding Café Milagro in Quepos, says loving the country and its people are essential to success in business. "And when I say success," he clarifies, "I mean not only monetary, but spiritual as well. Some foreigners manage to make enough money to survive, but they're miserable," complaining about the bureaucracy and their workers to whoever will listen. Lance and other business owners emphasize that it's the newcomer who must adapt, not the other way around.

Even though you'll naturally want to turn a profit or make a decent salary, it's good to keep things in perspective. Costa Rica offers visitors the benefits of living in a nation that has made long-term investments in peace, social justice, and the environment. It abolished its army in 1949, has put aside a quarter of its territory for national parks and wildlife refuges, and continues to put money into the country's infrastructure and social services. Think of all the sacrifices this tiny nation has made to transform itself into a place where all are entitled to health care and education, where despite problems the country basically *works,* and where a disproportionate share of the world's biodiversity has been given a fighting chance at survival.

Add to all that a slower, more humane pace, and you're already enjoying a host of advantages that money can't buy. Factor these into your balance sheet, and listen to the expats who note that those only interested in money seem to do worse here than those with broader goals. Whether you choose to teach English, start a bed-and-breakfast, or run a factory, you'll do better and be happier if you want to contribute to Costa Rica rather than wring from it everything you can.

Being a contributing member of your new society and earning money are not mutually exclusive. It's not only possible to make a living here; it's often easier to start and run a business in Costa Rica than it would be in the United States or Canada. Making money hand over fist is another story.

And there's a lot to learn quickly. You're in a new environment, often using an unfamiliar language, and different labor laws apply. Legal and cultural differences come into high relief as you contract a lawyer to do the paperwork, hire staff to help you, and try to carve out your niche with tools you're not even sure how to use yet. It's easy to get discouraged. The successful business owners I've met all have their tales of struggle and woe, but they tell them with a comic twist rather than with bitterness. And it's a sense of humor—along with good planning, experience in the field, hard work, and just plain sticking to it—that makes a business work here (much like elsewhere in the world). It's the couple who buys a hotel though they don't know the first thing about running one, or the tourist who thinks doing business here will be like taking an extended vacation, who lose their shirts and often their affection for the country.

The Job Hunt

Costa Rica is like the United States in that it has one of the strongest economies in its geographical area, and so attracts people who need work. If your home country is in bad economic straits, with high unemployment—think Argentina, Peru, or Nicaragua—Costa Rica looks very good to you. "It's easy to make a living here," a Peruvian living in Liberia told me. "As long as you're ready to work hard. But at least here you find something to work hard at."

For North Americans used to making a good wage or salary, however, Costa Rica is no haven. North Americans don't usually come here for job opportunities; they come because they love the country. Those who need to generate income can do so, but that income won't approach what you could make back home. Sure, the cost of living is lower here, but not that much lower. Rent is less; food is about the same. Buses and taxis are a bargain, but cars are more expensive here than back home.

You can't legally work without a work permit, and they're not easy to get. Sometimes employers will arrange for permits, or give you a letter of employment so that you can hire a lawyer to apply for the permit.

Most of the jobs are in the Central Valley, the economic engine of the country. Yes, there's a lot of tourist activity on the coasts and in some inland areas like Lake Arenal. But there's also a lot of competition for those tourism-related jobs. How many wanderers stumble into cool little beach towns and decide they want to stay? Too many. These areas can only absorb so many massage therapists, surf instructors, real estate agents, and bartenders. And Ticos will always be hired before you—it's only fair. Says the owner of a large Pacific coast hotel, "Eighty percent of [foreigners] who move to Manuel Antonio seem to be looking for work. They usually

7th Street Books: A Clean, Well-Lighted Place

The best English-language bookstore in San José, and perhaps all of Costa Rica, 7th Street Books is also a great hangout. Located half a block off the pedestrian-only section of Avenida Central and a few blocks from the landmark Teatro Nacional, the store enjoys an excellent location and sees lots of foot traffic. Co-owner John McCuen helps to make the store not only a great place to buy a guidebook or quality novel but also a place to meet other tourists or resident foreigners—John has lived here for a decade and seems to know everyone in town. He can hold his own in any discussion, whether the subject is nematodes or the NBA, and customers cluster around the front desk, asking John's opinion about canopy tours or world politics. The store has been owned and operated by John and his partner, Marc Roegiers, since 1995, and they currently have five employees. Below, John answers a few questions about the business.

Can you live off the proceeds of the business?
Yes, but by drinking beer rather than wine. You often hear people say that it is hard to make money in Costa Rica, but that seems to be the case anywhere in the world.

What's next for the business?
We have begun publishing books on the natural history of Costa Rica. If that goes well, we would like eventually to publish books about other countries in Latin America, and also consider books on cultural and other themes.

What's the most satisfying thing about doing business here?
San José is small enough that one can sense the changes (however small and modest) that the business has wrought on the local scene. You also get to know your customers. In terms of employees, if you pay people fairly, you have access to lots of people who are eager to work.

The most frustrating thing?
I'm not sure the frustrating aspects are specific to Costa Rica. Small-business owners always wish they were making more money. Though foreigners doing business in Costa Rica often complain of how inefficient the business culture is here, I'd prefer to point out one positive aspect. There are fewer regulatory agencies here than in the United States; a friend who owns a fairly simple business in California must meet the requirements of 14 regulatory agencies.

If I had to mention one change in how business works in San José, a change to our detriment, it would be the change in rental laws here, which happened about seven years ago. Before, the laws were decidedly to the advantage of the renter, and in fact unfair to building owners. Basically, the renter could stay in a location forever, if he wanted to, without a corresponding lease obligation on his part to the owner. Now, I think, the rental laws are decidedly unfair to the renter. After only three years of operating your business, the building owner can send you packing.

Any advice to others thinking of starting a business in Costa Rica?
Don't assume that what might work in other countries will work here. Move here first to learn about the country. Study Spanish. These all sound obvious enough, but when you have met someone who planned to open a topless car wash in Costa Rica (according to his astute plan, the workers, women, would be topless, not the customers) and another who was going to rocket the ashes of dead people to the moon, and yet another who wanted to create a Che Guevara theme park, then you realize that common sense is needed.

Any other untapped business opportunities you see down here? Enterprises you'd start if you had the time, money, and/or expertise?
Many people come here with the eager plan of learning how to salsa. Apparently, it is impossible to learn, based on observations of the whirling dervish mockery that the average foreigner makes of the art of salsa. Some of them get the steps down, but miss the groove; others just step on their partner's feet. One might become very rich indeed by the discovery of something in Latin dance equivalent to the Suzuki method in violin.

Contact Information
7th Street Books
On 7th Street, between Central and 1st Avenues (150 meters/164 yds. south of Morazan Park), San José
tel. 506/256-8251
fax 506/258-3302
marroca@sol.racsa.co.cr
Open daily 9 A.M.–6 P.M.

don't find it, because it's very hard for businesses to hire foreigners. If it were easier, the whole tourist industry would change."

If you do get a job in a tourist town, it will probably end when high season does—in April—or even before. The few North Americans I met who had managed to land jobs in resort areas spoke of low wages, lack of shifts, and (for waiters) no tips.

The government would really rather you start your own business and provide work for others. To get an idea of how foreigners are encouraged to open businesses but discouraged from holding jobs, consider this: The most common categories of foreign residency—*rentista* and *pensionado*—allow you to be a business owner but not an employee. Understandably, Costa Rica wants to protect its own work force.

But there are foreigners who work at salaried jobs, some even legally. What do they do, and how do they do it? Some work for multinational corporations with branches here—those jobs are usually arranged before they get to Costa Rica. By law, these companies are allowed to fill 10 percent of their positions with foreign workers; in practice the percentage is much lower. There are many qualified Ticos to fill the positions, and they are likely to work for lower salaries.

Some foreigners work for NGOs (non-governmental organizations). Others, with specialized skills like electricians, plumbers, or finish carpenters, get hired because there may be few people in the area (especially outside of cities) with their skills.

Probably the most common job for expats is teaching English. Victoria Schwarz, who works for two English schools in San José, says there's an explosive need for teachers.

English teachers usually make between US$3.50 and US$7 an hour. The bigger, more successful English schools can often give teachers enough hours a week to make a living wage, but smaller or struggling schools may only have a few slots available. Be wary of promises. A young woman I met in Monteverde had communicated by Internet with an English school there, which promised her work, along with room and board. When she arrived, she found that the room was a hovel, the board not available, and she only got paid for teaching if students signed up for classes, which seemed to be a rare occurrence.

"If they don't know you," cautions Peggy Windle, who has taught at several schools in Costa Rica, "they won't give you a full-time job. They'll try you out part-time, and if they like you, maybe in four or five months they'll give you enough work to live on. Bring money."

She also advises bringing your actual physical credentials with you—diplomas, teaching certificate, et al. "They wanted my sheepskin from college!" says Peggy. "Not the transcripts, but the piece of paper that says I graduated. They're very into pomp and circumstance here. I had to call my son and get him to FedEx everything down."

I asked Peggy if would-be teachers should do a lot of advance work before they arrive in Costa Rica. "You can email or call if you want," she says. "But the schools will only believe you really want a job when they see the whites of your eyes."

Annika Loughram, co-owner with Karlene Mistretta of a well-established English school, says they're always looking for qualified English teachers. The school, called Inglés sin Fronteras, caters to professional students, with teachers going onsite to give classes at the offices of multinational corporations in the San José area. Annika says that her teachers make about US$100/week, teaching four class-hours a day. Common schedules are Monday–Thursday, two hours in the morning and two in the afternoon, plus a three- or four-hour class on Saturday. "We ask for a commitment from teachers of at least four months," says Annika. "Otherwise it's too hard on the students, always having to get used to a new face and a new approach." Annika herself came to Costa Rica in 1996 from Marin County, California. She came with the Harvard Institute for International Development and worked with Costa Rica's Ministry of Education to improve English curriculum for primary grades.

Many English-speaking foreign residents also teach in bilingual primary and secondary private schools, most of which are located in or around San José. Kirt Wackford, who has a Ph.D. in ecology, teaches science at St. Paul's College in San Rafael de Alajuela. The school emphasizes English instruction as well as other academic subjects, and Kirt teaches his classes in English. Full-time teaching earns him about US$1,000 a month before taxes.

Teachers I spoke with said they had a hard time adjusting to some aspects of the Costa Rican classroom. The biggest was noise level and a certain lack of respect for the teacher. "Kids will talk away while you're trying to give your lecture," says one teacher. "And the culture here is to just let them."

Scheduling does not seem to be a Tico strength. "When I taught at a private school," says Peggy, "I didn't have my own classroom—I always had to look for a place to teach my class. And that's not rare here. I went to a teacher-training program at UCR [the University of Costa Rica in San José], and every morning, we never knew where our class would be. If you were late, you were lost, because everyone met at a certain place on campus at 8 A.M., then we'd wander around looking for an empty classroom. If you arrived late, there was no way you'd find the rest of the class."

INTERNET-ASSISTED WORK

Some jobs based in your home country will travel well, and if you are lucky enough to have one, you've hit pay dirt. Salaries that are modest by U.S. or Canadian standards will allow you to live well in Costa Rica. And if you're paid in dollars, you gain each time the *colón* loses.

With online banking and direct deposit, you don't have to worry about the check being lost in the mail. And if you're a freelancer marketing your services, no one even needs to know you're abroad. With online fax and payment services, you can ply your trade from anywhere there's an Internet hookup. Costa Rica is pretty well wired, with dial-up service widely available, though only select areas have faster cable or broadband connections.

Any sort of independent activity that can be parlayed via Internet is a good bet. Writing, editing, transcribing, proofreading, and web design are just a few of the professions that could keep you in *gallo pinto* (beans and rice) and *guaro* (the local firewater).

Self-Employment

With a stable political environment, solid infrastructure, a highly educated workforce, and no limits on foreign control of corporations, Costa Rica is a very good place for foreign residents to do business. Money flowing in and out of the country does not attract undue attention. There are no limitations on transferring capital (in whatever currency, from whatever country) earmarked for investment, and there are no restrictions on re-investment or repatriation of earnings, royalties, or capital. Costa Rica considers that it protects itself against exploitation by protecting its workforce. Labor laws are strict and well enforced. The government makes it easy for foreigners to do business here in part because it wants more jobs created for Ticos.

For a few specific kinds of enterprise there are further incentives, which include tax exemptions that can last for more than a decade. You'll need an experienced and up-to-date lawyer to tell you which of the many incentive programs you might qualify for, and to guide you through applying for them.

If your company qualifies for Free Zone (export processing zone) incentives, you'll get 100 percent exemption on import duties on raw materials or components, 100 percent exemption on export taxes, and 100 percent exemption on taxes on profits for eight years (and 50 percent exemption on taxes on profits for the next four years after that).

Got a tractor? With the lack of bridges in some parts of the country, you could make a tidy sum pulling cars out of rivers.

If your company relates to tourism or reforestation, there are many other incentives to be had, and some investments even qualify you for residency. A US$50,000 investment in approved tourist or environmental enterprises qualifies you for residency, and US$150,000 in any area accomplishes the same. But many business owners don't bother with this program, as residency is not difficult to obtain through other channels.

SOCIEDAD ANÓNIMA (S.A.)

Get used to the two letters "S.A." You'll be seeing a lot of them, especially if you want to start your own business. A Sociedad Anónima (Anonymous Society) is a corporation, and in Costa Rica, everybody and their dog seems to have one. People form corporations just to buy a car, for instance. The main feature of an S.A. is limited liability. If something goes wrong, it's not you who owns the car or company or whatever; it's the corporation. Liability is limited to how much money you've put into the S.A. It works for Exxon and other multinationals; why shouldn't the average Joe or Jolene have the same protections? Here in Costa Rica, they do.

To form a Costa Rican corporation, two people appear before a notary public and execute the articles of incorporation, and subscribe to at least one share of stock each. The incorporators needn't be citizens or

Victoria Schwarz: Teaching the Body and Mind

© Houman Pirdavari

From the massage table in Victoria Schwarz's Escazú apartment, you can see out the window and across most of the Central Valley. Especially during the wet season, the view is dramatic: Storm fronts move in and out, rain pours down, and lightning bolts pulse like veins across the sky.

What's happening on the massage table is equally dramatic, if more subtle. Victoria definitely has a gift, one she doesn't claim as her own—despite decades of training—but attributes to forces working through her.

Whatever the source of her skill, the lucky client on the table benefits. Knots release as thunder rumbles, pain washes away with the sound of rain on the roof, and the body just generally lays its burden down.

Victoria has many terms for what she does: massage therapy, intuitive healing, Reiki energy work. She sees herself as a sort of interpreter, "translating the needs of the body such that integration, balance, and joy might occur." She also considers herself a teacher who gently instructs the body, mind, and spirit how to be at their best. I can attest to her abilities—the first few times I had a massage with Victoria, I told her where I needed the most attention; gradually I realized I didn't have to tell her; she already knew. My body was telling her, and she was listening.

Teaching is part of Victoria's life, and has recently taken another form—teaching English to adults at two schools in San José. Below, Victoria talks about her dual professions, and about doing business in Costa Rica.

Can you live off the proceeds of the business?

Combining massage and English teaching, I am solvent. There's an explosive need for English teachers down here. Ticos understand that from the janitor on up, they need to know English. I make between 1,800 and 2,800 *colones* (about US$4.50–7) per hour, and I get a transportation allowance when I go to teach at businesses. It may not sound like much, but it's pretty good for Costa Rica.

In 2002 I lived for three months in Quepos and four months in Playa Chiquita, on the Caribbean side. I loved both places, but it was very hard to make a living outside of the Central Valley. In Playa Chiquita I got hooked up with a wedding party at a hotel and did 35 massages in three days—lived off that money for months. But by the time I left Playa Chiquita, we were all bartering—no one had any cash.

When I lived in San Francisco, I would earn between $80 and $125 for an hour of massage. Here I charge locals US$20/hour, and people from hotels between US$35 and US$50. I like repeat customers, so I can see the progress made.

The most frustrating things about doing business here?

It's common for Ticos to just not show up for an appointment. And unless they've dealt with a lot of gringos, they don't even call to say they won't be there. I'm busy, and their slot could have been filled by one of many others. Ticos here tell me it's just something you have to get used to. I think it's about them not wanting to disappoint, or have any sort of confrontation.

Another thing is that you have to stay on top of people you hire. If you're out of sight, you're out of their minds. Sometimes it seems as if to get anything done here, you either have to do it yourself or keep pushing and pushing for someone else to do it.

The most satisfying thing?

I feel like the possibilities here are end-less. Despite the problems, if you're creative and clever, you'll do well.

Any advice to people starting a business down here?

Get your friends to come down and fill their suitcases with stuff you need. I had a box mailed, which included a lot of massage oil, and it was confiscated—they thought it was food, and there are a lot of restrictions on mailing in food. Also, get your friends to bring small electronics—phones, answering machines, coffee machines. The stuff here is expensive and not very high quality. You can buy a phone for $6 in the States.

Any untapped business opportunities you see down here? Enterprises you'd start if you had the time, money, and/or expertise?

What's needed here are good mechanics—they say that a Costa Rican mechanic is someone who's worked on a car once or twice.

But a more important gap I see is convalescent care and nursing homes. There's a saying: "It's not whether you're going to be handicapped; it's when." We will all need help. So there's a huge need here to fill that gap. More nursing homes are needed, but I'm more interested in creating communities here, maybe in a condo complex, where people will take care of each other, or pool their resources to hire the help they need.

On a more general level, I think what we gringos have to offer this country is creativity. For whatever reason, I think we're problem solvers.

The House of Screws: There's no mistaking what this store sells.

even residents of Costa Rica; citizens of any nation are free to form a corporation here. An S.A. also needs a board of directors, with a minimum of three members: president, secretary, and treasurer. The two incorporators often play two of these roles, drafting a friend or relative to play the third. That third director needn't appear before the notary public if he or she sends a letter accepting the position.

Forming a Corporation (S.A.)

To form a corporation, you'll need to:

1. Execute the articles of incorporation before a notary public.
2. Publish legal notice of the corporation in Costa Rica's official newspaper, *La Gaceta*—this is to give people the chance to object to the corporation name being recorded, if, for instance, the name is already taken.
3. Register the company at the National Registry (the notary public who executes the articles of incorporation usually does this).
4. Legalize the corporation's books: A set of three accounting books—daily, main *(mayor),* and inventory and balances—and three "legal" books—shareholders' record, shareholders' assemblies, and board of directors' meetings—are presented to the Ministerio de Hacienda for

their initial authorization by the Book Legalization Department. Once legalized, these books will register all internal affairs of the company (as well as stock transfers) and are kept privately by the shareholders.

The incorporation process usually takes a few months, though I've heard of people paying extra and getting it done in a matter of weeks.

Corporation Tax

The fiscal year in Costa Rica runs from October 1 through September 30, with tax returns due by December 15. A corporation is taxed only on income earned within Costa Rica, and tax rates vary from 12 to 36 percent of net profit. There are no capital gains taxes in Costa Rica. Some businesses will need to charge customers and then pay sales tax *(impuesto de ventas)*, also known as a value-added tax. The current rate is 13 percent, and the tax is on goods and services not deemed basic necessities. If your business imports goods, there will be those tariffs to deal with as well. Anita Myketuk of the Buena Nota in Manuel Antonio notes that a store owner

---

Businesses for Sale

Open up any local paper to the classifieds, and you'll get a sampling of the businesses changing hands in Costa Rica. Below is a sampling from one issue of the *Tico Times.*

Established Escazú restaurant with excellent clientele, $39,000 firm.

Bargain! Gym near University area. Make offers!

San José hobby shop, excellent investment, good location, $30,000.

Two warehouses for sale. Rented now for $11,000; sales price $1,200,000.

American-style sports bar and restaurant. Fully functioning. Eleven televisions, including 65" HDTV. DJ booth with full audio. Pool table, the works.

Reduced! $30,000. San Pedro sports bar and grill. Best location in Costa Rica, across from Mall San Pedro. Only 3 months old. Owner must return to U.S. Priced for quick sell.

Hotel and condo near airport, $800,000.

Fine beauty salon, Italian style, excellent location, near Clinica Catolica. $10,200.

Jacó hotel for sale, 20 rooms, pool, perfect location. Gardens, parking, and beach access.

Interested in acquiring a business? I'm selling or bartering a good-running doughnut factory.

needs to figure import taxes into her balance sheet. "A lot of the items in my store are imported," says Anita. "That's why, for instance, sunscreen is so expensive here. There are a couple of brands made in Costa Rica, but no one wants them, because they're not name brands—Coppertone or Hawaiian Tropic. But some things don't have import taxes or have very low taxes, like sporting gear."

Credit Card Fees

Bookstore owner John McCuen points out that "credit card companies really stick it to merchants down here," deducting up to 7 percent from sales paid for by credit cards. In the United States, the rate is closer to 2 or 3 percent. As a shopper, I always ask if there's a discount for paying cash—sometimes the merchant will lower the price by 5 percent, since that still allows him or her to do better than giving up 7 percent to the credit card companies.

FURTHER INFORMATION

The Costa Rican/American Chamber of Commerce (AMCHAM, tel. 506/220-2200, fax 506/220-2300, www.amcham.co.cr) may be of help to businesspeople.

The Costa Rican Investment and Development Board (CINDE, tel. 506/299-2800, fax 506/299-2869, invest@cinde.org, www.cinde.or.cr) is a private, nonprofit organization, founded in 1982, that offers free advice and assistance to foreign investors trying to start businesses in Costa Rica.

CINDE also maintains offices in New York City (tel. 212/704-2004, fax 212/997-9839, cindeny@cinde.org) and in San Jose, California (tel. 408/573-6146, fax 408/988-8090, cindeca@cinde.org).

The Ministry of Economy, Industry, and Commerce (tel. 506/235-7855, fax 506/236-7192, info@tramites.go.cr, www.tramites.go.cr) has put together a booklet called *Investor's Manual: Establishing a Business Enterprise in Costa Rica,* in English and Spanish. The information is also available in CD format and on their website.

The Chamber of Representatives of Foreign Companies (CRECEX, tel. 506/253-0126, fax 506/234-2557) is an independent, nonprofit association of private companies that promotes free trade and enterprise.

Hiring Help

A recent glossy brochure funded in part by the Costa Rican Investment and Development Board (CINDE) sings the praises of Tico workers: "A highly ed-

ucated, versatile, and productive workforce at only US$1.85 fully loaded."
And while you have to wonder what it means by "fully loaded" (maybe including the contributions employers must make to Social Security), the
claim isn't an exaggeration. Education in Costa Rica is free and compulsory
through ninth grade, with computers and English emphasized from an early
age. There are lots of good people here who are ready to work. But the country knows what it has, and protects its workers with a series of regulations that you should study carefully before hiring *any* employee. Another
caveat: Labor law is constantly evolving, so please check for any new developments with your lawyer (oh yes, you'll have one, if not two or three).

LABOR LAWS
Whether you hire one person to clean your house or 30 people to sew
stuffed monkeys, the same basic labor laws apply. The Labor Code of
1943 is the basis for the lengthy document now in effect, which seeks to
minimize conflict between employer and employee by spelling out every
detail of that relationship. These regulations are taken very seriously,
workers generally know their rights, and if there is a conflict, Labor Court
judges often decide in the favor of the employee.

In brief, the regulations specify that:
1. Employers must make Social Security (Caja) contributions for each
   employee, and also deduct a percentage of the employee's pay for
   further contribution to the Caja.
2. Forty-eight hours is the maximum work week; hours beyond that are
   paid as overtime.
3. Minimum wages and salaries for most jobs and professions are set by
   the Caja.
4. Employers must notify the local Caja office within eight days of a
   hire.
5. The first 30 days of employment is a trial period; after that, employees
   must be given notice *(pre-aviso)* if they are to be fired, and they have the
   right to severance pay *(cesantia)*.
6. Employers must provide employees with paid vacations.
7. Employers are obligated to pay a Christmas bonus (called the *aguinaldo*).
8. Employers must provide for maternity leave.
9. Employers must pay employees for nine holidays off per year.

These rules are covered in more detail in the following sections.

Social Security (Caja) Contributions
The Caja Costarricense de Seguro Social (the Caja) pays for workers'
health care, sick leave, and disability, but employers are expected to

Café Milagro: A Good Cup of Coffee

Though Costa Rica is known world-wide for its *grano de oro* ("grain of gold," or coffee), visitors often find it oddly difficult to find a really good cup of java here. When Lance Byron and Adrienne Pellizzari came to Costa Rica in the early 1990s, they puzzled over that riddle, then decided that they might just be the ones, at least in the Quepos/Manuel Antonio area, to solve it.

Adrienne began researching the industry. What she found was that although Costa Rica produces some of the world's finest beans, much of the best coffee is exported. She discovered that the only way to get quality beans was to become a coffee roaster herself, and that's exactly what she did, scraping up the cash to buy an old roaster that, to this day, no one but Adrienne and Lance dare to operate.

Café Milagro Coffee Roasters was born in 1994, and has since grown to include the restaurant El Patio in Quepos and Café Milagro in Manuel Antonio. El Patio offers full dinners; Café Milagro provides lighter fare. Also on offer are bags of fragrant beans, world music CDs, and international newspapers and magazines. Below, Lance answers some questions about the business.

What's the most satisfying thing about doing business here?
It would have to be the sense of pride and self-confidence resulting from being successful in a foreign country, despite all the obstacles. It's a great feeling to know that you're resilient and self-reliant enough to not only live, but also operate a business, in an environment with a different language and culture.

The most frustrating thing?
There is a certain degree of discrimination toward foreigners in Costa Rica. You get the feeling you're the only one playing by the rules. It's not so bad if it's limited to paying a little extra for your dream home. But if you're trying to run a profitable business, paying a little extra for everything makes it hard to compete with the guy who has the "insider's advantage."

One example would be that although Costa Rican law states you cannot sell alcohol within a certain distance of a church or a school, recently a Tico opened a bar/restaurant that is obviously too close to both a school and a church. This business has created a considerable amount of competition for other legally established restaurants in the area. But since the established businesses are owned by foreigners and the illegal business is owned by a Tico, nothing has happened.

What's next for Café Milagro?
The next step is the official launch of our export business. It will be an online store, and primarily focused on our existing customer base, people who have passed through our shops and either signed up for home delivery or who have inquired about our coffee via email.

Any advice to others thinking of starting a business in Costa Rica?
Love it or leave it. Adrienne and I came to Costa Rica to experience the culture and improve our language skills. We stayed, not because we saw an opportunity to get rich, but because we love the country. Most new businesses fail, no matter where they are in the world, but I believe an even greater percentage of new (foreign-owned) businesses fail in Costa Rica, because the people are here for the wrong reasons.

Many people come here on a brief vacation, have a fabulous time, and decide it would be great to live here. And since you can't live on bananas and coconuts alone, the foreigner starts a business, because it will be "easy" to make a bunch of money in a country where everything, including the labor, is so "cheap."

But the foreigner finds out the vacation is over real fast and she has to work! She can't say anything but *cerveza* and *pura vida* in Spanish. Because of her inability to communicate with the locals, she generalizes that all the locals (at least the ones she meets and "interviews" at the local tavern) are untrustworthy thieves.

So now the foreigner is no longer on vacation, and is working with a bunch of "thieves" at a business that is losing money by the minute. She decides she doesn't particularly like Costa Rica. In fact, she *hates* Costa Rica and its people! But for some reason, she stays, in an apparent state of constant misery, complaining to who-ever is unfortunate enough to sit on the bar stool next to her.

The moral of the story: You have to love Costa Rica. And you can't fall in love in a matter of days—that's infatuation. It's best to move to Costa Rica on a temporary basis, study the language, and live here for at least one entire year before investing a single dollar, let alone your entire life savings. If at the end of a year, you're still in love with Costa Rica, your language skills are strong enough to read and understand the labor code, and there is indeed a niche to be filled by your business plan, then go for it!

Contact Information
Café Milagro
tel. 506/777-1707
fax 506/777-2272
info@cafemilagro.com
www.cafemilagro.com

Hours
December–April:
Café Milagro Coffee Roasters (Quepos): 7 A.M.–10 P.M. (closed Sunday)
El Patio Café & Restaurante (Quepos): 6 A.M.–10 P.M. daily
Café Milagro (Manuel Antonio): 6 A.M.–10 P.M. daily

May–November:
Café Milagro Coffee Roasters: 9 A.M.–5 P.M. (closed Sunday)
El Patio Café & Restaurante: 6 A.M.–10 P.M.
Café Milagro: 6 A.M.–6 P.M. daily

do their part. An employer must calculate 26 percent of a worker's gross salary and pay that amount to the Caja. Employers also need to deduct 9 percent of a worker's wages and pay that additional amount to the Caja. Example: A cashier at your bookstore earns US$400 a month. Twenty-six percent of that salary is US$104, which is the employer's contribution to the worker's Social Security. Nine percent of the salary is US$36; the employer deducts that amount from the employee's pay (leaving the worker with a salary of US$364), and pays that additional amount to the Caja.

The Work Week
Forty-eight hours is the maximum workweek, ten hours the maximum day shift (eight hours for hazardous work), and six hours the maximum for a night shift. Managers and executives can be asked to work 12-hour days. Anything exceeding these limits is overtime and must be paid at time and a half.

Minimum Wages
Almost all jobs in Costa Rica have a minimum wage, set by the National Council on Wages. In 2003, minimum wages ranged from about US$8 a day for agricultural laborers though US$213 a month for a polygraph operator to US$540 a month for someone with a Licentiate degree (roughly equivalent to a masters degree). Remember that these are minimums—to attract and retain quality workers, many employers pay more. In Spanish the list of wages is called the *Decreto de Salarios Mínimos,* and can be obtained at Social Security offices or from most bookstores.

Domestic Servants: The food and lodging provided to a live-in domestic is considered "in-kind" payment equivalent to 50 percent of the worker's wages, and must be factored in when calculating severance pay or the mandatory Christmas bonuses. What that means is that if you pay a live-in gardener or maid a salary of say, US$300 a month, the real total, when you calculate severance or bonus, would be US$450.

Notification of Hire
You must notify the Caja within eight days of hiring someone. This is to limit the employer's possible liability as well as to start the paperwork moving. If an employee registered with the Caja is injured on the job, the Caja pays most of the medical bills—the employer's liability is limited to four days' salary. But if the worker isn't registered with the Caja, the employer could be liable for not only the worker's medical bills but also half of his or her salary while the employee is injured or sick.

Minimum Wages

Below is a small sampling of minimum wages for various jobs in Costa Rica. The minimums are set each year by the National Council on Wages; those below are for 2003 (exchange rate about 400 *colones* to the dollar). Some wages are daily, others monthly. Remember that many employers pay significantly more than minimum wage to attract and retain good workers. An up-to-date list of wages (called *Decreto de Salarios Mínimos*) can be found at most bookstores.

Babysitter	US$7.96/day
Bartender	US$9.12/day
Bricklayer	US$9.10/day
Bus driver	US$9.12/day
Carpenter (skilled)	US$9.12/day
Computer programmer	US$10.97/day
Construction worker (unskilled)	US$7.96/day
Dental assistant	US$10.95/day
Drafter of architectural or engineering plans	US$287/month
Gardener	US$9.12/day
Journalist	US$669/month
Pizza maker	US$8.75/day
Popular dance teacher	US$9.12/day
Sailor	US$7.96/day
Secretary	US$278/month
Specialized laborer	US$321/month
Roaster of meats	US$8.75/day
Telephone booth cleaner	US$7.95/day
Worker with no degree or qualifications	US$238/month
Worker with bachelor's degree	US$452/month

Length and Cessation of Employment

The first 30 days of employment is considered a trial period, with both employee and employer having the right to end the relationship without notice. After 30 days, unless an employee's termination is for just cause, employers must give advance notice of dismissal and are liable for severance pay. An employer can fire an employee and have no further responsibility to that worker only under very specific circumstances, outlined in Article 81 of the Labor Code. Just causes for dismissal range from deliberately damaging an employer's property to being thrown in jail. In Costa Rica, it is the employer's responsibility to document reasons for dismissal and to be ready to argue his or her case.

Pre-Termination Notice *(Pre-aviso)*: If termination is not for a cause listed in the Labor Code (maybe business is slow, and there isn't enough for an employee to do), an employer must give advance notice of dismissal, the amount of time dependent on how long the worker has been on the job. If the worker has been with you more than three months but less than six, one week's notice is required. Employment of six months to a year requires two weeks' notice. One month's prior notice is necessary for workers who have been employed for one year or more. In lieu of notice, an employer can pay the wages that would have been earned during the notice period. Notice should be in written form, or can be delivered orally in the presence of two witnesses.

Severance Pay *(Cesantia):* If an employee is terminated without just cause, he or she is entitled to severance pay. If an employee has worked more than three but fewer than six months, he or she receives seven days' wages. Employees who've worked from six months to a year get 14 days' wages. Employment of a year or more requires between 19.5 and 22 days' wages for each year, depending on the number of years worked.

What If the Employee Quits? If an employee quits for just cause (also outlined in the Labor Code), the employer has the same responsibilities that he or she would have to a worker terminated without just cause. If, however, the employee has no just cause for quitting (maybe she got a better offer elsewhere), the employer's responsibilities end with the employee's departure.

Paid Vacations

Employers must provide workers with two weeks of paid vacation for every 50 weeks worked.

Unused Vacation Pay: When a worker is terminated without just cause, unused vacation pay is due him or her. Workers get two weeks of paid vacation for every 50 weeks worked. If a worker is terminated before a year is up, he or she should be paid for one vacation day per month worked.

The Christmas Bonus *(Aguinaldo)*

Sometimes known as the 13th month of pay, law mandates this "bonus." Every worker who has been on the job at least a year is entitled to an extra month's wages, to be paid between December 1 and 20. If a worker is fired before December, the *aguinaldo* must be pro-rated and paid to the employee at the time of termination: Take the total wages paid to the worker from December 1 through November 30, and divide the amount by 12.

Remember that to calculate *aguinaldo* for live-in domestic servants, you must add 50 percent to the salary for in-kind payment in the form of room and board.

Maternity Leave

Pregnant employees are entitled to one unpaid month off before the baby is born, and three half-paid months off afterwards. During those three months the employer pays full salary, half going to the worker, half to the Caja.

Paid Holidays

Employers must either provide paid time off for the following nine legal holidays, or pay workers (if they agree to work) double their usual wage. Legal holidays fall on January 1 (New Year's Day), April 11 (Juan Santamaría Day), two days during Easter week (Holy Thursday and Good Friday), May 1 (International Workers Day), July 25 (Annexation of Guanacaste), September 15 (Independence Day), and December 25 (Christmas).

Unpaid legal holidays include August 2 (celebration of the country's patron saint, the Virgin of Los Angeles), and October 12 (Day of Cultures—formerly Columbus Day).

CULTURE CLASHES

It seems to be an international pastime to complain that you can't get good help anymore. Costa Rica's version of that game includes grumbling that Ticos lack initiative and a sense of personal responsibility. The Beisanz family writes in *The Ticos* that the "emphasis on dignity and courtesy often takes the form of saving face for others as well as oneself. Ticos rarely accept blame for mistakes and usually take care not to embarrass others, especially in public." To save face and to make the moment agreeable, Ticos will tell you whatever they think you want to hear: that your check will clear soon; that they'll be there this afternoon, for sure; or that they know which of those wires is live.

Ticos want to *quedar bien,* which means to make a good impression and to get along with others. They want to be respected as individuals and to be treated with the same consideration that they extend. Being scolded or corrected, especially in front of others, is not something a Tico will easily forgive.

Anita Myketuk, who for decades has run a successful souvenir shop in Manuel Antonio, says, "you have to charm people here in order to get them to want to help you. And never, ever yell at anyone or get nasty. North Americans are used to yelling; it's not the end of the world. Here it *is* the end of the world."

Plying an Honest Trade

In 1993, Canadian transplant Barry Wilson was dating a Tica nurse who told him it wasn't easy to find decent uniforms here. Ever obliging, Barry opened a store that sold nurses' uniforms and shoes. "It was a great place," he says. "Great stock. There were big armchairs where people could relax, and we even had coffee and doughnuts." The store did fine, though not as well as Barry had hoped. Wanting to continue in the medical field, he decided to ease out of retail. He now runs a uniform supply company that provides surgical gowns and drapes (which cover a patient during surgery) to private clinics and hospitals in the San José area. Below Barry answers a few questions about doing business in Costa Rica.

What's the most satisfying thing about doing business here?

Supplying a worthwhile product to a market that needs and wants it.

The most frustrating thing?

A large sector of our potential market [the government] is too mired in bureaucracy to realize that our product is better than what they're now using, and is worth the extra effort to adopt. Public hospitals here still use 100 percent cotton gowns and drapes, which have been shown to harbor more bacteria than polyester gowns and drapes.

What's next for the business?

We'd like to gain government contracts. Because the socialized medical system here is so good, the percentage of private clinics is low in comparison to other countries. To expand, we need to look to the government-run public hospitals. We'd also like to

eventually expand into other Latin American countries.

Advice to others thinking of starting a business in Costa Rica?

You'll do well with any kind of business that doesn't depend on selling to the government or on the growth of tourism. Factories, gas stations, auto repair shops—if you are good at a normal, honest trade, you can probably operate it successfully here.

People need to know that it's not unsophisticated down here. You need to pay attention to the regulations, work hard, and provide good product for the money.

Any other untapped business opportunities you see down here? Enterprises you'd start if you had the time, money, and/or expertise?

Costa Rica should be the world capital for retirement homes and assisted living communities. Here in the Central Valley, the weather is almost perfect—you wouldn't need to pay for heat or air conditioning. And you've got first-class medical care available here. You could pay doctors and nurses a quarter of what you'd have to pay their counterparts in the United States, and still have very high-quality staff.

Another opportunity would be condos built to U.S. specs for U.S. tastes. The condos put up in places like Escazú already go fast, even though there's always something not quite right about how they're built—the parking places in the carport are a little too short, the rooms are strangely shaped, or the trim ends before the wall does. Think how fast those condos would go if they didn't have those annoying little glitches.

Ray Beise of Guanacaste tells how he learned to deal with the Tico tendency to nod and say yes even if they don't know what's being asked of them. "I say to my worker, 'Go over there and dig a hole.' And I leave, and come back, and he hasn't done it. Then I think, maybe there's something he didn't understand. I tell him again. 'Please, go over there and dig a hole.' And this time I ask, 'Did you understand what I said?' And he nods yes, but later I come back and he still hasn't done it. Finally—and this took a long time—I tell them what to do, and then I ask them to repeat back to me what I've just said. Usually they'll hem and haw, but then they'll say, 'OK, tell me again.'"

The culture values harmony (even if it's a superficial sort of harmony) over honesty, an approach that makes for a polite society but can be frustrating for those who prefer candor and are counting on people to keep their word.

Lateness is common, to the extent that when making plans one needs to specify *hora tica* (Tica time, which means an hour or two after the appointed time) or *hora Americana* or *hora exacta* (American time, or exact time).

Still, with all the frustrations (and there's no doubt that Ticos are frustrated with foreigners' idiosyncrasies at least as much as the other way around), almost all of the expat employers I spoke with were happy with their employees. Many think they got lucky, and claim to have the best cook, clerk, or carpenter in all of Costa Rica. But it seems that a great many employers "got lucky," which suggests that Ticos are essentially good workers, especially if you're a good boss and make it your business to learn about cultural differences that may affect the employer-employee relationship.

In the end, it's all about people. Many foreigners move to Costa Rica because things here are on a more human scale. Personal relationships are paramount, even in the business world. Lance Byron of Café Milagro in Manuel Antonio tells of a local girl who worked in the café. "Silvia worked for us during her high school vacations, went off to college, then got a great job with Procter & Gamble International, who sent her to the United States several times as one of their prodigies. We'd see each other once in a while and she'd always tell us Café Milagro was her favorite job. Whenever Adrienne [the café's co-owner] and I would sit and dream of the day we'd export coffee, Adrienne would have an implementation panic attack and ask, 'But who's going to run it?' I'd calmly reply, 'Silvia.' Well, wouldn't you know it, after a few years in the multinational corporate world, Silvia comes back to us and says she's tired of being 'a number.' So we created the export manager position for her and she's been working on Café Milagro's export logistics."

Costa Rica is like a small town. You never know who will leave the *pueblo* only to circle back and into your life again. This kind of coziness comes as a shock to vagabonding, job- and city-switching North Americans, who may launch and then jettison a dozen different lives before they hit middle age. In Costa Rica it's a bad idea, both personally and professionally, to burn too many bridges (in Spanish it's called *quemar sus barcos,* to burn your boats). A good rule of thumb here is: Treat everyone as if you'll have to see him or her every day. It might turn out that you actually do.

Volunteering

Though many think of volunteering as giving something for nothing, seasoned volunteers see it differently. Besides the satisfaction of knowing you're helping where help is needed, volunteering often gives you a crash course in an unfamiliar subject, from the life cycle of the butterfly (if you're a guide at Monteverde's Butterfly Garden) to how to build a house (if you're helping out at Habitat for Humanity). Some organizations even provide room and board for their volunteers, though most require you to pay your own way.

Volunteering also significantly expands your social circle, often hooking you up with people whose politics and priorities are similar to yours. Sometimes volunteer positions lead to paid work within the same field, as when Robert Durkin volunteered for Habitat for Humanity and later became a paid employee, organizing the agency office in Ciudad Colón. He says at Habitat, volunteers not only pay their own way but often give financial contributions as well. "It probably started with church groups, who give of both their time and financial resources. But it seems to have also extended out to individual volunteers."

ORGANIZATIONS
Just about every agency in Costa Rica that is working to improve society and the environment could use dedicated volunteers. If you have a special area of interest, contact organizations working in that field. See the list in Contacts in the Resources section for ideas.

CREATING YOUR OWN OPPORTUNITIES
Though there are many ready-made volunteer positions, you may prefer to do good in your own way. It can be as simple as identifying the needs of your community and then organizing the effort to fill them. Maybe your neighborhood has no place for kids to play. What would it take to build a playground or even a community center? What kind of help could you get from local and national government, from private organizations, and from your neighbors?

An Italian couple runs the thriving Luna Llena Hotel in Tamarindo.

In rural areas, even basic necessities like garbage pickup and a reliable water supply may be lacking. In Tortuguero, the local Woman's Association took on their Caribbean town's trash problem. "About 80,000 tourists come through here every year," says Jenny Madden of the Association. "Each tourist, and every person who lives here, produces a mountain of trash—Coke cans, cigarettes, juice containers. We took on the responsibility of picking up all that trash." But they found they couldn't do it alone, and have begun charging a small fee per house and business (much like any trash-collecting enterprise), and soliciting funds from government agencies. Their project is still a work in progress, but it shows what a small group of people can do.

Look around your town. Does the local health clinic need a vehicle so doctors and nurses can make house calls? Are the nearest preschool or library hours away? Do a lot of people drown every year at the local beach? If you're a problem solver, maybe you can help fix these things.

The best thing about getting involved, one volunteer told me, is that "it gets you to the heart of things. You're right in the middle of town life. It can be frustrating, trying to get things done, but sometimes it all comes together, and you get to help change the face of the place."

© Erin Van Rheenen

Finance

Cost of Living

What most people thinking of moving to Costa Rica want to know is, "Can I afford it?" Some have heard you can live like a queen on next to nothing; others say rumor has it that it's as expensive to live here as it is up north. As always, the truth lies somewhere in between. Calculating cost of living is by no means an exact science—so much depends on your personal definition of what is essential. Some can't live without hot water on tap throughout the house—this is not the Tico style, and will cost you more. Others feel fine scrimping on housing but can't for the life of them economize on books, magazines, and CDs. Most end up compromising—living a life that is frugal but with a few frills. They take buses but splurge on excellent meals twice a week. Or they live in a small apartment in a modest neighborhood, but take a beach vacation every month.

You *can* live in Costa Rica for a lot less than what you'd be spending in

Lottery tickets are easy to come by in San José.

the United States or Canada, but not without conscious effort. What helps is that most people who move down here want to pare down, to let go of all they've accumulated over the years. They want to own less, work and spend less, and enjoy life's simple pleasures. With this approach, it's not hard to live economically.

"When I was married to a lawyer in San Francisco," says Victoria Schwarz, who moved here in 2002, "we had a combined income of US$450,000—and that was in 1990! I had a US$150,000 line of credit, and I used it. Sometimes I miss that life, but mostly I don't. I purposely did not transplant my U.S. life down here, as I notice many gringos do. I would say that I live better than most Ticos but far 'lower' than I lived before, in the United States. I count my pennies. If I see something I want, I wait three to five weeks, then look again, to see if that item would really enhance my life. With this technique, it's amazing how little is necessary. It's been good for me to not just go out and buy whatever I think to buy. It feels good not to consume."

What about the numbers? Again, it's hard to pin these things down, but from my observations of many foreign residents, I would say that an exceptionally frugal person could live on as little as US$300–400 a month. This would mean not owning a car (vehicles are very expensive here), renting a small room, eating at home, and thinking twice about going to the movies or ordering a double scotch. But most people, the frugal-with-frills types, will need at least US$1,000 a month to live well. These are budgets for single people—if you're a couple, add another 40 percent to the figure, though this may be an overestimate, since often two can live almost as cheaply as one. Rent is shared, food isn't that much more expensive for two, and—if you like each other—you can be your own entertainment. Dominos, anyone?

Victoria says she lives on about US$1,050 a month, with US$475 going to rent (she's got a great one-bedroom apartment in Escazú), phone and electricity at US$25, food and household miscellaneous US$300, and restaurants and entertainment claiming US$250 a month. What she'd like to add to her budget in the future is international health insurance (she thinks it'll be about US$800/year) and Internet access at home (US$15/month). She doesn't have a car and doesn't want one, but she would like to be able to travel more within Costa Rica.

My personal ideal budget would have a similar total, with less going to rent (I pay US$200) and more to phone, Internet, and entertainment.

Of course, there are foreign residents who spend four or five times these amounts, and more power to them—they often throw excellent parties. But the point is, if you need to live on less, you most certainly can. Some things that will drive your budget way up: expensive private school for your kids; luxury cars with high insurance rates; gambling habits or bad investments; child support (laws here are strict); high drug or alcohol consumption. Know thyself, and you will know thine budget.

SHOPPING

Newcomers are often surprised to see the vast U.S.-style supermarkets and upscale malls that have sprung up all over the country, but especially in the Central Valley. The megastore of megastores, Hypermas, is like a big Target or Price Mart with food. You can load your cart with toaster ovens, mattresses, Häagen-Dazs ice cream and fresh pineapple (from Costa Rica or Hawaii!), and get your day's exercise just walking from one end of the store to the other. Prices are often disconcertingly similar to those in the United States, though careful shopping will yield some bargains. Soon you'll learn that the local ice cream, Dos Pinos, is quite tasty and costs a fraction of what imported brands do. Or you'll figure out that you can get cheap sheets and towels in downtown San José rather than pay Hypermas prices. But if you want everything under one roof, price be damned, these megastores are for you. There are several other grocery store chains (with branches all over the country), from the well-stocked Perimercados to the bare-bones Palí.

What It Costs

McDonald's Big Mac: US$2.50
Casado (meat, beans, rice, salad, drink): US$2.50
Rent on a three-bedroom U.S.-style house (hot water throughout), nice neighborhood: US$1,000–1,500
Rent on a three-bedroom Tico-style house (hot water only in the shower), decent neighborhood: US$300–700
Movie ticket: US$3.75
Bus ticket (across town or to outlying area): US$.45
Taxi ride (across town or to outlying area): US$6
Taxi ride from downtown San José to airport: US$12
Gasoline: about US$2.50/gallon for regular
Loaf of whole-wheat bread: US$1.50
Pineapple: US$1.25
Five kilos of laundry washed, dried, and folded: US$4.50

In terms of non-food shopping, the pedestrian-only Avenida Central in downtown San José is a good place to start, as are the many malls, MultiPlaza in Escazú being the largest and most upscale for now (many more are under construction). There's even a Price Smart, this country's answer to membership shopping (owned by the same man who owns the U.S. Price Mart).

Costa Rica has an interesting blend of chain stores, mom-and-pop businesses, and what economists would call "informal commercial activity." In downtown areas, you'll find rickety kiosks offering a little of everything: banana chips, fruit, single cigarettes, hair barrettes. Vendors with their wares spread on the sidewalk sell everything from mangoes to Winnie the Pooh paraphernalia (here the ever-popular bear is just Winnie-Pooh). There are roving vendors called *polacos,* after the Eastern European Jewish immigrants who arrived in the 1920s and often made their living peddling wares from house to house. Especially on weekends, ambulant vendors go up and down my suburban street: ice cream carts with their bells chiming, vegetable vendors singing out *ricos aguacates* (delicious avocados), knife grinders, and the little old man pulling his cart piled high with simple wooden furniture.

What's Available

Costa Rica is a consumer society, and most of what you'll need is available here, often in the Central Valley. Residents of outlying areas make regular shopping trips to San José.

I keep a running wish list, in part to see what is and isn't available here. Usually I find what I need. Nice clothes and shoes are easy to come by, though women will have to get used to the idea of sprayed-on attire—none of the clothes you bring down will begin to be tight enough for Tico tastes. Specific toiletries may or may not be available; I found Neutrogena skin cream but not Aveda hair conditioner. I couldn't find a pink straw cowboy hat but found a great canvas rain and sun hat. In San José's Central Market were the dried herbs a fellow in Limón had suggested I use as medicine. At a health food store I found melatonin tablets and gel from the noxious noni fruit, said to have miraculous healing properties (the stinky fruit itself is also widely available). At Cemaco there was a good inexpensive desk lamp (made in China, US$10). I couldn't find a decent-but-cheap boombox, and had visitors from the States bring one down for me. A big surprise is that in a downtown Asian supermarket I found Thai green curry paste and fish sauce. Now I can make my famous green curry chicken, which local friends—who prefer mild fare—consider closer to insecticide or jet fuel than to actual food.

Farmers Markets

In almost every town or neighborhood there is a weekly farmers market, offering up mounds of onions, whole hands of bananas, and row upon row of head lettuce. Quality is often better and prices lower than in supermarkets, and it's also a lot more satisfying than choosing from among plastic-wrapped cucumbers at the local supermarket. Organic produce is still a novelty, but it's becoming increasingly available. The markets are social occasions, with housewives chatting with neighbors or with the vendors they've come to know. Cheese, meats, and fresh juices are often available, as are plants, from hardy daisies to delicate orchids. Arrive early in the morning for the best selection, and bring your own bags or a cart.

Bargaining

Travelers who know the vast public markets of Mexico, Guatemala, and other developing countries may be surprised to see few such places in Costa Rica. Western-style malls are more the norm in Costa Rica, and bargaining is a very different matter here. Forget offering a quarter of the asking price, then settling in for twenty minutes of animated haggling, including the old ruse of pretending to walk away so that the merchant will call you back with a better deal.

In Costa Rica you pretty much pay the asking price. There's a little bit of room to move, but be careful and don't insult the merchant or her wares. You might ask if there's a discount for volume, or, if you're in a more upscale shop that accepts credit cards, if there's a discount for

Mercado Central in San José

© Erin Van Rheenen

paying cash. Merchants here pay up to 7 percent to credit card companies for each transaction, so they may be motivated to give you a 5 percent cash discount. For services—tours, hotels, and the like—ask if there's an off-season rate, a midweek rate, or any discounts offered senior citizens, Costa Rica residents, or ARCR members. It's best to do this with a light touch and not to insist—merchants may prefer to lose the deal than to keep haggling with someone they perceive to be difficult. And if you do negotiate a good price, be sure to get it in writing (if it applies to something in the future, like a trip or a car repair), as people here have a tendency to forget what they've promised.

TIPPING AND SALES TAX

In restaurants the bill will be 23 percent more than you expect it to be, with 13 percent added for sales tax and 10 percent for service. So you've really already paid the tip; outstanding service may warrant a little extra, but most Ticos don't leave any additional tip. The 13 percent sales tax is on all goods and services except fees to doctors, lawyers, dentists, and most other independent professionals. The sales tax on airline tickets is 5 percent. The sales tax on hotel rooms is the usual 13 percent but with an additional tourist tax of 3.9 percent, for a total of 16.9 percent.

Taxi drivers are not tipped, though you'll want to tip bell boys (about a dollar a bag), hotel maids (a dollar or two a day), and tour guides (depends on service, the length and cost of the tour, and how many people were on the tour, but a good measure is to think what you'd tip a similar person in your home country).

Banking

CURRENCY

Costa Rica's currency is called the *colón* (plural is *colones*), named for the explorer Christopher Columbus (his name in Spanish is Cristobal Colón). Often the U.S. "cents" symbol (¢) is used to denote *colones,* but sometimes the $ is used, which can make it difficult to know if *colones* or U.S. dollars are meant. But if a car is priced at over a million, or a cup of coffee at 400, you know you're in *colón* country.

The bills you'll most often see are in denominations of 500 (orange-brown), 1,000 (red, and often called a *rojo*), and 5,000 (blue, and sometimes called a *tucán,* for the bird on the back and in the watermark). There are also 10,000 *colón* bills, which no one seems to want to change. The bills are the same size as U.S. notes. Coins are of different sizes, and come in denominations of 500, 100, 50, 25, 20, 10, and 5, though the lower denominations are slowly being taken out of circulation. The size of coins tells you little about their value: The 20-*colón* coin is bigger than the 100, for instance, and it's easy to mistake the 100 for the 500-*colón* coin, though new, bigger 500-*colón* coins are in the works. Money is sometimes called *pista* or *plata,* and loose change is *menudo.*

Counterfeits

Counterfeit bills seem to be very common here, and most merchants have little light-table machines that allow them to quickly check for fakes. The low-tech method of checking a 5,000-*colón* bill (the most often counterfeited) is to hold it up to the light and look for the toucan watermark to the right of the official signatures. Other bills are also faked. Once when I was trying to pay for a bag of *pan dulce,* the bakery owner pointed out that the design on my 1,000-*colón* note was totally off-register, and so it was—the counterfeiter had been quite sloppy. I did what a Tico would do—kept the bill and paid a taxi fare with it later that night. Money is just a collective hallucination, after all—a consensus that these scraps of paper mean something. The off-register bill will be someone's change in that taxi, and will make its way around the country much as any

Getting Your U.S. Federal Benefits in Costa Rica

Frequently asked questions answered by the Federal Benefits Unit at the American Embassy in San José, Costa Rica.

Q: I was receiving Social Security benefits in the United States. Can I receive them in Costa Rica?

A: Yes, if you are the direct beneficiary. If you are the child, surviving spouse, or dependent, please contact the Federal Benefits Unit. At the present time, the direct beneficiary may either have checks sent to a bank in the United States and withdraw money in Costa Rica using a debit card or bank transfer, or you may have the checks sent to your address in Costa Rica. The Embassy will receive the checks and have them sent registered mail to the address on file at the Embassy.

Q: Is there direct deposit with Costa Rica–based banks?

A: At the present time this service is not available in Costa Rica.

Q: Can I use a U.S. mailing address to receive my Social Security checks while living in Costa Rica?

A: According to Social Security Administration regulations, you cannot use a U.S. mailing address unless you are physically present in the United States.

Q: Who handles claims for foreign medical treatment under the Veterans Administration?

A: The Denver Veterans Affairs office handles the claims. It may be reached at tel. 303/331-7590, fax 303/331-7803. The embassy cannot process these claims. For more information, visit the Veterans Benefits and Services website at www.va.gov.

Q: I am a full-service U.S. veteran. Can I receive coverage over here for my service-connected disabilities?

legitimate bill would. Maybe it's a metaphor for the world economy: If you don't look too closely, everything works just fine.

Exchange Rates

Every day the local papers print the U.S. dollar/*colón* exchange rate, and every day, at least for the past several years, the *colón* is on the losing end. Yearly devaluation ranges from 5 to 15 percent, and you can count on the dollar gaining about a *colón* a week. That's why people like U.S. dollars—they hold their value better than local currency. Landlords like to write leases in U.S. dollars; they gain a little each month. Example—my

A: Yes, you can be reimbursed for medical treatment, but this is limited to service-connected disabilities only. The Veterans Administration/ Foreign Medical Program Office in Denver, Colorado, sets the protocol on how to approve claims.

Q: I am married and would like my spouse to receive survivor Social Security benefits upon my death. Can s/he?
A: Your spouse would be eligible at age 60, if s/he had been married for more than one year to you and had not remarried. Please contact the Federal Benefits Unit of the embassy for specific requirements.

Q: If I work outside of the United States, will this affect my benefits?
A: Only after age 65 may you work without your earnings affecting your pension.

Q: How soon can I apply for my retirement benefits?
A: Three months prior to your 62nd birthday.

Q: Do I need to travel to the United States to apply for Social Security benefits?
A: No, you may apply at the U.S. Embassy Monday–Friday 8–11:30 A.M., and Monday 1–3 P.M.

Note: You can also apply for Social Security benefits online at www.ssa.gov.

More Resources
For more information, contact the Federal Benefits Unit at the American Embassy in Rohrmoser (San José), tel. 506/220-3050, www.usembassy.co.cr, Monday–Friday 8–11:30 A.M. and Monday 1–3 P.M.
   Remember that Medicare benefits are not available outside the United States. For information about Medicare, see www.ssa.gov/mediinfo.htm and www.medicare.gov.

first month's rent of US$200 was equivalent to 74,000 *colones*. Less than a year later my monthly rent was worth over 80,000 *colones*. Foreign residents and Ticos alike can have their local bank account in dollars and get loans in dollars. In fact, financial analysts worry that the dollar's dominance is weakening the national economy.

GETTING CASH
The U.S. dollar is much in evidence in Costa Rica. Upon arrival, you needn't hurry to change money (forget changing money on the street— you'll get ripped off), since taxi drivers will accept dollars, as will many

businesses, especially in tourist areas. Often they won't accept soiled or torn U.S. bills, though some of the *colón* notes you'll see look as if they've been in circulation since giant sloths roamed the land.

Of course you'll eventually need to get with the program, and the easiest way to get *colones* is to withdraw them from one of many ATMs, using your U.S. or Canadian bank card. Some bank's cards (like Wells Fargo) will only work in some Costa Rican banks (Scotiabank and Banco de San José, in this case). Check to see where yours will work. Be aware that most U.S. banks charge a fee each time you use an ATM that doesn't belong to them, and that often "currency conversion" rates are tacked on as well. It would be worth your while to get the specifics from your home bank before you make the move, and perhaps change to a bank with less punishing policies.

ATMs are everywhere and are well stocked. Out-of-date guidebooks tell of ATMs routinely running out of cash, but I've never had that experience. Occasionally I won't be able to get dollars, but will be able to get *colones*. Sometimes the "system" is down and the machine spits my card out. Sometimes the system is down for a few days, which means I have to go inside the bank and get an advance on my credit or debit card. This can take time, and the transaction is more subject to human error.

Once I sat for an hour and a half as the clerk ran my debit card through a machine again and again and again, saying it wasn't working. Finally I left with cash in hand, only to go home and find (online) that the bank (Banco de San José) had debited my account three times the amount I had received. I spoke with the bank manager, who after an hour told me there was nothing he could do. I had to work it out with my home bank, over long-distance telephone. Now I try to do everything by ATM.

BANKS AND BANK ACCOUNTS

Up until 1949 most of Costa Rica's banks were private and owned by U.S. citizens. Early efforts to nationalize banking didn't go well. In 1914 President Gonzales Flores was ousted by wealthy Ticos and U.S. oil interests for his attempt to open a state bank. But decades later, a nationalized system became part and parcel of Costa Rican identity, offering up loans on the basis of social responsibility rather than profit. National banks helped fund infrastructure, health, education, and rural development. These banks were the only ones authorized to offer checking accounts and time deposits, and the Central Bank was in charge of national monetary policy.

Despite the benefits of public banks, there were also major drawbacks. Critics complained of inefficiency, misuse of public funds, and cronyism—it was thought almost impossible to get a loan unless you knew someone high up in the bank hierarchy. National bank employees were (and are) essentially government employees, and it's nearly impossible to fire them, no matter how incompetent they might be.

The industry began to change in the early 1980s, in part because USAID threatened to halt new grants and loans to Costa Rica if the banking system didn't move toward privatization. By 1996, private banks were given the same rights as public ones—to offer checking and savings accounts, for example.

Now there are both public and private banks in Costa Rica, and neither are models of efficiency. The four public banks (Banco Nacional de Costa Rica, Banco de Costa Rica, Banco Credito Agricola de Cartago, and Banco Popular) at least have branches all over the country. If you live out in the sticks, it might be easier to deal with one of these entities. Also, the National Banking System guarantees deposits in government-owned banks. National banks are known to be extremely slow and bureaucratic, with checks often taking weeks to clear, and wire transfers taking up to a week to register in your account. And you have to keep calling and checking— otherwise your funds may get lost in the shuffle. You can open U.S.-dollar or *colón* accounts, and the minimum for opening a checking account is usually US$500. The ARCR cautions that national banks are not a good source of capital for foreign investors or for mortgages. "The procedure can take months," it says in a booklet for members, "unless you know someone with contacts high in the bank. After waiting months it is not unusual to be turned down for any number of reasons."

Service at one of the 17 private banks may be a bit less inefficient, with slightly more possibility of getting a loan or a mortgage. Fees are often higher as well. And even in private banks, it seems to be a matter of whom you know. One long-term foreign resident says, "If you want decent service in any bank, you need to woo the manager, charm the pants off the tellers, and even make friends with the guard who stands by the door. Then maybe your check will clear and you can take the manager out to a fancy lunch."

Most expats recommend keeping at least some (if not most) of your money in a bank back home, and accessing it here via ATM or advances processed through real live tellers. A bank back home will allow you to pay bills online (that's just starting up with banks here) and get direct deposit of your pension or rental or investment income. As you get deeper into your life here, it will become useful to also have a local account. If you have a business, you'll definitely need one, and for residency applications, you'll need to deposit money in a local account. One of the many services provided to ARCR members is an up-to-date and detailed comparison of local banks, including minimum balance, what sort of identification and references you need to open an account, and fees charged.

CREDIT CARDS

Credit cards are widely accepted, especially in upscale or tourist-oriented businesses. Visa is the most widely accepted card, with MasterCard a close second and venerable American Express a distant third. Conversion is at the official exchange rate, though merchants may tack on a surcharge to offset the 6 or 7 percent they're charged by credit card companies for each transaction. You can use your credit card to buy *colones* or dollars at a bank (there may be a minimum, often US$50). You can also get cash advances on your credit card via an ATM, provided you have arranged for a PIN. If you lose your credit card while in Costa Rica, call:

Visa International: tel. 506/257-4744
MasterCard: tel. 506/257-4744
American Express: tel. 800/012-3211
Diners Club: tel. 506/257-1766

Your Signature

When you use a credit or debit card in the United States, most clerks never even glance at the signature. In Costa Rica, be prepared for the clerk to carefully check your signature on the back against the one on the receipt you sign.

Here, your signature still means something, and many Ticos have worked up elaborate marks that could be hieroglyphics for all their resemblance to letters. Hard-to-copy signatures guard against fraud, as well as express the individual's personal style. North Americans, who hardly write by hand anymore, think of fraud in terms of identity theft and personal information that hackers can get off your computer, but here the signature still carries the weight of your identity.

Investing

There are many investment opportunities in Costa Rica—everything from pineapple processing to stocks traded on the national exchange (the *bolsa*). Costa Rica's *bolsa* was established in 1970 and is dominated by large national companies such as the *La Nación* publishing empire and the Costa Rican Brewery. Land development is big business, with mega-malls, hotel/condo spreads, and housing developments springing up all over the country.

Lawyers

Lawyers permeate many aspects of Costa Rican life. You'll need them for (among many other things) real estate transactions, residency permits, and forming a corporation (a Sociedad Anónima, or S.A.; see the Employment chapter for more information). One exasperated local jokes that you can barely get out of bed in the morning without a lawyer filing a *tramite* (the general term for legal papers).

It is imperative that you find an honest and effective lawyer, and that you nurture the relationship as you would one with your in-laws, recognizing it as a necessary evil. Personal referrals are the best way to go,

though even with a highly recommended lawyer you need to be vigilant—reading over all the documents he or she will file with various agencies (errors abound), and keeping on top of dates and deadlines (because he or she might not). It's also helpful to know the basic prices for various services (ask other expats and other lawyers) to make sure you're not being overcharged.

Through the country is swarming with lawyers, ironically, Costa Rica is not a litigious society, probably because lawsuits can take seven years to come to trial, and monetary awards are limited to lost wages and hospital bills.

Everything you read about investing in Costa Rica, and every hard-luck story you hear from bilked expats, tells you to be very, very careful when parting with your hard-earned money. A lot of people seem to think, sure, lots of people get ripped off in Costa Rica, but *I'm* too sharp for that. Rest assured that the criminals out to defraud you are even sharper. It's their business to know exactly what will make you want to turn over your cash, and there's not many people trying to stop them, at least in the initial stages of the game. The investment climate here, says financial consultant Alan Weeks in one of his newsletters, is largely unregulated. "For every person who has struck it rich," he warns, "there are dozens of people left behind to tell the sad story of a lifetime's worth of savings . . . down the drain."

Besides the real estate scams, the teak farms that don't exist, and various and sundry swindles, there are also many financial firms offering high-yield investments that seem too good to be true.

And indeed they usually are, as the fall in recent years of two of the largest entities demonstrates. Ofinter S.A. (a.k.a. "The Brothers") offered returns of 3.5 to 4 percent interest a month (42 to 48 percent a year), and got around the regulations by claiming investors were "friends" of the man who headed the firm, Luis Enrique Villalobos. Loaning money to friends is not regulated here (nor is it in most countries). In late 2002, some of the Brothers' accounts were frozen while they were being investigated for money laundering. Shortly thereafter the company heads skipped town with an estimated US$200 million that had belonged to their many "friends." A similar thing happened to Savings Unlimited (a.k.a. "The Cubans") in early 2003.

Many of these firms' investors were foreign residents who didn't ask many questions about how they were able to earn such astronomical interest. When the rocket shook apart in midair, however, many investors blamed the Costa Rican government for their losses, sharply criticizing the loosely regulated financial environment that had allowed them to earn such impossibly high rates in the first place.

An article in *La Nacion* diagnosed the problem as "an explosive mix of excessive trust, tempting high profits, and lack of regulation." Speaking of Ofinter and Savings Unlimited, former Central Bank president Eduardo Lizano said, "I do not know of traditional investments with such high returns." A *Tico Times* editorial asked, "With gray areas, who needs corruption? Costa Rica needs urgently to get clear about what's legal and what's not, and to enforce its laws."

The problem wasn't and isn't limited to the Brothers or the Cubans; almost every week you'll see headlines in the local press like "Another Financial Firm Under Scrutiny" or "Another Fraud Suspect Caught." The unregulated environment attracts a great many scamsters, many of whom are on the run from financial trouble up north or across the sea. Another headline you'll see frequently is some version of "Fraud Suspect Extradited to the U.S." Con men and women come to Costa Rica thinking they'll be able to ply their trade unfettered, and indeed they often do, sometimes for decades. With all the people getting caught, you have to wonder how many more are still doing brisk business. But some are nabbed, and whisked away to Miami, Toronto, or Bartlesville, Oklahoma—wherever there's a warrant out for their arrest.

It's all mildly entertaining unless you happen to have invested with one of these snake-oil vendors. Then it's not so funny, and could have devastating consequences if you're relying on that income for living expenses. Shortly after the Brothers went under, a German-born retiree living alone near Arenal took his own life. He'd lost a great deal of money in the scam, and confided to a neighbor a few days before he shot himself that he didn't know how he was supposed to live now.

I don't want to scare potential investors, but I do want to stress the dangers of trusting one's savings or pension checks to suspect enterprises. Costa Rica is an extraordinary place, but basic common sense still applies here. Do your homework, ask the hard questions, and don't invest in risky ventures unless you can afford to part with that money. You've heard it before but I'm going to say it again: If you wouldn't do it at home, don't do it here.

Income Tax

COSTA RICAN TAXES

Tax is paid only on income earned in Costa Rica, and taxable income is based on net income (gross income minus any expenses or deductions). Personal income tax on salary ranges from 0 percent (if you make less than 750,000 *colones* per month) to 18 percent (if you earn over 1,500,000 per month). If you're self-employed, you pay no tax if you earn less (after deductions) than 1,316,000 *colones* per month. After that, tax rates vary from 12 to 30 percent. The fiscal year runs from October 1 to September 30, with tax returns due before December 15.

U.S. TAXES

The Internal Revenue Service (IRS) has long arms, and they're not for hugging. Living abroad doesn't mean you can forget about U.S. taxes, though there are a few advantages for citizens living out of the United States.

Automatic Filing Extension

The first advantage is that the April 15 deadline is automatically extended to June 15. To qualify you must write boldly across the top of your return (which is due before June 15): TAXPAYER LIVING OUTSIDE THE U.S.A., AND QUALIFIES FOR THE AUTOMATIC 2-MONTH EXTENSION. You may end up paying interest or penalties if you owe more than US$1,000. You can file your income tax return through the American Embassy in San José.

Foreign Earned Income Exclusion

The second potential advantage for U.S. citizens living outside the United States is the Foreign Earned Income Exclusion. If your "tax home" has been on foreign soil for more than 330 days, you may be able to exclude up to US$80,000 of what you've earned abroad. The exclusion doesn't apply to interest, dividends, capital gains, pensions, annuities, or gambling winnings. You need special forms to apply for this exclusion, and the rules are complicated enough that you'll probably want to hire a tax professional. Even if you qualify for the exclusion, you still need to file a return.

Communications

Telephone Service

Costa Rica's telephone system ranks among the best in Central and South America. It's no accident that so many multinational corporations choose this country for a major branch office—they're drawn by the solid telecommunications network. The high concentration of sportsbooks (online betting agencies), with their reliance on phone lines, tells you that the system is working.

More than 80 percent of the population has easy access to telephone services. There are more than 500,000 landlines in this country of four million people, with cellular use increasing by leaps and bounds every day. Every third person you see—on the street, waiting for the bus, drinking coffee in a café—seems to be checking in their bag to see if that's their phone ringing.

Of course there are frustrations. If you don't inherit a phone line when you rent or buy a place to live, you could wait months for a line to be installed. If you're out in the sticks you might have to wait until they get around to putting up poles and stringing wires. Locals know tricks to speed up the process—like requesting a commercial line if a residential one seems slow in coming. The state utility monopoly (the Instituto Costaricense de Electricidad, or ICE, pronounced EE-say) is a behemoth that does things at its own pace, including striking for 21 days in 2003. During that time there was no repair service and no one answering the directory assistance line, although basic service continued uninterrupted.

If implementation of CAFTA (the Central American Free Trade Agreement) goes as planned, parts of the telecommunications sector (broadband internet service, cell phone service, and private data networks) will be open to private competition by 2007. Proponents of privatization say this will lead to better service.

In general, you can get what you need with patience and persistence. When I was having serious trouble with my line (sometimes I couldn't call out, people trying to call in got cut off, or there was so much static I couldn't hear what the caller was saying), it took me several phone calls to figure out to whom I should be talking. Finally I got the right department, which sent out a repairman within the day. There was no charge for the repairman's visit.

Another surprise was that I had an answering service included in my telephone service but didn't know it. When I was online or away from home, a mechanical voice invited people to leave a message. It took months of people mumbling about how unavailable I was to figure out that something was wrong. I finally called the telephone company, and they explained how to use the system that, up to that moment, I hadn't known existed. Needless to say, my mailbox was full, and some of the messages were pretty testy.

Residential and Commercial Service

As of mid-2004, basic residential telephone service cost about US$6/month; the basic commercial rate was about US$7/month. Basic cellular service was approximately US$8/month, including 60 minutes of time. After that hour, additional per-minute rates (in-country) run from US$.35 during prime time to US$.23 during off-peak hours.

International Rates

Calling the United States or Canada can cost up to US$.60 a minute from your home phone in Costa Rica, unless you have an international calling card (buy one before you leave home, at Wal-Mart or Sam's Club, or check out the deals offered at www.att.com, www.idt.net, www.ekno.com, or www.nobelcom.com, among many others). Also check out call-back services; you could try www.BestNetCall.com, though there are countless other companies plying the same trade. Another option that promises to be cheaper than even cut-rate international calling cards comes from the rapidly changing world of Internet phone connections. Simply put, you call through your computer, and pay only as much as you would for emailing. This technology is called voice-over-Internet protocol, or VoIP, and is improving at breakneck speed. If the traditional telecommunications corporations don't hound it out of existence, it will soon change the way we think about phones. At press time, the following companies offered some sort of VoIP calling: www.net2phone.com, www.dialpad.com, www.iconnecthere.com, and www.vonage.com.

Bring Your Phone
If you have a favorite phone that you can't bear to part with, by all means bring it down in your luggage. The system here, down to the jacks, is the same as in the United States, and you can get cheaper, better phones in the States.

Where cell phones are concerned, you need to be more careful. ICE, the sole provider of cell-phone service, says you need a GSM tri-band phone here in Costa Rica. See the sidebar "Cell Phone Service" for more information.

DIALING TO AND FROM COSTA RICA
It's easy to dial direct to most countries in the world from Costa Rica. To reach the United States, for example, you would dial 001, then the area code, and then the telephone number. If you'd rather make the long-distance call through an operator, dial 116. All the operators speak both Spanish and English.

When dialing *from* the United States to Costa Rica, the international code is 011, then you dial the country code (506), then the seven-digit telephone number.

You can also use your telephone credit card, dialing the numbers below:
AT&T: 0-800-011-4114
MCI: 0-800-012-2222
Sprint: 0-800-013-0123
Canada Bell: 0-800-015-1161
British Telecom: 0-800-044-1044

To make a collect call from any phone, dial 09, the international access code of the country being called (these numbers are listed in Costa Rican phone books), and then the number.

Cell Phone Service

As elsewhere in the world, cell phone use in Costa Rica went from 0 to 60 in a matter of what seemed to be seconds. Not too many years ago, no one here had a cell phone. Now even grade-school students have them. Remote parts of the country that were still waiting for wires to be strung for land lines ended up getting transmission towers instead. Some Costa Ricans who never had land lines now have cell phones.

As recently as 2003, getting a cell phone was a matter of putting down a deposit, putting your name on a list, and waiting—sometimes up to two years—for your number to come up. Now, delays are a matter of weeks, not years, and often you can get service the same day you apply for it.

The only provider of cellular service in Costa Rica is ICE (pronounced *EE-say*), the state electricity and telecommunications monopoly, but ICE allows local stores to serve as its agent, so you can buy a phone and sign up for service at almost any corner cell phone store (and there are more opening every day). While companies other than ICE are not strictly banned from providing service, the restrictions put on them make for few takers. In fact, one of the recurring sticking points in free trade talks between Costa Rica and the United States is that the United States wants Costa Rica to open its state-run telecommunications industry so that private foreign corporations can get a crack at the burgeoning market.

At this point, though, ICE is the only game in town. It has many different plans to choose from (including some with international roaming), but you need to have the right kind of phone for any of them to work. ICE's website says you need a GSM tri-band phone, and it mentions in particular Motorola models V66 and V66i; Sony Ericsson models T68i, T200, T300, T310, and T600; Nokia model 7210; and Saumsung's SGH-S300, though I know people who have other GSM models and find them to work as well. Cell phone technology changes rapidly; check the cell phone portion of ICE's website (www.ice.go.cr/esp/serv/per/cel/index.html) for the most up-to-date information.

Rates, too, change rapidly, but in 2004 the basic monthly rate was about US$8, with international calls to the United States and Canada billed at 45 cents a minute and calls to Europe 60 cents per minute. International calling cards offer better rates.

How many bars do you get in Costa Rica? Reception is generally good in the Central Valley and more problematic elsewhere. In beach and mountain communities you'll notice spots on the road where a number of cars seem to have pulled over for no reason. Look closer, and you'll see all the drivers have phones clamped to their ears—they're taking advantage of that rare spot where the signal slices through like a hot knife through butter.

Costa Rican phone card

Calls within Costa Rica are cheap, though even within the city of San José calls are time-charged. There's just one area code for the entire country: 506.

PAYING YOUR BILL

If you live in the city, paying your telephone bill is as easy as going to the bill-paying window at your local supermarket (you can also pay water and electric bills there). If you live in a more remote location, you'll need to find the place designated as a payment point. It won't always be an ICE office; it could very well be the local *pulpería* (corner store).

To pay your bill, however, you first need to receive it. Ask locals how and when telephone bills are delivered in your area; in some cases you may need to go pick up your bill at a central delivery point. If you've inherited the line, it will be in someone else's name (it's hard to transfer the account to a different name, so many people just keep paying on an account that isn't in their name), which may complicate things further.

In ICE's eyes, not receiving a bill is no excuse for not paying it, and non-payment of bills will, of course, lead to your phone line being shut off. The burden is on you to make sure you receive your bills and pay them on time. When in doubt, call or visit the nearest ICE office and check in on your account.

PAY PHONES

Most pay phones used to be coin-operated, and at any given time a large portion of them were out of order. The situation has improved, with booths in better repair, and many (if not most) phones now take the phone cards you can buy on the street or in corner stores. Cards come in various denominations, from 500 to 5,000 *colones*. Unlike in some other countries, you usually don't slide the phone card into the phone itself (there are a few phones where you do). Instead, you dial a series of access codes listed on the back of the card: first 197 or 199 (depending on the card), and then, after you connect with the automated service, the 12-digit code that is revealed when you scratch a dark band off the card. You will be told how many *colones* you still have on the card, and then asked to dial your desired number. Directions on how to do all of the above are printed on the back of the cards. On the 199 cards, the directions are in both Spanish and English, and the automated system you connect with gives you the option of listening to instructions in English.

Email and the Internet

INTERNET ACCESS

Everyone loves to complain about ICE, the state telecommunications monopoly, and there's a lot to complain about. Its Internet branch, RACSA (Radiográfica Costarricense S.A.), is just now emerging from the dark ages, with much of the country's access limited to slow dial-up service. ICE has been criticized for squelching any attempts to improve its service. In late 2002 it nullified bidding for the infrastructure that would have led to a high-speed direct service link (DSL) line, and there have been many other cases of RACSA dragging its feet on changes that would vastly improve the system.

But it can't hold out forever. Public demand will (one hopes) oblige RACSA to either provide better service or cooperate with companies that can. Already RACSA is creating what it calls "strategic alliances" with companies such as Teletica (www.teletica.com) and Amnet (www.amnet.co.cr) to offer cable Internet access to more and more neighborhoods and towns. The rate is about US$80/month for up to two computers. It's not as fast as the cable or DSL access you're used to up north, but it's a lot better than dialing up on a 56K modem, which, by the way, never seems to reach that speed—you're lucky if you're operating at 46K, and sometimes the speed drops into the 20s. Forget downloading photos or songs at that rate—you'll be online all night.

Large foreign-owned businesses tend to be able to negotiate better Internet service (Costa Rica is the land of the special case, especially on the corporate level), but for individuals the choices are limited. In 2003

RACSA said that 100,000 of its 108,000 clients were using dial-up service. It's easy to get and only costs US$15/month, plus the small fee you pay for being on the telephone. One of the many complaints about RACSA's dial-up service is that the system can only handle 5,000 users at any given time. If you try to connect at a peak time, you may get a busy signal or be disconnected just as you're about to send that email that took half an hour to compose.

If you live in or near San José, you can start things rolling at the main RACSA office downtown at Calle 1 at Avenida 5 (First Street at Fifth Avenue), but setting up an account can also be done quickly and painlessly at many computer stores throughout the country. Either way, they'll give you an email address and a password after you fill out a few forms. You can even pay with a debit or credit card, having them automatically deduct each month's bill from that account. You can only use your dial-up service from your home number.

INTERNET CAFÉS

There are scores of Internet cafés in the greater San José area, and you'll find a handful in tourist towns like Tamarindo, Montezuma, or Puerto Viejo. The access points in San José tend to be cheaper because there's so much competition—sometimes prices are as low as US$.50 an hour. In remote areas prices can be much higher, since often the café is the only game in town. Many hotels, even low-end backpacker hostels, now offer free Internet access, and Spanish language schools often provide their students free access. If you want to stay in touch, you can.

A WIRED COUNTRY

Despite the barriers to speedy and efficient Internet access, Costa Rica has fully embraced the digital age. Studies show 384,000 individuals using the Net at last count in 2002, and most government agencies have extensive websites. If you can speak Spanish, these sites are an excellent introduction to how the country works. Some of the sites even have English translations. A good place to start is www.mideplan.go.cr/Instituciones.htm, which has links to a variety of agencies and ministries.

Mail

EL CORREO

The national mail service can at times surprise you with its efficiency. Say you're swinging in a hammock outside your rather remote home near the

> *As long as you marvel when the postal system works and don't have to rely on it, you'll be fine. Most letters arrive in a timely fashion, but some take weeks.*

beach when a man on a dirt bike roars up your gravel drive. Don't be alarmed—it's just the mailman, his pouch slung across his shoulder and his fat-tired motorcycle perfectly suited to his potholed route. It's like a modern-day Pony Express, and when he hands you an envelope with a New York postmark of just a few days back, it feels like magic.

As long as you marvel when the postal system works and don't have to rely on it, you'll be fine.

Most letters arrive in a timely fashion, but some take weeks, and parcels larger than a magazine-sized envelope are often held at customs until you come and pay the outrageous duties, often 100 percent of perceived value.

Sometimes the lack of addresses and house numbers in this country seems to stymie even experienced mail carriers. Mail sent to my San José address (which is a long recitation of turn this way and that, and look for the pink house) from across town never arrived, though bills always made their way into my *buzón* (mailbox). Many people like to pay the small fee for a post office box at their local post office. Depending on where you live, there can be a long wait to get a P.O. box.

The post office has an extensive website (www.correos.go.cr), which is in both Spanish and English, or Attempted English—we learn that P.O. boxes are available to both "phisic persons and juridic figures."

PRIVATE MAIL SERVICES

Many foreign residents swear by private mail services. You get a post office box in Miami, the U.S. city closest to Costa Rica, and from there the company couriers your letters

main post office *(correos),* downtown San José

and packages to you in Costa Rica. Plans generally have a monthly fee that covers, say, three kilos of mail a month. Excess weight is charged at various rates, mostly below US$10/kilo.

See Contacts in the Resources section for companies to consider.

SHIPPING OPTIONS

There are many ways to ship packages within Costa Rica and from Costa Rica to the United States or Canada. It's a competitive market, with rates and services changing rapidly to meet customer needs; be sure to confirm the specifics listed below with a call or a website visit.

National Postal Service

The cheapest way to send packages is the *correos,* the national post office. A one-kilo (2.2-pound) package sent regular mail would cost about US$8 and arrive in 10 to 12 days. Another category of service costs more and arrives sooner—a 100-gram (0.22-pound) parcel would cost about US$20 and arrive in under a week. There's a "package tracker" feature on its website (www.correos.go.cr), but it only guarantees arrival time on parcels sent within Costa Rica. Go to the nearest *correos* branch, or call 506/253-1901. The post office provides no packing materials.

I sent three book-filled boxes (approximately 15 x 12 x 10 inches) from Costa Rica to California. It cost me US$60, and the boxes arrived in about three and half weeks.

DHL

DHL has offices in Liberia (Guanacaste), Limón, Heredia, and in the San José neighborhoods of Pavas, Curridabat, and Paseo Colón. It'll get your packages to other points in Central America or to Miami overnight, to the rest of the United States in two days, and to Canada and Europe in three days. A 30-kilo package to the United States would cost just over US$200. DHL also offers door-to-door delivery of Jumbo Boxes (25–50 kilos/55–110 pounds) and of Jumbo Junior boxes (10–20 kilos/22–44 pounds). Boxes are available at DHL offices. For more information call 506/210-3939 or go to www.la-reg.dhl.com.

FedEx

FedEx has many different ways to send packages within, from, and to Costa Rica. You can send a package of up to 68 kilos (150 pounds) to the United States and it will arrive in one to three days, depending on the destination. Its website (www.fedex.com) has a lot of information on shipping internationally, listing customs procedures for more than 30 countries. Business customers within Costa Rica can use the FedEx website to track inbound and outbound packages. In San José there's an office on Paseo Colón, 100 meters (109 yds.) east of the León Cortéz statue and right next to the Iberia airlines office, open Monday–Friday, 8:30 A.M.–5 P.M. Call 800/052-1090 for more information.

United Postal Service

UPS has offices in San José, Quepos, Limón, Jacó, and Tamarindo, most with a good selection of boxes, tubes, and other packing materials. Worldwide Expedited Service to the United States will get a two-pound package there in three days for between US$6 and US$90, but there are many other shipping options. One new service is the TicoPak, which offers shipping directly from souvenir shops in Costa Rica to homes in the United States, with special CoffeePaks, HammockPaks, and MachetePaks to accommodate the most frequently bought keepsakes. Call 506/290-2828 or visit www.ups.com.

Media

Freedom of the press has long been an essential feature of Costa Rican culture. It began with the founding of local papers in the early 19th century and was formally declared a fundamental right in 1948. More recently, in

2002 Costa Rica ranked high in a study of press freedom conducted by media watchdog group Journalists Without Borders. Of 139 countries around the world, Costa Rica finished 15th, second in the hemisphere, behind Canada but ahead of the United States, which ranked 17th.

Press freedom is a nebulous term, of course, and can be measured in a variety of ways. In the past, Costa Rica's three major dailies offered different perspectives, with *La Nación* providing a more conservative outlook, while *La República* and *La Prensa Libre* had left-of-center viewpoints. But now, says *Culture and Customs in Costa Rica* author Chalene Helmuth, "Newspaper reporting in the three major dailies has converged into a monolithic, rightist perspective." Press freedom is also no doubt affected by the fact that the *La Nación* publishing empire owns three of the major papers, a couple of television stations, and countless magazines. "Most media are owned by the business elite," write the Biesanz family in *The Ticos*, "who are also the chief buyers of advertising space and time."

Journalism is a respected profession here, and journalists are feared and courted by special interest groups and the government. The *Decreto de Salarios Mínimos*, which comes out every few years and stipulates the minimum wage of almost every job in the country, lists a salary for journalists, around US$700/month, that is definitely on the high end of what professionals make here.

SPANISH-LANGUAGE NEWSPAPERS

Costa Rica has at least eight major Spanish-language newspapers, one *(La Gaceta)* belonging to the state. *La Nación* is the largest and most widely read daily paper. *El Financiero* (owned by the *La Nación* publishing empire) is a business weekly. *La Nación* also owns *Al Dia*, known for its sports section.

As for the non-*Nación* papers, there's the daily *La República*, now mostly devoted to business news, *El Heraldo*, and *La Prensa Libre*, the latter an afternoon paper. Then there's *Diario La Extra*, full of photos of half-naked women and bloody bodies and home to a much-read romantic advice column, *Sentimientos en conflicto* (Feelings in Conflict). If you like sex, gore, and advice on "Ten Types of Men You Should Avoid," the *Extra* is for you.

At the other end of the spectrum is the University of Costa Rica's *Seminario Universidad* (http://cariari.ucr.ac.cr/~semana/), a leftish paper that takes on the underlying roots of current events.

A great way to get in the spirit of Costa Rica (even if you're in the United States) and to practice your Spanish is to check out the local papers' websites. Not only will you know which government ministers have resigned and which bridges have washed out; you'll also keep up to date on daily temperatures and fluctuations in the exchange rate. Many of these sites also have background information on Costa Rica and links to other excellent sources of information. *La Nación* even has on its website (www.nacion.co.cr) a weekly news summary in English; it comes out every Thursday. Also try www.diarioextra.com, www.prensalibre.co.cr, www.elheraldo.net, and www.go.cr/fs/gaceta.html.

ENGLISH-LANGUAGE NEWSPAPERS AND MAGAZINES

There are enough English-speaking residents of Costa Rica to support a variety of media, the most influential being the weekly *Tico Times* (tel. 506/258-1558, fax 506/233-6378, www.ticotimes.net), founded in 1956 and read front-to-back by many foreign residents. The paper has won awards for its reporting, and covers everything from politics to tourism. It's also a great source for finding out what's happening culturally in the Central Valley, with listings for plays, benefits, and the many clubs in which foreign residents congregate—from bridge to the Association for People Who Have Had Brain Surgery.

Though it has some news coverage of the Central American region and the rest of the world, the *Tico Times* still retains a hometown feel, with news of So-and-So in Playas del Coco having their second child or opening a third bar. The advertisements reveal the preoccupations of at least some of Costa Rica's foreign community: ads for Spanish language schools, tax lawyers, hair replacement, and plastic surgery.

Business Costa Rica (tel. 506/220-2200, www.amcham.co.cr)is a monthly business magazine put out by the Costa Rican-American Chamber of Commerce.

The *Central American Weekly* (tel. 506/296-1341, www.centralamericaweekly.net) is a more tourist-oriented paper published in English, Spanish, and German. You can find it around major hotels.

The bimonthly *Costa Rica Outdoors* concentrates on fishing, birding, and tourist-oriented sports.

Mesoamérica (tel. 506/253-3195, www.mesoamericaonline.net) is produced by the Institute for Central American Studies and provides analyses of politics in all the Central American countries.

Outside of the Central Valley, you'll find lots of little regional publications. In the Tamarindo area there's *The Howler* (tel. 506/653-0545), a free monthly that focuses on community news and surfing reports. In Playas del Coco there's the *Costa Rican Travel Magazine* (tel./fax 506/670-0563, www.costa-rica-travel-magazine.com), published periodically and covering the northern Guanacaste coastal region. The *Tico Trader Magazine* (tel./fax 506/643-2813, ticotrader@hotmail.com) covers the Jacó area, while *Quepolandia* (www.quepolandia.com) takes on the Quepos/Manuel Antonio region. For English-speaking residents in the southern region, there's *Sol de Osa* (www.soldeosa.com).

RADIO

Radio is king in Costa Rica, and you hear it everywhere you go—in homes, workplaces, buses, and taxis. Radios vastly outnumber televisions, with a 1997 survey registering almost a million radios and just over 500,000 TVs. There are about 130 radio stations in the country, broadcasting talk shows, sports, humor, news, and popular music from Latin America and the United States. Golden oldies and up-to-the-minute pop songs in English are surprisingly omnipresent on the airwaves here.

Ticos seem to have a high tolerance for noise, and you may be surprised when a friend keeps the radio blaring while you're trying to have a conversation. Get into a taxi and you may have to shout above an ear-splitting soccer match to tell the driver where you're going. Public buses play dance music so loudly you'd think they were trying to compete with discos. Maids, housewives, and other homebound folks may keep the radio on all day for company.

Radio is a traditional link between the capital and the provinces, and a community service in many small towns. On local stations you'll hear neighborhood news and even pleas that Juan call María at 5 P.M. at the local payphone.

Widespread radio ownership also makes the medium a natural for distance learning. In 1973, the newly founded Costa Rican Institute of Radio Education created *The Teacher in Your House,* a program that broadcasts primary and secondary school lessons from 12 noncommercial stations around the country. Many farmers living in isolated rural areas have

Radio Stations

Most stations here play a mix of local and U.S. popular music, but if you look hard you'll find alternatives. Among the English offerings is the respected Radio for Peace (AM 1504). Radio Dos (FM 99.5) and 107.5 FM mostly play music but have occasional news updates in English.

Interesting Spanish-language stations include Radio FM 96, which plays mostly classical music; Radio Universidad (870 AM and 96.7 FM), which features classical and jazz; Radio U (101.9 FM), with a variety of eclectic programming; Radio Estereo Azul (99 FM); and Econews 95.9 FM, which offers not only economic news but also classical and jazz music.

taken advantage of the program, enrolling in courses that lead to certificates of completion.

TELEVISION

If radio is king, then TV is most certainly queen, and a foreign queen at that. While the 13 broadcast stations here have programming mostly in Spanish, the vast number of cable stations are most often in English (sometimes with Spanish subtitles, sometimes without). Cable services are extremely popular, and even lower-middle-class households pay for the privilege of choosing from among dozens of channels, including ones in French, German, Italian, and Japanese. But English rules, and even the Spanish-language stations reveal the influence of English and of U.S. culture. During a long series of commercials (as in Europe, commercial breaks here are longer but much less frequent), you may hear "Ya regresamos a *Six Feet Under.*" ("We will return to *Six Feet Under.*") Even if there's not an English syllable within shouting distance, the U.S. influence is often obvious, as in a local KFC commercial that has a cartoon Colonel speaking Spanish with a horrendous gringo accent.

Beyond the gringo influence, there are programs and commercials

Catching up: low-tech communication
Lankester Gardens

from all over Latin America, especially Mexico and Argentina. I've never heard so much Argentine-inflected Spanish, with its *j* slant on the Spanish *ll,* usually pronounced *y.* Apparently the Argentine ad business is highly developed, and spots made in that country are beamed all over Latin America. But at least Argentina and Costa Rica share the preference for *vos* instead of the more common *tu* to express the informal "you."

Some Ticos worry that so much foreign influence is eroding the national character and filing away the rough edges of local lingo. Still, it's unlikely that this country will do what France has done, trying to protect its language by mandating that a certain percentage of cultural offerings, like films, must be homegrown.

Ticos watch a lot of TV, and they don't seem bothered by the flood of foreign programming. Just as the radio is left playing all day as background noise and electronic companionship, so is the TV on almost everywhere you go. In restaurants, bars, doctor's waiting rooms, and corner stores you'll see CNN en Español, *Mr. Ed* reruns dubbed in Spanish, old *Munsters* episodes, soap operas from Mexico and Venezuela, and the ubiquitous soccer games, punctuated by the announcer shouting an impossibly drawn-out "goooooaaaal!"

Cable and Satellite TV Companies
Craving your CNN, your BBC, or the Fox roster of adult cartoon shows? Compare the offerings of Amnet (tel. 506/210-2929, fax 506/231-2909, www.amnet.co.cr/index_tv.htm), Cable Tica (tel. 506/210-1450, fax 506/231-7914, www.teletica.com), and Direct TV (tel. 506/205-5151, fax 506/205-5152, ventas@directtc.co.cr).

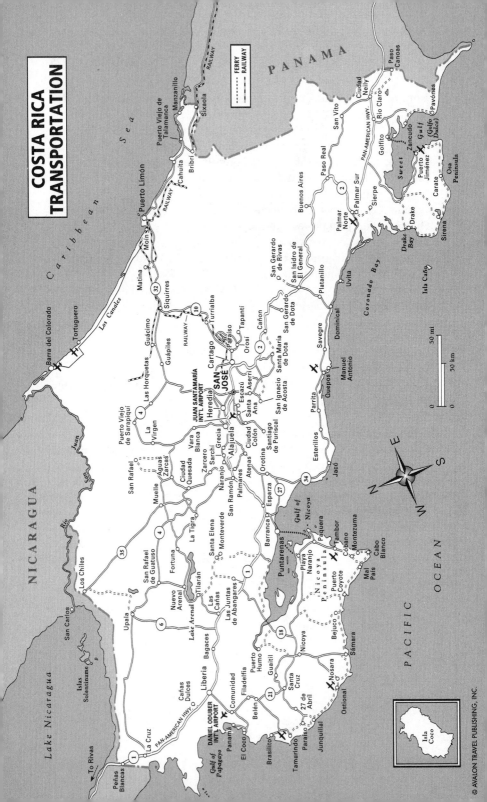

COSTA RICA TRANSPORTATION

© Erin Van Rheenen

Travel and Transportation

Getting There

By air is by far the easiest way to get to Costa Rica, and although fares fluctuate, for the past several years there have been some great deals, especially if you're flexible about when you can fly. More than one million people come to Costa Rica every year, and most arrive by plane. The other methods of getting here are overland—by car or bus—and by sea. The latter option requires you to either have your own yacht or to come by cruise ship (and be content to dock in Costa Rica for only a day or two). Coming overland through Mexico and Central America is a trip you will not soon forget, and it's best left to adventurous souls with lots of time.

BY AIR

Costa Rica is less than three hours by air from Miami, about five hours from New York City, seven hours from Los Angeles, and 8.5 hours from

Toronto. More than 30 international flights arrive daily at Juan Santamaría International Airport, half an hour northwest of San José. Every year, carriers add more flights and more carriers get in the game. Presently, you can choose from Air Canada, American Airlines, America West, Continental, Delta, LACSA (Costa Rica's airline), Mexicana, Northwest, TACA (the Central American airline), and United, not to mention charter flights that come and go as demand dictates. Charter flights seldom show up when you do web searches for the best airfare deals—call a travel agent or make direct contact with package tour companies.

Prices vary widely, but at press time round-trip coach tickets on commercial carriers could be had for about US$300–400 from Miami, US$400–500 from Texas, US$550–650 from New York, US$450–550 from Los Angeles, and US$600–700 from San Francisco.

Direct flights are available from many cities, including New York, Miami, Atlanta, Dallas/Fort Worth, Houston, and Los Angeles. Other cities require a brief stop and sometimes a plane change, though every year it gets easier to get to San José quickly and painlessly. From San Francisco, for instance, you can get a flight that stops briefly in San Salvador and then arrives in San José about eight hours after takeoff in California. A favorite for those able to sleep on the plane is LACSA Flight 561, which leaves San Francisco at 1:15 A.M. and arrives in Costa Rica before 10 in the morning.

Airports

Costa Rica's main airport, Juan Santamaría International Airport, is in Alajuela, 16 kilometers (10 mi.) from downtown San José. The airport recently had a major facelift and now occupies a new glass-and-steel terminal. After your plane arrives, you'll go through customs, pressing a button that illuminates either a green or red light. A green light means you go through without having your bags searched; a red light means you will be searched. Even with the tightening of security after 9/11, most tourists get the green light. As you exit the airport, you'll see a little booth where you can buy a taxi ticket to wherever you need to go, paying in dollars if you like. Taxis that don't work with the ticket system charge about the same as those that do, and are often unregulated and therefore uninsured. A taxi ride from the airport to downtown San José will cost around US$13.

Getting to the airport from the San José area is a matter of hailing or calling a cab, or arranging for a shuttle (see the Getting Around section later in this chapter). Leaving by air, travelers pay a US$26 exit tax (payable in *colones*, U.S. dollars, or a combination of the two). The baggage limit is generally 32 kilos or 70 pounds, in one or two bags whose dimensions (length

+ height + width) are not supposed to exceed 62 inches. You're also allowed a carry-on bag that weighs less than 40 pounds. Airline policies on surfboards vary; call ahead.

About six kilometers (4 mi.) southwest of central San José in the suburb of Pavas, Tobías Bolaños Airport handles domestic flights only. For more information, see the Getting Around section later in this chapter.

Flights to Daniel Oduber International Airport in Liberia deposit you in the northern province of Guanacaste, about half an hour from Playa Hermosa and a little over an hour from Tamarindo. For those heading for the northern Pacific coast, this flight eliminates a car or bus ride from San José, which can take four or five hours.

Up to December 2002, there were no direct, scheduled commercial flights from the United States to Liberia, but all that changed when Delta started flying here direct from Atlanta. Delta runs six flights a week; the trip takes six hours. American Airlines runs three flights a week (Thursday, Friday, and Saturday) direct from Miami, while Continental flies three times a week from Houston.

Private charter flights into this airport can be great deals. Two Costa Rican companies coordinate the charter flights: Aerojet de Costa Rica (tel. 506/668-1161) and AVS (tel. 506/668-1151). Aerojet coordinates flights from Sky Service (which comes from Toronto every Tuesday); Air Transat (which comes from Toronto every Friday); and USA 3000, which originates in Philadelphia. AVS handles other companies that don't have fixed schedules. Also look into SunTrips' flights, one of which goes direct from Oakland, California, to Liberia.

BY SEA

An increasing number of cruise ships are making Costa Rica a port of call, if only for a few days or even hours. Passengers may disembark for a quick sightseeing trip, a hike, or a river-rafting jaunt. Tourism Institute statistics indicate that close to 200,000 cruise-ship passengers docked in Costa Rica in 2002, about half of them in the Caribbean port city of Limón, and the rest in the Pacific coast ports of Puntarenas, Caldera, and Golfito.

Ports of Entry

If you're coming on your own boat, there are several official ports of entry with both customs and immigrations stations. On the northern Pacific coast you have Playas del Coco (tel. 506/670-0216), while the central Pacific has Puntarenas (tel. 506/661-1446) and Caldera (tel. 506/634-4055). At Playa Herradura you can put in at the private Los

Sueños Marina (tel. 506/643-3886 or www.lossuenosresort.com), which has its own customs and immigration, as well as a full-service fuel station and good docking facilities. Radio ahead to VHF16. The south Pacific has facilities at the old banana port city of Golfito (tel. 506/775-0423). Boaters arriving on the Caribbean coast go through customs at Puerto Limón (tel. 506/758-4466) and dock at nearby Barra del Colorado.

Commercial Ports

Costa Rica's main commercial ports are Caldera on the central Pacific coast, Golfito on the southern Pacific, and Limón and Moín on the Caribbean coast. The ships that come and go from Caldera are usually carrying agricultural products; those in Golfito are stacked with the electronics and appliances sold at the *Deposito Libre* (duty free) in that ex-banana town; Limón is now the banana port (among other things); and Moín is associated with the oil that runs in a pipeline from the Caribbean coast to the Central Valley. Puntarenas used to be a big commercial port but now only receives cruise ships.

BY LAND

I've met a lot of people who have driven overland from North America to Costa Rica, but they all seem to have done it 10, 20, or 30 years ago, "when we were young and brave and stupid," as one traveler put it. Maybe it's the forgiving fog of memory, but most of these folks claim that despite dismal roads, corrupt and inept border officials, run-ins with police and thieves, and the inevitable mechanical breakdowns, it was a long strange trip that they wouldn't trade for anything in the world. One advantage of coming by car is that you can load up with all that you need to start your new life—no 70-pound maximum on luggage.

If you do make it to the Nicaragua/Costa Rica border, you'll come across at Peñas Blancas on the InterAmerican Highway. As border crossings go, it's not bad at all. The website www.drivemeloco.com, which offers up-to-date information about driving through Central America, calls the Costa Rican border "by far the most efficient and trustworthy crossing" in the area.

Your first step in crossing the border is to pay US$3 to have your car fumigated: An official will spray a white liquid on the underside of your vehicle. If you object to being doused with who-knows-what chemicals, you might offer up a few bills for the privilege of skipping this step.

The Costa Rican and Nicaraguan immigration offices are four kilometers (2.5 mi.) apart. Once inside Costa Rica, you'll park, go to one window for an entry stamp (US$2), then take your passport and car title to the Aduana window.

You'll also need to buy insurance for a minimum of one month (US$17). Officials will provide three forms: *Certificado de Entrega de Vehiculos, No Comerciales Importacion Temporal; Instituto Nacional de Seguros;* and *Recibo de Dinero,* then you're on your way. There are several checkpoints just beyond the border area; show all your papers, and they'll let you pass.

Before you get to the border, make sure you have your passport and all vehicle documentation, and be prepared to stand in one line after another. There are lots of kids that will run up to you and offer to speed you through the process. Veteran border-crossers advise caution, but I've had good luck picking a kid who looks street-smart but not yet like a full-fledged criminal. These helpers will show you which line to stand in first, then hurry you to the next window, rattling off advice in Spanish that you may or may not understand. The kids expect a tip of at least a few dollars for their efforts.

See Suggested Reading in the Resources section for books on driving to Costa Rica. Also check out the website of Sanborn's insurance (www.sanbornsinsurance.com), which specializes in overland travel from the United States and through Mexico and Central America. Sanborn's has a U.S. office in MacAllen, Texas, one of the preferred border crossings for people making the drive down.

Bussing the whole way is cheap, and easier than driving in terms of bureaucracy (no licenses or insurance or traffic cops to deal with). It's also harder on the body. Most Mexican and Central American buses are at least as comfortable as Greyhound buses in the United States, and some are positively deluxe, with movies, clean bathrooms, and snacks served. But some still fit the stereotype of rickety haulers of the unwashed masses and their livestock; you'll probably find yourself on one or two during your trip, maybe for that 13-hour stretch with only pork rinds to eat and no bathroom breaks. Those with delicate stomachs and weak bladders need not apply. Costa Rica–based Tica Bus has daily buses to and from San Salvador (in El Salvador), Tegucigalpa (Honduras), Guatemala City, Managua (Nicaragua), and Tapachula in Mexico.

Getting Around

BY AIR
Domestic airlines use small planes to make their short hops (20 to 40 minutes) to places like Tortuguero, Golfito, Nosara, or Tamarindo. Planes carry from four to fifteen passengers, and round-trip fares cost US$80–200. Residents pay significantly lower fares.

© Erin Van Rheenen

Carate airstrip

SANSA is the domestic branch of TACA; it flies out of Juan Santamaría Airport. NatureAir flies out of Tobías Bolaños Airport in the Pavas section of San José.

Other charter companies are Paradise Air, Aero Bell, Aero Costa Sol, Pitts Aviation, and Helicópteros Turísticos Tropicales. Contact information for these companies can be found in the Resources section.

Though Costa Rica's civil aviation authority gets high marks from the U.S. Federal Aviation Administration, it's still safer to go with known companies here. Between 2000 and 2003, nine U.S. citizens died in domestic air accidents in Costa Rica, with pilot error deemed the cause in the majority of the accidents. Private air taxi services were involved in a disproportionate number of crashes, and the government subsequently provided more funds for the oversight of their pilots, procedures, and aircraft.

BY BUS

Costa Rica has a great bus system—cheap, extensive, comfortable, and often on time. You can get just about anyplace in the country for under US$10. It's also a great way to see the country without the expense or hassle of a car, and to make contact with locals, who use buses as their daily transport. Popular destinations—like Jacó, Liberia, and Limón—are served by both direct *(directo)* buses and those that stop a lot along the way (called *normal* or *corriente*). Routes to crossroads towns like Liberia often leave every hour from early morning to late evening, while less-visited destinations may be served by just one or two buses per day. Buy tickets a day or two in advance—seats sell out fast. Popular routes are served by buses with comfortable seats and decent legroom; many resemble Greyhounds in the United States. Urban or shorter-distance buses may be renovated U.S. school buses, with those unpadded seats that hold two small children but only one and a half adults.

In San José, there's no central bus station; instead there are many departure points throughout the city. The tourist office right next to the Gold Museum downtown has good maps that show where a variety of long- and short-distance buses leave and arrive. Most points are in decent areas, but be especially careful at the central San José bus depot known as the Coca-Cola (near 1st Avenue and 16th Street)—your bags can disappear in the time it takes to check your watch. Accurate bus schedules are hard to come by, but one source is the website www.costaricabybus.com.

City Buses

Most urban routes cost less than US$.50, and passengers pay as they enter the bus. Bus drivers usually have change for small bills. When you want to get off, either pull the cable, or—if there is no cable—call out *la parada, por favor* (next stop, please).

© Houman Pirdavari

Old schoolbuses from the U.S. are common sights in Costa Rica.

Bus stops often have shelters (essential during the rainy season) or battered signs that say the route name or number. Route numbers seem not to be much use, though: I once asked the driver parked at the Route 66 sign if that route went to my neighborhood. He looked at me quizzically—he'd never thought of his route as having a number. Buses are known for their destinations: the Desamperados bus, the bus to the University.

Shuttle Bus Companies

Fantasy Bus (tel. 506/220-2126, fax 506/220-2393, operated by Grayline Tours, www.graylinecostarica.com) and Interbus (tel. 506/283-5573, fax 506/283-7655, www.costaricapass.com) will take you to more than 40 destinations in air-conditioned vans. Routes leaving from San José pick up passengers at hotels throughout the city; one-way fares range US$20–38. If you want more comfort than you'd get on a regular bus, these shuttle services can be very useful, though they're not always as reliable as you'd like. Especially if you're catching one in a town outside the Central Valley, check and double-check departure times, and book ahead. Both companies also offer airport shuttle service.

BY BOAT

The Caribbean coast north of Puerto Limón is riddled with rivers and swamps, which have made it tough to build roads. This is perhaps the only

Caño Blanco

noncoastal area in the country where boat travel is the daily norm, with motorized *canoas* making runs from one tiny town to the next, carrying people and freight. Boats can be hired from Moín just north of Puerto Limón, and from Caño Blanco, among other ports.

Ferries

There are four major ferry crossings in Costa Rica, with three of the four carrying people and vehicles between Puntarenas and the southern end of the Nicoya Peninsula. Two of these—the Tambor Ferry (tel. 506/220-2034) and the Ferry Peninsular (tel. 506/641-0118)—go from Puntarenas to Paquera, and the third runs between Puntarenas and Playa Naranjo (Ferry Playa Naranjo, tel. 506/661-1069). All take about an hour. The trip is scenic, and fares are low (US$14 for a car; less than a dollar for a walk-on). It's a great way to start a trip to Montezuma or Malpaís.

On the southern Pacific coast, a passenger-only ferry goes across the Bahia Dulce, connecting Golfito and Puerto Jimenez on the Osa Peninsula (tel. 506/775-0472). The trip takes about 90 minutes.

There used to be a ferry across the Tempisque River in Guanacaste, but it shut down in 2003 upon completion of the Taiwan Friendship Bridge.

BY TRAIN

For years, the train was the best way to get from the Central Valley to the Caribbean port city of Limón. In the 1970s, however, roads were improved and the train began to be utilized less. Then a 1991 earthquake destroyed miles of tracks and put an end to this scenic trip, and with it, all passenger train travel within Costa Rica. There is talk of resuming the Limón route and the old San José–Puntarenas line—time will tell.

BY CAR

Renting

Though it's expensive to rent a car here and the roads are quite a challenge, a car gives you a great deal of freedom and lets you see every nook and cranny of the country. You don't have to worry about bus schedules or packing light—just load up the car and take off into the wild green yonder.

Most rentals are standard shift, and you'll probably want to rent a 4x4 with high clearance, unless you're sure you'll be on major roads for your entire trip. In my experience it pays to rent a medium-sized rather than the smallest four-wheel drive—you'll appreciate the extra weight when you're trying to ford a river. You can probably find a compact car for about

US$300/week, but a decent 4x4 will cost you closer to US$400–500 per week. Sometimes you can get better deals by making reservations from the United States.

One good thing about renting a car in this country is that some companies will deliver the vehicle to your door, especially if you live far from a rental office. In Guanacaste's Playa Negra, I had a 4x4 delivered to the door of the rather remote place I was staying. The company sent two cars, so that the fellow driving my car would have a ride back.

For specific car rental companies, see Contacts in the Resources section.

Rental Insurance

When you rent a car in Costa Rica you need to pay for mandatory basic insurance, which doesn't give very much coverage. Most renters opt to buy

Off-Roading, Tica Style

The Río Montaña doesn't look menacing until you start tracing the route your car would take to cross it. We're not talking a rickety narrow bridge here; we're talking no bridge at all. In Costa Rica that's not unusual, and driving through water is common, at least during the rainy season, which was supposed to be over but wasn't. Fording rivers can be great fun, I'd been assured, if car and driver are up to the challenge.

I wasn't sure about the driver (me) and I had even graver doubts about the car, which was a rented 4x4 with *"doble traccion,"* but about the size of a large kitten. I left my mud-spattered, pothole-rattled car on the riverbank and went to study the crossing. The Ostional side looked fairly shallow and slow-moving. On the Nosara side the water was about waist deep, with the current accelerating fast out of a bend and then shooting off to sea.

Asking people for directions, I'd heard this river mentioned more than

once. You won't have a problem, they said, except maybe the river right past Ostional. The Río Montaña. That can get pretty big, and it's been raining a lot lately. Now if you had a *chapulín,* more than one person said, that would be different.

As far as I knew, a *chapulín* was a grasshopper. Either the people here considered grasshoppers good luck, or a *chapulín* was maybe a special kind of all-terrain vehicle, or some way you could soup up your car to make it good in rivers.

A local appeared as I was studying the current. I asked him what he thought. I'll wade across to show you how deep it is, he offered, starting in before I even had the chance to answer. At first the water was only to his calves, and it was easy going. Then his gait slowed, and he held his possessions over his head. At the deepest point the water was only to his waist, but you could tell he was struggling against the current. He braced himself and more insurance; some let their credit card cover the high deductible (often from US$750 to US$1,500!) that goes along with basic insurance. Be sure to check that your card indeed offers this benefit. And be ready for surprises—a friend thought American Express would cover him, but found that there was a clause that said the coverage didn't hold if the driver went "off-road"—that is, on unpaved roads. Since most of the roads in Costa Rica are unpaved, he ended up having to pay a few hundred dollars to repair a small scrape.

Rental car companies will charge for the most minute scratches, so be sure to look the car over very carefully before driving off the lot. Things like rearview mirrors and tires are often not covered by insurance; you pay if they get ripped off. That's why it's so important to park the car in a safe place.

looked back over his shoulder at me, shaking his head. *Mejor que no,* he called out. You better not. Then he scrambled up the riverbank and was gone.

I turned around and went back to Ostional to have lunch and think it over. At Las Loras I was the only customer, and with the steep rutted road up I could see why. But the setting was amazing—handmade wooden tables and chairs set under a high circular thatched roof (there were no walls), and a chest-expanding view of almost the entire length of Ostional beach. I ate a whole fried fish, along with heaps of rice, beans, cabbage salad, sliced tomatoes, and tortillas, which set me back about US$3.50. The couple that ran the place and I got to talking, and I told them about my river-crossing dilemma.

What you need, said the man, is a *chapulín.*

Yes, I agreed. How sad that I don't have one.

Well, he said. Señor Rodrigues lives just about a kilometer past the river, and he has one. A really nice *chapulín.*

I took a breath. What is a *chapulín?* I asked my host.

He responded in excellent English: A tractor.

I nodded, starting to smile. No, I said again. I don't have a tractor.

No, no. Señor Rodrigues has a tractor. He can pull you across the river. He doesn't charge much, either. Maybe 1,000 or 2,000 *colones.*

And that's what happened. I found Señor Rodrigues, and rode with his son on a very big tractor back to the river. The tractor had wheels taller than a man and it took the river like it was stepping across a puddle. My rental car was hooked up and pulled across in a matter of minutes. I rode in the car and felt the current pull hard at the deepest part. Water rushed by, but it didn't make it up past the open window. People had gathered on both sides of the river, and they smiled as the grasshopper tugged the gringa's car to safety.

Owning

Due to high import tariffs, cars in Costa Rica are expensive. If you try to get around that by bringing in a car from outside, you'll confront another set of problems. You could import a car to use for the time on your tourist visa (three months plus a three-month extension) without paying high fees or tariffs, but after that time expires, things get complicated. Of course you have to first get the car here—which means driving it through five countries or shipping it by container. Shipping from Miami or New Orleans to Puerto Limón is the cheapest option, but it still might cost you close to US$1,000, and that's before you pay any of the various taxes and fees to pick it up on this end. You can also ship from the west coast of the United States or Canada to Puerto Caldera on the west coast of Costa Rica, but that's even more expensive.

If you want to make your car a Costa Rican native after the six-month grace period has expired, the process is long and costly. You'll pay from 60 to 85 percent of the car's appraised value in duties, and then there will be lots of paperwork, stamps, and miscellaneous fees. It's often easier to buy a car down here; if it's used, get it checked out by a reputable mechanic, as you would do in the United States.

Driving

Costa Rica has about 37,000 kilometers (22,990 mi.) of roads; fewer than 8,000 (4,971 mi.) of them are paved. And paved is sometimes worse than unpaved—a gravel road can be well-graded and in excellent repair, while a "paved" road may be riddled with deep holes. The U.S. State Department rates roads here, and the availability of roadside assistance, as "fair to poor." I guess that's better than "poor to abysmal," but still, you need to make some adjustments when you're driving in this country.

You must be ready for anything—trucks passing on a hill, potholes big enough to do your vehicle real damage, and cops hiding behind the next palm tree. Police here have radar guns and they love to use them. Speeding tickets can be very expensive—up to US$150 if you're really making time. Pay attention to speed limit signs, even if it seems that there's no one else on the road. Speed traps are common on the most-traveled routes to tourist areas.

Costa Rican drivers have developed a way of signaling to other drivers that there is trouble up ahead—they flash their lights at oncoming cars. Of course this can also mean, "Turn off your brights!" but if someone flashes you, slow down and be on the lookout for an accident, a damaged roadway, or a police car. If you're behind someone and they flash their lights, it can mean "The road is clear for you to pass," but be aware that what

Costa Rican drivers consider a safe distance to pass is a fraction of what most North American drivers deem necessary.

Wear your seat belt—it's the law. A selectively enforced law, but a law nonetheless.

Even as you try to drive by the book, other drivers will be throwing that same book out the window—turning across two lanes of traffic without signaling, hoisting a bottle while passing on a blind curve, or realizing that, yes, they really should have had the brakes fixed last week. If the worst happens and you have an accident, stay in your car until the police arrive. If you're out in the middle of nowhere or in the middle of a highway, this will be impractical, of course. But wait if it's possible to wait, so as not to open yourself up to liability.

Traffic enforcement in Costa Rica is the responsibility of the Transit Police *(Transitos)*, who wear light blue shirts and dark blue pants, and drive light blue cars or motorcycles equipped with blue lights. (Regular police drive dark blue cars.) Transit cops often wave vehicles to the side of the road for inspection, asking drivers for their driver's license, vehicle registration, and insurance information. Fines are not supposed to be collected on the spot, although reports of officers attempting to collect money are common. Accidents may be reported by dialing 911.

© Erin Van Rheenen

A road near the mountain town of Monteverde.

Most accidents occur at night—do what you can to avoid driving after dark. Most roads are unmarked and unlit. Fog and torrential rains can make the way even rougher.

You can drive with a valid license from your home country, as long as you have a valid passport with an up-to-date entrance stamp.

Security

Whether you're driving your own car or a rental, you'll want to seek out a secure place to park it overnight. Car theft is common, and the deductible on rental car insurance policies can be as much as US$1,500. Many hotels provide secure parking, or you could seek out one of the many freelance car or neighborhood guards and take your chances giving him a few bucks to look after your vehicle.

In looking for a place to live, it's important (if you're a car owner) to find a place with a secure garage. In my middle-class neighborhood in San José, no one leaves a car on the street overnight. Never leave anything of value in a parked car.

The Fine Art of Honking

"I just got my Costa Rican driver's license," Polo Lacoste, who did a brief stint as the ARCR president, told me when we met. "Which means I now have a license to honk."

The language of the car horn in Costa Rica is a rich one that may take years to master. Only long-term residents can tell the difference, for instance, between the "Get out of my way!" honk and the "What a pleasure to see you, my friend, on this same stretch of road where I see you every morning and evening" honk.

There's also the "Hey baby" honk, the "I'm a taxi and I'm available" honk, and perhaps most maddening, the "I'm here! Come out of your house and say hello!" honk, which can go on for a long time, especially if no one's home.

After you've been in Costa Rica for a while, you'll start to recognize even more varieties, maybe even inventing a few of your own. After all, what occasion—no matter how humble—is not enhanced by the sounding of a car's horn?

TAXIS

In the San José area, taxis are cheap and plentiful. Official taxis are red, with the taxi's ID number in a yellow triangle on the passenger-side door. Taxis should have meters (called *marías*), and drivers should use them—otherwise you'll have to haggle, which is hard to do when you don't

How to Talk to a *Taxista* (Taxi Driver)

Take me to . . .	*Lléveme a . . .*
Straight ahead	*Directo*
Stop at the corner	*Pare en la esquina*
Take a right	*A la derecha*
Take a left	*A la izquierda*
A block	*Una cuadra* or *cien metros*
Half a block	*Cincuenta metros*
North, south, east, west	*Norte, sur, este, oeste*
At the intersection	*En el cruce*
Next to	*Al lado de*
Across the street from	*Frente a*
Around the corner	*A la vuelta de la esquina*
The next street	*La proxima calle*
Are we lost?	*¿Estamos perdidos?*
Stop here	*Pare aquí*
Stop there	*Pare allí*
Wait for me	*Espéreme*
Taxi meter (in Costa Rica)	*maría*
Please use the meter	*Use la maría, por favor*
How much to take me to . . .	*Cuanto cobra por llevarme a . . .*
How much do I owe you?	*¿Cuanto le debo?*

know how much the fare should be. Currently the first kilometer costs 265 *colones* (US$.62), with additional kilometers at 155 *colones* (US$.37). A trip across town costs about US$6.

There are thousands of taxis in the San José area, and it's easy to flag one down from just about any corner, unless it's raining at rush hour. While local men tend to ride up front with the driver—perhaps to show they're just folks—foreign residents, especially single women, should probably ride in the back.

Most taxi drivers are very friendly and helpful, and will sift through your broken Spanish with a smile. They know that foreigners have different ways of thinking of addresses (like street names and house numbers), and are good about helping you figure out where you need to go. You don't need to tip the drivers, though I do if they help with bags or go out of their way for me.

Besides all the official cabs tooling around the city, there are also thousands of *piratas*, pirate cabs that may be red and even have a *maría*, but are not registered. The proof is in the ID number on the door—if a car

Montezuma bus station

doesn't have it, it's not an official cab. In outlying areas (like Escazú) *piratas* are the norm, and residents come to know the drivers who wait at the central square for fares. But if you have the option, take an official cab. Some *piratas* aren't really taxis at all, but criminals cruising for marks. Women traveling alone should be especially wary, but everyone needs to stay alert.

Cabs waiting outside hotels or discos will often try to charge you several times the normal rate. Ask before getting in if they have a *maría;* if they don't, either negotiate the fare before entering the cab, or look for another cab.

Taxis outside the greater San José area are a completely different story. They're usually high-clearance four-wheel-drive vehicles, for starters, because provincial roads are so bad. They rarely have meters, and they charge whatever the market will bear. You'll pay through the nose until you know the area and the usual fares from one point to the next. That said, the occasional taxi can be a good alternative if you're traveling around the country but don't want to rent a car. Using buses whenever possible, it won't break your budget to hire a taxi to take you where buses don't go.

Renting a Taxi and Driver

When you get serious about looking for a place to live, renting a taxi and a driver by the hour or day is a good way to explore. Especially in the

Central Valley, there are so many little towns down so many little roads that it helps to have a driver who knows his or her way around. Sure, you could rent a car—for about the same price as hiring a taxi for the day—but you'll spend most of your time trying to figure out where you are or how to open the gas tank.

Most taxi drivers will rent themselves and their vehicles out for about US$10 an hour or about US$60 a day. If you're going to need a car for several days, you can probably negotiate a lower rate. Hotels and travel agents can suggest reliable, English-speaking drivers, or ask foreign residents for their recommendations. These drivers often double as translators and cultural informants, and they might end up as friends. Buy them lunch and listen to their advice.

Housing Considerations

You have a dream, and it goes like this: You'll quit your job, buy a dirt-cheap piece of beachfront property in Costa Rica, then build a little house with your own two hands, using driftwood and palm fronds. You've got the skills—you hammered together that tree house when you were 12, and once fixed a door that wouldn't close. In a few months you'll be spending your days surfing bathtub-warm tubes, reading all the novels you've always meant to read, or just lying in a hammock, swaying in the ocean breeze.

Or maybe your dream is more industrious: you'll take over a down-at-the-heels lodge at the foot of an active volcano. Howler monkeys will hoot you awake each morning and toucans will serenade you at dusk. With hard work you'll turn the place around, adding an upscale spa, a five-star restaurant, and stables. Soon your place will be featured in *Travel & Leisure,* tourists will flock to you, and the money will roll in.

Hold on a minute. Better yet, hold on a few good months or even years. "Things take a long time to accomplish in Costa Rica," says Brenda

Burnside, a former professional boxer who now runs a health and exercise center in Nosara. "And sometimes that's a good thing." If you've done your homework—traveled the country, staying here and there a month or two and longer in the place you think you might like to call home—you'll already know that the above scenarios are about as likely as crossing a raging river in a golf cart.

You'll also know that Costa Rica has some of the most beautiful land you've ever seen, and you'll be ready to do whatever it takes to get your own private piece of it.

There are always people for whom price is no object; most of us don't belong to that select club. You *could* pay as much for property here as you would in some of the hotter U.S. markets—we're talking millions of dollars—but most people want to avoid such madness.

How do you keep costs down and still get the house of your dreams? Adaptability and patience are key. If you need to duplicate exactly how you'd live in the United States, you'll pay a high price. And if you want to live completely isolated from the rest of the country's inhabitants, you'll also pay for that dubious privilege.

But if you actually want to live in this country, rather than in an en-

Rowhouses in San José

closed bubble that could be Beverly Hills for all its diversity, you're off to a good start. And if you rent for a while in your area of choice, getting to know the ups and downs of the place, talking to people, and observing what properties are going for, you're more than halfway there. Some real estate agents say that property values have doubled in the past decade and are likely to double again soon. That may very well be true, in some areas and for some types of property. That doesn't mean you should snap up whatever's on offer. I've said it once and I'll say it again: *Be patient.* "It's easy to buy," cautions Chris Simmonds of Remax in Tamarindo, "and not so easy to sell." Which is in itself good news, as it suggests that in Costa Rica right now, it's a buyer's market.

Another piece of good news is that regardless of your nationality or immigration status, you have basically the same property rights as native Costa Ricans. This is not true in all Latin American countries—in Mexico, for instance, foreigners are not supposed to own beachfront property. Costa Rica's solid and egalitarian property rights are a big incentive to investing here.

What's Different?

In terms of buying property, building houses, and renting apartments in Costa Rica, most of the same rules apply as would apply in the United States and Canada. It takes perseverance and a certain measure of luck to find the place of your dreams. As elsewhere, location is everything: If everyone wants to live there, prices shoot up. The more you know about a place and the people in it, the better deal you're going to get. Would you bluster into a small town in the American Midwest and snap up the first house on offer, just because the price is half of what you'd pay in New York City? Of course not. You'd hang around for a while, get to know some real estate agents and residents. You'd learn that every spring the local meandering creek swells and jumps its banks; the houses nearby have mud marks to prove it. You'd learn that the owner of the best restaurant in town is desperate to sell because she wants to join her daughter in Santa Cruz. You'd hear about the new mall they're putting out on Highway 32, which will increase traffic fourfold on the single-lane road leading to what you'd thought was a pleasantly remote little plot of land.

In a new culture, where laws and customs are different and where you may not even speak the language, such investigations are doubly important. Some of the major differences you will encounter here are:

- **Real estate agents are everywhere, and none of them have to be licensed.**

There are no requirements to be a real estate agent in Costa Rica beyond hanging out a shingle and printing up business cards. Some of the bigger realty companies advertise that their agents are licensed in the United States or elsewhere. This may mean that the agents are more knowledgeable, but it's unclear what that would mean if there were a problem—after all, what sort of jurisdiction would a U.S. organization have in Costa Rica? As for those with no credentials whatsoever, some of these self-styled real estate agents (many of whom are from the United States, Canada, and Europe) do a fine job. Others are incompetent at best, and downright crooked at worst. Word of mouth may be all you'll have to go on. You have to be a private eye of sorts—asking everyone in town, not just the people you'd want to have dinner with, who they would recommend. Get as many sides to the story as possible. Realize, too, that there's a lot of competition and backbiting, especially in small towns; you may have stepped into a family feud, or one real estate agent may badmouth another so he'll get your business.

There is a fledgling national association of real estate agents, the Costa Rican Real Estate Agents Chamber (tel. 506/283-0191, fax 506/283-0347, www.camaracbr.or.cr), which is lobbying for mandatory licensing of real estate agents. Members of the organization may or may not be more trustworthy than nonmembers. As with other professionals in Costa Rica, it's best to get a personal recommendation. In Guanacaste Province, there's the Guanacaste Association of Realtors (tel. 506/670-0472, fax 506/670-0807, www.gar.or.cr); its approximately 50 members have knowledge of local beach and rural properties.

- **When they hear your accent and see your face, the price will skyrocket.**

This may seem unfair, but in the larger scheme of things it makes sense—most North Americans and Europeans who come to Costa Rica have more resources than the locals. But I'm not rich, you may protest. Not by your standards, perhaps, but by Tico standards you're probably pretty flush. Which is not to say you should pay inflated prices. But you should understand and not be personally offended by sellers trying to get as much from you as they can. Is it really any different in other markets, where they won't even look at you unless you've been pre-approved for a loan, and where real estate agents start bidding wars that send costs sky-rocketing 50 percent above the asking price? By the way, in Costa Rica buyers almost never bid over the asking price. Bidding substantially lower is much more common. *To avoid paying the gringo price, become a local.* Stick around for a while. Learn the language so you can bargain with the best of them. Or do what so many newcomers do: Get a trusted local to do your negotiating. When you scan real estate ads in the paper—*La Nación* is a good place to look, especially for Central Valley properties—often a price will be listed. This is a good starting point, and it makes it harder for the seller to double the price once they see they're dealing with an *extranjero*.

- **You'll need a lawyer for just about everything.**
"Costa Rica is the land of lines and seals," says writer and ex-Californian Richard Livett. He's talking about standing in line for every official document you need, and then having to get it stamped and often stamped again with all manner of official seals. Buying and selling property involves a great deal of paperwork, just as it does in the United States. Very few people want to wade through all that bureaucracy themselves, so they hire lawyers to do it for them. See the Buying section later in this chapter for more details.

- **Financing is a very different story in Costa Rica.**
Forget that 30-year mortgage with a 5.35 percent interest rate. Costa Rican banks don't offer such deals, and U.S. and Canadian banks aren't going to lend you money to buy a house outside of their jurisdiction. Creative financing is the name of the game here, which often means big down payments and paying the rest off in a few years. Scott Cutter of Latitude 9 Realty in Manuel Antonio outlines a typical financing situation: "Usually they'll want a 10 percent 'good faith' deposit after the first papers are signed. You'll close in 30 to 90 days, after which you'll need to come up with another 40 percent of the purchase price. Then maybe the owner will carry the remaining 50 percent for six months or a year. But don't count on it." Scott thinks that eventually financing will get easier, and will come to more closely resemble financing in the United States. "But when that happens," Scott points out, "there will be a lot more competition among buyers, because more people will be able to buy. Prices will most likely go up."

The Tico House

It's hard to talk about the average Tico house, which might be anything from a condo in the city to a wooden shack on the beach. Back in the 1800s, most Tico houses were of adobe brick, formed from a mash of mud, grass, and sugar cane waste. Roof tiles were made of soft clay formed on the workman's thigh and left to dry in the sun. Doors and window frames were of one of the many excellent tropical hardwoods found in this country. Walls were whitewashed, with a wide strip of blue at the bottom to discourage pecking chickens.

Few of these traditional houses remain, though you may see modern houses that adopt some of the traditional elements. Nowadays most Ticos live in small houses of wood or concrete block (hard to hang pictures or tack up postcards!). In the mid-90s, nine out of ten Tico households had electricity, and 93 percent had running water (half from wells, half from government aqueducts). About 30 percent of houses were connected to sewer systems, while the rest had septic tanks or outhouses.

Tico houses can be as luxurious and well equipped as any you'd find in the world, but most will have certain characteristics that may take some getting used to if you're used to North American standards. But whether you're looking to buy or rent, many of the better deals will be Tico-style houses, so it's worth seeing if you can live happily à la Tica.

• Bars, bars, and more bars.
Even in better neighborhoods, there are bars *(rajas)* on every window, and usually big iron gates protecting the front of the house and parking areas. Thankfully, you don't see much of the broken bottle-topped fences common in other Latin countries. Still, watching the sun rise each morning through barred windows takes some getting used to. David Garrett of Garrett Insurance says that all those bars don't necessarily mean you're living in a high-crime area. "It's a cultural thing," says David. "If everyone on the block has bars except you, where's a thief going to go? So in a sense having bars on your windows is keeping up with the Joneses."

• Noise.
In Tico neighborhoods and towns, expect to hear roosters crowing, kids playing, music blaring, and car horns honking. "Noise pollution" is not a known concept here, and it is culturally unthinkable to demand that your neighbor tone down his or her act. The idea is that people need to live their lives, and who are you to infringe on this right? There are upsides to this situation: I've never once been asked to "Keep it down, please!"—not even by my landlord, who lives right next door.

• No hot water.
Often the only hot water to be had in a Tico house is in the shower, and is not so much hot as *heated* water, warmed by an electric device attached

just above the shower head. Some of these devices have exposed wires bristling out and seem sure bets for causing nasty shocks or worse, but in practice they usually work well, and probably save a bundle on utility costs. Many houses, especially in the hotter areas of the country, have no hot water at all. "Hot water is for wimps!" one Guanacasteco (resident of the province of Guanacaste) told me. Washing dishes, clothes, and sometimes yourself in cold water seems strange at first; you'll soon learn that there are special soaps designed to work well in cold water. And there's nothing like a cold shower to make you, well, long for a hot one.

- **No bathtubs.**

If you want to soak in hot water, you'll have to rent a room in a hotel geared to North American tastes, or head to one of the country's many hot springs.

- **Telephones are a hot commodity.**

Consider yourself lucky if your house or apartment comes equipped with one, and get it in writing that the phone is part of the deal. Landlines are hard to come by—that's why so many people use cell phones, although the country is blanketed with dead spots. Some landlords ask for a separate phone deposit, not wanting to be left with an enormous long-distance bill (the phone line will almost always stay in the landlord's name).

- **Bare floors.**

You won't find much wall-to-wall carpeting in Tico houses. Tile floors are the norm—swept, washed, and waxed each day by the homeowner or, more likely, the maid.

- **Lawns are tiny or nonexistent.**

Especially in middle-class suburbs, front yards consist of a concrete slab where you park you car. Backyards are more often patios than wide swathes of lawn. In the country you won't have a lawn, because the field or forest will come up to your door.

- **Not "up to code."**

North Americans are used to a certain level of quality when it comes to finish work and details. In Tico homes you may marvel at a piece of baseboard or molding that stops a foot short of the corner, or an electrical outlet placed too high for all but a basketball star to reach. An expat couple in La Fortuna was perplexed to find that the light bulb on their porch would be smashed each time they opened the door. Sometimes closets are nonexistent, other times they are the size of a breadbox or, even stranger, bigger than the room itself. Even in areas with many flying insects, screened windows and doors are an anomaly. When looking at a house to buy or rent, check every detail: water pressure, outlets (do they work? are there enough of them?), windows (do they open? close? lock?), electricity, door locks, toilets, shower, pipes, etc.

Of course, if you build your own home, you can put the outlets where you want them, install North American–style hot water heaters and window screens, and lay down floors of tropical hardwoods. You can orient the house toward the best view (many Tico houses seem to look inward rather than outward). You can put in lush lawn, or landscape to your heart's content with the native trees and flowering shrubs. "You don't really have to plant things here," one gardener told me. "You just stick something in the ground, or you wait (not long) for your yard to be invaded." In short, you *can* build the house of your dreams, for considerably less than you'd have to pay up north. But it won't be dirt cheap, and it will take a lot of sweat and patience. And as I've said before, it's important to rent first, to make sure you like it here.

Renting

The best way to know if you want to live in a place is to live there, but without investing in property. North Americans are conditioned to want to own, own, own, but renting has a lot going for it. The legal period for a rental lease is three years, but as with so many other things in Costa Rica, theory and practice—what's "on the books" and what's actually done—are separated by a wide gulf. The practice here is that most leases are from six months to a year, with some landlords willing to rent month to month. Renting month to month, you could live for a few months in the expat-heavy Central Valley suburb of Escazú, then live for a while in the shadow of a highland volcano, then retreat for a season to a beachside haven on either the Caribbean or Pacific coast. (Try to strike a rental deal on the coast outside of the December–April high season; September and October are excellent times to negotiate.) After living in a few places, you'll know what sort of weather and ambience suits you.

Renting can be very economical or can strain your budget beyond the breaking point, depending on where and how you want to live. Rates in a recent issue of the English-language *Tico Times* ranged from US$203 per month for a three-bedroom apartment in San José to a whopping

Deciphering the Classifieds

The classified ads are a good place to start your search for housing. One thing to remember: if the ad's in English, the price will almost certainly be higher. So while you may find some interesting options in the back of the excellent English-language paper the *Tico Times,* you'll find cheaper options in Spanish in newspapers like *La Nación.* Here are some terms and abbreviations that you may encounter.

¢ — the symbol for *colones* (confusingly, $ is also sometimes used)
3 dor (3 dormitorios) — 3 bedrooms
2 bñs (2 baños) — 2 bathrooms
204m2 — 204 square meters
alfom (alfombrado) — carpeted
alquileras — rentals
amplia — wide, spacious
amueb (amueblado) — furnished
apartamento — apartment
bodega — storeroom, warehouse
casa — house
cerám (cerámica) — tile floor
coch 2 (coches 2) — room for 2 cars
cocin (cocina) — kitchen
comercial — business
condominio — condominium
c/tel (con telefono) — with telephone
edificio — building
exc. ubic (excelente ubicación) — excellent location
finca — farm or country estate
ganga — great deal
jardín — garden

lindo — pretty
local — office
lote — lot
lujo — luxurious
mil — 1,000 (one thousand)
millón — 1,000,000 (one million)
muy seg (muy seguro) — very secure, safe
nva (nueva) — new
parq (parqueo) — parking lot or area
peq (pequeño) — small
pisc (piscina) — swimming pool
piso — floor, as in two floors (levels)
planta baja — lower floor
playa — beach
quinta — country house
se alquila — for rent
se vende — for sale
tranquilo — peaceful
ventas — sales
vista — view
zona franca — free trade zone
zona verde — green area, perhaps a lawn

US$3,800 for a hilltop home in Escazú. In a recent issue of the Spanish-language *La Nación,* the prices were as low as US$130 a month for a two-bedroom apartment and as high as US$1,100 for a larger, more luxurious home.

The above-mentioned newspapers will be invaluable to you as you search for an apartment, especially if you want to live in the Central Valley. The *Tico Times* puts most of its classified ads online (www.ticotimes.net), so you can apartment-shop even before you arrive.

Outside of the Central Valley, make contact with local English-speaking expats and see if they know of anything available. Most people I talked to found their places by word of mouth. Also try posting on one of the many

Costa Rica–related message boards (see Contacts in Resources in the back of the book), asking if anyone knows of a place to rent in your chosen area. Home-owning expats just may be looking to rent out their place so they can make a long visit home. You can also ask at language schools, who will have lists of families willing to rent out rooms (though they will give their own students priority, of course). Keep your eye out for For Rent signs, and talk to shopkeepers in the neighborhoods you've targeted.

The mechanics of renting here are much like they are in the United States. Landlords often adapt a boilerplate lease according to their own and their tenant's needs. My first apartment (in the safe and pleasant San Francisco area of San José) cost me US$200 a month, with a US$200 deposit paid in two monthly installments. The landlord was willing to make it a month-to-month lease, as long as I gave a month's notice of my departure, and we wrote that into the lease (which was in Spanish—if you don't speak Spanish, make sure you get a translation of any document). The apartment was small (but two-storied), clean, and comfortable. It was furnished with a refrigerator, stove, and microwave, cable TV, a phone, table and chairs, a bed, and a desk. The landlord's wife even made sure I had sheets and towels! I paid the electricity and telephone bills, though they remained in the landlord's name. My monthly electric bill was about US$3, and I paid about US$25 for the telephone (unlimited Internet access was an additional US$20 per month, debited from my U.S. checking account).

From my apartment I could walk to two supermarkets, a bank, a few bakeries, and countless shops and restaurants. Three blocks away was a Centro Deportiva (Sports Center), where I ran around a track or watched kids play soccer. The bus stop was a five-minute walk from my apartment, with buses leaving for the city center every 20 minutes or so; the trip took 15 or 20 minutes and cost US$.25. Sometimes I'd splurge and take a taxi into town for about US$3.50. I thought I'd discovered my own private pocket of livability, until I realized that there were two gringo families within shouting distance of my front door. For better or worse, we gringos live in every nook and cranny of this country.

If you're renting an unfurnished apartment, remember that you will probably have to supply your own appliances. In the United States an unfurnished apartment almost always comes with a stove and a refrigerator—not so in Costa Rica. So if you're looking to rent for the short term, your best option is a furnished place. If you opt for unfurnished, it's useful to make a list of what you'll need, estimate the prices, and factor that figure into your decision-making process. Setting up a house or apartment is not cheap.

It's important to check out a potential rental thoroughly. Turn on the faucets to check water pressure, see if the water drains out, and make sure the heater attached to the showerhead actually heats up the water. Check to see if there are enough electrical outlets, check the windows and doors for functioning locks, and if there's a phone, pick it up and make sure it works. Try to imagine what you'll be doing day to day and ask questions accordingly: Where's the nearest market, bus stop, bank, running track? When is garbage picked up, and do you have to pay for that service? Can the landlord tell you anything about the neighbors or the neighborhood? Is it safe to walk around after dark? Is it easy to get a taxi?

Legally, landlords are entitled to raise the rent by 15 percent each year, but of course (if you have a one-year lease), you're also entitled to then opt out of your lease. Anecdotal evidence suggests that landlords rarely raise the rent by that much, that fast. On my suburban block alone, there were two For Rent signs and one For Sale sign. The For Rent signs lasted a month or two, and I would guess that the For Sale sign is still there. Costa Rica is struggling economically, with the devaluation of the *colón*, austerity measures intended to help the repayment of foreign debts, and modest wages. With the recent influx of foreigners, many houses and apartments were built with the intention of cashing in. Right now, though, it seems that the supply exceeds the demand.

If you're thinking of being a landlord yourself, be aware that the law tends to favor renters. Lillian Iverson, who has lived in San José for almost fifty years, says it took her four years to evict her tenants, who were "very bad people." Lillian adds that the laws have changed somewhat in the past five years, and that she was finally able to get the tenants out. A property owner in Manuel Antonio says he thinks long and hard before renting out his places. "There are no zoning laws to speak of," he says. "Tenants could start a disco in your apartment if they wanted to. They could bring in 10 family members and seven dogs, and it would still be hard to get them out. I rented to an Oklahoma Jesus freak who thought he was here to save Manuel Antonio from the devil. He decided to move on, but if he hadn't, he'd probably still be in my apartment."

SHORT-TERM RENTALS

Besides a month-to-month lease, there are other options for short-term stays. The San José area has dozens of aparthotels, some of them quite luxurious. They often cost as much (if not more) than a regular hotel, but come equipped with a kitchen and other amenities you wouldn't get in a hotel room.

But a comfortable hotel room might suit you as well as an apartment-style room. Before I found my apartment, I was thinking of staying several weeks in a midrange hotel while I looked for a longer-term place. I arrived in October, which is the low season, so many hotels were empty and quite willing to negotiate. For example, a pleasant hotel advertised at US$35 a night, close to the center of town and offering free breakfast, came down quickly to US$20 a night when I offered to pay by the week and in advance. But don't try this sort of haggling during December, January, or Easter week, when it can be hard to find a room at any price.

Another option is a homestay with a Costa Rican family. Though utilized most often by students in one of the many Spanish language study programs (and often arranged through the school), you can also arrange such a stay separate from language study (and living with a Spanish-speaking family is its own sort of language study).

Buying

You've rented an apartment or two for a while, have explored the country, and are convinced that this is the place for you. You have an idea of where you want to live, and how much you can spend. What's next? You start looking, taking it slow, secure in the knowledge that with patience and perseverance you'll be able to find (or build) the house of your dreams.

Most real estate transactions in Costa Rica are between individuals—real estate agents are a relatively new phenomenon in this country, and there is no board regulating their training or conduct. Real estate agents affiliated with local branches of multinational agencies (like Remax and Century 21) may be slightly more accountable than unaffiliated real estate agents. A good agent can help you decide where to live, but chances are he or she will show you only the more expensive offerings. You're North American, after all; you must be rich. If you decide to use a real estate agent, be very clear about your budget, and make sure you understand exactly how much you're paying for the agent's services. This will not be easy—being direct is not a Costa Rican trait, and the real estate agent may arrange different deals with different clients—whatever the market will bear. All in all I would advise that unless you have a real estate agent who comes highly recommended from a trusted source (and they do exist), going it alone will probably be your best option. See Contacts in the Resources section for general real estate contacts, and the Prime Living Locations chapters for specific real estate agents' names.

© Erin Van Rheenen

A new house in Escazú

WHERE TO LOOK

Look everywhere. In the Classifieds sections of local newspapers, on fences and trees for For Sale signs. Ask the waiter at your favorite seafood restaurant, talk with hotel owners, surfers, the woman selling fresh-squeezed orange juice on the street. As has happened in other countries, the Internet has revolutionized the real estate market in Costa Rica, allowing you to check out beachfront property as you shiver in Minneapolis. The Web is a valuable tool, but remember that mainly higher-end properties are represented there. The best deals may not even be advertised; you'll find them on the ground, talking to the owner of the *pulpería* or to other expats. One more tip: Try looking in *La Gaceta,* the government newspaper, for notice of public land auctions, especially in more remote areas. Good deals are still out there.

RESEARCHING PROPERTY

So you've found a nice little plot of land, with or without a house on it. Your first step is to check to make sure the person selling the property actually owns it, and that there are no snags such as liens, lawsuits against the property, public road restrictions, water easements, or any other type of restrictions.

The steps outlined below can be accomplished by a very resourceful and patient prospective buyer, although most people choose to hire a lawyer to take care of things. Both methods have their advantages: If you do it yourself, you'll learn a great deal about the country and its laws, and you'll be sure that you've really covered all the bases. On the other hand, and especially if you don't speak fluent Spanish, getting a trusted lawyer to help will save you much time and aggravation.

• Go to the Registro Publico.

You will find information on the property's title at the Registro Nacional (the National Registry, located in San José, and also available online at http://registronacional.go.cr). You'll need the name and ID number of the owner, along with the title number. The property section of the Registro Publico is fully computerized and indexed, and may be searched by the owner's name or ID number or the title number, but it's best to have as much information as possible. The title number assigned to each property is known as the Folio Real, and is a six-digit number followed by a dash and three additional numbers, which tell you whether the property is owned by one, two, or more people. For example, a title number of 240871-000 means there is only one owner of the property. Property held jointly by husband and wife will have a -001 suffix, and -002 would mean there are two separate (non-married) owners of the property. Condominiums will

© Erin Van Rheenen

A house for sale in the San Francisco section of San José

have F in the title number: 240891-F-000. The certificate of title will tell you everything about the property in question, from its dimensions to whether or not there are liens or encumbrances on it.

- **Get a property map.**

Ask the seller to get you the latest version of the property map. Check to make sure the measurements and boundaries on the map are consistent with the property itself (take a good long walking tour of the property to make sure). If the seller has no map, you can get one at the Catastro Nacional (National Records Office), which is the real estate section of the Registro Nacional (National Registry) in San José. If no map exists, get a registered surveyor to draw up a map, and then register it at the National Registry (www.registronacional.go.cr, tel. 506/224-6668).

- **Make sure the property isn't part of a national park or reserve.**

Search for this information at the Ministro de Recursos Naturales, Energias, y Minas (Ministry of Natural Resources, Energy, and Mines) and at the Servicio Nacional de Parques (National Park Service).

- **Confirm they're not going to build a freeway through your land.**

The Ministro de Obras Publicas and Transportes (the Ministry of Public Works) is the place to look for this information.

- **Make sure the land isn't too close to national frontiers.**

Only Costa Rican citizens can buy land within two kilometers (1.24 mi.) of international borders.

- **Look into any zoning restrictions.**

Ask at the Ministro de Salud (Health Department) and the Instituto de Vivenda y Urbanismo (Housing and Urban Development Department) to see zoning plans that may affect your property. Consult the Dirección General Forestal (Forestry Department) for any land use restrictions. Also consult your local municipality.

- **Certify that the seller has paid all past property taxes and assessments.**

- **Make sure any domestic employees you intend to retain have been paid off by the seller.**

Otherwise, you may be liable for any past monies due to them.

- **Check all utilities.**
Does the property have access to water, electricity, telephone lines, and waste disposal?

- **Check out your neighbors.**
Are they known cranks, water hogs, or drug runners? Ask around.

Tired yet? I never said it was going to be easy. And sure, there are a lot of people who either trust others to do the legwork for them, or who just slack off and forget many of the steps. You might skip some of the due diligence and be just fine. On the other hand, you might end up with a beautiful piece of land that you can't build on or even access.

TITLE TRANSFER

If everything checks out and you're ready to make the purchase, you or your real estate agent will present the buyer with a written offer and an earnest money deposit. If you and the seller agree that you want a period of time before closing, you enter into either an Opción de Compra (Option to Buy) or Promesa Reciproca de Compra-Venta (Reciprocal Promise to Buy and Sell); both documents outline the price and time frame of purchase. At closing, the formal transfer begins.

Property is transferred from buyer to seller by executing an Escritura de Traspaso, or transfer deed, before a notary public. In Costa Rica notary publics must also be lawyers, and they can do a lot more than their counterparts in the United States, having extensive powers to act on behalf of the state. The transfer deed will include details of the financing of the property.

You can buy property individually, jointly with other individuals, or in the name of a corporation (Sociedad Anónima, or S.A.). Lawyers and expats alike speak of the benefits of buying property in the name of an S.A. (more about forming an S.A. can be found in the Employment chapter). Doing so can protect the property from any liabilities the individual may incur. "Costa Rican courts in general. . . will not pierce through the corporation to get to the individual," explains Roger Peterson, author of *The Legal Guide to Costa Rica*. What this means in layperson's terms is that if you as an individual have financial problems or claims against you, property owned through an S.A. would not be affected by those problems or claims.

Another advantage of owning property through an S.A. is that if you sell the property, you may do so by selling the stock of the S.A. that owns the property, thereby decreasing closing costs. The property tax transfers won't apply, since the sale is of company stock rather than of property per se. U.S. residents are accustomed to big corporations having these sorts of protections; in Costa Rica an individual who forms an S.A. has the same sorts of rights.

If you're a married couple, another option available to you is to declare your property an Afectación Familiar, or a homestead. Such a property cannot be mortgaged or encumbered by one spouse since it belongs to both. In effect, property designated as a homestead is shielded from the creditors of either spouse; only the joint debts of the couple can be filed against the property.

PROPERTY AND MUNICIPAL TAXES

Property taxes are very low—0.025 percent of the recorded value of the property. Recorded value is often lower than actual purchase price, bringing the property tax figure even lower. Property taxes are assessed yearly (the year runs from January 1 to December 31), and are collected by the local municipal government, which also collects a general tax that covers garbage pickup, water, and sewage. The amount varies depending on where you live, but it is usually quite low.

SQUATTERS

Imagine you buy a lot in, say, Arizona, that you hope to build a vacation house on someday. While you're toiling away in California, trying to save money for just that purpose, a family sets up housekeeping on your Arizona land, plants crops, and lays legal claim to your property. Not possible, you say. And you'd be right, because in the United States, property ownership is sacrosanct. Even if you own thousands of acres, if you don't use it or even visit it, U.S. law still upholds your ownership and your right to kick intruders out.

In Costa Rica things are a little different. Early in the past century, laws were introduced to allow poor farmers to settle on land that was unoccupied or not in use, and claim it for themselves. In its usual democratic fashion, Costa Rica wanted all of its citizens to have access to land. The laws sought to prevent a few wealthy and often absentee landlords from owning most of the country, while the majority worked for them as landless laborers.

Known as *precaristas,* squatters here have certain rights. If they occupy and work "abandoned" land, in three months they start to accrue property rights, and in a year they can apply for its expropriation from the "absentee landlord." Expats who buy property in Costa Rica and visit just a few times a year need to be aware of this potential problem. It's not common, but that won't be any consolation if it happens to you.

Robert Wells, a U.S. lawyer who has helped many foreigners in conflicts with squatters, said in a *Tico Times* article that landowners should file for an eviction order within the first three months of squatters occupying their land.

"As long as you can prove they've been there for three months or less, the procedure is relatively fast and painless," said Wells. "However, if you wait, the procedure is much more long and involved."

Avoiding Squatters

Before buying property, do a thorough visual inspection to make sure squatters haven't already settled in. If the seller says there's a resident caretaker, make sure that's what he or she is. Ask to see pay stubs (a caretaker will be paid; a squatter will not).

Record the property on film, and keep records of improvements made (so you can prove the property isn't "abandoned").

If you're not going to live on the property full-time, hire a caretaker. Have a written contract with him or her, and keep up-to-date with salary and Social Security payments (so the caretaker won't become a squatter).

Make sure you or someone you trust does a full inspection of the property at least every three months. Nipping this kind of thing in the bud is the way to avoid trouble.

Building a House

HIRING AN ARCHITECT OR CIVIL ENGINEER

Applications for construction permits must be filed by a member of the Colegio Federado de Ingenieros y Architectos (www.cfia.co.cr). The application will be submitted to the Oficina Receptora de Permisos de Construcción (Construction Permit Reception Office), where it will be reviewed by a host of agencies. Housing development and commercial projects require additional permits. You will also need to apply at your local municipality for a construction permit.

The architect or civil engineer can offer various levels of design and planning assistance at various costs, and can supervise the project in a variety of ways, including:

Inspection: S/he visits the building site once a week, making sure the plans are being followed by the general contractor, checks on materials being used and verifies invoices. The architect or engineer's fee would be about 3 percent of total construction costs.

© Erin Van Rheenen

Part of a housing development near the Guanacaste coast

Supervision: S/he visits the site daily and is more involved with construction. Cost would be about 5 percent of total construction costs.

Management: S/he manages the project. Cost would be around 12 percent of total construction costs.

RESTRICTIONS ON COASTAL PROPERTY

If you've found some beachfront property that you love and can afford, congratulations! But know that there are different rules for owning and building on this type of land. The Maritime Zoning Law says that no one can *own* the first 200 meters (219 yds.) of beach frontage, at least not legally (unless you bought the land before 1977, when the law went into effect). Of those 200 meters of beach frontage, which begin at the high tide mark, you can't build on the first 50 meters (55 yds.)—it's part of the *Zona Pública* (public zone). The next 150 meters (164 yds.) inland is classified as *Zona Restringida* (Restricted Zone), which can be built on if the government chooses to grant a lease or "concession" of the property. Concessions last from five to twenty years, and can most often be renewed without a problem, says Ryan Piercy of the ARCR.

The Maritime Zoning Law also restricts ownership of concession land. The following are *not* supposed to acquire concession land:
- Foreigners who have been residents of Costa Rica for fewer than five years
- Corporations with bearer shares
- Corporations based outside of Costa Rica
- Costa Rican corporations incorporated by foreigners
- Corporations with 50 percent or more ownership by foreigners.

In practice, how strictly these rules are adhered to seems to depend on where you are (How valuable is the land? Are people clamoring to use the *Zona Publica?*), and how much influence you wield. Tellingly, approximately 300 concessions are recorded in the Registro Publico, but there are more than 15,000 hotel and tourist developments along the coast that somehow managed to bypass the law.

If you're a multinational corporation with money and lawyers to burn, you probably don't need to worry. For the rest of us, keeping a low profile and not stepping on anyone's toes seems to be the key to avoiding problems. Then again, law enforcement in Costa Rica comes in fits and starts, so it's prudent to operate on the straight and narrow.

If you're building on coastal property, besides the usual building permits, you'll need to run your plans by the Instituto Costarricense de Turismo (the Costa Rican Tourism Institute).

WARNING

I heard this advice over and over again: When you hire workers, never pay them their money up front. Give them enough to get started, but keep as much as you can in reserve. Contractors often have several jobs going at once, and it's good to give them an incentive to come back and finish your job.

COSTS

Building Costs

Costa Rica's Colegio Federado de Ingenieros y Architectos (Federation of Engineers and Architects) calculates that building a house here will cost US$210–346 per square meter (US$19–32 per square foot), though there are expats who'll tell you that you can spend a lot more—up to US$500 per square meter (about US$46 per square foot).

Building in remote areas is often more expensive, since you have to factor in delivery costs of materials.

Closing Costs

Usually the buyer and seller will split closing costs, but make sure to verify that arrangement. Below is an example of closing costs on a piece of property bought for US$100,000 but with a registered value of US$15,000. (Ryan Piercy of the ARCR estimates that most people in Costa Rica register their property at 10–30 percent of what they actually paid.)

Sale price: US$100,000
Registered value: US$15,000

A. Real estate transfer tax (1.5 percent)		US$225.00
B. Public registry fee (.5 percent)		US$75.00
C. Documentary stamps		
Municipal stamp		US$30.00
Fiscal stamp		US$30.00
Agrarian stamp		US$15.00
Bar association stamp		US$3.75
National archive stamp		US$.10
Subtotal taxes and fees		US$378.85
D. Notary fee		
1.5 percent of first million *colones*		US$43.86
1.25 percent of remaining sales price		US$1,213.45
Subtotal notary fee		US$1,257.31
Total closing costs		US$1,636.16

Real Estate Agent Costs

One of the problems with a country where anyone can be a real estate agent is that each of those middlemen can charge anything they want to on top of the purchase price. If you allow it, that is. It is imperative that you agree, in writing and up front, what the real estate agent's commission will be. There are real estate agents like Iris Maillox of Playas del Coco who were trained in North America and who follow North American guidelines—3 percent commission for the seller's agent and 3 percent for the buyer's agent. But don't count on that being the case—nail the numbers down ahead of time. Iris also cautions buyers to be aware that the more people in on the deal (the taxi driver, his brother, and their cousin the barkeep at the local watering hole), the more you'll pay on top of the purchase price, with everyone wanting their cut. Sometimes all the added commissions will double the purchase price, and the seller won't even know

Sheet metal for sale in Barrio Amón, San José

© Erin Van Rheenen

it! As for whether or not you need to use a real estate agent, I spoke to a few people who did fine dealing directly with the seller. But these were people who'd been in the country for years and who spoke fluent Spanish. Unless you are confident that you know the ins and outs of Costa Rican real estate law, and have an excellent grasp of the market, a good real estate agent can save you a load of trouble.

Prime Living
Locations

© Erin Van Rheenen

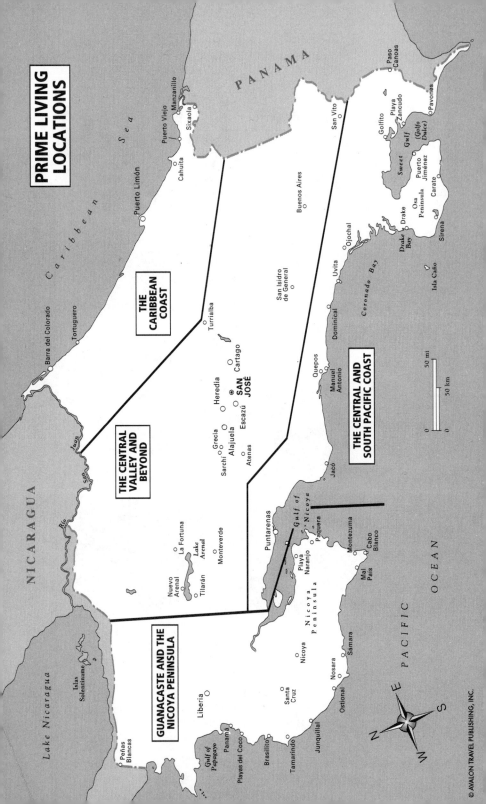

PRIME LIVING LOCATIONS

© AVALON TRAVEL PUBLISHING, INC.

Overview

The chapters in this section describe the characteristics and appeal of the different regions of Costa Rica, also outlined in brief below. The areas profiled are by no means the only desirable ones, but they are places where a number of expatriates have decided to make their homes. For such a small country, Costa Rica has an astonishingly varied terrain. Guanacaste in late April (the end of the Costa Rican summer) will be hot and dry, its fields and rolling hills blanketed in deep yellows and browns. Just a few hours away, mountain towns like Monteverde—or La Fortuna, in the shadow of Arenal Volcano—are still wet and green. Puerto Viejo, on the Caribbean coast, will be its usual humid and rainy self, while the weather near peaks south of the Central Valley will be downright frosty.

Deciding where to live is a very personal exercise, a process of self-discovery and of getting to know your adopted country. You may love to vacation at the beach, for instance, but find that after two months there you're bored stiff. You may think you want to be far from other expats, but then realize how much you need an occasional dose of your own kind. Or the opposite may occur—you begin in an expat-heavy area and then, as your Spanish gets better and you feel more at home in the culture, decide you want to move farther afield, into a more truly Costa Rican environment. As I suggest elsewhere in this book, the best approach is to rent houses or apartments in a variety of locales, seeing which place suits you best, before settling in.

It's worth thinking for a moment about the privileged position of being able to *choose* where you want to live. Most movement from country to country, from region to region, is spurred by war, political strife, natural disaster, or economic hardship. You are probably not thinking of relocating to Costa Rica for any of these reasons, so relax and know that you have time to find the right place to begin your new life. And as you review the basics, like real estate prices and climate, also ask yourself how you might contribute to the towns that make it on to your shortlist. What will you do there; who will you *be* there? The owner of a thriving business that employs a dozen locals? The founder of the new town library? Or the

Range of Motion

What it takes to make it in Costa Rica is not unlike what it takes to make it in any new environment—those who've been through the experience agree that flexibility is key. But you may not even know how inflexible you are until you try to do the cultural equivalent of touching your toes (let's not even talk about the backbends and headstands you'll be called on to perform as you adapt to your new world). In our everyday life, within our own familiar culture, we often stay within fairly narrow confines, from the route we take to work to the emotions we allow ourselves to feel. Our range of motion, both physical and otherwise, is quite limited. As we age, this becomes even more pronounced, as bodies stiffen and thoughts and feelings travel along familiar paths.

But one can consciously fight against this closing in by exercising the body and mind to increase all forms of "range of motion." And if deliberately stretching your boundaries while in your own culture is good exercise, moving to a new country and adapting to a new culture is an extreme sport. You need to train for it—to read up on the culture, to prepare yourself mentally for a period of upheaval, even to physically build up a resistance to all the new microbes that will invade your system.

Adapting to a new culture is not easy but the rewards are immense. Increased flexibility and range of movement means you move through the world with more grace and pleasure. You will look back on your old life, your old frame of reference, and it will look small.

sour-faced gringo on the hill who complains about the roads and starts drinking before breakfast? Such considerations are not solely altruistic—it's well-known that to successfully relocate, a person must forge new roles and new relationships. You'll be a happier camper if you not only make friends with the locals (both Tico and expat), but also if you become an integral and valuable part of your adopted community.

Over- and Underdevelopment

A caveat: When you hear that a beach town in Costa Rica is "overdeveloped," take that designation with a grain of salt. It's all relative, and what for some might seem touristy will for others seem enchantingly rough around the edges.

Take Guanacaste's Playas del Coco area, for example, which includes Playas Ocotal, Hermosa, and Panama, as well as a few inland towns. In the entire area there are 10,000 people—about the number of people who turn out to see a midsize college basketball game in the United States. Real estate developers, of course, would like to see the area explode with new business and new residents. Playas del Coco is by far the most developed town in the area, and it consists of one strip that leads to the beach and is lined with funky outdoor bars and restaurants, low-rise hotels, and the odd Internet café or souvenir shop. If you want to take an after-dinner stroll, walk slowly, because in five minutes you'll run out of road.

Or consider Jacó, on the central Pacific coast. People warned me that it was touristy and tacky. And while the town has its problems, like increasing drug use and prostitution, it's another one-strip wonder with a very laid-back vibe and a fair measure of charm. Tourists and locals move about like they're underwater, and there's no high-rise buildings in sight. There's a great new sushi restaurant that has its other branch in Huntington Beach, California, but if that means the town is spoiled, then bring on the *futomaki*.

And whether you're in these "tourist traps" on a Saturday or a Tuesday makes a world of difference. One Monday in mid-December (the start of the high season), I shared the long expanse of Jacó Beach (one of the most visited beaches in the country) with a crowd of around six or seven people. (This does not apply to Christmastime or Easter week, when popular beach towns are mobbed by foreign tourists and vacationing Tico families.)

Of greater concern is the *under*development of so many beach towns. Places whose popularity has skyrocketed in the past decade often cannot keep pace with the basic needs of visitors, not to mention residents. We're talking woefully inadequate roads, water, electricity, phone lines, garbage pickup, and sewage treatment.

But many towns are rising to the occasion, forming residents' associations to figure out what the community needs and then lobby for it, either asking the national and local governments for help or getting locals to pitch in and do it themselves. Whether it's Danish students organizing beach cleanups in Playas del Coco or hotel and restaurant owners in Tamarindo commissioning a sustainable growth plan, it's often foreign residents who spearhead such efforts. Which is only fair—it's the influx of foreigners who overtax the system and who often hope to make a living off that same influx. It makes sense that they should give something back to their adopted communities.

Not that Costa Ricans aren't deeply involved in improving their own communities. Take the recent example of a bus driver in Ciudad Neilly (not far from the Panama border), fed up with the rutted roads and how long it was taking MOPT (the agency in charge of the highway system) to fix them. He loaded his pickup with cement and sand, and spent his days off filling potholes on a 28-kilometer (17.4-mi.) stretch of road that was especially damaged. No one paid him; he just decided to take the initiative and improve the road he had to use every day. The government's slow response to community needs has had the side effect of forcing people to be more self-sufficient. This is also why, perhaps, people who live outside the Central Valley (where all the best services are concentrated) feel more identified with their town or area than with Costa Rica as a whole.

THE CENTRAL VALLEY AND BEYOND

Seventy percent of Costa Rica's population lives in the beautiful and fertile basin called the Valle Central. At the heart of this highland plain (1,150 meters/3,773 feet) lies the capital city of San José, the nation's undisputed political, economic, and cultural center. Here is where you'll find the museums, the theaters, the government buildings, and the University of Costa Rica, the country's largest and most important institution of higher learning. Costa Ricans from outlying areas are drawn to San José for better job opportunities, and many expats are sent here to work at branches of multinational corporations.

Temperate weather is one of the area's main draws. For those who don't do well with heat or humidity, the Central Valley's mild and dry climate is a godsend. It never gets very cold or very hot here—temperatures average in the mid-20s Celsius/mid-70s Fahrenheit.

Some of the most popular expat areas around San José include Escazú, where the American ambassador makes his home; nearby Santa Ana, with its lovely old stone church and upscale restaurants; Alajuela, a reasonably priced town near the international airport; and Heredia, larger and more congested but still worth a look. Further afield you'll find Grecia, 30 minutes from San José but a world apart—it was voted "cleanest town in Latin America" and boasts an interesting sheet-metal church in its quiet main plaza; Cartago, the original capital of the country and home to Costa Rica's most stunning church; and Sarchí, a center for arts and crafts.

North of the Central Valley and over the mountains of the Cordillera Central lies the highland plain of San Carlos, home to Arenal Volcano and a series of pristine villages such as Zarcero, centered around a topiary-filled town square and part of an area cool and misty enough to grow lettuce and strawberries. Northwest of San José are the mountain towns of Santa Elena and Monteverde, the latter founded by Alabama Quakers in the 1950s and now an interesting mix of long-term expats and native Costa Ricans, many of whom have intermarried and speak both Spanish and English at home.

South of the Central Valley is the Valle de la General, an oft-overlooked zone that includes the pleasant inland towns of San Isidro de General, Buenos Aires, and San Vito, settled by Italian homesteaders and now the center of one of Costa Rica's most fertile coffee-producing areas.

GUANACASTE AND THE NICOYA PENINSULA
With Guanacaste's dependable dry season (December–April) and seemingly endless supply of beaches, it is the preferred choice for lovers of sand and surf who want to escape the rain and snow back home.

Most of the beaches are on the Nicoya Peninsula, which is 150 kilometers (93 mi.) long, averages 50 kilometers (31 mi.) wide, and lies almost entirely within the province of Guanacaste (the southernmost tip, where you'll find offbeat Montezuma and the surfer haven of Malpaís, is part of Puntarenas Province). But provincial boundaries don't mean much here; the Nicoya Peninsula is all of a piece, with most of the fun to be found along the coast, and the practical stuff—banks, supermarkets, etc.—available in a series of inland towns strung along Highway 21.

Driving Guanacaste's potholed back roads (almost all the area's roads qualify as back roads), you'll see barbed wire looped around gnarled and crooked tree trunks, improvised fences that keep the pale, hump-backed Brahmin cattle from wandering off. In the dry season, trees blaze with bright yellow and orange blossoms made even more dramatic because they grace bare branches, before the trees leaf out. The evergreen Guanacaste tree has a full, spreading, often perfectly symmetrical crown

Expat Profile: Bill Linnemeier

In 2002, Bill Linnemeier moved from California to La Fortuna, a little town in the shadow of Arenal Volcano. He'd been a merchant marine for 20 years and was finally ready to settle down. "It was either here or New Zealand," he says. "But they've got a tough immigration policy there; you kind of have to buy your way in. If you're a millionaire and want to retire someplace nice, get a little ranch in the suburbs of Christchurch. The average guy, forget it."

He came instead to Costa Rica, where he'd been coming for years, and he isn't sorry he passed on New Zealand. Bill loves everything about Costa Rica: the people, the climate, even the economy. "As a merchant seaman, you spend a lot of time in third-world countries, and they all have the same problems: the kids are underfed, the health system is non-

existent, the infrastructure is minimal at best—all the money goes toward the military, toward wars. Banana republics change their dictators every few years whether they need to or not. But Costa Rica has a long-standing tradition of democracy, of sorts. The kids are well educated and well fed. The medical system works. The backbone of the country is solid."

Not only did Bill want to live here; he also wanted to do business. "I sat here for a month and a half, studying their economy. The restrictions placed on you as a non-Tico are considerable; it's hard to try to figure out how to make a living. You have to find a niche that isn't being filled by anybody else. Fly below the radar, don't offend anyone, and they'll let you do what you're doing."

So what's Bill doing? Baking bread. And cinnamon rolls. And focaccia.

"I looked at the economy, and I found a niche. I'd been baking bread in the States, mainly as a hobby. Good bread, bread that would sell for three or four dollars a loaf in San Francisco. They didn't have anything like that here. They had a farmers market once a week, and a lady from a nearby town would sell bread on Fridays. People bought a lot of it. It's the niche I found to step into. The only competition in town was Tico air bread—Musmanni [a national bakery chain]. They sell these long slender tubes of air, and call it bread.

"I converted a storeroom into a bakery. Had to pass Ministry of Health Inspection—you need a sanitary certificate. Got US$2,000 seed money. Spent US$1,000 on an oven that will make 30 loaves at a time—it's a commercial pizza oven. By the way, interest rates are usurious here, anywhere from 25 to 35 percent per annum. Short-term notes can carry up to 10 percent per *month*. If you're going to do business in this country, and you need cash, get the money from the States."

So Bill had his oven, but he needed to fine-tune his product to the market, the market that bought up all that air bread. He didn't think he'd be able to sell a pure German or sourdough bread, so he made a lighter version of the two. At first he'd go door-to-door every day with a gym bag, selling six loaves at a time. "I went to every house in town for three and a half months," Bill recalls. "I know everybody. Every housewife. All the dogs."

And they all loved Bill's bread, or as it's known locally, Willie's *Pan* (Spanish for bread). In La Fortuna, Bill is Willie and his wife, writer Joy Rothke, is Mrs. Willie Pan.

Bill stepped up production to 30 loaves a day: 15 white, 15 wheat. It was hard to lug all that bread around in a gym bag, so he invested in a three-wheeled bike with a big tray in the front like the ones they use to deliver groceries here. He remembers the routine. "It would take me four and a half or five hours to make the bread, I'd hit the streets in the morning, then sell it until about 2:30 in the afternoon. I'd come back and prep for the next day, eat, do laundry, go to bed around 6:30 P.M., then get up again at 2:30 A.M. to do it all over again. Day in, day out. Charged 350 *colones* for 750 grams (1.6 lbs.). Cost about 150 *colones* to make. Sold it as fast as I could make it. Everybody was asking for other products, so I started with the cinnamon rolls, some empanadas, and the focaccia."

Bill knew everyone and everyone started to know him. "Everywhere I'd ride my tricycle, people would say, Crazy gringo! But they'd recognize me and my product. Brand recognition—people pay gazillions of dollars to firms on Madison Avenue to get what I had just by pedaling around yelling *Pan, pan, Willie's pan.*"

So now that he's known and his bread is in demand, what's next? He wants to garage the trike and rent a place in the center of town, so people will come to him. "And I'm not going to be making the stuff anymore. I'll train someone to do it."

© Erin Van Rheenen

House on Playa Hermosa, Guanacaste

that provides welcome shade during hot afternoons. The tree's long dark pods curl like ears, which is why the original inhabitants of the area called it *quauhnacaztli,* from the Nahuatl words *quauitl,* for tree, and *nacaztli,* for ear.

As you move toward the Pacific you'll catch glimpses of the sea through branches or across scrubby fields. Arrival at the westernmost edge of the country is an inspiring experience, and Guanacaste's beaches seduce even non–beach lovers. From white-sand Playa Hermosa up north to rocky Cabo Blanco down south, there's something for everyone. Most expats in Guanacaste live (or try to live) off the tourist trade, running hotels, restaurants, Internet cafés, or real estate offices. Land prices around the most popular resorts are high, but then again, there's an entire coastline to be discovered—you needn't limit yourself to developed area such as Tamarindo and Playas del Coco. Long-term expats warn of a lack of health care facilities and a dearth of culture—most go to San José for more serious medical problems and might drive hours just to see a movie. Still, most agree they wouldn't have it any other way—they didn't move to the beach for state-of-the-art medical care or to be able to see the new James Bond movie the day it debuts in New York.

THE CENTRAL AND SOUTH PACIFIC COAST

The grouping together of the central and south Pacific coasts makes sense geographically, but the two areas couldn't be more different in terms of ambience and density of settlement. The central Pacific coast, located between the Nicoya Peninsula to the north and the Osa Peninsula to the south, is one of the most visited and most developed parts of the country. It is anchored by the resort towns of Jacó and Quepos/Manuel Antonio, the first famous for surfing (international contests are held on Jacó's long, palm-shaded beach); the second a sportfishing mecca and home to Manuel Antonio National Park, where sloths and monkeys hang out in trees that border some of the country's prettiest white-sand beaches.

As in most areas outside of the Central Valley, expats who come to this area (and need to make a living) tend to work in the tourist trade. In fact, the majority of hotels and restaurants in Jacó and Manuel Antonio are owned and operated by non-Ticos. Industries not based on tourism include vast plantations of oil-producing African palms, which line the road from Jacó to Quepos, extending inland and often planted where bananas used to grow before that industry was destroyed by blight in the 1950s.

The central Pacific coast has a wet season and a dry season (May–November, and December–April, respectively), but this area's dry season is not nearly as dry as that of Guanacaste, where virtually no rain falls. The further south you go, the wetter it becomes. Temperatures hover around 30°C/86°F in the dry season, a little lower in the wet season.

Traveling south along the coast road from Quepos, you won't see much for about 40 kilometers (24.9 mi.), at which point you'll hit Matapalo, a tiny beachside settlement gaining ground as a place foreigners like to hide themselves away. A little further along is the bigger town (all of a few hundred people) of Dominical, known for its surfing and, even more than Matapalo, increasingly popular with foreigners looking to buy property on the coast but away from big resorts. Even further south, Uvita and Punta Dominical also have their share of foreign-owned property, but settlement is sparser and services fewer and further between.

The southern Pacific coast is dominated by the hook-shaped Osa Peninsula and the vast, tranquil Golfo Dulce (Sweet Gulf), which borders the Osa's eastern shore. Termed Costa Rica's Amazon, this area is wetter, hotter, and more lushly verdant than the central coast. It's also wilder— less populated and less developed. Up until the early 1980s, the area had a lawless, Wild West feel, with gold prospectors making and losing fortunes daily. Old-timers say everyone carried a gun and prostitutes were paid in gold nuggets. The Osa Peninsula's Corcovado National Park was formed partly in response to mining that was destroying the country's biggest and best example of coastal rain forest. Now the park—almost 42,000 hectares (103,784 acres)—protects 139 species of mammals and 400 species of birds, including the brilliantly plumed scarlet macaw.

Bigger towns in the area include Puerto Jimenez (where a good number of expats have settled) and Golfito, a port that was United Fruit's company town until the banana producer pulled out in 1985 after a series of labor strikes. Golfito today is most famous for the Deposito Libre, a duty-free shopping compound where Ticos can buy appliances and other goods without paying the duties that can tack 50 percent onto purchase prices.

The southern Pacific coast is also known for excellent surf spots, including Pavones, home to what some call the longest wave in the world.

THE CARIBBEAN COAST
In a country where each new province seems a world apart, the Caribbean coast of Costa Rica might just qualify as another universe. Nearly all of the country's blacks, most of its Chinese, and a good part of its indigenous population can be found in the *Zona Caribe,* as it's known in Spanish. Though these minorities make up only a few percentage points of the total national population (Afro-Caribbeans and indigenous peoples with about 2 percent each, and the Chinese population weighing in at barely .25 percent), the fact that most live in the sparsely populated Caribbean province of Limón means that this area is the most ethnically diverse in the country.

The Caribbean coast is where the colonizing Spaniards first arrived, but it is the Jamaicans, more recent arrivals, who have had perhaps the biggest impact. They (along with people from other Caribbean islands, and a number of Chinese) migrated here in the late 19th century to work on the railroad and in the banana fields, and their culture now dominates the area. What this means is that reggae overtakes salsa, spicy island-inspired concoctions offer welcome relief from bland *casados,* and a lilting Caribbean English is heard as often as Spanish.

Puerto Limón (often simply called Limón, which is also the name of the entire province) is the biggest city in the area, a bustling port that has more economic than aesthetic appeal. North of Puerto Limón, swamps and rivers dominate the area. Waterways are the zone's roads, and boats outnumber cars. In the little town of Tortuguero, at the entrance to the famed Tortuguero National Park, there are no roads. Sand paths connect the wood-frame houses built on stilts to guard against flooding, and almost everyone has a dock and a boat or two in their front yard. South of Limón there is one decent coastal road linking the beach

House on the Tortuguero River

towns of Cahuita, Puerto Viejo, and Manzanillo, where most expats tend to settle. Inland, the heavily forested Talamanca mountains are home to several large indigenous reserves, among them the BriBrí and the Talamanca.

It rains more here than in other parts of the country, and the humidity is higher. The beaches south of Limón look like a South Seas fantasy, the water tending toward turquoise when the seas are calm, coconut palms arcing out over coral-protected coves. Limón also looks more like your stereotypical third-world country than other parts of Costa Rica—it's the poorest province, and you won't see upscale shopping malls or luxurious resorts here. What you will see are charming ramshackle villages, wildlife-rich jungles, and beautiful beaches. Fans of the area say they wouldn't trade their little piece of Limón, with its rain and its rough edges, for a dozen more developed beach towns on Costa Rica's Pacific coast. "Life is a little harder here," one expat told me, "but it's also more rewarding, somehow. It's a real place."

PRICES

The areas most popular with expats and well-to-do Ticos will be the most expensive, both for renting and buying. In some areas, like the San José suburb of Escazú or the Pacific coast town of Tamarindo, prices can rival those at home, with one-bedroom condos going for US$250,000 (US$1,200/month in rent), and beachfront or mountaintop spreads fetching US$1 million (these places tend to rent by the *week,* always a bad sign if you're looking for a bargain).

At the other end of the spectrum, you hear tales of mind-boggling bargains: US$10,000 for four hectares (ten acres), a starfruit orchard, a waterfall, and a little house thrown in to sweeten the deal. As elsewhere in the world, it's a matter of supply and demand, and of location. Those amazing deals are most often way out past who knows where—you may have to build your own road or lay your own water line. But if you're looking to really get away from it all, you could live like a king on a workingman's budget.

Most people will be interested in the middle ground—nice places in nice areas, with neighbors within walking distance. It all comes down to how you define "nice." For some it means a four-bedroom, four-bath house with a pool, maid's quarters, a slope planted with mature fruit trees, and a view of the entire Central Valley. That kind of place will run US$300,000 and up in the coveted areas, but might cost as little as US$150,000 in a not-so-fashionable but equally pretty location. If you're renting, the luxury places could run you thousands of dollars a month, but there are a great many pleasant two- and three-bedroom houses in the Central Valley area that go for under US$500—check the *Tico Times*'s online classified ads for a small taste of what's available (www.ticotimes.net). There seem to be quite a few expats who bought houses—as vacation homes or investments—and are anxious to rent them out, especially to expats, who tend to have more money than locals. Sometimes these homes are furnished, and have been built or renovated to more closely resemble North American houses—with hot water throughout instead of just in the shower, for example.

Outside of the Central Valley (and excluding the hottest beach towns), prices tend to be lower. There are countless towns, nestled on the slopes of a volcano, or down a sandy track on a hidden peninsula, where you can find your own little piece of paradise for under US$100,000 and often considerably less. If you find something you like, don't rush. Settle in to that area—maybe in an economical hotel or a short-term rental apartment—and look around. Visit the real estate agents in the area, talk to hotel owners and with expats you see in cafés. Walk the streets in the early morning and at night. See how long it takes to get to the next town, and what is available there. In short, do your homework, and don't be swayed by people urging you to buy right here, right now! There are no shortcuts to finding the right place at the right price. And in the end, the right place is more important than the right price. Just because something's a bargain doesn't mean you'll be happy there. Choose where you want to be first, then look for a good apartment to rent, a house to buy, or a lot to build on.

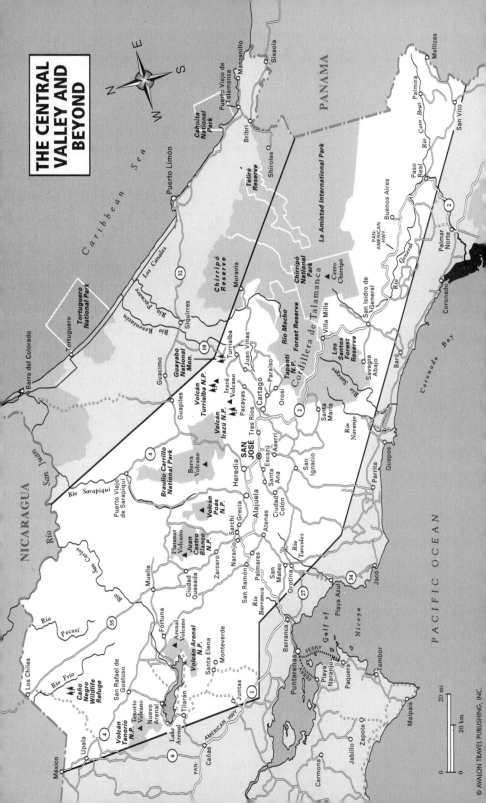

© Erin Van Rheenen

The Central Valley and Beyond

The Lay of the Land

It's upon returning from the humid Caribbean or the dry Pacific coast that you really start to appreciate the charms of the Central Valley, where the great majority of both Costa Ricans and expats choose to make their home. The *Tico Times* estimates that 100,000 foreigners live in this area—half of them English speakers—and it's not hard to see why. Drive up from Guanacaste in the summer and you'll go from flat expanses of dry grass to a rolling panoply of every shade of green. Stands of trees alternate with deep-green patches of coffee growing up the hillside. The variety of plant life here is astounding; you'll see pine trees next to palms, and bright yellow daisies at the foot of enormous stands of bamboo. Bougainvillea, hibiscus, and roses—yes, roses—add dashes of red, and stately trees burst with fiery orange and yellow blossoms.

But the big story is green, and to see the morning light illuminate the most delicate yellow-green all the way to the deepest emerald is to know that you're in one of the most fertile areas of a fertile country, rich in volcanic soil and irrigated by rivers, streams, and the rain that comes down in brief afternoon downpours during the green season.

The scenic beauty of the place owes much to the dramatic juxtaposition of imposing peaks and gentle valleys. To the north, the Central Valley is encircled by the soaring Cordillera Central, with its chain of volcanoes including the active cones of Poás and Irazú. The Cordillera Talamanca forms the area's southern perimeter. Measuring 80 kilometers (49.7 mi.) east to west and 40 kilometers (24.8 mi.) north to south, the plateau is actually two separate valleys, split by the Cerros de la Carpintera, which mark the continental divide. The Río Virilla drains the valley to the west, and the Río Reventazón—well-known in rafting circles—plummets down the eastern slopes of the Cordillera Central.

Elevations within the Central Valley range from 900 to 1,787 meters (2,953 to 5,863 ft.), with weather at lower elevations suggesting perpetual summer. Ascending the volcanic peaks that ring the valley, the air becomes

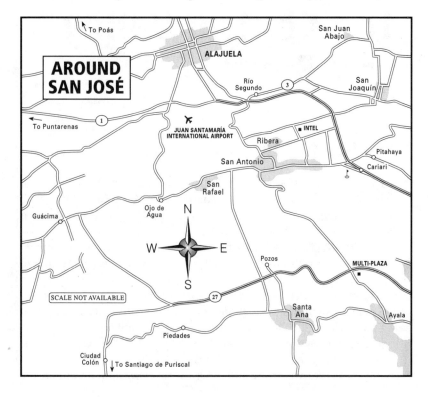

a little cooler. Temperatures in the heart of the valley are mild year-round, averaging around 21°C (70°F). Moisture levels also weigh in at a happy medium. If you've been to a humid area, you'll find the drier air here a great relief, and if you've been in dry heat, your skin will drink greedily of the increased moisture in the air.

San José

It's not just the climate that draws people to this area. Everything is here, much of it in and around the capital city of San José—jobs, government offices, the best public hospitals and private clinics, shopping malls, restaurants, and theaters. Bill White, who in the early 1990s founded an artist's colony in Ciudad Colón, says that when he arrived he drew a circle around the national theater in downtown San José, and only looked at property within a half-hour drive of the ornate building that hosts the national symphony. For a smallish city (about 350,000 inhabitants, with

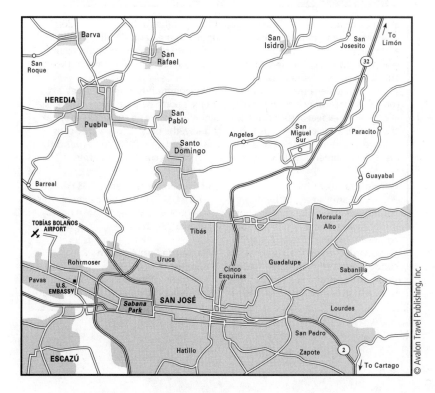

Gated Communities Around San José

© Erin Van Rheenen

Called *residenciales* in Spanish, gated communities of houses or condominiums are growing more and more popular in the Central Valley. Both Ticos and resident foreigners appreciate the instant community and the security, which means you can leave your place vacant while you're away and not worry about break-ins or squatters.

The downside is that you must abide by community rules, and pay extra condo and/or security fees on top of your home's purchase price. Some people dislike the artificial feel of such planned communities (there no corner stores or bakeries in these "neighborhoods"), but for many, the pros outweigh the cons.

Once you're in Costa Rica, a real estate agent can show you around the many developments. Below is a sampling of what's currently on offer.

Condos Palmeto 801

Pozos de Santa Ana, just behind the Forum, a deluxe office complex housing branches of many multinational corporations, like Procter & Gamble. This guarded *residencial* comprises 24 condos, most with three bedrooms, three baths, and a two-car carport. Common areas include four saunas and a pool. Prices start at US$138,000, with a US$15,000 down payment. The bilingual Blue Valley School is nearby. tel. 506/282-9274

Hacienda San Agustín

Heredia
A large development with 750 houses. A two-bedroom home will cost about

US$50,000. With a down payment of 14 to 17 percent, the monthly mortgage would be US$400 to US$500. tel. 506/260-6810

Los Reyes
La Guacima de Alajuela, off the highway that goes past Santa Ana

If you can't live without a polo field nearby, Los Reyes is for you. Purchase of a house, condo, or lot to build includes membership in the development's country club, along with use of the golf course, tennis courts, pools, and polo field. Sample price: 1,500-square-meter (.37 acres) lot, 320-square-meter (3,444-sq.-ft.) house (four bedrooms, two-car garage): US$295,000. A local real estate agent estimates that 60 to 70 percent of the families here are Costa Rican, with the remainder being resident foreigners.
tel. 506/438-0858
fax 506/438-0005
info@losreyescr.com
www.losreyescr.com

Residencial Milenio
San Joaquín, Heredia

One- and two-story houses priced from US$45,000 on up. It advertises "hot water in the entire house," cable TV, and easy access to nearby private schools.
tel. 506/250-3740 or 506/372-4531

Residencial Sol del Este
Sabanilla, on the road to Tres Ríos

This mountainside development will eventually boast 140 houses on its six hectares (14.8 acres) of land. House models range from a cozy 70 square meters (753 sq. ft.) to an ample 200 square meters (2,153 sq. ft). Lots go for less than US$90 per square meter.
tel. 506/273-0707

VillaCondo Torre Sol
San Joaquín de Flores

Nine two-story homes with great mountain views. Electric gates enhance security; there's also a pool. Prices start at US$135,000, with a down payment of US$20,000.
tel. 506/392-6575

Villas Luisiana
San Joaquín de Flores

Of the 40 houses in this quiet *residencial,* half had been sold by mid-2003. Houses start at US$86,500; the average lot is about 250 square meters (.06 acres).
tel. 506/254-7543
www.fomentourbano.co.cr

ON THE COAST
Gated communities are also popular on the Pacific coast, where condos or houses offered for sale or rent are on the grounds of large tourist developments that also include hotels, golf courses, and other resort amenities. See the Guanacaste and the Nicoya Peninsula and the Central and South Pacific Coast chapters for more details.

San José skyline

closer to a million people if you include the urban sprawl that extends into other counties), San José has a lot to offer. On any given night you can choose from a dozen plays (some in English), opera, dance performances, classical and popular music, and dozens of movie screens on which you'll find some of the latest films, often premiering just a few days after their U.S. release.

While San José isn't known for its 24-hour antics, the city has a pleasant buzz. That it's the literal center of the country adds to the draw; all roads lead to San José, and residents of outlying areas come here to find what can't be found in the hinterlands. They may come for a better selection of building supplies, a hip new pair of shoes, or just to stroll down the Avenida Central, a bustling pedestrian mall great for window shopping and people-watching. At the far end of Avenida Central is the Central Market, a jumble of stalls and smells where you'll find no Tommy Hilfiger (unless it's a knock-off), but plenty of fresh fruit, dried bunches of medicinal herbs, and whole pigs on hooks. This is the real thing, and even politicians know it. On the TV news, President Abel Pacheco was shown slurping *sopa negra* (black bean soup) at one of the market's bare-bones *sodas*. Wiping soup off his chin, he told reporters he was a humble man, a man still true to his working-class roots.

People love to complain about San José—the traffic, the crime, and all those KFC franchises—but I find it an agreeable and fairly safe city. The excellent and very cheap public transportation puts my hometown of San Francisco to shame; you can find pretty much anything you need, from showerheads to CDs, and there are lots of opportunities to soak up culture or make some of your own. English-speaking activities are plentiful—from theater clubs to self-help groups. As for safety, you'll want to take the same kinds of precautions you would take in a similar-sized U.S. city. Violent crime is much, much rarer here than in the United States, but petty theft is common. Awareness is the key, and the more people flowing around you, the sharper you'll want to be. I probably don't need to tell you that you shouldn't take your wallet out in the middle of the Central Market and count just how many *colones* you have left. Any sort of flash is ill advised—keep your new digital camera under wraps, and leave your grandmother's sapphire pendant in the safe-deposit box. Thieves will choose another target if you look like you know where you're going. Of course, you'll have to be a good actor to pull this off; with the utter lack of street signs in San José, it's unlikely that you'll even know where you are.

Those expecting a historic jewel of a city will be disappointed. It's the rare building that is more than 100 years old, and San José boasts its fair share of remarkably ugly modern edifices. Still, the city grows on you. You find your own favorite attractions, from the guy selling fresh orange and carrot juice on the corner near the bus stop, to the shady out-of-the way park at the foot of the city's only all-metal (and all-yellow) building. It's a city of neighborhoods, and if you walk just ten or fifteen minutes from the jam-packed downtown, you'll hit quiet, spacious, often upscale neighborhoods in every direction.

LOS YOSES AND SAN PEDRO

East of downtown, you'll find Los Yoses and San Pedro, residential neighborhoods built around cores of bustling commercial activity. Houses here range from middle-class modern to gracious old estates tucked behind lovely gardens. Los Yoses has a quiet energy during the day. Several government buildings are located on the neighborhood's western edge, and nearby restaurants serve lunch to suit-and-tied civil servants and matrons taking a break from shopping. At night, the area all but shuts down.

San Pedro is livelier, by day but especially by night. The presence of the University of Costa Rica, with its student body of 30,000, guarantees an abundance of bars, clubs, cheap restaurants, and funky clothing stores. When school's in session the streets around campus bustle with activity, with small businesses catering to student needs—copy shops, pizza-by-the-slice joints, and kiosks selling pens, notebooks, and single cigarettes. At night people come from all over the city to hang out at the bars, restaurants, and clubs. Live music of all kinds is easy to come by, including jazz at El Rincon de Jazz or the Jazz Café.

San Pedro was once its own town; the village church and square (just a few blocks from the university) now stand across from the up-to-the-minute Outlet Mall. Despite its name, the mall offers no cut-rate bargains but boasts four floors of clothing boutiques, music and electronics stores, multiple movie screens, and plenty of mall food.

Foreign residents who live in these areas like that they are integrated into the life of the city, but also have a quiet place to close the door and regroup. In Los Yoses, the North American Cultural Center organizes conferences, film series, art exhibits, and theater. Even if you don't want to enroll as a full-time student, the University of Costa Rica is a great place to study Spanish or brush up on your art history.

ROHRMOSER AND LA SABANA

West of downtown, the streets gets wider and green areas start to crop up with more regularity. Though not usually thought of in recreational terms, the large General Cemetery does provide a break from the surrounding hubbub, with marble mausoleums and special sections for *obreros* and *israelitas* (workers and Jews). Down the street and quite a bit livelier is La Sabana, San José's largest park, which used to be the national airport and now is one of the few places in town where you can jog without having to fight traffic. You can also play basketball, volleyball, or tennis; swim in an Olympic-sized pool; or take one of the free aerobics classes offered on weekends. On the park's northwest corner is the National Stadium; on the southeast corner is the National Gymnasium.

The park is a big draw for people who like to be in the city but within walking distance of a little piece of the country. Add to that many good restaurants and cafés, upscale strip malls, and proximity to downtown, and you've got a very desirable area.

The best known of the neighborhoods around La Sabana is Rohrmoser, northwest of the park and home to many upper- and upper-middle-class Tico families. It's also a favorite of expats, who perhaps feel at home where there seems to be a foreign embassy on every corner.

BARRIOS AMÓN, ATOYA, AND ARANJUEZ

These three contiguous neighborhoods to the immediate north of downtown are definitely not expat centers. Parts of the area are rundown, and along one stretch you'll see a fair number of streetwalkers who, if you opt for a closer look, turn out to have more than you bargained for under their miniskirts.

So why do I even mention these neighborhoods? Because they are fascinating barrios, with some of the oldest and most interesting buildings in the city. There's a feeling here you don't get in the rest of San José—namely, that the city has a history, and remnants of it are still visible if you take the time to look. Walking these streets, I have seen dozens of gorgeous old wood frame houses that cry out for loving restoration. Hand-carved wooden latticework graces roof eaves, and the wraparound front porches remind me of grand old houses in the American South and Midwest. Architects and historians may cringe, but if pressed I'd dub these charming buildings Caribbean Victorian.

These neighborhoods are uphill from the center, which gives them a feeling of being above and beyond all the downtown bustle. The area's northern perimeter is the Torres River, which is best seen from the cliff that marks the abrupt end to Barrio Aranjuez.

If I had a few million dollars I'd buy up a whole block here, creating a café, a bed-and-breakfast, and several grand homes I could take turns living in. Downtown shops and movie theaters would be a short walk away.

© Erin Van Rheenen

San José, near the main post office

Actually, people have already done that, and charming little hotels and up-scale restaurants are easy to come by.

ZAPOTE, CURRIDABAT, AND SAN FRANCISCO DE DOS RÍOS

The neighborhoods to the southeast of downtown San José are a varied lot, but in general are pleasant middle-class areas that are drawing more and more foreign residents. Those who want to be close to the action of the city center, and don't wait to pay the higher prices of upscale western suburbs like Escazú, have quietly moved in, and now, especially in San Francisco de Dos Ríos, it's not uncommon to see gringos (including lots of families) going about their daily business at the supermarket or running track. There's a great kid-friendly park in San Francisco (Parque Yokohama), where the kids of foreign residents swing on the swings and mix it up with the locals on a dirt soccer field.

Real estate agents expect these neighborhoods, along with the areas around Cartago, to take off soon. There's a lot of commercial development, from Multiplaza East under construction in Curridabat, to the Terramall on the highway to Cartago. Remax real estate agent Les Núñes calls it a "lead-lag situation." In a March 21, 2003, *Tico Times* article, he explained that "commercial development leads off, and residential follows." Though this area is now on the rise, he believes the price difference will remain constant. "The way it works is the west side [Escazú, Santa Ana, etc.] levels off, the east side picks up, and then the west side will take off again. Let's say a two-bedroom, two-bath sells for US$150,000 in Escazú; the same house might go for about US$100,000 in San Francisco de Dos Ríos. That US$50,000 spread tends to maintain itself over time. If our San Francisco house goes up to US$150,000, the Escazú one will eventually hit US$200,000."

Around San José

The suburbs of the city and the outlying towns range from wealthy and Americanized to working-class and *puro Tico,* but all share a truly spectacular setting, perched at the foot of, or climbing up, hills carpeted with the glossy green of coffee plants, or, even higher up, towering cedar and pine. The flora here is not what newcomers expect; while there is a definite tropical undercurrent, the hills above San José look more like summertime Switzerland than the Amazon Basin.

Getting to know the Central Valley can be a challenge. Just figuring out where all of the towns are will take a few months, and exploring them could take half a year of weekend jaunts. The fact that roads are so poorly signed doesn't help matters. Luckily, getting lost can have its rewards, not least of which is discovering a tidy little town halfway up the slopes of an active volcano, terraced fields cascading down the mountain and nurturing everything from potatoes to ornamental plants.

For each town described below, there are literally dozens of others waiting to be discovered. The places I've focused on tend to appeal to foreign residents, and there are often good reasons for their popularity. Still, I encourage those serious about living in the area (especially if you plan to buy property) to take your time in exploring the densely settled and enormously varied Central Valley.

West of San José

ESCAZÚ

One of the oldest settlements in the country, Escazú is also one of the most up-to-date and sophisticated. This is arguably the most prestigious place to live in Costa Rica, and residents love the fact that they're only 15

© Erin Van Rheenen

Taller Pilo, a woodshop in Escazú

minutes from San José but worlds apart in terms of atmosphere. I can't tell you how many successful lodge and hotel owners I met all over Costa Rica who told me their real home was in Escazú.

The town climbs the lower slopes of the surrounding mountains, the highest of which is 2,455 meters (8,054 ft.), and the air is usually a few degrees cooler than it is in San José. Tucked amid the foothills you'll find impressive individual homes, gated condominium complexes, fine hotels with manicured grounds, and even a few affordable apartments. There's a well-regarded English-language school (the Country Day School, K–12) and not one but two country clubs. Despite the fashionable shops and restaurants, parts of Escazú still have a surprisingly rural feel. Next to a high-end furniture store you might see a couple of cows grazing in front of an adobe hut.

> *If you see in the San José newspapers a notice for tai chi, meditation, or re-birthing, chances are you'll be directed to an address in Escazú.*

In proper terms, Escazú is not one but three towns, each with its own church, central plaza, and prefix (San Rafael de, San Miguel de, and San Antonio de). But as tends to happen in burgeoning areas, what were once separate areas started to bleed together, and soon it was hard to tell where one stopped and the other began. Now, the different towns function more as different neighborhoods, with the air growing clearer and the streets more tranquil the further up the hill you go. San Rafael de Escazú is the lowest, close to one of the few stretches of superhighway in the country, and home to most of the modern shopping malls and services. This area's busy strip offers up the chance to drop a small fortune on an imported suit or handmade tile for your kitchen, or to sample Italian, French, or Argentine cuisine (among many other international options). Though the tenor of the place is undeniably upscale, there's still room for more down-to-earth establishments such as supermarkets, health clinics, gas stations, and, of course, a McDonalds or two.

A kilometer (.6 mi.) up the road is San Miguel de Escazú, which centuries ago began life as a crossroads between indigenous villages, and later, in the 1700s, became a Spanish settlement that served the area's cattle ranchers. A few remaining cobblestone streets can be found around the village square, with its lovely red-domed church painted at its base with a strip of color to ward off witches. Despite such precautions, Escazú, traditionally known as the witch capital of the country, hasn't lost its power to captivate and enchant. Some residents seem to soak up that ability; a local *bruja* suggests that any woman who lives long enough in Escazú becomes a witch in her own right.

Still further up the hill is San Antonio de Escazú, the most rural of the three Escazús and home to the annual Ox Cart Drivers Day festival. The slopes above San Antonio are planted in coffee bushes, until even these give way to cloud forest. Just minutes from town you can be walking along a remote trail, maybe heading for the 15-meter (49-ft.) iron cross on a nearby peak, with nothing but trees and the occasional dairy cow to keep you company.

There are a lot of gringos in Escazú, some in gated communities that allow them to leave for months and not worry about security, others more integrated into the community. Real estate prices are among the highest in the country.

To cash in on the town's cachet, developers are building all manner of single-family homes and condo complexes in and around Escazú. I looked at a bi-level, 465-square-meter (5,000-sq.-ft.) condo with lots of light, a beautiful terra-cotta tile floor, and an asking price of US$300,000. "They call it Santa Fe style," shrugged the Tico real estate agent. "Ticos don't really go for it but I guess gringos do." Driving around the hills above town, you'll see sprawling homes that combine a dizzying array of architectural styles; a starkly modern building might sprout Greek revival columns or a quasi-Victorian turret. Closer to Escazú's colonial center(s), thankfully, the municipality requires new construction to conform to a more traditional style.

Socially, there's a lot going on in Escazú, and the number of expats here ensures that you'll have plenty of potential playmates who speak your language. I'm not sure what this says about the area and its inhabitants, but if you see in the San José newspapers a notice for tai chi, meditation, or rebirthing, chances are you'll be directed to an address in Escazú. On a different note, the town also seems to be a center of charity work, with benefit dinners and book sales generating funds for local schools and clubs.

SANTA ANA

Unlike Escazú, which is spread out and has many "centers," nearby Santa Ana has a village-like atmosphere with one undisputed heart: the 1870 medieval-looking stone church. Even on a Saturday night the church will be packed to its wooden rafters, worshippers dressed to the nines, throwing flirtatious glances between the call-and-response of 6 o'-clock mass. It's a place to see and be seen, with young men and women dolled up as if for the disco, which is indeed where they'll probably be later in the evening.

Across the street the soccer field will be lit up, with teams of twelve-year-olds playing as if the World Cup were at stake. Within a few-block radius you can find Peruvian ceviche, American steakhouse fare, or local specialties like wood-grilled chicken with fried sweet onions.

The town is famous for its ceramics, and there are at least 30 independent pottery shops in the area. An 8,000-hectare (19,768-acre) forest preserve and bird sanctuary above town ensures that Santa Ana will always be bordered (if not surrounded) by nature.

Santa Ana used to be billed as "the alternate to Escazú," with lower prices and a more traditional Tico feel. From what I can observe, though, it's not far from Escazú in terms of real estate prices, fancy restaurants, and expat presence. Santa Ana is a little lower in elevation than Escazú, so is a few degrees warmer.

CIUDAD COLÓN

Eight kilometers (5 mi.) west of Santa Ana is Ciudad Colón, which used to be considered "way out there," laughs Bill White, who's lived in Colón for more than a decade and runs a hillside artists' colony on seven luxuriant hectares (17 acres). "But it's only 20 or 30 minutes from San José. Or it used to be, before the traffic got so bad."

Even so, Ciudad Colón feels far from the city. Even the weather is different—warmer, and a touch more humid. It feels more tropical. For years everyone's been saying this place will really take off when they finish the San José–Puerta Caldera highway, an alternate route to Pacific coast resorts like Jacó. The highway will mean people living in places like Colón or nearby Santa Ana will be able to reach the beach in an hour. But in Costa Rica, you never know when and if such projects will be completed, and that suits longtime foreign residents just fine, since most came exactly because the area was a little out of the way.

Bill estimates that there are around 50 or 60 expats in Colón, six of them on his property, where he not only maintains bungalows for visiting artists but also rents out houses built of tropical hardwoods and tucked amid the property's abundant trees. Mavis Beisanz, coauthor of the groundbreaking cultural work *The Ticos,* makes her home in Colón and is a frequent guest at the Julia and David White Arts Colony, as Bill's spread is known. "We've got our own little expat community right here," says Bill. "People come for weekly chamber music concerts, or to see what the visiting artists are doing. There's always something going on."

Bill recalls that he paid around US$85,000 for seven hectares (17 acres) about a decade ago. He estimates that the improved property is now worth millions. That may be, but Colón is still a relative bargain when compared to other Central Valley towns like Escazú. Scan the real estate ads in the *Tico Times* or *La Nación* and you'll find that houses and apartments in and around Colón are priced consistently lower than equivalent properties in Escazú or Santa Ana. Being considered far afield can have its advantages, even if it's only a matter of a few more minutes along the road from San José.

ATENAS, SAN MATEO, AND OROTINA

On the less-traveled of the two routes to the Pacific coast resort of Jacó, you'll pass through some very pleasant country, as the road gradually loses elevation and the foliage becomes slightly more tropical but the weather still retains a mountain freshness. The town of Atenas (50 km/31 mi. from San José, population 6,500), was said by *National Geographic* magazine to have the best climate in the world. At 800 meters (2,625 ft.) in elevation, it hovers between spring- and summertime temperatures, and is known as an excellent orchid-growing area. Aside from weather, Atenas, along with nearby San Mateo (population 2,500) and Orotina (population 8,700), are clean and appealing towns, with lots of trees and some interesting old wooden houses. There's a sense of *there* there; the towns have a pleasing density that speaks of history and of gradual, organic growth. These aren't non-towns strung out along a highway, and in fact the road slows considerably as it meanders through narrow streets and past town squares. There are scattered expats here, as there are everywhere, but these towns have Costa Rican souls.

South and East of San José

CARTAGO

Twenty kilometers (12.4 mi.) southeast of San José lies historic Cartago, a city of 125,000 best-known for sheltering in its cathedral the stone statue of La Negrita, Costa Rica's patron saint. Only eight inches high and supposedly found amid the rocks beneath what is now the basilica, La Negrita has pride of place in the Cathedral of Our Lady of the Angels, attracting pilgrims from all over the country each August 2. On the tourist circuit, Cartago is famous for Las Ruinas (the ruins), the remains of the Parroquia church built in 1575 and damaged many times before its final destruction in the earthquake of 1910.

Earthquakes are not the only type of natural disaster Cartago has had to endure. The town is only a few kilometers from the steep slopes of Irazú Volcano. In 1723, the volcano erupted, destroying the city, which at the time was little more than a collection of adobe huts and a single church. Since then, Irazú seems content to burble and boil and periodically shower Cartago with a fine layer of volcanic ash.

La Negrita's Gifts

Have you ever wondered where all the offerings left for La Negrita end up? They give her flowers by the truckload, piles of pencils used in exams, medals in the shape of body parts, even bridal veils.

If you haven't wondered, maybe you would if you knew who this Negrita was and why people give her such strange gifts in the first place.

La Negrita is the "little black woman," which sounds condescending in English but conveys nothing but affection in Spanish, for this is the nickname of the beloved Virgin of the Angels, Costa Rica's patron saint, an eight-inch-tall stone statue that inspires a yearly pilgrimage to her basilica in Cartago, with some of the faithful walking for days to demonstrate their faith.

The story of La Negrita goes back to 1635, when Cartago was more a scattering of crude huts than a city. One day a *mestiza* (mixed-blood woman) named Juana Pereira saw a strange light coming from between the trees of the path she took every day. Following the light to its source, she found a small black stone in the shape of the Virgin, nestled in the recess of a much bigger rock. Delighted, she took the figure home, but twice La Negrita found her way back to her place of birth. Even when Juana gave the statue to the town priest for safekeeping, La Negrita returned once again to the rock from which she had come. The Virgin's attempts to escape captivity were interpreted as a desire for a basilica of her own, built where Juana had first found her.

And so the Basilica de Los Angeles was constructed, and today its vaulted hardwood ceiling, stained-glass windows, and flower-painted walls host all who come to visit the shrine of La Negrita. They come steadily all year long, but arrive in the hundreds of thousands for the Dia de la Virgin de Los Angeles, a national holiday on August 2, when the pious make the old story new again.

The story has some unexpected twists. For instance, in recent times, late April and early May have seen spikes in the national birth rate. It seems that the pilgrimage is one of the few times "good girls" are allowed to stay out all night, and the religious revelry can turn carnal. If you walk the 22 kilometers (13.7 mi.) from San José to Cartago the night of August 1, you'll see pilgrims with flowers in one hand and a beer in the other. Even back in 1782, the party sometimes got out of hand. That year, a priest ordered the statue moved from the basilica to a local church called El Carmen, so that La Negrita wouldn't have to witness how her day had been taken over by drunken carousing. Partying now takes a back seat to devotion, but the tradition has endured, and from August 3 to September 7, La Negrita takes a post-party vacation in the parish church.

Now what about those offerings? They're thank-yous, of course, for miracles performed. For prayers answered, exams aced, bodies made whole again, and husbands delivered to the altar. What is done with the countless tokens of gratitude? The flowers are used to decorate the church. The non-rusting medals are put in glass cases in a side chapel, while the lower-quality ones are kept in some unspecified back room. And the bridal veils are cut up to make veils for poor girls about to undergo their first communion. Call it the recycling of miracles, short work for La Negrita.

Cartago is one of the oldest Spanish settlements in the Central Valley, and was the nation's capital until shortly after the 1823 civil war. Central America had just declared its independence from Spain, and the subsequent battle in the Central Valley was over whether to join with other former Spanish colonies in a federation or to declare Costa Rica its own independent republic. The cities of San José and Alajuela favored independence; Heredia and Cartago wanted to be part of the larger federation. Those seeking independence won the day, and Cartago lost its capital-city status to San José.

The city's loss may have also been its gain, in that urban growth here hasn't been as helter-skelter as it's been in San José. Cartago feels a lot more traditional and reserved than the current capital. This tidy, bustling town has not attracted as many foreign residents as places like Escazú and Santa Ana; probably no more than a few dozen expats live in Cartago fulltime, with many more in the surrounding towns like Paraíso. But that may change, as Cartago seems a very livable place indeed, and is not yet so "hot" that property values are rising daily.

TURRIALBA

About 40 kilometers (24.9 mi.) east of Cartago and 65 kilometers (40.4 mi.) from San José lies the small but bustling town of Turrialba. Not yet a magnet for foreign residents, the town is pleasant, and the surrounding cane fields, coffee farms, and dense forest are quite beautiful. The drive from San José, up to Cartago and then down to Turrialba, reveals new shades and textures of green at every turn, with mist drifting down from the higher ridges. You'd never pick this town out as the place where Rawlings manufactures the baseballs used in Major League games in the United States, but it is.

Twenty kilometers (12.4 mi.) north of Turrialba is Costa Rica's best-known archaeological site, Guayabo National Monument, where you can study the workmanship of a 3,000-year-old cobblestoned street or watch water rush through an equally ancient aqueduct system that still functions today.

Walk around Turrialba and you'll see some gringos, the majority of whom are here to run the Reventazón and Paquare Rivers and one or two of whom actually live here. As San José continues to sprawl, places like Turrialba, not far from the capital but far enough to avoid its fumes and grit, will become more and more attractive for relocators.

North and Northwest of San José

HEREDIA

Founded in 1706 at the foot of Barva Volcano, Heredia is home to the

National University, whose student body (the second-largest in Costa Rica) injects into the town a good measure of youthful energy. There are also several Spanish-language schools in this city of 31,000, and these students—mostly from Canada and the United States—add to the cosmopolitan feel of the place.

The *Tico Times* calls Heredia "arguably the Central Valley's most charming urban center," and there's no denying that the town's tree-shaded central park is a first-rate place to people-watch and listen to free live music on the weekends. The nearby Cathedral of the Immaculate Conception was built in 1797 and has managed to withstand several earthquakes since then. Another historic building, El Fortin, is a lesson in how not to build a fortress. Alfredo Gonzáles Flores, president of Costa Rica from 1914 to 1917, designed the gun slits on the circular tower so that they easily allowed bullets in but made it nearly impossible for soldiers to shoot out.

Local expats do better at defending the charms of their adopted city. "It feels cozy," says a woman who's lived here for years. "But you can still run all the errands you need to run—the bank's down the block, the Central Market is one of the best places for fruit and vegetables in all of Costa Rica, and now we've even got The Literate Cat [a used bookstore selling mostly books in English]."

With its understated charm and its proximity (just 11 km/6.8 mi.) to San José, Heredia has attracted its share of expats, though many tend to settle in and around nearby small towns—Santa Barbara is set in the heart of coffee country, while San Joaquin de las Flores is known for its upscale residences and lively Easter week processions. Santo Domingo de Heredia, a quiet, bougainvillea-draped town, is an easy 20-minute bus ride from downtown San José. A gleaming white and silver basilica presides over the soccer field and the weekly farmers market. Just outside town is Casa Zen (www.casazen.org), founded in 1975 and, as far as I know, the only Zen Buddhist community in the country. Casa Zen has ties to Zen centers in Vermont and Toronto.

Heredia is slightly higher in elevation than San José, so it's a little cooler and greener all year long; towns further up the slopes of the volcano are even cooler.

ALAJUELA

The City of Mangoes is often called a mini San José, but it's warmer than the capital in both senses of the word. The temperature is consistently higher, and though Alajuela is a bustling city of 53,000, the plaza at the heart of the city makes it feel more like a small town. Shaded by enormous mango trees (hence the city's nickname), the Parque Central is where it all happens. Local teenagers cruise, money changers trade *colones* for dollars, and the town's substantial population of North American retirees comes here to trade information about available apartments, where to find a good masseuse, or the current price of a round-trip ticket home. The talk slows when professional musicians file into the park's bandstand and begin to tune up for a program of classical or popular music.

Every April 11, the Parque Central is the center of a raucous party celebrating Juan Santamaría, Alajuela's native son and Costa Rica's beloved national hero. Also known as El Erizo (the Hedgehog) for his bristly hair, Santamaría set fire to the invading enemy's barracks after a ragtag army chased them out of Costa Rica and over the Nicaraguan border. The enemy happened to be William Walker, a pint-sized Nashville native drunk on Manifest Destiny. Dreaming of a Central America firmly under U.S. control, Walker and his band of mercenaries invaded Nicaragua in 1855, then turned their sights on Costa Rica. Santamaría, who died in that final battle, became a symbol of Costa Rica's capacity to oust foreign invaders. Even so, everyone—regardless of nationality or secret desire to rule the world—is welcome at the town-wide fiesta celebrating the Hedgehog's bravery.

On Saturdays, there's an excellent farmers market. During the rest of the week, there's no shortage of supermarkets and *pulperias,* the corner stores where you can find at least one of everything.

GRECIA

Aside from the oddly columned structure at the turnoff to this town of 17,000, Grecia feels about as Greek as a scarlet macaw. But it's a pretty little place, just thirty minutes from San José's international airport, small enough to be safe and friendly and large enough to have a critical mass of expats and some decent services. The road into town winds past coffee *fincas* and fields of sugar cane, which look like enormous clumps of grass topped with pale yellow tassels. Every bend in the road reveals stunning views of gently sloping valleys and steep volcanic peaks.

At the center of town is, of course, the church, in this case made of an unlikely material: metal. Constructed of steel plates imported from Belgium in 1897, the church is prettier than it sounds, with stained-glass windows and an attractive tiled floor. Streets around the church and town square are wide and pleasant. Locals like to remind you that the town was voted "cleanest town in Latin America" not once but several times, and indeed Grecia does have a tidy and prosperous feel. Expats (along with everyone else in town) congregate in the palm-shaded main square, or shop for fresh fruit and vegetables at the nearby Central

Market. If you need a little excitement, you can always visit a must-see attraction just east of town: El Mundo de los Serpientes has a living collection of 300 snakes from around the world, including some of Costa Rica's most beautiful and deadly.

SARCHÍ

A few kilometers northwest of Grecia is the crafts center of Sarchí. Famous for the brightly painted oxcarts that are one of Costa Rica's most visible examples of folk art, the town is now on the tourist map, with crafts emporiums offering everything from miniature oxcarts to handmade wooden furniture. In fact, Sarchí rockers—simple but attractive chairs combining hardwood and leather—have become famous, with the added advantage of being collapsible and thus easy to transport.

> *Sarchí's setting can't be beat—it's surrounded by hills blanketed in coffee and sugar cane, and has spectacular views of higher peaks further off.*

The main street, which connects Sarchí Sur (population 4,000) with Sarchí Norte (population 6,500), is lined with somewhat tacky tourist shops (avoid the area on weekends during high season, when tour buses clog the road). Beyond this unpromising introduction, however, the town is quite charming. Whitewashed buildings and the bridge into town are painted with the intricate geometric designs originally found on oxcarts—the colorful patterns remind me of Pennsylvania Dutch motifs found on barns in that state, but amped up a notch or two until they hit tropical exuberance. Equally festive is Sarchí Norte's church: birthday-cake pink with bright turquoise trim. Inside are vaulted hardwood ceilings and striking carvings made by local artisans. The town's setting can't be beat—it's surrounded by hills blanketed in coffee and sugar cane, and has spectacular views of higher peaks further off.

There's not yet a large expat contingent in Sarchí, but the town is definitely worth a look, being fairly close to San José and only a few minutes from better shopping and services in Grecia.

ZARCERO

Tucked in the folds of the mountains you cross to get from the Central Valley to the Zona Norte, Zarcero is dominated by a pretty church and a plaza filled with shrubbery cut into fanciful shapes, from bears to cartoon characters. The town is clean and the air cool enough so that strawberries and lettuce thrive, planted in neat rows just outside the town limits. Farming in general is good here, and there's a fair amount of wealth that displays itself in well-kept homes and farms.

Zarcero, though cute as a bug's ear, is not the only town of its kind. All across Costa Rica you will find the kinds of places you'd never expect to find in this country. Costa Rica enchants in part because it so often surprises. The fun is in wandering far enough afield (and opening your eyes wide enough) to be amazed and delighted by what you find.

Zona Norte

There are several routes north over the peaks of the Cordillera Central, but all offer spectacular views and a glimpse of a Costa Rica the casual tourist rarely sees. Narrow roads rise up out of the Central Valley, winding past mountain towns and highland farms before dropping down to a fertile plain that extends all the way north to the Nicaraguan border.

Comprising the Llanura (plain) de San Carlos and the Llanura de Guatuso, this 40,000-square-kilometer (15,444-square-mi.) area has been called the breadbasket of the nation, though rice bowl would be more accurate. Ticos eat rice with every meal (including breakfast), and most of the rice consumed in Costa Rica is grown here in the Zona Norte (Northern Zone). Three great rivers and their countless tributaries irrigate the region, flooding during heavy rains and creating the swampy conditions ideal for rice cultivation.

I've heard the area described as a tropical Tuscany or a steamier Oregon. Boulder-strewn streams alternate with lush farmland. You pass fields of knee-high pineapple plants, a single fruit at the center of each burst of blade-like leaves, and papayas growing on small trees, all the fruit hanging from the central stalk. Bean fields give way to rice paddies and banana groves.

Rising up out of this lush plain like a whale breaching the ocean's surface, Arenal Volcano is one of the most dramatic sights in the country. If you can see it, that is. Arenal is so often shrouded in clouds that some tourists wonder if the steep-sloped gem really exists or is just a clever figment of a tour agency's imagination. (One local guide reports that a tourist asked if they turned on the volcano at night.)

Whether or not you see it, you can always hear the volcano, grumbling deep in its fiery throat and just generally making sure you never forget that although it slept through the colonial and most of the modern era, when it woke in 1968 its eruptions wiped out two towns. Not quite as furious now, it still coughs up smoke and truck-sized cinders daily, and on clear nights you can see red-hot rocks bouncing down the mountain. There's nothing like soaking in the hot springs at the foot of the volcano, a light cool rain pocking the water, secure in the knowledge that if

Arenal blows again like it did in '68, you'll have about nine minutes to get out of the danger zone.

Around Arenal there are two seasons: wet, and really wet. Theoretically, there's supposed to be less rain February through April, but locals rarely go out without a rain hat or umbrella. During the really wet season, they don't go out without heavy-duty slickers or ponchos. When it rains here, it pours, and it's part of local hospitality to offer you dry clothes if you arrive soaked.

Joy Rothke, a writer from California who now lives in La Fortuna, says that in this very humid climate, she has gained a new appreciation for the clever survival strategies of mold, which takes hold in unlikely places, like books, jewelry, even bills in a wallet. Her husband, Bill Linnemeier, likes the weather; he says it's like living in Miami but with mountains.

There aren't many expats in the area yet, at least not when compared to the throngs in the Central Valley and along parts of the Pacific coast. Joy could tell me the names and histories of each of the handful of foreign residents living in and around La Fortuna. To thrive here requires integrating into the local community, which isn't always easy. "The locals [Costa Ricans] are friendly," says Bill, "but it's like you move to Maine from Wyoming, and two generations later, you're still the family from Wyoming. You can be accepted here, but you'll never be a Tico. You will forever be an outsider." This isn't something peculiar to the Zona Norte—I heard the same sentiments echoed all over the country. But in smaller towns with fewer expats, that truth may be felt more keenly.

LA FORTUNA

A town built in the shadow of Arenal Volcano, La Fortuna has, in the past few years, become something of a tourist hub. More than a dozen tour agencies line the main street, as do souvenir shops, whose most appealing wares come from Guatemala, Panama, and Indonesia (Costa Rica isn't known for its crafts). At the center of this town is not the usual soccer field (that's down the street, near the high school) but a plaza dominated by a basketball court, the backboards neon-orange advertisements for a rent-a-car company. Taxis line up along one side of the plaza; local buses stop along another. The inevitable Catholic church is unremarkable save for the view of the volcano as you look up from the main steps: The white cross on the church's roof is like a tattoo on Arenal's huge green shoulder.

Visitors on their way to Caño Negro Wildlife Preserve, windsurfers heading for Lake Arenal, or those who come to catch a glimpse of the volcano all pass through and often stay in Fortuna. To accommodate the influx, everybody and their dog seems to be building small hotels or tourist

The Río Tabacón runs hot, like the nearby springs.

cabinas, some of which are little more than huts in someone's backyard. There's a lot of construction going on in town, and the place seems quite prosperous given that a decade ago it was hardly a bump in the road. Real estate is still inexpensive (especially when compared to other parts of the country), but Fortuna is changing so rapidly that it's hard to predict how long that will last.

Most, but not all, business opportunities revolve around the tourist trade. Foreign residents run a variety of enterprises, including an adventure-tour agency, an Internet café, a massage parlor, various restaurants and hotels, and at least one art gallery. Former Minnesotan Bill Linnemeier bakes bread, cinnamon rolls, and focaccia and sells to the locals (see his Expat Profile in the Overview of Prime Living Locations chapter).

There are some very pretty places to live just outside of town, especially near the river on the road to La Catarata, the local waterfall.

NUEVO ARENAL

Though it's often called simply Arenal, the *Nuevo* (new) in this town's official name reminds us that the old town is at the bottom of lovely and pristine Lake Arenal, a 32-kilometer (19.9-mi.) reservoir created in 1973 when the Costa Rican Institute of Electricity (ICE) built a dam at the

Expat Profile: Richard Thomas

"I wouldn't necessarily recommend that people do what I did," warns Richard Thomas. "But it worked, and here I am."

"Here" is a rickety but appealing two-story house perched on a hill above the tiny town of El Castillo. To get to El Castillo you take a three-hour bus ride from San José to La Fortuna, then take a dirt road so bad taxis charge extra—or won't even go there. El Castillo doesn't have many people, but it has everything a Costa Rican town needs: school, church, bull ring, and a *pulpería* (general store) that lets the locals run a tab. Richard had been renting for a mere US$50 a month, but is now going to buy the place, for about US$5,000. "Those aren't normal prices," he admits. "They're less than a third normal prices, to be honest. But I got lucky. And a Tico is loaning me the down payment! They say never loan money to a Tico, and here one is loaning *me* money."

Four years ago he left the States with US$800 and his massage table. It hasn't been easy, but things are evening out. During the high season he does massage for clients of Arenal Observatory Lodge, an appealing blend of luxury hotel and working volcano research station. When massage is slow he works on his many entrepreneurial schemes, including selling real estate (you don't need a license in Costa Rica) and making candles.

Richard's furnishings show his priorities; there's one electric frying pan to do all his cooking, and a queen-sized bed with carved headboard and footboard. Clothes hang everywhere, over the backs of wooden chairs, from nails on the wall. "I'm a bachelor for sure," he says. He's got a red curtain between his bed and the rest of the living area, "so it seem more like a one-bedroom place." His cat, Fidel, keeps the varmints out, though one night Fidel dragged a pit viper under Richard's bed.

Up the ladder-like stairs to the breezy second floor there are workrooms for his cottage industries—making candles, and packaging a fine black silt to make instant mud for facials. On the second-floor porch hangs his hammock, from which he can see out across the impossibly green hills and all the way to Lake Arenal on the left and looming Arenal Volcano to the right. It is a gorgeous view, one it would be hard to tire of. The volcano is one of the most active in the world, and is what Richard says he watches instead of TV. Every day he hears the rumbling, which sounds like a freight train blasting through a peal of thunder. When the rain and fog clear, he can see glowing orange-red rocks hurtling down the side of the mountain.

Originally from Oregon, Richard doesn't mind the rain. Which is good, since around El Castillo there are not

© Erin Van Rheenen

one but two rainy seasons. Like many people from rainy areas, Richard shows equal measures of pride and practicality in his insistence on doing what he has to do, rain or shine. "My mother used to say, 'You made of sugar? You think you're going to melt?' No one in my town ever used an umbrella."

He knows everyone and has no problem communicating in Spanish, though he never studied it formally. "I bought a Spanish-English dictionary once, but I gave it away." His method is total immersion, and from the looks of it he is totally immersed in his new life. He likes to walk through the for-est, looking for toucans, snakes, and jaguars. He's found plenty of the first two but has only seen the tracks of the elusive cat locals call *el tigre*.

On the more day-to-day level, he's got a trade, good friends, and a dirt bike to ride the back roads (most of the roads around are back roads). Going far too fast down the deserted road from his house to the Lodge, his raincoat is open and flapping in the wind. The forest presses in on all sides, a green lung breathing out oxygen. The rain is starting up, and it feels good on his face. "Not a bad commute!" he yells above the roar of the engine.

eastern end of the valley. ICE also erected wind turbines along the new lake's southwestern shore, taking advantage of the stiff winds (30- to 80-kph) that blow almost constantly and make Lake Arenal one of the world's best windsurfing spots.

Thankfully, Nuevo Arenal is more protected, and is a pleasant, prosperous-looking town built on the lake's upsloping shore. Perhaps because it was a planned community, it looks more spacious and less haphazard than most Tico towns, though some newer construction seems to be slumping along in usual Costa Rican fashion.

One guidebook says this town of 2,500 has "nothing of tourist interest," but what draws tourists is not always what draws new residents. Though the area will never be as popular (or as expensive) as some of the Pacific coast beaches, it is nevertheless experiencing its own small boom, with real estate prices rising and more people arriving all the time. Views of the lake from town are stunning, and the weather is temperate. Lakefront property is not subject to the same restrictions as beachfront property; if you find your Eden on Arenal's shores, you can own it outright rather than having to lease it from the state.

The town itself consists of a few dozen houses scattered in the folds of

Nuevo Arenal

© Erin Van Rheenen

hills, the main street offering up a handful of businesses: a hardware store, a place to buy cowboy hats and saddles, a few restaurants and several bars, and—a more recent addition—a real estate office run by two Florida transplants, Richard and Ann McCarthy. Off the main street there's a well-established German bakery called Tom's Pan, where expats can linger over big German lunches or take home delicious bread and pastries. The land around town has quietly been changing hands over the past decade or two—from Tico to German, Swiss, Italian, U.S., Canadian, and other nationalities. But Nuevo Arenal still feels like a small Tico town, where people leave their doors open and keep their front yards neat and blooming.

TILARÁN

Although it's only a few dozen kilometers from Nuevo Arenal to Tilarán, the unpredictable state of the highway means the trip could take anywhere from 30 minutes to well over an hour. Sometimes you'll fly along on what appears to be well-maintained blacktop, but don't be fooled—around the next bend may be a lacework of potholes or a mudslide blocking the way. Take your time and enjoy the view. The road skirts the top of lovely Lake Arenal and is the site of an increasing number of hotels, lodges, and private homes. Five kilometers (3.1 mi.) after the road heads west, away from lake, it arrives in Tilarán, a pretty highland town with a population of 10,000, including a number of expats. At 550 meters (1,804 ft.) above sea level, Tilarán is high enough to have pine trees as well as palms in the town square, and the temperate climate, springlike and drier than Arenal, is a big draw.

Tilarán sits atop a hill, with the land sloping away to the west, down to the Guanacaste flats, and climbing a little more to the east, up to gorgeous Lake Arenal. The streets are wide and immaculate, and the soaring church tower is flanked by two tall monkey-puzzle trees. Last time I was in town, traffic slowed to let an iguana cross the street from the churchyard to the main plaza. In the shadow of the church is the town's vocational center, complete with horse and cattle stalls—ranching is one of the area's main sources of income and employment. From the main street, you can see Arenal Volcano in the distance, looking too small to do the damage it did during its last big eruption in 1968.

Not as many foreigners have chosen to settle in Tilarán as in Nuevo Arenal (the lake is a big draw), and the town feels like a Tico version of a Norman Rockwell painting. As in Nuevo Arenal, there are few bars on windows, and people leave their front doors open to the street. On weekends you'll see people working in their neat gardens or washing their cars out in front of well-maintained homes. Kids playing hopscotch on the sidewalk smile as you walk by; the older folk sit in rocking chairs on bougainvillea-draped tiled front porches.

There's an alternate route to Tilarán that spares you the Lake Arenal road. From San José you drive toward the Pacific coast, then go north for an hour or so on the Pan-American Highway. At Cañas you bear east on Highway 142, which winds through very pleasant rolling hills reminiscent of the Sierra Nevada foothills in northern California, except for the big volcanic boulders strewn among the grazing cattle. Golden grasses wave in the wind, stately trees spread their shade, and creeks run in the clefts of the hills.

Other Temperate Locations

MONTEVERDE

In 1951 a small group of Quakers left Fairhope, Alabama, to settle on 1,214 fertile hectares (3,000 acres) high in Costa Rica's Cordillera de Tilarán. Of the fewer than 50 emigrants, five had just been released from prison for refusing to register for the draft. The judge had told them that they should obey the law of the land or leave the country, and after their release, the latter is exactly what they did. They chose Costa Rica because it had recently abolished its army, and had done away with the death penalty years earlier. Besides draft resisters, the group also included farmers, teachers, and a retired rural mail carrier.

It's hard to imagine that in the 1950s there was still an opportunity to be a pioneer, but at that time many parts of Costa Rica were still inaccessible or very sparsely settled (some parts still are today). The Quakers needed horses and oxcarts to convey their belongings to their new home; the roads were so bad that not even Jeeps could make the journey.

The land they purchased was at 1,400 meters (4,593 ft.) and straddled both the Guacimal River and the Continental Divide. Plant life was riotous and varied, a mix of tropical, subtropical, and, with the mist drifting in from the Atlantic side of the mountain, cloud forest as well. Wilford Guindon, one of the original settlers, spoke of the land's "drippy tropical tangle"; that tangle supported (and still supports) a great variety of wildlife. The more than 400 species of birds includes 30 species of hummingbirds and the resplendent quetzal, a little-seen bird that draws naturalists to Monteverde.

Upon arrival, the settlers cleared land for crops and dairy cows, built houses and barns and roads, and founded a creamery that nowadays produces some of the best cheese in the country. Half a century after their arrival, the area is also one of the best-known tourist destinations in

Costa Rica, in large part because of the private Monteverde Cloud Forest Reserve, one of the best wildlife reserves in the New World Tropics.

Monteverde and nearby Santa Elena are still influenced by Los Cuaqueros (the Quakers), but the settlers have intermarried with local Costa Rican families and now the two communities have formed a hybrid, with many a bilingual household and customs that include traditional Tico fiestas, Quaker meetings, and the weekly Scrabble games instituted by some of the original settlers.

Over the years, many non-Quaker expats have joined the community, and modern-day Monteverde (which now numbers around 2,400) is an appealing mix of scientists, artists, retired folk, and dairy farmers. Wendy Rockwell, granddaughter of one of the original settlers and now a member of the town council, was born in Monteverde but went back to the United States to go to high school and college. She brought her California-born husband back to her birthplace, where they now run Chunches (Costa Ricans for "stuff"), a kind of enlightened general store/launderette in the heart of Santa Elena. At Chunches you'll find everything from books on midwifery to a decent cappuccino, which you can sip as you wait for your clothes to dry.

Speaking of dry, Monteverde isn't. Like the area around Arenal, Monteverde (which means Green Mountain) is perpetually green. How does it stay so green? Rain, more rain, and then a little more rain. Locals learn not to wait for the skies to clear before getting on with their business. A little rain never hurt anyone, and a lot of rain—well, you'll probably live through that too. If you like perpetually clear skies and dry heat, by all means visit Monteverde, but don't plan to stick around.

It seems to me that settling here would appeal to a very special type of person—someone who is moved by the unusual history of the place and willing to participate in its multifaceted present. Residents here are aware and involved, especially in regards to environmental issues. Echoing Quaker practice, community decisions are made by consensus. One expat (who lives elsewhere in Costa Rica) called it a mini-Berkeley, after the city in California known for its progressive politics. But you won't find half as many butterflies in Berkeley, nor will you be able to walk through old-growth forest, marveling at how one tree can support so much life, from sinuous vines to blossoming bromeliads. Monteverde is like that tree: A surprising variety of species has found a home here.

SAN ISIDRO DE GENERAL

Besides being the only stretch of the Pan-American Highway not called Highway 1, Highway 2 south of San José will also put even the most confident driver to the test. One hundred kilometers (62 mi.) from the capital, the road reaches the 3,500-meter (11,483-ft.) peak at Cerro de la Muerte (Hill of Death), then plunges dizzyingly down. Landslides often block the way, potholes proliferate with each heavy rain, and dense fog adds spice to the brew. Big trucks and diesel-spewing buses often hold up long lines of cars, with drivers waiting their turn to hazard passing on the winding road. But it's a stunning drive, especially when the mist clears to reveal jaw-dropping views.

What you'll see below, if the weather cooperates, is the Valle de El General, a 100-kilometer-long (62-mi.-long) depression between the Talamanca range and the Fila Costeña. About 700 meters (2,297 ft.) in elevation, the valley is balmier than the Central Valley, but not as hot as either coast. At the north end lies San Isidro de General, the regional capital and a natural stopping-off point for those looking to hike up nearby Cerro Chirripo (at 3,819 m/12,530 ft., the highest peak in Central America south of Guatemala), raft the Ríos Chirripo and General, or continue on to Dominical and other Pacific beaches. It's also a bustling agricultural market town, the center of a fertile zone where pineapples are the major crop.

After the drama of the journey, the town itself may underwhelm, though it's a pleasant enough place. Laid out in a grid, the town is centered on the plaza at Calle Central and Avenida 0, with a concrete church at one end and an astonishing number of taxis lined up on three sides of the square. San Isidro de General is a young town—founded in 1897, but built mostly after World War II—and there's a palpable sense of commerce rather than history here.

The non-Ticos you'll see around town—those who aren't on their way to climb a mountain, run a river, or surf the beach break at Dominical—most likely don't live in the town proper but have made their stand near the beach or in the hills around San Isidro. They come to town to do their shopping, wait in line at the bank, or make use of the hospital, the biggest one for miles. Expats who live in or near the beach town of Dominical, for instance, regularly make the 40-minute drive up Highway 243 for San Isidro's better variety and lower prices, whether they're stocking up on food or shopping for building materials. Sturdy plastic lawn chairs were going for just US$6 when I was there last—you can't do better, even at Home Depot.

Guidebooks often describe San Isidro (also called Perez Zeledon, after the name of the district) as without interest or charm, but those who come here often find themselves developing an affection for this very Tico town. There's an excellent *polideportivo* (sports complex) at the edge of town, with a gym, a running track, and lush grounds for hiking or picnicking. And there's a good variety of restaurants, bars, and cafés. Sample the real Mexican food at Taqueria Mexico Lindo, or have an espresso at the Strapless Kafe, where Betty Boop, Jackie O, and Princess Di dolls peer out of locked glass cabinets. You'll almost certainly run into other expats—from North America, Europe, and South America—taking a break from their errand-running. Most foreign residents are appalled by the new McDonald's on the main highway, but local Ticos aren't averse to heading for the golden arches.

Though the coast is a definite expat magnet, there are those who have settled along the waterfall-rich stretch of road (Highway 243) from Dominical to San Isidro, in little mist-shrouded towns like Platanillo and Tinamastes. Some settle in the hills around San Isidro itself, like Ed Bernhardt, founder of the New Dawn Center (www.newdawncenter.org), an organic farm and education center 15 kilometers (9.3 mi.) northwest of San Isidro. Two decades ago, Ed left the United States and settled here, choosing the area because it was far from what he saw as the Los Angelization of Costa Rica's Central Valley. The land was cheap, the people friendly, and, as a child of the turbulent 1960s in the United States, Ed wanted to settle in a country dedicated to peace. "The Ticos don't have the scars we carry," says Ed, "growing up with war."

Ed married a Tica, and the couple's two sons, now teenagers, were born on the farm. "They were like nymphs, running around naked. Then they got socialized, and now they're Ticos." One of his sons attends "the first environmental high school in Costa Rica," founded by former neighbor Alexander Skutch (who died in 2004 at 99), coauthor of the classic *Birds of Costa Rica*. Ed himself contributes a weekly gardening column to the *Tico Times,* and is the author of the highly detailed and useful *Costa Rican Organic Home Gardening Guide.*

Ed "goes into town" (San Isidro) a few times a week. The farm has no phone, no email, and no papaya or pineapple, though they do well with mangoes and avocados. "Each microclimate supports different crops," says Ed, just as each nook and cranny of Costa Rica sustains different varieties of expats. But Ed worries about how fast San Isidro is growing. "Did you see the McDonald's? That's a death knell if I ever heard one. Maybe it's time to move up to San Vito."

SAN VITO

Heading south from San Isidro, Highway 2 leaves the Valle de El General and enters the Valle de Coto Brus. The road is surprisingly good, at least until Paso Real, where those heading for San Vito leave the Pan-American

Highway and take winding and scenic Route 237 up to the prosperous regional capital. This is coffee country, with glossy-leafed bushes marching up steep mountains and blanketing gentle slopes. Views of the valley below are spectacular.

Until the 1950s, the area was all but inaccessible, and indigenous peoples (the Guaymi and Boruca, among other groups) made up more than half of the area's population. The Pan-American Highway finally cut through to nearby Buenos Aires in 1961, and by then non-indigenous Costa Ricans had begun to outnumber the original inhabitants.

Non-Ticos also had a hand in changing the face of the area. In 1949, an Italian named Vito Sansonetti visited the remote valley and was so drawn to the fertile and heavily forested frontier that he set in motion what was essentially an Italian colonization of the area. Scores of war-stricken families, most from the south of Italy, saw in the plan the opportunity for a fresh start. The Costa Rican government helped to finance a proposal in which 250 families, 20 percent of them Ticos, would settle in what became San Vito. The plan became reality in the early 1950s, and in San Vito today, though most of the Italian settlers have married into Tico families or returned to Italy, there are still traces of their influence, from blue and green eyes to the excellent pasta at places like Liliana's Restaurant, just uphill from the tiny central park.

Early townspeople made good use of the area's temperate climate, planting the bushes that would make the valley the country's largest coffee-producing region. More recently, the crop that made the town's fortunes is not bringing such high prices on the international market, and farmers have been pulling out their coffee bushes and trying their hand at other crops.

One of the town's draws is its climate—warm days and nights cool enough for a real blanket. Stands of pine alternate with tall tropical hardwoods draped with vines and orchids. The abundance of budget hotels in town might lead you to believe that this is a tourist center, but don't be fooled—these rooms fill up with Ticos, most of them traveling on business. Besides the Italian colony, other stray foreign residents have made their way here, but they are the exception to the rule and usually arrive for a very specific purpose. Their stories demonstrate how far hard work and a consuming passion can take you, and also how recently this area has been "settled," though indigenous peoples had been scattered across the zone for centuries.

Darryl Cole-Christensen, for example, came with his family from the United States in the 1950s to carve a farm and a life out of what was nearly impenetrable rain forest. In his book, *A Place in the Rain Forest:*

Settling the Costa Rican Frontier, he tells of how the roads, when they existed, were too much for Jeeps and, during the rainiest parts of the year, even impassable to horses. In his book he takes a thoughtful look at the frontier mentality that allowed settlers to "tame" the land, but which resulted in the destruction of vast tracts of tropical forest.

"The frontier was generally seen at this time in two ways," writes Cole-Christensen. "There was the land, and there was the forest. On the land homes could be raised, communities would rise," and crops could be planted. The forest, on the other hand, "was the great obstacle and antagonist to overcome." Settlers were hard-working and resourceful folk. They saw a fertile land and believed the abundance would shine forth even after they'd cut down the forest and planted crops. What they eventually realized, explains Cole-Christensen, is that the fertility of the rain forest lies in its canopy rather than in the soil. But the farmers prevailed, using their newfound knowledge to raise crops and a community on the land. Cole-Christensen still lives in the area, and his farm, Finca Loma Linda, has been given over to research of tropical sustainable farming methods.

The rich flora of the area also drew Robert and Catherine Wilson, who first came in 1959 and shortly thereafter bought a ridgetop farm that had been denuded by years of cattle grazing. The couple had run a tropical plant nursery in Florida, and wanted to see what marvels they might be able to raise and sell in the lush environment just above San Vito. When they realized that their location was too remote to be the base for a successful tropical plant business, they allied themselves with the Organization for Tropical Studies (OTS, a worldwide consortium of 66 universities and research stations, six of them in Costa Rica). The Wilson Botanical Garden was born. Now part of the Las Cruces Biological Station, today the garden welcomes mostly students and scientists, though birdwatching and plant-loving tourists have begun to discover this 283-hectare (700-acre) gem, which boasts 5,100 species of plants, 330 species of birds, and dozens of mammal species, including 37 kinds of bats.

Catherine Wilson died in 1984, Robert in 1989. The Wilsons loved their adopted land so passionately that they wanted to be buried here, on the reserve itself. Friends who tried to honor their wishes ran into problems, however. By Costa Rican law, bodies can only be buried in a cemetery. After much bureaucratic wrangling, a solution was found: A tiny piece of the reserve was declared a cemetery. "A very selective cemetery," says resident biologist Rodolfo Quiros. "Just two people are buried there"— the two expats who dedicated more than half their lives to turning a cattle pasture into a remarkable garden and reserve.

Real Estate Agents

Note: The agencies and individuals listed below are a small sampling of what you will find; inclusion in this list does not imply personal recommendation.

Lake Arenal Realty
Lake Arenal area
Richard and Ann McCarthy
tel./fax 506/694-4132
info@lakearenalrealty.com
www.lakearenalrealty.com

Remax First Realty
San José area
Les Nunez
tel. 506/290-3183
fax 506/290-3178
www.remaxcostarica.com

Remax Lider
San José area, especially Escazú
Andrés Zamora, Manager
tel. 506/228-0767
cell: 506/391-5088
fax 506/228-1145
andresz@racsa.co.cr
www.remaxlider.com

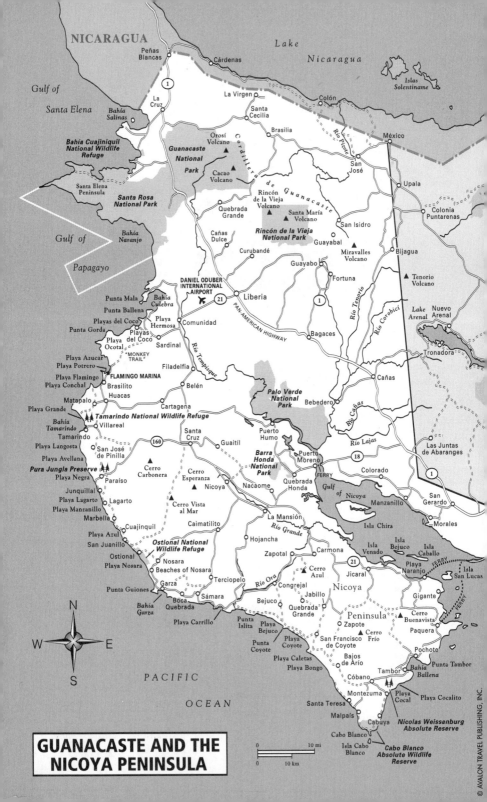

GUANACASTE AND THE NICOYA PENINSULA

© Erin Van Rheenen

Guanacaste and the Nicoya Peninsula

I n its early years, Guanacaste was independent from the rest of Costa Rica, and to this day the area retains its own flavor quite distinct from the rest of the country. First its own province, then a part of Nicaragua, Guanacaste didn't officially became part of Costa Rica until 1858. Home of the *sabanero* (cowboy), this area is the country's Wild West—where a maverick spirit combines with the interdependence necessary in a frontier society—and also its Gold Coast, with 70 percent of the nation's beach resort infrastructure. Local residents consider themselves Guanacastecos first and Ticos second. In fact, the Guanacasteco heritage is so strong that it has seeped into the national character, with the spreading guanacaste tree the Costa Rican national tree and the local *punto guanacasteco* celebrated as the national dance.

The Lay of the Land

Even the weather here is at odds with the rest of the country, much to a visitor's delight. They say the sun shines brighter here, and it most definitely shines longer. From November through April, the area receives almost no rain, a boon to those from northern climes used to seemingly endless rain, sleet, and snow during the North American winter (which is Costa Rica's "summer," or dry season). Newcomers can't believe their luck, but even so, by May, everyone is ready for the rain that transforms the yellow-and-brown landscape back into a riot of lush green. Chris Simmonds, originally from Vancouver but nine years in the beach town of Tamarindo, says, "Everyone remembers the first day of rain—last year it was May 18. By the end of April, you're thinking, It's got to come. People who can't wait shoot up to Arenal for a couple of days," where the two seasons are wet and really wet.

This is the second-largest province (about 10,000 square km/3,861 square mi.), but with one of the smallest populations (about 280,000). The heart of Guanacaste is a sparsely populated plain that extends northward to Nicaragua. To the east rise two mountain ranges, the Cordillera de Guanacaste and the Cordillera de Tilarán, and to the north loom several volcanoes, many of which are protected in national parks. The largest towns are small by North American standards: Liberia, the provincial capital and the largest town in the area, has all of 35,000 inhabitants. The small airport began to receive commercial flights in 2002; Delta pioneered the route with several weekly nonstop flights from Atlanta, Georgia. This development is transforming not only Liberia (some locals predict it will be "the next San José"), but the nearby Guanacaste beaches as well, some of which, like Playas del Coco, are only 30 or 40 minutes from Liberia by car. Another change in accessibility came in 2003 with the long-awaited completion of the Taiwan Friendship Bridge across the Tempisque River, which separates the 130-kilometer-long (80.8-mi.-long) Nicoya Peninsula from the mainland. Previously there was a slow ferry that could only carry 40 cars at a time, and waits were up to two hours. Now you can whiz across the bridge, cutting hours off the trip from San José to mid-peninsula beach towns like Tamarindo, Nosara, or Sámara.

On the Nicoya Peninsula, the bustling towns are all inland, strung out along Highway 21, which runs from Liberia through Filadelfia, Santa Cruz, and Nicoya, Costa Rica's oldest colonial city and the place beach dwellers go to do their shopping if they're not up for the trip to the capital. From the inland cities, a web of roads—some paved, most not—extends to remote beaches and coastal towns so laid back that each day seems to last a week. These are the kinds of places where the local grocery store lets everyone run a tab, and where you run into the same people seven times a day.

Most newcomers to Guanacaste choose to live on or near the beach,

Do You Really Want to Live on the Beach?

We're talking Guanacaste (the northern Pacific coast) here, but most of the concerns below apply to any Costa Rican beach community.

1. Weather is a big issue—it's much hotter and drier than the Central Valley.
2. Culture—there'll be no movie theater in your town. No recreational shopping. Hard to buy things, hard to get things repaired.
3. Doing business here is good, though it's not easy. Competitive (it ain't pretty). You need the same things to succeed here in business that you'd need to succeed anywhere: hard work and the ability to overcome obstacles. But here what's more important is a big dose of patience.
4. Social life—do you want to get involved, volunteer, do activities? If not, you'll be pretty isolated and won't have much to do.
5. Rent first, for a year.
6. If you're a perfectionist and can't roll with the punches, don't even think about moving here.

—*Chris Simmonds of Remax Real Estate in Tamarindo*

where ocean breezes alleviate the dry-season heat. The Nicoya Peninsula—most of which lies within the province of Guanacaste—is where you'll find most of the coveted beachfront property, with more ground cleared every day for new development. There are towns where you'll be hard-pressed to find many locals. Many hotels, restaurants, and real estate agencies are owned by foreigners, among them Germans, Americans, Canadians, Italians, Swiss, and French. There are also growing numbers of immigrants from other Latin American countries such as Argentina, Colombia, and Peru, drawn to Costa Rica's peaceful and stable environment and looking to escape their home country's economic, political, or military strife. "It used to be," a Peruvian told me about his home of Lima, the capital city, "they'd kill you on your way to work. Now they kill you on your way to *look* for work. Here it's *tranquilo,* and you can find a job without much problem."

Every year, a local tells me, the number of foreigners who come to live (rather than just visit) increases. It takes some of them years to build their houses—they go back to the States to work, then come down and build another room. But there are also those, with more resources and more time, who build fantasy houses overlooking the Pacific or who invest in already-built homes or condos, many in gated communities with golf courses, stables, and their own supply of water and electricity. Some of the country's biggest developments are located in northern Guanacaste, like the Club Med–style Playa Melía Conchal (just north of Tamarindo). In December 2003, a mammoth resort opened along the Gulf of Papagayo, anchored by a Four Seasons hotel and offering up lots and houses to those who want to own a piece of that coast.

It's an odd combination of rapid development—the building trade is booming, employing many grateful locals—and underdevelopment, with rutted dirt roads leading to million-dollar spreads. Infrastructure can be a problem, with overextended municipalities unable to fix the roads or improve electrical, water, and waste-removal systems. Often developers or homeowners shoulder what in other countries would be the state's burden, paying for new roads, stringing electrical wires, and arranging for secure water supplies and waste removal. During the dry season, water can become a real problem, especially with elaborately landscaped grounds and sprawling golf courses sucking up so much of the precious fluid.

In terms of prices, real estate agents and contractors say that building costs here are higher because so much of the material must be trucked in, often via some truly atrocious roads. In Playa Negra, south of Tamarindo, I watched as a truck sent to repair some enormous potholes (which the rains had turned into muddy lagoons) became stuck in one of the very holes it had hoped to fix. A tractor had to come and pull it out.

From the Gulf of Papagayo down to funky Montezuma at the southern tip of the peninsula, Guanacaste and the Nicoya Peninsula boast stunning beaches and beach towns that range from party central to places so remote they verge on inaccessible.

Playas del Coco to Tamarindo

The concave sweep of coastline south of Santa Elena and north of the Nicoya Peninsula is dominated by the Gulf of Papagayo, an enormous gulf that holds within its waters smaller and more protected bays and coves, like the nearly-enclosed Bahia Culebra, or Snake Bay.

More than half of the Gulf's stunning coastline is protected in Santa Elena National Park, home to oft-deserted Playa Naranjo and a dramatic outcropping just offshore called Witch's Rock, mythic in surfing circles. The route to this remote wave-riders' mecca is either by boat or overland on one of the worst roads in the country.

For regular civilians, more accessible (and ownable) land begins around Nacasolo, at the northern headland of Snake Bay. But even that area is fairly remote; most people choose to live in the Playas del Coco area, which includes (from north to south) Playas Panama, Hermosa, Coco, and

Ocotal. A perfect semicircle of gray sand, Playa Panama is so protected that there are hardly any waves breaking on its quiet shores. On my last visit you couldn't drive further north; they were grading and paving the road—good news indeed.

Playa Hermosa is one of the most beautiful beaches in this area, and the number of visitors it receives reflects that. Condos and hotels climb the hill north of town. Boogie boards and kayaks lay in multicolored stacks on the beach, ready to be rented. Roving vendors sell coconuts (for the refreshing milk) and souvenirs; you don't see that on the other beaches in the region, except maybe Coco during the highest season. The water is cool enough to be refreshing on a hot day, but warm enough to stay in for hours without feeling chilled. Waves break close to shore; out beyond the breakers you can still stand. Swells lift you off your feet and deposit you gently back down on the white-sand bottom.

The Vuleys, an extended family from Atlanta, Georgia, moved here in November 2002 and are renting out and running Puesta del Sol, a lovely open-air bar and restaurant at the northern end of the beach. The grand opening was December 1, says Richard Conlon, the Vuleys' British son-in-law, and lots of other business owners came. Among Playa Hermosa

Playas del Coco

© Erin Van Rheenen

hotel and restaurant owners there's a spirit of cooperation rather than of fierce competition. They help each other out, posting flyers for each other's businesses on their bulletin boards.

Richard and his wife, Alison, have two young children who go to school in Liberia, 30 or 40 minutes inland. When he's not working at the bar, Richard likes to snorkel—around the rock outcroppings just offshore are found a stunning array of multicolored fish. Ethan, the teenaged son of Art and Mary Vuley, loves it here. He got his GED back in the States and is thinking of going to college, but not right now. He has lots of friends here, and best of all, he says, "a beautiful Tica girlfriend who speaks no English." He likes to go to a deserted little beach just north of Playa Hermosa—to get there you scramble over the rocks at low tide. It's a beautiful white-shell beach, and he goes there to relax and play his guitar.

There are some frustrations, Richard admits. The price of beer just went up 25 percent (one company has a monopoly), and they had a CD player stolen from their car. Getting anything repaired is a challenge, and they had problems with a used car they bought in Liberia. But in balance, says Richard, gazing out over the gently breaking surf, they are very, very happy here.

Although there's just one beach, Playas del Coco is always expressed in the plural. The name also applies to the lively strip of a town that runs a few kilometers from the beach inland, where you'll find not only good seafood restaurants and fun dive bars, but also real-life services like banks, hardware stores, and supermarkets. On the hills above Playa Ocotal, just south of Playas del Coco, million-dollar vacation homes and more modest condos overlook the secluded gray-sand beach. Many of the properties available here lie within gated communities, a security plus for owners who only make it down a month or two every year.

Playas Flamingo, Brasilito, and Potrero lie just north of Tamarindo, with radiant Playa Flamingo serving as the central community and boasting the prettiest beach—Christopher Baker, in his *Moon Handbooks Costa Rica,* calls it one of the most magnificent beaches in the country. Some say nearby Playa Brasilito has been compromised by the Melía Conchal Resort, which bulldozed a lot of the funkiness out of the place. Still, a sizable community of expats has settled here and in nearby Playa Potrero. A few years ago the prestigious Country Day School of Escazú opened a branch just outside Potrero, making the area more attractive to expats with school-age children.

Ironically, the Country Day School building was constructed by Melía Conchal, and was meant to be a small shopping center. Country Day School converted the shops to classrooms and added a gymnasium and a swimming pool. The school goes from kindergarten through 12th grade, and in 2003 had 85 students. Most are children of expats, but some are local Ticos, including two boys on full scholarship. Yearly fees amount to some US$6,000, an unthinkable sum for most Ticos and prohibitive for many expats as well. But outside the Central Valley, good private schools are few and far between, and some expats would no more send their kids to a Costa Rican public school than they would trust their health to the Caja, the government-sponsored health care system. Other expats choose to partake of Costa Rica's extensive social services, and have good things to say about the system, which is considered one of the best in Latin America.

Tamarindo to Ostional

I had heard that Tamarindo was one of the most developed resorts on the Pacific coast; imagine my surprise when I rolled into a funky little beachside village that could be explored on foot in all of fifteen minutes. It's true, though, that the town is one of the most popular tourist destinations in the country, with nightly "turtle tours" to see massive leatherbacks lay their eggs in the sand, and with dozens of places to stay—budget *cabinas,* boutique-y bed-and-breakfasts, even generic midrange options like Best Western. Still true to its roots as a haven for surfers and other tattooed nomads, Tamarindo also draws an older and more sedate crowd, who may not pull all-nighters at the local disco but who quietly come, buy property, and open businesses. People who come to visit often want to stay, and this small town has a disproportionate number of real estate agencies to help them in that pursuit. You've got Remax, run by Canadians; French-owned Century 21; Hidden Coast, with mostly Dutch agents; and several agencies run by escapees from the United States. Property values in and around Tamarindo are among the highest in the country.

Still, it's hard to think of a place as overdeveloped (or even just developed) when most of the streets are unpaved, with dirt turning to slippery mud after a rainstorm. On one visit the lights went out during a nighttime storm, catching me on a pitch-black stretch of road between one cluster of businesses and the next. When the lights came back on 20 minutes later I had progressed some 100 meters and was covered in mud. A flashlight would have come in handy.

Though in some ways the town is your typical beach resort—lots of Internet cafés and rowdy bars, no hardware store or supermarket—Tamarindo feels more international and sophisticated. Many of the local hotels and restaurants are owned and run by Italian, German, Dutch, Swiss, Canadian,

© Erin Van Rheenen

San Juanillo, on the Nicoya Peninsula

and American expats, to name just a few of the nationalities represented in this multicultural burg. Some of those business owners came together in 1993 to form the Asociacion Pro-Mejoras de Tamarindo (Association for the Betterment of Tamarindo), "dedicated to satisfying the needs of tourists without compromising the environment and rich bio-diversity of the area." It's no secret that without tourism, towns like Tamarindo would most likely dry up and blow away. But it's also clear that people visit for the beauty of the natural environment, which must be preserved while seeing to the town's basic needs. The association organizes and lobbies to keep the streets in decent repair, protect sources of potable water, and make sure there's a waste-management system in place.

Italian expat Simona Filippini, who with her sister founded the hotel/dance studio/community center Arco Iris, says it's gratifying to work at this sort of grassroots level. Though there are frustrations, she feels like these sorts of citizen groups can have more impact here in Costa Rica "where thing aren't so fixed, and where there's more room to move." The association puts out a bilingual newsletter, *Noticias de Tamarindo/Tamarindo News,* whose masthead quotes Molly Ivins: "Where there is greed there is no vision," and then adds its own motto: "Don't let individual short-term gain prevent us from doing what's best for the future of our community."

Real estate agent Chris Simmonds says the area is going through a transition right now, from a resort to a place where people want to settle. "One of the big changes is the nearby Country Day School," he says. "Now English speakers have someplace nearby to send their kids."

South of Tamarindo is one of the most ambitious developments in the area, a sprawling gated community called Hacienda Pinilla. Billing itself in its glossy brochure as "an exclusive resort community," the development spreads across more than 1,821 hectares (4,500 acres) of a former cattle ranch, and stretches along five and a half kilometers (3.5 mi.) of coastline. Pat Pattillo of Pattillo Construction, an Atlanta-based developer, bought the land 28 years ago but only recently began transforming it into an upscale complex that he hopes will entice wealthy North Americans who want to relocate or buy vacation homes. Already many lots and homes have been sold.

Pattillo had to start from scratch, building roads; putting in phone, electrical, and sewage systems; and planting tens of thousands of trees in an effort to bring back to life vast tracts of land denuded by cattle grazing. If things go as planned, the project will contain three housing developments, several luxury hotels, condominiums, and a "retail village," presumably so residents will never have to leave the hacienda's gated confines. Lot prices run from about US$80,000 (165 square meters or 1,700 square feet) up to US$500,000 (beachfront, about 2,345 square meters/.58 acres). Prices per square meter run from about US$50 (for lots in the interior of the development, with no view) to US$335 for beachfront lots.

"We don't want to interfere with nature," said Hacienda's general manager Mauricio Estrada in a recent article in *Costa Rica Travel Magazine*. "We want to be part of it." "But you've got to wonder," pointed out one local, "how Pinilla's 18-hole golf course qualifies" as not interfering with the nature of this semi-arid land.

The further south you go (until you hit Nosara), the less developed the beaches and inland areas. Not that you won't run into expats—they're everywhere in this part of the country, including in and around Playa Junquillal, Playa Avellana, and Playa Negra, which draw surfers willing to rough it rather than tourists who want more amenities. And the expats you meet on this stretch of coast are likely to be fiercely independent men (and rarely, women) with a mission. Take Ray Beise, a former Minnesotan crackling with energy and ideas. Just up the road from Paraíso and a few kilometers inland from Playa Negra, Ray has created Pura Jungla, 100 hectares (250 acres) of ecologically sound development containing 32 building sites of about .8 hectares (two acres) each (much of the land will be left undeveloped).

Tamarindo Bulletin Board

What you find tacked up on local bulletin boards can tell you a lot about a place. This board was outside of Panadería Paris in Tamarindo, and included these notices:

Apt. for rent: 3 bedroom, 2 bath, hot water US$400/month

Surf lessons

Sportfishing trips

"4 Patas" Dog Obedience School

Digital photos available

Workshop for unleashing your creative potential. Once a week for 12 weeks, US$90

Murals and logos painted

Dharma body piercing

Massage/chiropractic services

Mayan astrology readings

For sale: various boats

For sale: 1968 VW classic camper. Experience Pura Vida in a bonafide time machine complete with extras: surfboard, guitar, friends. The possibilities are endless. US$2,000 negotiable.

"What you're looking at right now," Ray told me, as we stood in lush woodlands, listening to birds try to outdo each other in song, "was a cattle pasture. There were no animals, no trees, no iguanas, no bugs, no spiders, no cockroaches—nothing. It was burnt, dried-up cattle pasture. What we had here 15 years ago you couldn't even call earth—the land was hard as concrete. A herd of buffalo could walk across it and you'd never know they'd been there—it was so hard they wouldn't even leave a mark. Now it's soft. In the wet season you'll sink up to your ankles. We've done all kinds of work in soil building, soil regeneration. Water is the key to the regenerative process. If you have water, a lot of the regenerative process will happen on its own. All of these little *quebradas* (creeks) that are dry now, would have run, 100 years ago, all year long. We're trying to work with the land so that the water stays, doesn't just run off, taking all the soil nutrients with it."

Residents must agree to leave about a third of their land undeveloped, ensuring that living in Pura Jungla will continue to be like "living inside a national park," and guarding against the building of monster houses that push against lot boundaries. Two homes have already been built, and five more are on the drawing board. The house I saw was like a luxury tree house, built on stilts and floored with tropical hardwood, and with sweeping views of the ocean from its upper levels.

South of the Playa Negra area you'll find small unspoiled fishing villages like San Juanillo, or slightly bigger Tico towns like Ostional, whose beach is known for its *arrivadas,* great invasions of egg-laying Ridley turtles.

Between Ostional and Nosara runs the Río Montaña, often impassable during the rainy season. I had to hire a big tractor (called a *chapulín,* or grasshopper) to pull me across. It was either that or backtrack all the way to Playa Negra and then head inland for the better roads. The trip back would have added three or four hours to my journey; the *chapulín* cost me about five dollars.

Nosara, Sámara, and Playa Carrillo

Nosara is a quiet place that grows on you. Guidebooks say there's not much to do here, and in terms of sights, they're right. What people do is stick around and soak up the good vibes. The Nosara Yoga Institute up on the hill casts a benevolent eye over the community, and the town attracts residents whose idea of heaven is to perfect their headstand, amble along one of the three absolutely pristine beaches, or paddle out to surf when the waves are big. Mornings, locals meet at Café de Paris for good coffee and even better blueberry muffins.

The town has two main parts: Bocas de Nosara, five kilometers (3.1 mi.) inland and a typical Tico small town, clustered around the soccer field; and Beaches of Nosara, closer to the beach and home to a large foreign community, made up mostly of American and Canadian expats who live in houses tucked among lush trees and flowers.

Although Nosara is blessed with stunning natural beauty, it isn't by accident that the area has avoided some of the worst pitfalls of seaside tourist towns. Residents are active in keeping their town low-key, and the Nosara Civic Association leads the way. The association began back in 1962, when Allan Hutchison bought 121 hectares (300 acres) in Nosara, built roads, put in electrical wires, and drilled wells to create one of the only private water systems in the country. He sold off parcels within this area, and charged residents a monthly fee for the water and services.

"Water is the key," says Linda Cox, current manager of the association. "If you have good water, everything else is gravy." But Costa Rica is known for its potable water, and the association is about more than a steady supply of water. They also work to improve trash pickup, send out crews to maintain the roads when the municipality can't afford to, and perhaps most important, work doggedly to see that development doesn't spin out of control.

Expat Profile: Brenda Burnside

I stumbled across a boxing gym in the jungle entirely by accident. The place I'd wanted to spend the night in the Pacific beach town of Nosara had closed, but the ex-manager said I might try Brenda next door—sometimes she rented out *cabinas*. I should look for the little path just past the stone that's painted bright blue.

And there the path was, littered with tiny purple blossoms and wending its way across a stream and to an unlocked gate. Brenda? I called out. Dogs started to bark, and soon a woman with short-cropped blonde hair appeared. She had tiger-stripe tattoos up and down her bare arms and legs.

It was Brenda Burnside, former professional boxer and owner of the shady domain she calls the Enchanted Forest. And the tattoos? She was called the Tigress, she told me. There'd even been a film made about her, called *A Tiger by Her Stripes*.

The heart of this tigress's domain is

an open-air gym, with a high thatched roof from which bats swoop out during late-afternoon training sessions, feasting on mosquitoes. There's also a lovely domed-ceiling sauna made of fragrant cedar wood that she fires up after classes, an outdoor kitchen, and a scattering of one-room cabins.

As birds squawked and fire ants nipped at my ankles, I wondered: What had brought this woman to a quiet town on a pristine stretch of Costa Rican coastline?

A dream, as it turned out. Her first visit, in 1999, coincided with one of the largest *arrivadas* in years. An *arrivada* is when sea turtles arrive on the beaches by the hundreds, scrambling up the sand to lay their eggs. Brenda had never seen anything like it, and she went to sleep that night with images of the vast army still in her head.

She dreamed of a turtle diving into a hole made not of air nor water but of

© Erin Van Rheenen

something in between. She followed the turtle in and there encountered a sea of eyes—the slanted eyes of this area's Brahmin cattle, the round dark eyes of the local howler monkeys, and the ancient eyes of Ridley turtles—all looking at her and beckoning.

Brenda woke up feeling that she was needed here in some way, and that she had to find a way to live here. On the remaining days of her vacation, she looked into real estate, and learned that a nearby piece of land was available. It had been for sale for 18 years, the real estate agent told her. Nobody wanted it. The price was about US$30,000.

First she used the land as a campground, but she knew that although she'd retired from pro boxing in 2000, she didn't want to entirely give it up.

When she first arrived, she'd done exhibition matches during halftime at bullfights. The guys were impressed; they couldn't believe a woman could fight. Someone said she should give lessons to the kids in Nosara, which is what she started doing. The kids loved her classes. First it was seven people, then twenty, then forty. But Brenda had trouble with her feet and the cement floor at the local community center where she'd give the classes.

She started building a wood-floored gym on her land, tearing the floor out twice to get it to her liking. The resulting space is beautiful, and well equipped, though Brenda jokes that it's her Flintstone gym—along with the regulation heavy bags are sand-filled inner tubes, and some of her weights are Coke bottles filled with sand. But people come, and more will come when school's out in December. The boys love it, but she wants especially to encourage the girls. Brenda's dream was to be an Olympic athlete, and though she was good at many things—fencing got her closest, she thinks—she never quite made it. Women's boxing will soon be an Olympic sport, and Brenda would love to see a girl from Costa Rica make it to the Olympic ring.

Meanwhile, she has big plans for the Enchanted Forest. She'd like to make it a full-fledged fitness center, to open a restaurant, and to rent out the premises for private gatherings.

Her time here hasn't been without challenges, but she loves living in Costa Rica. "In the States you always have to be doing something. Here, you can be productive but still live day to day. It's hard to describe. In a way it's much easier here."

But still, she cautions, you need to be smart about it. Her advice to someone coming down? "Bring lots of money. Come down and check out the different places. Do you like the city, the mountains, the ocean? Then learn about the place you like. If you live near the ocean, for instance, anything electrical doesn't last very long. This is my eighth coffeepot since December, and it's going. That's almost a coffee pot a month. It's the salt and humidity. You got to keep those things dry, and nothing's dry here. Everything goes here. Zip! It's gone. You got to have a room that has a dehumidifier. I've got a little box that I built, with two light bulbs in it. I keep my computer and DVDs in there."

"Look around," she continues. "Ask questions. But in the end, you need to follow your dream. If the turtles tell you to stay, you stay."

The association influences development within and outside its boundaries. The fact that few structures in Beaches de Nosara are over two stories is no accident. Builders aren't following municipal zoning laws but rather are adhering to guidelines set by the association, which will fight in the courts any development it considers antithetical to the understated ambience of the area. One of its biggest fights was against Marbella Corporation, who wanted to build a high-rise hotel on the beach. That battle raged for 18 years, and the association recently won. "But there will be more," predicts Linda Cox. "It's a never-ending battle."

Roberto Sitwell of Nosara Real Estate says more and more people want to live here. In the last six months of 2002, he personally sold more properties than the entire Nosara Real Estate office had sold in the previous three years. Right now, he says, the supply is almost nil and the demand astronomical, at least within the association itself. He says that land goes for about US$60/square meter within the association, and as low as US$20/square meter outside. Roberto himself, who's been in the area for more than a decade, opted to buy property a few kilometers south, in the more traditionally Tico town of Garza, where prices are lower.

About 15 kilometers (9.3 mi.) south of Garza, the next town of any size is Sámara, as unlike Nosara as *guaro* (the local firewater) is from chardonnay. Fans of Nosara are likely to turn up their noses at Sámara's party atmosphere and beachfront development, but both places have their charms. It's interesting to note that recently the powerful National Tourism Institute (ICT) developed a plan that sets aside certain areas for high-density tourism—large hotels and beachfront development—and designates other areas as low-density. Perhaps building on how things are already shaping up, Nosara was designated low-density and Sámara high-density. This means that developers in Sámara will face far fewer hurdles than those wanting to build in Nosara, and that the already very different character of these two beachside communities is likely to be accentuated in years to come.

But before you start to picture Sámara as some sort of evil anti-Nosara, picture this: a beautiful half-moon of a protected bay, with palm trees and vines acting as a green fringe to the gray-sand beach. It's a great place for learning to surf, as the waves never get too big and you can stand in chest-deep water waiting for the perfect one to come your way. There are hotels and restaurants built right on the beach, it's true, but so far they're low-rise and casual, open-air bars with sand floors or small *cabinas* partially hidden by beachside vegetation. Consider, too, that the center of the community is *puro Tico*, the usual town built around a soccer field; the town hasn't yet bifurcated into separate areas for Ticos and expats. The place is very popular with Tico tourists, which suggests that Sámara is the Costa Rican idea of what a beach resort should be. Ticos like the feel of Sámara, and after all, it's their country.

A few miles south of Sámara is Playa Carillo, a gorgeous pink sand beach protected by an offshore coral reef. Yachts anchor at the south end of the bay, and hotels and residential communities are being built along this quiet stretch of coast that boasts its own airstrip. Investors have long felt that Carillo has enormous potential, and with the new bridge over the Río Tempisque (at the upper end of the Nicoya Peninsula), access to all of Nicoya is easier and faster than before.

South of Carillo, the road gets really, really bad, and is often impassible during the wet season. A string of stunning beaches goes all the way down to Cabo Blanco, the southernmost tip of the Nicoya Peninsula. The area is sparsely populated and requires some gumption to visit; you need even more to live there.

Montezuma Area

The approach to Montezuma is dramatic—you wind down a gravel road, catching glimpses of nothing but blue, blue ocean, all the while wondering if there's really a town down there. Turn a sharp corner and there it is—a charming little place tucked into the folds of overgrown hills. Low buildings line the narrow main street, with hibiscus, palm, and acacia crowding in and making the way even narrower. Tourists arrive in rented 4x4s, and a few times a day the bus from the Paquera ferry squeezes through and deposits its load of surfers, backpackers, and people like Lauren, a middle-aged pipe fitter from Alberta who comes down a few months every year to swim, read, and relax.

This is a very good place to relax. The influx of mostly young North Americans and Europeans has made Montezuma a cool little "alternative" spot, with excellent vegetarian food at the American-run Sano Banano and the German-run Bakery Café, a bookstore (the Libreria Topsy) where you'll find "wicked good books" to buy, trade, or rent, and a couple of bars that pump out dance music deep into the tropical night. On one visit I watched as a film crew trailed the finalists for Tica Linda, a national beauty contest, through the streets and down to the beach. The entire town, always slow-paced, ground to an absolute halt as young beauties tottered along in high heels, draped in strategically placed strands of jute. Local surfers were recruited to stand in as atmospheric background. No doubt the town was chosen as much for its funky vibe as for its natural beauty, but the point is, the place has cachet.

The coastline here is convoluted, jutting out into the sea and doubling back on itself. Walk a few hundred yards and you're out of town; walk ten minutes and you'll find beaches where you'll have the place to yourself except for the occasional pelican, iguana, or troop of monkeys. The jungle rushes right up to the edge of the beach, where brown sand alternates with volcanic rock and pulverized pink and white shells. Rivers and streams cascade over boulders and empty out into deserted coves.

The "alternative" feel of the area has roots that go back at least to the 1950s, with the arrival of two Europeans who would transform the landscape of the place, or, more accurately, work hard to make sure that the land they loved so passionately would still be there for future generations to enjoy. Olaf Wessberg of Sweden and Karen Morgensen of Denmark had a dream of escaping the Scandinavian winters and of growing organic fruit in tropical America. They tried California, Guatemala, and Mexico, and visited many parts of Costa Rica before they found their niche in Montezuma, where they moved in 1955. They spent their time raising 30 varieties of fruit and getting to know and love the diverse flora and fauna of their adopted home. Journalist Bill Wienberg knew the couple and described them as strict vegetarians who "had a reverence for nature that bordered on the mystical, talking great joy in the company of monkeys and coatimundis."

In the late 1950s, the couple watched in horror as more and more squatters moved into the area, clearing land for crops and then selling out to lumber companies and cattle ranches. Afraid that soon the land would be beyond repair, Wessberg wrote an appeal for donations so that he might buy up property around Montezuma and thus protect it from destruction. His call was heeded, with contributions coming from the British World League Against Vivisection, the Sierra Club, and the Philadelphia Conservation League, among many other organizations and individuals. Wessberg and Morgenson bought a big parcel of land to the south, on the headland between Cabuya and Malpaís, which in 1965 became Cabo Blanco, Costa Rica's first nature reserve. The reserve protects one of the last large tracts of mixed evergreen and deciduous moist tropical forest in the area, and is home to rare and threatened species such as currasow, crested guan, brocket deer, and jaguarundi.

Montezuma is a good place to visit, but what about living here? Out of gas? You're out of luck. Stove blow up and you need a new one? Get used to cooking over an open fire. In terms of stores, you've got one grocery store and that's it. And try not to get sick or slip on the rocks at the waterfall south of town (like I did), because there's no doctor, no clinic, not even a pharmacy.

If you want to eat, drink, lounge, get a tattoo, or buy handmade jewelry, Montezuma is the place. You need anything halfway practical, you go to Cóbano, 40 minutes inland. If you don't have a car and the bus isn't coming for hours, well, you can try to find a taxi, or you can start walking, hoping someone will take pity on you and give you a ride.

To the north of Montezuma is Playa Tambor, a gray-sand stretch of beach chosen by Spain's Barcelo company as the site of a massive ocean-front development. This all-inclusive resort, which was the first of its kind in Costa Rica, has everything from a golf course to a 350-seat theater to a helicopter landing pad. Barcelo is said to have destroyed wildlife habitats and drained wetlands to build the sprawling complex. Nevertheless, the Costa Rican government not only gave it the green light but also agreed to pave the road to the hotel, to add a new ferry to bring visitors from Puntarenas on the mainland, and to house construction workers who would later be employed by the resort. If the choice is between protecting the environment (enforcing already existing laws) and promoting tourism, Costa Rica seems to choose the latter.

South of Montezuma, Malpaís (Bad Country) and Playa Santa Teresa are more remote than Montezuma but still draw their share of expats, especially those who appreciate the great surfing on both beaches. From the inland town of Cóbano the road leads south to Carmen. Go left and you'll find Malpaís; go right and you'll hit Santa Teresa. Both towns are expanding rapidly and consist of hotels, restaurants, and homes strung along the main road, which runs parallel to the beach.

Real Estate Agents

Note: The agencies and individuals listed below are a small sampling of what you will find; inclusion in this list does not imply personal recommendation.

Century 21 Coastal Estates
Tamarindo area
Bruce Trudell
tel. 506/653-0300
fax 506/653-0600
bruce@c21tamarindo.com
www.c21tamarindo.com

Hidden Coast Realty
Tamarindo area
Joost Hauwert, Hans Veeken, Maarten Kampen, Mariano Caffaratti
tel. 506/653-0708
fax 506/653-0849

location@racsa.co.cr
www.hiddencoastrealty.com

Nosara Real Estate
Nosara area
Darin McBratney, Roberto Stowell
tel./fax 506/682-0012
darin@nosararealestate.com
www.nosararealestate.com

Remax Ocean Surf Realty
Tamarindo area
Chris Simmons, Jim Main, Brigette
O'Shaughnessy
tel. 506/653-0073
fax 506/653-0074
csimmons@racsa.co.cr

**Remax Resort
Properties Papagayo**
Playas del Coco area
Iris Mailloux
tel. 506/670-1129
cell: 506/392-7111
fax 506/670-0825
mailloux@racsa.co.cr
www.costa-rica-real-estate1.com

Tamarindo Real Estate
Tamarindo area
Jerry Smith
tel./fax 506/653-0107
tamarindobeach@hotmail.com

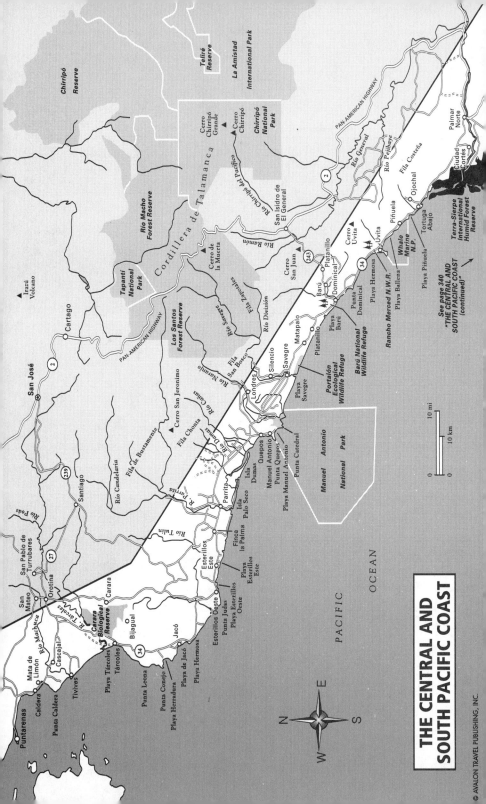

THE CENTRAL AND SOUTH PACIFIC COAST

See page 340 "THE CENTRAL AND SOUTH PACIFIC COAST (continued)"

© AVALON TRAVEL PUBLISHING, INC.

The Central and South Pacific Coast

S peaking in generalities, the farther south you go along Costa Rica's
  Pacific coast, the less developed the area and the more tropical the
  climate. For the purposes of this book, the central Pacific coast is
from Jacó to Palmar Norte, the south Pacific coast starting where the
Osa Peninsula pushes out from the mainland and ending at the Panamanian border.

The Lay of the Land

Geographically, the central Pacific consists of a narrow coastal strip
backed by steep and heavily wooded mountains. This juxtaposition
makes for some very dramatic beaches, where the jungle pushes right
up to the sand and where monkeys and sloths join your afternoon tanning
session. The climate offers up two fairly distinct seasons—wet (or green)
being May–November, and dry running December–April. Those who

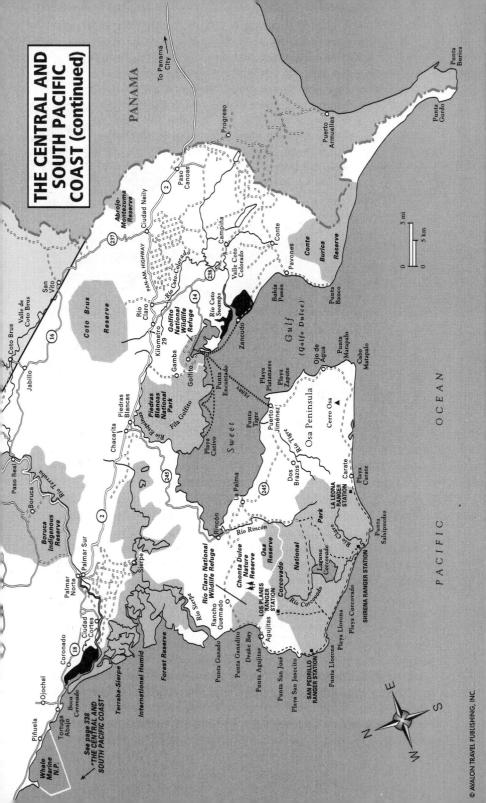

consider Guanacaste (in the north) too dry, and the southern zone too humid, feel that the central Pacific coast is, like something out of a fairy tale, just right. Towns like Quepos and Jacó, and national parks such as Manuel Antonio and Carera, are blessed with a happy medium of rainfall and sunshine. While the summer sees considerably less rain than the winter here, even in dry season you will see a riot of green cascading down the hills to the sea.

The south Pacific coast's seasons correspond roughly to those of the central Pacific coast, but the dry season here isn't all that dry. Locals are prepared for rain at any time of year, as the area receives 4–8 meters (157 to 315 in.) per year. But the wet season definitely lives up to its name, and May through November are when legendary surf spots like Pavones (with its kilometer-long left-breaking wave) really go off. Thunderstorms are not uncommon late in the year; Caño Island, off the Osa Peninsula, has the dubious distinction of being struck by lightning more often than any other place in Central America.

In stark contrast to the central Pacific's straight and narrow coast, the southern coast is positively convulsive, disrupted by swamps and estuaries near the Valle de Diquis, thrust out into the ocean at the Osa Peninsula, and deeply indented at the Golfo Dulce. As the crow flies, the central and southern coasts are roughly equivalent in length, but tracing the shoreline convolutions of the southern zone would probably take two to three times longer, if there were roads that allowed you to do so.

But even with all the time in the world and a hardy 4x4, you couldn't drive the whole of the coastline. A road traces the eastern perimeter of the heavily wooded Osa Peninsula, but stops at Carate. On most maps there's a dotted line running along the Osa's west coast; map keys call it a "track," passable in dry season. It may be passable, but you'll be passing on foot, because this "track" is most often a path, wide enough for one person when it isn't petering out into the bush. On the narrow Burica Peninsula, which Costa Rica shares with Panama, the road ends almost before the land begins its jut into the Pacific.

The lack of roads means that the towns you *can* get to feel like outposts, islands of civilization amid vast tracts of wilderness. Darryl Cole-Christensen, in his book *A Place in the Rain Forest,* writes of pioneering in the Coto Brus Valley in the late 1950s. The forest was their adversary, he says. Gloomy and dangerous, home to venomous snakes, jaguars, and wild pigs, it was something that had to be fought and cleared as settlers carved out a place for themselves, their livestock, and their crops. Nowadays there has been much clear-cutting of trees and destruction of animal habitat (even on so-called protected land), here as elsewhere in the country. But the southern zone still feels wild, a place that even now provokes primordial fear and wonder.

The area has a very interesting pre-Columbian history—the Indians here were influenced by South American tribes, while indigenous peoples elsewhere in Costa Rica had ties to more northerly civilizations. Like the Inca of Peru, the tribes in southern Costa Rica created gold ornaments using lost-wax technique; many are in the shapes of local animals such as crocodiles and jaguars. They also created perfectly round stone spheres, some weighing up to 16 tons. These mysterious spheres have generated many theories as to their origin—Erich von Daniken, in his *Chariots of the Gods,* claimed that they were projectiles shot from starships. Others suggest that the spheres were shaped by hydraulic pressure, tumbled with other rocks at the base of thunderous waterfalls.

Recent history is just as colorful. Gold fever hit in the 1970s, concentrated in what was to become Corcovado National Park. Puerto Jimenez was a rowdy boomtown, with *oreros* trading nuggets for booze and prostitutes. Longtime locals tell of wild times, with everyone packing a gun and fortunes being made and lost every day. Even a young José Figueres (president from 1994 to 1998) succumbed to the fever. The miners' destructive methods—chopping down the rain forest, dynamiting riverbeds—prompted outrage and led, finally, to the creation of Corcovado National Park in the mid-1980s.

ACCESS

If you're looking to relocate or buy a vacation home along the Pacific coast, geographic and climate may be less important than accessibility. As elsewhere in Costa Rica, the question here is not: Is it beautiful? but Can you get there? The days may be gone when you needed a horse and several days to reach what are now decent-sized towns, but you still need to consider how hard it will be for you to get home. Of course, if you never leave home—even if you dwell deep in the jungle—you won't have any trouble. But chances are, the more remote the area, the more likely you'll need to go—often!—somewhere else. Whether you need a stack of plywood, a big bag of rice, or emergency medical care, what are the roads like that will get you there? Most North Americans can't imagine planning their day (or life) according to the state of nearby roads, but that's the reality in the more remote areas of Costa Rica. And the "wild south" most surely qualifies as remote. For example, driving from San José to Puerto Jimenez (on the Osa Peninsula) is a full-day affair, more if rains have washed out the road or made rivers impassable.

Or let's say you want to live on land that borders the magnificent Corcovado National Park. The easiest entry point would be at Carate, a "town" that consists of an airstrip and a general store that charges an arm and a leg for a can of Coke. The road there from Puerto Jimenez isn't too bad, though of course it's not paved and there are a few rivers to cross. But with a 4x4 and a few hours, you can get there. If your car breaks down, you can hope your timing is right to catch the once-a-day "shuttle"—riders sit in the back of a truck and hold on for dear life.

The central Pacific wins the accessibility contest without even breaking a sweat. From the Central Valley, where the majority of expats and Costa Ricans make their home, central Pacific beach towns like Jacó and Quepos are the most convenient vacation spots in the country. And it goes both ways, of course—residents of these areas can easily shoot up to San José for a shopping excursion or a visit to a well-regarded specialist, or to meet a friend's incoming flight. Roads in the area are relatively well-maintained, so travel time from San José to Jacó is under two hours, with Quepos another forty minutes down the road. After Quepos, things get tricky for a while—the 45-kilometer (28-mi.) stretch from Quepos to Dominical is one of the few remaining unpaved sections of the coastal highway. From Dominical to Palmar Norte used to be even more dicey, but in 2000 the road was paved.

Central Pacific Coast Towns

JACÓ

People warned me about Jacó. "It's close to San José, so it's the most popular beach town in the country," they told me. "You know what that means—it's become a tourist trap." But maybe because I was expecting little, Jacó snuck up on me with its laid-back charm. If this is the worst Costa Rica has on offer, then the country is very lucky indeed.

The place is basically one long strip, parallel to the long white-sand beach, with no building over two stories high. There are the usual beach town open-air bars and restaurants, souvenir shops, budget *cabinas,* and some larger chain hotels (like Best Western) outside the town proper. But there are also the businesses that make a place not just visitable but livable: banks, medical clinics, hardware stores, and car repair shops. I think it's this combination that won me over—many beach towns force you to go elsewhere if your needs go beyond food, alcohol, or a new bikini.

Javier Barquero, manager of the Best Western Jacó, describes how the town has changed in the last few years. "Now there's more construction, more investment, more opportunity. Better services. Lots of nice places to

Jacó

go out for a drink or have dinner. But there's also been an increase in drugs and prostitution." Javier, himself from San José, sees Jacó as a town of people who've come from elsewhere. "There are lots of Canadians here," he says. "Some Americans, some Italians. The foreigners don't mix so much with the Ticos; sometimes they don't even mix with other foreigners."

Betty, from Argentina, would probably agree, but wouldn't see it as a problem. A stylish and affable woman in her forties, Betty runs a popular juice stand on the main drag. Often other Argentines, including the owner of the Argentine-style Tango Grill down the street, are perched on the juice bar's stools, sipping her concoctions. "It's my little colony," she says. She and her family arrived a few years ago, and she's very happy with Jacó. "It's a real town," she says. "Actually, it feels more like a neighborhood." She says she would prefer to live outside of town, up in the mountains where it's quieter and cooler, but her kids, ages 11 and 13, would always need to be driven somewhere. "Here," she says, "it's flat and you can bicycle everywhere. That's what my kids do. They're always flying by on their bikes. I just wave."

Property for sale at the time of my visit included 16.2 hectares (40 acres) 45 minutes from Jacó, with waterfall and ocean view, for US$86,000; and 600 square meters (6,458 sq. ft.) in downtown Jacó, suitable for business, US$30,000. There are many modest housing developments going up around the town, where houses on small lots go for as little as US$15,000. Among the better-known beaches close to Jacó, Playa Herradura (7 km/4.3 mi. north) is the site of Los Sueños, a Marriot megaresort and residential complex with hundreds of condos and its own marina (www.lossuenosresort.com). There are also tennis courts and a championship golf course. If you want to see what Playa Herradura looks like without the bother of traveling, rent the movie *1492*, starring Gérard Depardieu as Christopher Columbus—the beach is featured in many scenes. Local indigenous peoples were recruited to play the Indians Columbus encountered; they were paid US$15 a day, with women who bared their chests getting three times that rate. The ten weeks of filming was said to contribute US$8 million to the local economy. Ten kilometers (6.2 mi.) north of Playa Herradura is Punta Leona, where vacationers from the Central Valley and abroad own condos in a gated community.

Just south of Jacó is Playa Hermosa, a 10-kilometer (6.2-mi.) stretch of gray-brown sand battered by the kind of waves surfers love. It's become a favorite among those who want something more laid-back than Jacó, and many of the businesses serving tourists are owned and operated by expats. The bartender at a local club told me he came here five years ago to surf, and now has a Tica wife and a two-and-a-half-year-old daughter. "It's easier to be a good father down here," says this South Carolina native. "The people are so nice, and the society is less materialistic. There's free medical care, and then you've got an extended family that helps out. Sometimes it's too much," he admits. "Seems like there's a baby shower or birthday party every other day. But there's much less stress down here."

He loves Playa Hermosa, but he and his family live in Jacó because there are more services there—health clinics, supermarkets, and the like. "Jacó has some problems, for sure," he says. "But if you don't run in those circles, they don't much affect you. And my neighborhood's great—I leave my bike out, unlocked, no problem."

But the problems in Jacó are starting to spill over into nearby areas, and locals report that now there's more petty theft in Playa Hermosa and nearby beaches. Development has also arrived, and on the gravel road between Playa Hermosa and the next beach south there are not one but two housing developments going up, sporting Spanish-style stucco homes on narrow lots that go for about half a million dollars each. Check out www.hermosaparadise.com and www.hermosapalms.com to see what's on offer. Oh, and don't be confused when you find Playa Hermosa after Playa Hermosa all over Costa Rica—it means Pretty Beach, and there are a lot of those in this country.

QUEPOS AND MANUEL ANTONIO

Quepos sits sandwiched between a tranquil harbor dotted with fishing boats and the steep, wooded slope southeast of town. Incoming and outgoing traffic take turns across the narrow bridge into town. Locals walk by with fishing poles over their shoulders or pedal along on bicycles, often with a cell phone scrunched between shoulder and ear. A pleasant grid of streets lined with low buildings, Quepos was once a banana town; the United Fruit Company built a compound south of town in the 1930s and drew workers from other parts of the country. In the 1950s, disease blighted the banana trees, and they were replaced by oil-producing African palms.

> *Fans of Quepos feel like they have it all: swimmable white-sand beaches, a gem of a national park, lush tropical foliage, and enough tourist infrastructure to ensure good roads and services.*

Nowadays, Quepos does triple duty as a major sportfishing destination, a working Tico town where you can buy a stove or some new shoes, and the gateway to the most-visited tourist site in the country, Manuel Antonio National Park. Budget travelers often opt to stay in Quepos, but the more upscale tourist facilities are strung along the seven-kilometer (4.3-mi.) road that winds through jungly hills from Quepos to the park entrance. There is also a small cluster of hotels, bars, and restaurants at the Manuel Antonio end of the road, all within walking distance of the park.

Property here is some of the most expensive in all of Costa Rica; 2,000 square meters (.5 acre) of prime beachfront property might go for several hundred thousand dollars. But fans of the area feel like they have it all: swimmable white-sand beaches, a gem of a national park where monkey and sloth sightings are all but guaranteed, lush tropical foliage, and enough tourist infrastructure to ensure good roads and services.

There are many real estate offices in town that will be glad to help you look for the place of your dreams. It's important to have the inside scoop on the area, and a good agent can provide just that. A local told me about a squatters' town on the road from Quepos to Manuel Antonio (which is lined with luxury hotels and pricey restaurants; not the kind of place you'd imagine a shantytown). Apparently, one of the biggest properties in the area was owned by a drug dealer who didn't come around much. This absentee ownership attracted squatters, who built small houses and planted crops, thereby laying claim to the land. Eventually, some of squatters sold "their" land to other locals, who then sold to foreigners. "Buying property here," the local told me, "you really need someone who knows the area and its history, to make sure you know what you're getting yourself into." Just because land was once squatted on doesn't necessarily mean that there would be a problem if you bought it—the property could very well have a clear title, and everything would be ducky. But then again, the property might exist in some legal no-man's land that would allow you to buy it (or at least pay for it) without actually owning it.

Many of the hotels, bars, and restaurants in the Manuel Antonio area are owned by Americans, Canadians, Argentines, Italians, and other non-natives, and there is a strong gay (male) presence, with many establishments gay-owned or at least gay-friendly. "We are an open-minded place" boasts a sign in English that hangs in the doorway of an open-air bar right off Manuel Antonio beach. Businesses cater primarily to tourists, and as such there are many non-Tico items on offer, like the excellent iced lattes and toasted bagels with cream cheese at the two branches of Café Milagro.

Getting work (as opposed to running your own business) is not easy. A hotel owner told me, "Very wealthy people do come here to hang out, but 80 percent of the people who move here seem to be looking for work. They usually don't find it, because businesses can't legally hire foreigners."

I talked with two Canadian sisters who had managed to land waitressing jobs but quit after a few months. "They hardly gave us any shifts,

Capuchín monkey in Manuel Antonio National Park

and the wage was less than two dollars an hour. People here don't tip, and the tourists pick up that custom when they see how much of their bill is tax and 'service.' Somehow we didn't see much of that service charge. It was like charity work, except the customers were really demanding."

DOMINICAL

About 45 kilometers (28 mi.) south of Quepos, or an hour from the inland city of San Isidro de General, lies Dominical. The town is a low-key "resort,"

Expat Profile: Anita Myketuk

Anita Myketuk has lived in the Pacific coast town of Manuel Antonio for nearly 30 years, running the Buena Nota gift shop for a good part for that time.

"We arrived in 1974, and there was nothing here—no electricity or running water or telephones in Manuel Antonio. Quepos was a small fishing village; there was no tourist trade, just one hotel and a couple of *pensiones* that mostly the truckers and delivery people would use. The roads were bad. We camped—had a Volkswagen. It was really primitive. Vegetables would come twice a week on the back of a truck. There were no supermarkets. After a year and a half we brought our cat down, and you couldn't get cat food, not even in San José. Now there's everything here. Even the little *pulpería* up the road has cat food.

"It was always expensive here, because of the taxes. It's never been cheap. We came here, walked to the end of the beach, and said, 'This is paradise. I bet we can pick up some property for next to nothing.' But it was never like that. Everything was expensive, even in the '70s. We bought some property up on the hill for US$20,000; we could have bought

a place in Marin County [California] for the same price.

"Don [Anita's husband, who passed away a few years ago] was diabetic, and he was losing his eyesight. Our place had a great view. We bought it with the idea that he wanted to see the most beautiful view in the little time he had left to see. But he went back to the States and had various procedures—laser surgery—and he never lost his eyesight!

"We were really excited when we bought it; we'd never owned property before. But if people are going to come down here, I'd definitely emphasize: Come down here for at least a year, not as a tourist, before you even consider buying anything. People say to me, But we've been coming here for nine years! And they build or buy something, and then they're stuck, and find out they don't like it. Because the bureaucracy is really bad, or they're retiring, which is stressful even in the States, and then they come here and it's worse. And they don't know any Costa Ricans, so nothing works for them. You do much better here if you know a few people who can help you, give you a few contacts.

"But I love it here. And as complicated as it is, you really shouldn't worry a latticework of potholed dirt roads framed by the Barú River to the north, the Tinamaste mountains to the east, and a four-kilometer (2.5-mi.) gray-sand beach to the west. The beach's booming waves are heaven for good surfers, but not so great for swimmers. Each year many people succumb to the punishing waves and dangerous riptides; the town recently organized a force of lifeguards at the residents' own expense. The coastline around Dominical is gorgeous, and the forest that comes down to the sea is riddled with rivers and spectacular waterfalls.

about it—it's really not that stressful if you don't take it to heart. It's nice because there's a lot here now: a supermarket, some good restaurants, other foreigners. It's fine to think you can go out and live in a very primitive place, like we did when we first came, but it's not that easy. I like being able to go get my mail, to go to a coffee shop and chat with other people, or to have some live music if I want to go out at night. And we have good cable here—we can watch CBS and NBC movies every day if we want to.

"Anything besides general medical care, I go to San José. Bigger purchase items I usually go to San José, though now there are two stores in Quepos that have big electrical appliances, even refrigerators. Even furniture you can get here now. You don't have to go out of Quepos much anymore. What we're really lacking here is a library and a university. A lot of people wouldn't think that is important, but for me it is.

"We have transport service that will bring things out from San José. They come almost every day, and the cost of them delivering a big box is only a couple of dollars. They deliver right to my door—they brought all these tiles, and the furniture. You don't

have to get a moving van. Most parts of Costa Rica have similar services that are very reasonable.

"We lived here for quite a few years before we bought the property. It's not for everyone. Some people love it; some people adapt really well. Couples sometimes have a hard time. One likes it better than the other, one adapts better, learns the language faster. Makes friends easier. I've seen couples break up. Also, weird things happen—men go off with young girls and women go off with young guys. It's real common here. There are three or four women that came down with nice men, nice families, and then took off with some young construction worker. I think maybe the young Ticos want to be with a wealthier gringo, and they'll do whatever they can to make it happen. I can't imagine they'd have a lot in common.

"All of Costa Rica is like a small town. Even in San José, I run into people all the time who know me. I went into a little hole-in-the-wall liquor store in Heredia, and the guy there said, "Oh, you're Anita from the Buena Nota." I thought I'd never seen this guy before in my life. He said, 'I used to live in Quepos 20 years ago, and I remember you.'"

Most resident *extranjeros* live outside of Dominical proper; the foreigners you'll see in town are mostly young backpackers and surfers. They stay in low-budget beachside *cabinas,* check their email at Internet cafés, and eat pizza at San Clemente Bar & Grill, where the ceiling is paneled with broken surfboards. Dominical is known as a board-breaking beach, and if you donate your busted board to the existing collection, you get a free beer and a taco. One wit wrote on the remaining half of his board: "This wave was at least 2 feet tall!"

The town has the same ragged patchwork of rapid development and underdevelopment as many a burgeoning tourist town. There are at least four real estate offices, but no real health clinic (more on this later). There are plenty of bars, restaurants, and mini-marts, but few useful businesses like supermarkets and hardware stores. Residents are trying, however, to retain the town's laid-back charm even as they try to accommodate new arrivals. A newly built "centro commercial," for example, is not an ugly strip mall but a cluster of pleasant low buildings connected by raised wooden walkways wending their way through a tropical garden. The center has an Internet café, some tour agencies, and a small health food store where they sell homemade yogurt, herbal potions in bottles with hand-lettered labels in English, and brownies so good you'll want to buy up all they have.

Though Dominical is much more wired than communities just a half-hour south—there's high-speed Internet access and plenty of working pay phones—the place still feels like a bit of an outpost. A citizens' committee tries to keep the town's bare-bones health clinic supplied with basic first-aid supplies, but the clinic is often locked; you ask around and get someone to open it up, then dress your own wound. A doctor visits the clinic once a month. For anything serious, people go to the small emergency room in Platanillo, 13 kilometers (8 mi.) east of Dominical, or drive an hour over the hill to the hospital in San Isidro de General. Those living south of Dominical may head south to Palmar Norte's medical facilities. For non-emergency medical care, residents often drive the four hours to San José.

Much of the beachfront property in the area has already been snapped up, mostly by foreigners, but inland lots (some with stunning views) are still available. Recent offerings include 32.4 inland hectares (80 acres) on the road to San Isidro for US$425,000, a .4-hectare (one-acre) lot with an ocean view for US$266,500, and a one-hectare (2.5-acre) lot in a gated community for US$160,000. If you know the area well and bide your time (but not too long!), you'll probably be able to find better deals.

Dominical's quickly improving roads are one reason the area is developing so fast. Dominical sits at the intersection of Highway 243, coming down the mountain from San Isidro, and the coastal highway, gravel to the north and newly paved to the south. It won't be long before the entire coast highway is paved, providing easier access to coastal areas that right now still feel a little remote. Just how long that will be is a subject of much debate, especially among developers and real estate speculators, who want to get in early but not so early that they have to wait decades for a return on their investment. Most established expats would prefer that the roads remain a challenge, keeping development and large-scale tourism to a minimum.

A few kilometers south of Dominical is Punta Dominical, a beautiful high rock outcropping with views down the cliffs to crashing surf below. Some lucky few (almost all foreigners) have built houses to take advantage of this setting. Not far from the rocky point is Playa Dominicalito, reef-protected and providing good mooring and decent swimming. From the mouth of nearby Higuerón (also called Morete) River to Point Piñuela to the south, Ballena (Whale) Marine National Park protects 44.5 terrestrial hectares (110 acres) and 2,175 marine hectares (5,375 acres), including the largest coral reef on the Pacific coast of Central America.

UVITA AND OJOCHAL

Uvita is a small community 16 kilometers (10 mi.) south of Dominical, on a road newly paved in 2000 and in some places already reverting back to its pot-holed splendor. Before you get to Uvita, there's a bridge where big chunks of concrete have fallen into the river below, with ocean breezes blowing through the remaining metal grid. Considering how long the area had to wait for the road to be paved, the bridge might fall into the river altogether before repair crews arrive.

But right now the bridge is serviceable, and brings you to Uvita, a pleasant town of both Ticos and expats, which has so far managed to avoid being overwhelmed by the low-budget travelers that flock to Dominical.

Ojachal, 20 kilometers (12.4 mi.) south of Uvita, is a tiny town offering unexpectedly good food, in large part due to the resident community of French Canadians, some of whom saw ads in their hometown papers and bought lots sight-unseen, with the guarantee of their money back if they didn't like the place. They liked it, they told their friends, and now there's a little piece of Québec here on Costa Rica's Pacific coast. The French aren't bad cooks, something even Canada couldn't change. The talent seems to have also survived Costa Rica (not known for its cuisine), and one of the joys of being in the area is deciding whether to stop for filet mignon at the truly exceptional Exo-Tica, crepes at Chez Elle, or croissants from the French Bakery past Ojochal's soccer field. If French food isn't to your liking, defect to the Dutch and their former colonies, sampling the international cuisine at Villas Gaia or the amazing Indonesian rice platter at Balcón de Uvita, up a gravel track that begs for four-wheel drive but rewards with amazing views.

Strung along the highway from Dominical to past Ojochal are a number of nice hotels, frequented by Europeans and North Americans who've heard about the area's international community and low-key vibe. Though there's a lot to do here—bird-watching, snorkeling, kayaking in the ocean, or hiking to waterfalls—it takes some effort to find out where to go and what to do. This is true in spite of the fact that the area is one of the most well-signed I've seen in this country. Uniform signs—blue, with icons for food and lodging reminiscent of those on U.S. highways—suggest a community-wide effort aimed at attracting tourists, though Ojochal still seems more geared to residents than tourists. Speaking of residents, they aren't all French Canadians. There are also French-from-France (one of whom opined that French Canadians were "so American"), Belgians, Dutch, Italians, British, non-French Canadians, people from the United States, and of course, Ticos.

© Erin Van Rheenen

Ojochal police station

Ojochal Internet Café: Québec in the Jungle

At the turnoff to the tiny town of Ojachal, there's a *pulpería* (small general store) that has one of the few public phones in the area, which just so happens, this muggy midweek afternoon, to be out of order. "Sixty percent of the time," a local will later confess, "that phone is out of order. The other 40 percent the store is closed. You've got to drive to Dominical [40 km/24.9 mi. north] if you want reliable public phones."

But just across the river and down a rutted road, the weary traveler comes across an unlikely telecommunications mecca. Relying not on phone lines but on satellite connection, the welcome outpost has four new computers, and offers a full range of services common in your town but as rare as a four-toed sloth in this neck of the woods. There's Internet access, scanning, photocopying, faxing, website design, CD burning, Internet-based phone calls, and even translation services.

Perhaps even more welcome is the strong coffee, the air conditioning, and the sense that you've stepped into another country. Clocks on the wall tell the time in Victoria, Québec, London, and Paris. The wood plank floor is swept clean, the creamy yellow walls are soothing, and the high beamed ceiling gives the small café a feeling of amplitude. A blond teenaged boy behind the counter drawls in unaccented English, then launches into fast and furious French as he speaks into a shortwave radio.

You've entered the Ojochal Internet Café, and, from the number of customers speaking their New World–accented French, you could easily be in Montréal. The place opened in October 2000 and quickly became a mainstay and meeting place for the substantial French Canadian community in the area, not to mention a favorite of other expats and of those just passing through. Owners Marie-Danielle Croteau and Robert Fleury traveled around the world for two decades, much of the time living on their sailboat, *The Black Sheep,* before settling in this unlikely town.

"Costa Rica is one of the few places in the world where it's easy for foreigners to own land," says Marie-Danielle, who is not only a café proprietress but the author of 23 books, including four novels and many books for children. "We loved it here," she says of finding Ojachal after years of globe-trotting (her two children were born in Zaire: the blond teenager mentioned above is her son, Arnaud, and her daughter, Gabrielle, lives in Québec). "But we found that, ironically, we'd had more sophisticated communications equipment on the boat than was available here on land."

They decided to rectify the situation, and now the entire rather remote community of Ojachal can enjoy an excellent espresso while connecting with the outside world. The café is open Monday–Friday 8 A.M.–noon and 2–5 P.M., Saturday 8 A.M.–1 P.M. Its trilingual website (www.ojochal-internet-cafe.com) also has information on local real estate.

Ojachal also appears to be blessed with an abundance of enterprising residents who cooperate on projects to improve the community. In 2003, after several robberies in the area, residents asked the Ministry of Public Safety if they could have some police stationed in their town. If you build a station, replied the Ministry, we'll provide six officers. Project coordinators gathered contributions from people throughout town, then organized the construction of a spiffy new station—all in four months! At last visit the building had just been painted dazzling white with deep blue trim, and the grounds were being prepared for the planting of flowers. The Minister of Public Safety himself had promised to be at the inauguration of the new building, no doubt to get a look at the folks who in a few months had accomplished what in other Costa Rican communities might take years.

Southern Pacific Coast Towns

While foreign residents may go to Palmar Norte to shop and run errands, it (like San Isidro de General) is not much of an object of relocation desire for expats. They're useful towns, pleasant enough, but most people drive in and back out in a matter of hours.

THE OSA PENINSULA

Palmar Norte does have the distinction, however, of being one of the gateways to a fabled land that *National Geographic* calls "the most biologically intense place on earth": the Osa Peninsula. This is Costa Rica's Amazon, a tropical rain forest where tall trees drip vines and lianas, macaws screech, and most of the country's remaining 250 jaguars prowl. The numbers are staggering: 42,000 hectares (103,784 acres) of land (a good part of the peninsula) are protected in Corcovado National Park, which supports 13 distinct habitats and on which six meters (236 in.) of rain falls annually. Five hundred kinds of trees thrive here, as do hundred of species of birds, mammals, and reptiles. Crocodiles lurk in marshy areas, sea turtles lay eggs on deserted beaches, and tapirs pick their way shyly through the trees.

The peninsula juts 50 kilometers (31 mi.) out into the Pacific, sheltering the Golfo Dulce to the south, whose warm, calm waters draw humpback whales, three kinds of dolphins, and all manner of sport fish. On the northern side of the peninsula, beautiful and isolated Drake Bay is usually reached by boat from the riverside settlement of Sierpe; there's hardly a town to be seen on the hour-and-a-half trip, and the river is lined with huge stands of stilt-rooted mangroves.

Mama Chi

On September 22, 1962, in the northern Panamanian province of Chiriquí, a young Ngäbe Indian woman was called on by a mysterious couple. The two turned out to be none other than the Virgin Mary and her son, Jesus Christ. The visitors told the young woman that the Ngäbe should cultivate the land—even that dominated by banana companies—and worship the divine in ceremonies blending traditional Ngäbe beliefs, Catholic doctrine, and even elements of evangelical Protestantism. The resulting religion is called Mama Chi, and it has adherents not only in Panama but also across the border in southern Costa Rica.

Though the Osa has had its share of environmental problems, including invasive gold mining, slash-and-burn farming, and the poaching of endangered wildlife, the area's relative inaccessibility has saved it from large-scale exploitation. Visitors need to make an investment of time and effort to sample the peninsula's delights, and prospective residents should have that extra measure of patience and resourcefulness that makes living in the outback an adventure rather than a hardship.

That said, it's getting easier to get to the Osa, at least during dry season. SANSA and Travelair (see Contacts in the Resources section at the back of the book) fly small planes from San José to Puerto Jimenez every day, and charters land at Carate and other makeshift airstrips on demand. Until rain makes it impassable, there's a decent dirt road from Rincon on the south side of the peninsula to Drake Bay on the north. You can travel by bus from San José to Puerto Jimenez (a 10-hour trip), but driving your own car (4x4 recommended) will make the trip quicker and more comfortable.

PUERTO JIMENEZ

With a population of around 7,500, Puerto Jimenez is the largest town on the Osa Peninsula and the only settlement with private phone service. Visitors to Corcovado National Park most often come through PJ, as local expats call it, and there are a handful of hotels, restaurants, bars, and Internet cafés to serve them. There's also a bank, a post office, an emergency health clinic, a tourist information center, and a new library (supported by donations), and the town's airstrip, rising up out of bird- and crocodile-rich wetlands, is actually paved!

Flying into town is much easier than driving, and you're just as likely to hear the drone of a light plane as the revving of a car engine. It wasn't long ago that the road into the area was even worse than the potholed tracks

Puerto Jimenez

© Erin Van Rheenen

drivers now endure; until recently boats were the main method of transport. Still crucial to the area, vessels both big and small find excellent moorage in the deep and calm Golfo Dulce.

The town's history is a colorful one, with tales centering on the gold rush of the 1980s, when Puerto Jimenez (to hear locals tell it) was a modern-day Wild West, with blood feuds, horses tied up outside saloons in which gunfights raged, and prostitutes with hearts of gold (or at least pockets full of gold nuggets).

Things are quieter these days, and many of the area's foreign residents like it that way. Those wanting even more peace than town life can offer settle deep in the jungle or along the spectacular coastline between Puerto Jimenez and Carate, where the road ends and you must walk into Corcovado. Beaches are tucked away between rock outcroppings, and at Cabo Matapalo, on the southeast tip of the peninsula, waves get big enough to draw surfers. Matapalo also draws foreign residents, some of whom operate luxury hotels, and some of whom, like actor and activist Woody Harrelson, keep to themselves, though he and other foreign landowners have been instrumental in attempts to preserve the area's flora and fauna.

GOLFITO

Golfito is located on a small gulf within the larger Golfo Dulce, and this double dose of protection from the ocean swell means that waves breaking on the town's shore never get more than knee-high. Would that Golfito had similar protection from economic storms. The town started life as a banana port when, in 1938, the Boston-based United Fruit Company (now called Chiquita) moved its operations from the Caribbean to the Pacific, fleeing banana blight and labor strikes. During the 1950s, 90 percent of Costa Rica's banana exports were shipped from Golfito, and the banana company was the major employer in the area. But just as it abandoned the Caribbean side of the country, United Fruit pulled out of Golfito in 1985, leaving the land around town pumped full of pesticides that made it hard to grow anything else here.

Since the departure of United Fruit, the Costa Rican government has tried to promote other businesses to shore up the area's depressed economy. The major effort is the Deposito Libre, a duty-free shopping compound opened in 1990 that looks like a prison but draws Ticos from all over the country, especially at Christmastime. They're looking to avoid the high import tariffs on everything from refrigerators to perfume, and Golfito's lodgings are mostly geared to the tourists who must wait 24 hours before being able to shop.

Non-shopping tourists and sportfishers also come through town, usually to hire a boat or be on their way to beach towns like Playa Zancudo and Pavones to the south. December–May is sailfish season, June–September is good for marlin, and May–September you're likely to find snook.

Golfito isn't much of a tourist attraction in and of itself, though it's interesting to hang out at the town's dock, watching rough-and-tumble locals unload headless marlin, or notice that in the old section of town (the *pueblo civil*), rickety houses hang out over the water, and every other business seems to be a bar.

Two kilometers (1.2 mi.) south is another part of town that looks like it's in a different country. The Zona Americana was built by United Fruit to house its higher-ups. Generously proportioned wooden homes were built on stilts to combat the damp and catch the breeze. Spacious lawns and gardens give the area a luxuriant feel that has endured even as many of the buildings fall into ruin.

The town's foundering economy means that there are some great real estate deals to be had, while the area's slightly rough vibe seems to have attracted some rather shady characters. There's the sense that half the expats here are on the lam. Hang out at the Latitude 8 bar, a tiny place with a view of the water, and see who's drinking bourbon shots at 4 in the afternoon, or order an espresso at the bunker-like Coconut Café and watch the town, locals and expats alike, parade by. Check the café's bulletin board for a taste of what's happening in the area. There are calls for volunteers to help the turtles, generators for sale, sportfishing services offered, small-plane schedules listed, and real estate offered—everything from 16 inland hectares (39.5 acres) for US$35,000 to a half-hectare (1.2-acre) beachfront lot for US$195,000.

Golfito is a seven- or eight-hour bus ride from San José, and it's an hour or two drive to Pavones or Playa Zancudo. There's a daily (except Sunday) passenger-only ferry between Golfito and Puerto Jimenez. You can also hire water taxis to take you to Playa Zancudo or Pavones.

PLAYA ZANCUDO

Playa Zancudo isn't far from Golfito, at least as the crow flies or the water taxi skims. If you drive, however, you'll negotiate a 45-kilometer (28-mi.) unpaved route that includes crossing the Río Coto on a two-car ferry that stops operating at 9 P.M.

This seriously laid-back town is strung out along a sandy spit of land between the Río Coto Estuary and the waters of the Golfo Dulce. It's a

Playa Zancudo

lovely place where you can buckle down to the serious task of doing very little. In fact, if you need a lot of stimulation, Playa Zancudo is probably not for you. It has that end-of-the-road feel that can either charm the pants off you or drive you nuts. If you end up staying, no doubt you'll have days when it does both.

Some of the 100 or so foreign residents (only a handful live here year-round) run hotels or restaurants, and that keeps them busy, at least during high season (December–April). Debbie Walsh of Zancudo Beach Club says she looks forward to low season, when she can catch up on repairs and spend more time with her five dogs, 18 horses, three parrots, and one husband, Gary. The couple visited the area six years ago, drawn by the promise of seeing parrots in the wild. No strangers to the colorful birds, they ran an exotic-pet shop in Boston; Gary also worked homicide for the Boston Police and Debbie oversaw a stenography business. At the time of their visit, they were in their late 40s, with kids in college. It wasn't the time to turn their lives upside down, but they saw a hotel for sale in Playa Zancudo, and something clicked. "Debbie said, 'I could do this,'" recalls Gary. "And I said, 'Well, I don't know if I can.' But we could, and we did. Sold the house and the cars, and bought this place not long after first seeing it. I was worried about putting the kids through college, but everything worked out. In fact, one of them is now in law school."

The Beach Club's open-air restaurant is very popular, and is a good place to catch a glimpse of the local expats, who come here to enjoy drinks at sunset and to sample treats like wood-oven pizza. Snatches of overheard conversation reveal expat concerns: the need to drive seven hours to San José to buy some things for the house or to pick a friend up from the airport; the need to get away, especially in the very rainy months of September and October; the frustrations of having the power go out or the phone lines on the blink. But there's a general good cheer as well, and a celebration of being in a beautiful spot, pretty much left to one's own devices. The beach here is the focus of many a lazy day. It stretches six lovely kilometers (3.7 mi.), is bordered by tall coconut palms, and offers good swimming at the south end and decent surfing further north. Fisherfolk will be in heaven, as some of the best fishing in the area can be had close by. In fact, there's a yearly sportfishing competition, based at Roy's Zancudo Lodge, that draws a surprising number of musicians, including, in recent years, Taj Mahal and former members of the Allman Brothers Band.

> *Playa Zancudo is a lovely place where you can buckle down to the serious task of doing very little. In fact, if you need a lot of stimulation, Playa Zancudo is probably not for you.*

The fact that Zancudo is hemmed in by an estuary on one side and the sea on the other has sparked some questions about property ownership in the area. Maritime zone law stipulates that no one can actually own land until 200 meters (219 yds.) up from high tide line, and even land further from the water has certain restrictions where foreign owners are concerned. Lately the municipality has been questioning the right of foreigners to own property in this zone. If you're looking to buy here, be sure to get the up-to-the-minute news by talking to as many foreign residents as possible.

PAVONES

At least as small as Playa Zancudo, Pavones has more of a center, even if that center consists of a scruffy soccer field around which the town's few business are clustered. There's the open-air cantina, a few humble *pulperias* and casual restaurants, a variety of low-budget *cabinas,* and, in the emotional if not geographic center of town, a surf shop.

For make no mistake, Pavones is a surf town. The famous left-breaking wave is the reason people come, it's the reason a select few stay, and it's the reason non-surfers whine, "There's nothing to do here." It's why most of the town's visitors are young and male, with biceps hard from paddling and skin an international brown, making it hard to say whether the guy in the long shorts is Israeli, French, Argentine, Floridian, or Tico. These fellows are also why Pavones has a different tourist season than most other towns in Costa Rica. The usual high season is dry season, December–April, but surfers know that the rainy months (May–October) are when the waves in Pavones really go off.

Even the nightlife, such as it is, revolves around surfing. Guys gather at the cantina to hoist a Pilsen or seven, going into the kind of excruciating detail about the day's waves that only fellow fanatics can appreciate. You'll also see them propped before the big screen at the thatch-roofed Manta Club, looking for themselves in video footage of the day's action or watching reruns of *Endless Summer.*

Did I mention that Pavones and its environs are absolutely gorgeous? Sometimes the surf vibe is so strong you forget that even civilians can appreciate how the rain-forested hills slide down to meet sandy beaches or how the rocky tide pools burst with life. Especially to the south of town, the coastline is pristine and often deserted. In contrast to surf spots like Tamarindo and Puerto Viejo, Pavones is harder to get to, which means that only the dedicated make it here, and the town has not yet mushroomed into a more general tourist destination, with the attendant bars and Internet cafés. Electricity didn't arrive in Pavones until the mid-

1990s, and private phone lines are still hard to come by. Cell phone use is on the rise, but the technology is primitive; you'll see people scurrying around to find the best spot to catch a signal, yelling into their headsets, "Can you hear me now!?"

Most people give up, and wait to use the one public phone at Doña Dora's open-air *soda,* where you can also get a delicious fish *casado.* While waiting your turn for the coveted phone line you'll notice that half the town is there with you, and chances are good that someone lounging nearby can tell you which *cabinas* have fans, who can take you fishing, who's driving to Golfito that afternoon, or where to paddle out when the river mouth is spewing mud and detritus. As in many small towns, but especially technology-challenged ones, word of mouth is the way almost everything is communicated.

This makes for a lot of gossip, of course, and for a certain fuzziness as far as facts are concerned. You'll hear that land has shot up to US$100 a square meter, and then you'll hear that coastal lots can be had for as little as US$15 a square meter. After some research you'll find the latter price closer to the truth, though some out-of-town developers are hoping to get the former, most likely from buyers as out-of-town and out-of-touch as themselves.

Property ownership issues are complicated by the area's recent history. After United Fruit pulled out in 1985, foreigners bought up big stretches of coastline. Even financial fugitive Robert Vesco owned land here for a while, as did many others whose sources of income would not bear much scrutiny. In 1988, Danny Fowlie, who'd bought up a fair amount of land around Pavones, was convicted of drug trafficking and put in jail in the United States. His enterprising lawyer sold Fowlie's land to other gringos, and to himself, but the Costa Rican government wanted the land for itself (by rights it can expropriate the land of convicted felons). Squatters also tried, with some success, to claim the property.

In 1992, a showdown between squatters and those who had bought pieces of Fowlie's land ended in one man (a Tico guard hired to protect gringo-owned land) being killed. In 1997, a 79-year-old U.S cattle breeder got into an altercation with a squatter, and they shot each other. Or, to hear the gossip, the squatter's boss shot the old man, then shot the squatter and put the gun in his hand. Whatever the truth of the matter, prospective buyers should be careful, making sure that land being offered them has a clean title and actually belongs to the supposed seller. Locals insist that Pavones now welcomes foreign investment and residence, but there's still a feeling of caution here.

Foreign residents joke that they haven't had to shoot anyone for a few months, and that Pavones is perhaps the most dysfunctional town in the country. No doubt the jokes are based in truth; how much truth is up to the intrepid relocater to find out.

Real Estate Agents

Note: The agencies and individuals listed below are a small sampling of what you will find; inclusion in this list does not imply personal recommendation.

Latitude 9
Manuel Antonio area
Scott Cutter
tel. 506/777-1197
cell: 506/375-4806
mail@latitude9.com
www.latitude9.com

Osa Peninsula Realty
Osa area
Jeff Lantz
tel. 506/735-5626
www.osapeninsula.com

Pavones Properties
Pavones area
Bobby Nielsen
tel. 506/388-3630
nielsen2@racsa.co.cr

South Coast Realty
Dominical area
Kent, Dave, Liz, and Jeff
www.southcoastrealty.co.cr

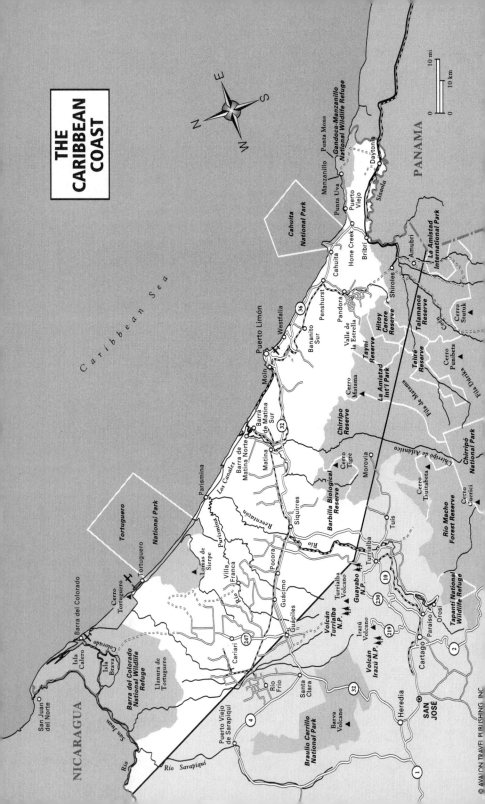

The Caribbean Coast

The Lay of the Land

As the toucan flies, the Caribbean coast is significantly closer to San José than fabled Pacific coast beaches like Tamarindo and Montezuma. Puerto Viejo, the east-coast version of those offbeat surfer havens, is an easy four-hour bus ride from San José. The provincial capital of Puerto Limón, a bustling port and the only real city in the area, can be reached in half that time. The entire coastline, from Nicaragua to Panama, is only 160 kilometers (99.4 mi.) long, while the more convoluted west coast measures 480 kilometers (298 mi.). Why, then, does Limón—the province that encompasses the entire east coast of Costa Rica and the mountains that back it up—seem so much more remote and exotic than the west coast?

Transportation—or lack thereof—is a good way to begin to understand the Zona Caribe. Until the late 1970s, travel to this coast meant taking a slow train from San José to Puerto Limón, and travel around the area

Punta Mona

In 1997, Stephen Brooks, a Grateful Deadhead from Florida, bought 35 hectares (86.5 acres) of land on a remote peninsula called Punta Mona (Monkey Point). There were no roads leading to his new property; getting there meant (and still means) a 30-minute boat ride or a few hours tramping through the rain forest. The only neighbor within miles was an old man named Padí, who ended up teaching Stephen a great deal about the area, and still lives in a little house a few hundred feet from the open-air kitchen and dormitories of what has become Costa Rica's best-known organic farm.

In a few short but busy years, Stephen, known locally and with affection as the *gringo loco,* has transformed this isolated plot of land into a living demonstration of permaculture, a term that at its most basic means working with, rather than against, nature. In practice here at Punta Mona, permaculture means everything from experimenting with organic black pepper, ginger, and vanilla, to recycling human waste to create the methane gas that fuels the kitchen stove. Thatch-roofed *cabinas* are scattered amid lush gardens, and provide a place to hang the hammocks in which visitors and residents sleep. When not helping out on the farm, farm denizens enjoy the yoga center, strum guitars and beat drums, or pick up one of the many books laying around, from the *Popul Vuh* to *The Lord of the Rings.*

More an educational center than a working farm, Stephen's place draws a constant stream of students, travelers, and fellow *locos* who stay for a few days, a week, or a year, soaking up knowledge and inspiration. One recent visitor, David Becerra of Spain, wants to go home and start a European version of Punta Mona. That's just the kind of response Stephen Brooks hopes to provoke in visitors: His project serves as a handful of seeds, some of which will germinate here in Costa Rican soil, others that will find their way halfway across the world.

Contact Information
Punta Mona Center for Sustainable Living and Permaculture
www.costaricanadventures.com/puntamona/

itself, especially in the north, was by motorized dugout canoe or via the slow *African Queen*–style boats that still bring mail and supplies to outlying areas.

In 1979, the road from Puerto Limón south (which takes you to Cahuita, Puerto Viejo, and Manzanillo) was improved and became passable most of the time, though heavy rains often washed out bridges and stretches of pavement. The 1991 earthquake destroyed the railroad, but by then the coastal strip south of Puerto Limón was fairly well-served by Highway 36, which was paved (sort of) to the town of Puerto Viejo. More recently, the pavement has been extended south to Manzanillo, a small village located within the Gandoca-Manzanillo National Wildlife Refuge—a reserve that doesn't get half the visitors of the more popular protected areas, but where you can see twice as much wildlife, including rare tucuxi dolphins and an alarming variety of pit vipers.

It wasn't until 1986 that Puerto Viejo (the most touristed town on the coast) got 24-hour electricity; Manzanillo and Tortuguero had to wait until 1988. Private phone lines arrived in Puerto Viejo in October 1996, and now some businesses and individuals have email accounts. In Manzanillo, it was just a few years ago that private phone lines became available (government offices had phones, and there were a few public pay phones in town). Now the government-run utility company is building antennae for cell phones in the area. If there are no major snags (always a long shot in Costa Rica), all who can afford a cell phone will be reachable, which is a huge change from fighting over the few private land lines the government deigned to make available.

Nowadays you can fly by light plane from San José to Tortuguero, in the north, and to many points south—most flights last no more than 30 minutes. North of Limón, there are still very few roads; canals dug in the 1960s to link up lagoons and meandering rivers now connect remote villages and lead tourists to Tortuguero National Park, where huge numbers of sea turtles arrive to lay their eggs, usually close to the very spot where they themselves hatched.

The area's historical isolation meant that the Zona Caribe was pretty much left to its own devices. Often ignored by the government, Limón province was the poor stepchild in terms of infrastructure, education, and health services (it still is, to some extent). A third of Limón's population is Afro-Caribbean, and blacks in Costa Rica didn't even have full citizenship until 1949; there were also restrictions on where they could travel and live within their own country. Indigenous peoples, like the BriBrí and the Talamanca, also had a hard time of it historically, though nowadays they are a much more organized and vocal minority that has done much work to preserve their culture and lands.

Remoteness and cultural diversity have deep roots in the Zona Caribe. Columbus landed here in 1502, on his fourth and final journey to the New World, but he didn't stay long. Cortéz came and went 22 years later. The *conquistadors* hoped they'd find gold, but they were for the most part disappointed—there were no gleaming, gold-encrusted cities in Costa Rica, like those found up north in Mexico or down south in Peru. There was no real reason for the Spaniards to stick around; the coast was left to its own devices and became a refuge for rumrunners, gun traders, and mostly British pirates, who between raids would retreat to the swampy interior or hide out along stretches of wild coastline. They traded and sometimes intermarried with indigenous tribes who farmed and fished the sea and rivers. Among the tribes were the Votos, who had female chiefs; most of the tribes here were, and are, matrilineal, meaning tribe membership comes through one's mother.

To this day, the Caribbean coast retains its reputation as a smuggler's haven; nowadays the area is, unfortunately, an important transshipment point for drugs on their way from South to North America. Florentino Grenald, a guide who specializes in hikes through the Gandoca-Manzanillo Wildlife Refuge, showed me a pristine and deserted white-sand beach that he called Cocaine Beach. A few years back hundreds of kilos were dumped here when smugglers had boat trouble; locals soon discovered the cache, generously giving the water-tight bricks better hiding places in their own homes.

Isolation from the rest of the country and neglect from Costa Rica's centralized government may have had its benefits for the Zona Caribe. The natural world fared a bit better on this coast, though banana companies razed large tracts of forest and then pumped toxic insecticides into the ecosystem. Still, more of Limón province is protected than any of the other six provinces in the country. Almost half the Caribbean coastline is sheltered in reserves. The isolation also meant that the culture—already quite different from the rest of Costa Rica—retained its individuality. Substandard health care facilities may have helped to preserve some of the folk healing and herbal remedies that came from indigenous cultures and from Africa, via West Indian immigrants. Knowledge and use of medicinal plants is common, and nontraditional healers do a brisk business in their communities, with many expats numbered among their patients. Their specialties are various and they go by many names—midwives, bush doctors, shamans, and *sukias,* to name a few. Many work hand-in-hand with more western approaches, referring people to nearby clinics if they believe that type of intervention is in the patient's best interest.

This coast has always been sparsely settled and less-developed than settlements in the interior of the country and on the west coast. In 1882, the Costa Rican government offered land grants here to encourage migration. Around the same time, the railroad was being built, and workers came from as far away as Italy and China, though most came from the Caribbean islands. Of these, the majority came from Jamaica, and that culture's influence is still strongly felt here, in the English patois spoken, the spicy coconut curries served with jerk chicken, and the oversupply of Bob Marley music—hang out in a few bars and you'll reach your lifetime Marley limit in under a week.

"Don't worry about a thing," could be the area's mantra. Don't worry about the rain—the biggest *aguaceros* (downpours) usually come at night, and overcast days provide welcome relief from the dazzling sun. Don't worry if you don't have money for dinner—just pull some red snapper out of the ocean, and pick from a dozen varieties of fruit growing year-round on trees that, if they aren't yours, don't seem to be watched over too closely either. And don't worry that if you have serious health problems, you'll need to go to the hospital in Limón or—if it's an emergency—that you'll most likely be airlifted to better facilities in the Central Valley.

Despite the rough spots, things move along at an easy rhythm, with a little syncopation to liven up the proceedings. And make no mistake, the Caribbean coast is full of surprises, from lacquer-red poison dart frogs jumping out from under leaves, to the prevalence of an English that confounds even more than Spanish, because you think you should understand it but don't. The people here constitute a heady brew of Afro-Caribbean, Chinese, indigenous, mestizo, European, and North American. The animal life is even more varied. I almost ended up in the Tortuguero River after my hydro-bike collided with an enormous creature that turned out to be one of the few remaining manatees in the area. Probably as startled as I was, the half-ton beast batted its fleshy tail against the boat's pontoons, then thrashed away upriver.

Such wonders are everyday fare in the Zona Caribe, and life is slow enough here to savor them.

The climate, too, is phenomenal, though whether it will inspire awe or lament depends on your constitution. The coast south of Puerto Limón (often called the Talamanca coast) averages a prodigious 2.4 meters (94.5 in.) of rain a year, with the wettest months being December, January, July and August. Drier times may be had in September and October, as well as from the second half of February through April. But those in the know say there's no real dry season, just a few months where it doesn't rain quite as much. Still, it's unusual to go more than a day or two without a glimpse of sun and blue skies. Often it rains at night or for a brief spell in the morning, and is clear the rest of the day.

North of Limón, the drier seasons are longer but when the rain comes down, it really comes down. July, the wettest month, averages almost a meter (39 in.) of rain in just 31 days.

Temperatures stay the same year-round, with lows around 21–23°C (the low 70s, Fahrenheit), and the highs in the 28–30°C (80–85°F) range. Humidity can be high, but cooling breezes help to alleviate the stickiness. The sun is very strong, especially around midday, when it's best to seek out some shade lest you end up looking like the Sunburned Tourist tree, red and peeling.

Tortuguero

A remote hamlet of 700 reachable only by boat or light plane, Tortuguero has drawn just a handful of permanent foreign residents. Every year, though, tens of thousands of tourists pour into nearby Tortuguero National Park, hoping to catch a glimpse of the tens of thousands of sea turtles that each year flipper their way up the beach, dig a hole in the sand, and lay their flexible-skinned eggs. Most visitors bypass the ramshackle town and spend their money in all-inclusive lodges along the river, though resident groups in the town of Tortuguero are working to change the situation.

Perched on a sandy spit of land between the oft-rough sea and a calm lagoon, the town can be walked end to end in minutes. You'll see wooden houses built on stilts, their corrugated tin roofs blazing in the tropical sun. Most houses are painted various shades of weather-beaten blue, with doors and shutters flung open to take advantage of the cooling breezes. There are narrow paths through the village, but most homes are oriented to the river or lagoon, the way residences elsewhere are oriented to the road. Brightly painted dugout canoes are pulled up onto the muddy bank or bob gently in the water. Herons and egrets lurk at the river's edge,

© Erin Van Rheenen

Tortuguero jail

keeping a sharp eye out for fish or the shrimp that congregate around the floating water hyacinth. Iguanas sun themselves on the branches of vine-draped trees.

It's a lazy, out-of-the-way place, a town you're either born to or are drawn to because of the nature that surrounds it. Volunteers come to work with the respected Caribbean Conservation Corp., founded by biologist Archie Carr in the 1950s to help preserve and study sea turtles. The few nonnatives who settle here tend to be involved in conservation or work as nature guides. Daryl Loth, a Canadian transplant who now works as an independent guide, arrived nine years ago to manage a biological station run by a Canadian nonprofit institute. He married a local girl and settled down in a riverside home that he recently expanded to include four pleasant, airy rooms that he rents to tourists. Daryl points out that Tortuguero has its own time zone. "When it's 9 A.M. in New York City," he says, "in Tortuguero it's 1973."

Some are attracted to just that town-that-time-forgot feel. Jenny Madden, for instance, had reached the end of her rope running a successful catering business in San José. She and her four children built the business up and they were doing very well, but the stress was literally making her sick. Her hands were the first to go, and soon she couldn't even make a fist. She felt tired all the time. Knowing she had to make a life change, she sold her business and moved to Tortuguero, but she couldn't quite give up the habit of feeding people. She and her oldest son run La Casona, an eclectic restaurant offering up welcome alternatives to the ubiquitous rice and beans.

Jenny (who despite her Anglo name is *pura Tica*) is president of the local Women's Association, which has taken on the unglamorous but essential problem of trash collection. She's also the secretary of the Development Association, whose current project is to build a public dock in town to encourage tourists to disembark. She's a busy woman, and as I spoke with her about the community, she was teaching her son, Andres (who studied law), to make banana pancakes. The next day she was leaving for San José, and Andres would be in charge of La Casona during her absence. "He's great with pasta and fish, but somehow never learned pancakes. If I know he can make them, I'll breathe easier in San José." She's heading back to the capital only until her daughter gives birth; then she hopes to bring the young family back to Tortuguero, a place that's good, she's found, for what ails you. Here she has recovered strength in her hands and her energy level has soared. She credits the smell of the ocean, the slow pace, and the songs of the birds.

Tortuguero gets my vote as one of the most unusual places in the country. It wouldn't be easy to relocate here—everything, including advanced health care and higher education, is at least a few hours' boat ride away. On the other hand, the town is located within spitting distance of one of Costa Rica's most-visited national parks, and there's talk of a road that would cut a swath through the swampy jungle and end just across the river from this carless village. Residents are actively trying to attract more tourists, and if they succeed, drowsy, aquatic Tortuguero is bound to morph into a very different kind of beast.

Puerto Limón

This down-at-the-heels port city bristles with energy, and is where expats and locals living in more tranquil towns come to shop or visit the doctor. Terri Newton of Cahuita says Limón, a city of 70,000, has several good private doctors and dentists. It's also where the biggest hospital in the province is located—if you're part of the Caja, the national health care system, this is where you'd come if you needed more than the basic care provided at the small clinics scattered throughout Limón province.

The rest of Costa Rica doesn't have much affection for Puerto Limón, citing crime statistics and calling it Piedrópolis (Crack City). But there's no denying Limón's vitality. It's the economic engine of the area, and the streets have a definite buzz you won't find elsewhere in the province. Five kilometers (3.1 mi.) west is the sister port of Moín, where crude oil arrives for processing and boats are piled high with bananas bound for Europe and North America. Trucks loaded with freight barrel through Moín and Puerto Limón night and day, and many of the rough-and-tumble waterfront bars are open 24 hours. A major earthquake in 1991 mangled the wrought-iron balconies and toppled the open-air arcades that gave the city its ragged tropical charm, though there's been much rebuilding in the last decade. The Limóneses walking the street are of every race, with lots of interesting blends that will have you trying to tease out the ancestry of a particularly arresting face.

But all in all Limón is not a place that inspires one to dream about buying a little house and settling down, and you'll want to hang on to your purse when you make the inevitable visit. The city's one indisputable claim to fame is that it explodes every October in Carnaval, with fireworks, dancing in the streets, and bands from all over the Caribbean and Latin America. Christopher Baker, author of *Moon Handbooks Costa Rica,* says the raucous festival is like the plague: You either flee or succumb. The same might be said for the city itself.

Cahuita

In early 2003, *La Nación,* the country's largest newspaper, called Cahuita "the best beach on the Atlantic coast." It should have used the plural, because Cahuita has a parade of delectable beaches, from black-sand Playa Negra to the 14 kilometers (8.7 mi.) of palm-shaded white sand within Cahuita National Park. Some of these beaches have earned high marks within the country's two rating systems: blue flags for cleanliness (only 27 beaches in all of Costa Rica have earned this flag, three of them in the Cahuita area) and the only "Double A" awarded to a Caribbean coast beach. Lush jungle flanks these pristine stretches of sand, the tangle of foliage so dense in places that 75 meters (82 yds.) in from the beach you can't hear the surf. Offshore coral reefs create protected coves excellent for swimming and snorkeling.

The land around the coast tends to be swampy and prone to flooding. In fact, much of the area in and around town was not so long ago under water; brush aside a few inches of topsoil a few hundred meters from the beach and you'll hit coral. Here and there coral outcroppings rise up out of the fertile loam, which supports all manner of flowering plants and

Cahuita's Playa Negra

trees, including jackfruit, ornamental ginger, carambola (starfruit), and varieties of citrus and palm.

Paul Vigneault, who runs the Hotel Jaguar, came here 15 years ago and thinks Cahuita has an ideal climate. "It's either surfing weather—a little rough—or snorkeling weather," when the sea is aquamarine and pacific. When Paul arrived, "there was a lobster under every rock, and just one restaurant in town, a lady who had two tables in her living room." Fifteen years later, Cahuita is still a modest village, with an unpaved main street leading to the entrance to Cahuita National Park. It's one of the few parks in the country so accessible to nearby towns, and it's also one of Costa Rica's loveliest preserves. A jungle trail parallels the beach, where red or green flags tell you whether to swim or stay out of the surf. Monkeys cavort in the trees and crabs scuttle across your path.

Nowadays the lobsters may have been overfished, but the restaurant situation has definitely improved; now there are a dozen places to eat, from traditional Afro-Caribbean fare to pizza and pasta. The school situation has also improved, with a K–12 private school that counts among its 100 students both expat and local kids. Parents formed the Escuela Complementaria de Cahuita (tel. 506/755-0075) because they felt frustrated by the local public school. "It would be pouring rain," says Swiss-born Brigitte Abegglen, who runs Cabinas Brigitte and has a nine-year-old daughter, "and kids would walk half an hour or more to school, arriving tired and soaked to the skin. Then they'd be told to go home—the teacher hadn't shown up, or there was a staff meeting that took precedence over classes."

Basic health care is available at a small clinic in town and a larger one in nearby Hone Creek; for more serious matters, residents travel to Puerto Limón or San José. Some residents head for the Talamanca mountains to one of many famed indigenous *curanderos* (curers), or seek out Afro-Caribbean bush doctors versed in herbal and folk remedies. One long-time expat "did the whole deal—made the trip, spent the night being eaten by bugs, then stood in line with the other supplicants." When her turn came, she told the *curandero* she wanted to quit smoking. "He gave me a potion, which I drank. Then I traded my lighter for a cigarette."

Just seven or eight years ago, Cahuita was the prime tourist spot on the Caribbean coast, but now Puerto Viejo has taken over that role. Why that shift occurred is an interesting question that locals like to debate. Some say it's just the fickle nature of tourism, where a town is a hot destination one year and cold as ice in the tropics the next. It could be the Salsa Brava, Puerto Viejo's fabled wave, which draws surfers from around the world.

Others blame the international press coverage of the murder of two young female tourists a few years back. The crime was committed further down the coast but is associated with Cahuita because the bodies were found near the highway outside of town. The culprits, who turned out to be from San José, were soon brought to justice, but that part of the story didn't get much attention, and tourists from around the world opted to skip Cahuita on their next trip to Costa Rica. Other locals discount that theory, pointing out that tourism started to fall off as early as 1994.

Cahuita is still a popular destination, if not quite as hot as a decade ago. And the decline in visitors may be a boon for potential residents, in terms of lower land prices and a quieter, more livable environment. "People always have time for each other," notes Slavko "Topo" Topolovsek of Cahuita's Magellan Inn. "You drop by, and people are glad to see you. No calling ahead here." Growth in Cahuita tends to be slow but steady, continues Topo, who also sells real estate. His town is prettier and safer than Puerto Viejo, he says, echoing what I heard all over town. Locals are constantly invoking Puerto Viejo as Cahuita's debased twin, where discos rock on into the night, drugs are plentiful, and real estate overpriced. Interestingly, no one in Puerto Viejo had much to say about Cahuita, good or bad. Opinions are mixed as to which town, in the final analysis, will be better off.

The area's foreign residents number around 50. More than a dozen countries are represented, with the majority being from Switzerland, the United States, Germany, Canada, and Italy. Topo said that back in the mid- and late 1980s, when Costa Rica was still a "secret place," land could be had here for a dollar a square meter. Properties up for sale at the time of my visit included ocean-view land at US$7.50 a square meter; an 800-square-meter (.2-acre) lot on Cahuita's main street, suitable for a business, offered at US$60,000; and a 1,100-square-meter (.27-acre) lot 200 meters (219 yds.) from the beach for US$20,000. If you don't need to be near the beach, prices go down—the further inland, the cheaper the land. A repeat visitor from Long Island had just bought a 1,250-square-meter (.3-acre) lot near Hone Creek for US$3,500—that's under US$3 per square meter. "It's kind of swampy," he admits. "But I'll build up [on stilts]. When the rainy season comes, I think I'll be okay."

Puerto Viejo and Vicinity

Puerto Viejo is the hip, slightly seedy cousin who earns enough money and has enough fun to make the rest of the family resent her terribly. It's a tumbledown place on a melancholy coast that has somehow managed to become a staple of international alternative travel. The place definitely has its charms.

© Erin Van Rheenen

Boat in Puerto Viejo

It's hard to beat drinking a cold beer while digging your toes into warm sand, watching expert surfers cut across the face of belligerent waves. You may have heard of the Salsa Brava—a hard, fast, dangerous wave that draws riders from near and far—but did you know you could languish in a beachside bar and still see all the action? When the surf dies down, you get to watch the newcomers choose the wrong route in, picking their way around shelves of razor-sharp coral. Buy them a beer if they arrive really cut up.

Driving the town's paved main street, you'll need to slow for bike and foot traffic—people pedaling by on beat-up beach cruisers or ambling from lunch to hammock or from coffee to Internet café. Not everyone here is tattooed and 23, though sometimes it seems that way. On closer examination, you'll see that even some of the surf gods look like they've been around long enough to remember Jimmy Carter's beer-swilling brother Billy, who, come to think of it, would probably feel right at home in Puerto Viejo. If you head south out of town, you'll pass Playa Cocles and Punta Uva, areas that have high concentrations of long-term North American and European expats. "They're all old hippies out there," a townie told me. "Good people." Nobody would hazard a guess as to how many foreign residents there were in the area, but locals lament that more and more land seems to end up in foreign hands. Richard Cunningham, born in Puerto Viejo and owner of Momchies Bakery, estimates that 75 percent of the town is now foreign-owned. "They flash a lot of money, and people are people—they take it." I asked him if he too was looking to sell out. His reply: "What're you offering?"

The influx began in 1991, when a newly paved coastal road made Puerto Viejo easily accessible from San José. Locals began selling off their land to newcomers, in part because many considered their farms worthless, since their principal crop, cacao, had recently been destroyed by the *Monilia* fungus.

Foreigners are still coming. Many tourists arrive and know from day one that they want to stay. Some go back home, make a little money, and return to build a beachside home or start a business. Others never leave, and eke out a living any way they can—I met a young man from Portland, Oregon, who seemed to be the waiter for half the restaurants in town.

Speaking of food, it's very good here. Where many tourists come, businesses spring up to cater to their every whim. So there's sushi as well as rondon (or rundown), a spicy fish stew with Afro-Caribbean roots, and Thai curry as well as rice and beans. Several places serve respectable coffee, and one (Café Rico) serves an espresso that will knock your flip-flops off. Nightlife is there if you want it, but the vibe is gentle—lots of reggae and its companion herb. Bambu Bar has reggae nights twice a week, and it's fun to watch the motley crew on the dance floor, most of them with eyes closed, swaying to their own beat. The jerkier dancers may have gotten into the coke, which is available and cheap enough to make it a problem. Says a *norteamericano* who's been here five years: "People come down here; they don't come for the drugs. But then they get a bump at a party, and they say, 'This stuff costs how much?' And oh, they're locked. Some of them never come back." Most foreign residents, however, are too busy with their businesses, their projects, or just trying to get their house built to have time for such hard-edged diversions.

For example, a decade ago Lindy and Peter Kring bought an abandoned cacao farm and transformed it into Finca la Isla Botanical Garden. "We've had our successes and failures," they explain in their brochure. "In many respects as a commercial farm, it is very inefficient. We tend to get carried away with collecting and experimenting. However, as boutique black pepper growers and nursery-landscapers we have been able to support ourselves."

Some expats help out with a local grassroots organization called ATEC (Asociación Talamanqueña de Ecoturismo y Conservación, or Talamanca Association of Ecotourism and Conservation). ATEC's office on the main street is Puerto Viejo's unofficial community center and tourist information bureau. Born in 1990 out of a concern that increasing tourism was benefiting outside investors but leaving native

Real Estate in Puerto Viejo

There's no shortage of people dealing in property in Puerto Viejo. Remember that in Costa Rica, you don't need a license to act as middleman for a real estate transaction. Consequently, and especially in hot markets, you'll run into a great variety of folks who have just the place for you. I saw listings where I checked my email, and without even looking I ran into several people who knew of this or that lot for sale. One of them who seemed to know his stuff was Charlie Wanger. Charlie and his wife, Shannon, also manage the Cabinas El Tesoro just outside Puerto Viejo in Playa Cocles.

I asked Charlie what someone could do here with US$50,000. "You could buy yourself a quarter acre of land," he told me. "Close to the road, not in front of the ocean. With electricity and water—by well or aqueduct, depending on what area you're in. You could build a small, simple but nice one-floor, two-bedroom house,

and still put US$10,000 in the bank. Right now I've got a 1,300-square-meter lot for US$15,000."

Charlie's friend Geoffrey Birtz of Ontario, Canada, just bought two beachfront hectares (4.9 acres) for US$11,000 out near Gandoca, which is almost at the border with Panama. It's not easy to get there—you have to drive inland on bad roads and then back out to the coast. There's a house on the property, but Geoff says it needs to be torn down.

What will it cost to build a new house? Charlie gives the following figures:

- For US$200/square meter, you can build a rustic house
- US$250–300/square meter gets you semi-rustic
- US$350–400 you're getting into nice
- US$400–450 and you're pretty upscale—nice tile, nice finishing touches, a real bathtub.
- Higher than that and you're entering deluxe territory.

Puerto Viejans high and dry, ATEC has trained locals to be guides, and is creating a small-loan program to help locals finance hotels, restaurants, and other small businesses. It also arranges trips to the nearby KéköLdi Indigenous Reserve, where Cabecar and BriBrí indians live and work.

Other newcomers want to make a positive impact on the community, but chose to go it alone. German-born Carlston "Ken" Teimann founded a company, Surayöum, which also offers tours to the KéköLdi Reserve, along with seminars on sustainable agriculture and the BriBrí way of life. Ken married Yuri, a BriBrí woman, and the two are proud parents of Surayöum, the daughter after which their company is named. "It means 'the sacred land where all BriBrí clans were created,'" explains Ken. "BriBrí's not an easy language—it's tonal. It took me a year to be able to pronounce my own daughter's name."

At Ken's 40-hectare (98.8-acre) farm, he planted 400 fruit trees and built a conference center and dormitory in the traditional open-air BriBrí style. He believes that we must pay attention to nature and how indigenous peoples have coexisted peacefully with the natural world of which we are all a part. "Somewhere most of the world took a wrong turn. We can learn a lot from indigenous people as to how to get back on track."

Most residents agree that allowing offshore drilling is not the right track, and locals and expats recently joined forces to drive Harkin Energy, which wanted to construct eight drilling platforms, out of town. The fight still rages on, and time will tell where the path Puerto Viejo is following will lead it. But there's no denying that things are changing here, and fast. The 13 kilometers (8 mi.) between Puerto Viejo and Manzanillo and nearby Gandoca-Manzanillo Reserve used to be bad enough to make people think twice about living out that way. Now it's all paved, and some fear that soon that stretch of highway will be as developed as the road between Quepos and Manuel Antonio National Park on the west coast, with dozens of upscale hotels, restaurants, and residences. On the other hand, points out one expat, "the way roads are paved in this country, it'll be full of potholes again in six months. They lay on such a thin layer of asphalt they might as well just paint the dust black. But maybe that's not such a bad thing. We don't want to be too accessible."

Real Estate Agents

Note: The agencies and individuals listed below are a small sampling of what you will find; inclusion in this list does not imply personal recommendation.

Caribe Sur Real Estate
Southern Caribbean coast area
Apdo 81-7403
Puerto Viejo
tel. 506/759-9138
cell: 506/826-3998
info@caribesur-realestate.com
www.caribesur-realestate.com

Topo's Real Estate
Chauita area
Slavko Topolovsek (aka Topo)
tel./fax 506/755-0035
magellaninn@racsa.co.cr
http://toposrealestate.org

Resources

© Houman Pirdavari

Contacts

EMBASSIES AND CONSULATES

For general information, visit www.costarica-embassy.org.

United States and Puerto Rico

Costa Rican Embassy
2112 "S" St., NW
Washington, D.C. 20008
tel. 202/328-6628
after-hours emergencies:
tel. 202/215-4178
fax 202/265-4795
consulate@costarica-embassy.org
Attention to the public: Mon.–Fri.
10 A.M.–1 P.M.
Jurisdiction: all U.S. states, particularly District of Columbia, Delaware, Maryland, North Carolina, South Carolina, Virginia, and West Virginia

Atlanta
Consulate General
1870 The Exchange, Ste. 100
Atlanta, GA 30339
tel. 770/951-7025
after-hours emergencies:
tel. 770/797-7700
fax 770/951-7073
consulate_ga@costarica
-embassy.org
Attention to the public: Mon.–Fri.
10 A.M.–3 P.M.
Jurisdiction: Georgia

Boston
Honorary Consulate
175 McClellan Hwy.
East Boston, MA 02128
tel. 617/561-2444
fax 617/561-2461
consulate_bos@costarica
-embassy.org
Attention to the public: Mon.–Fri.
9 A.M.–1 P.M.
Jurisdiction: Massachusetts

Chicago
Consulate General
203 N. Wabash Ave., Ste. 1312
Chicago, IL 60601
tel. 312/263-2772
after-hours emergencies:
tel. 312/399-3997
fax 312/263-5807
crcchi@aol.com
Attention to the public: Mon.–Fri.
9 A.M.–3 P.M.
Jurisdiction: Illinois, Indiana, Iowa, Michigan, Minnesota, Missouri, North Dakota, Ohio, South Dakota, Wisconsin

Dallas
Honorary Consulate
7777 Forest Ln., Ste. C-204
Dallas, TX 7523
tel. 972/566-7020
fax 972/566-7943
Attention to the public: by appointment only
Jurisdiction: Dallas

Denver
Honorary Consulate
3356 S. Xenia St.
Denver, CO 80231-4542
tel. 303/696-8211
fax 303/696-1110
cronsul@hypermall.net
Attention to the public: by
appointment only, Mon.–Fri.
9 A.M.–4 P.M.
Jurisdiction: Colorado

Houston
Consulate General
3000 Wilcrest, Ste. 112
Houston, TX 77042
tel. 713/266-0484
after-hours emergencies:
tel. 281/597-1194
fax 713/266-1527
consulatecr@juno.com
Attention to the public: Mon.–Fri.
9 A.M.–2 P.M.
Jurisdiction: Colorado, Kansas,
Nebraska, New Mexico, Oklahoma, Texas

Los Angeles
Consulate General
1605 W. Olympic Blvd., Ste. 400
Los Angeles, CA 90015
tel. 213/380-7915
or 213/380-6031
fax 213/380-5639
costaricaconsulatela@
hotmail.com
Attention to the public: Mon.–Fri.
9 A.M.–1 P.M.
Jurisdiction: Alaska, Arizona,
Hawaii, Nevada, Southern California, Utah

Miami
Consulate General
1101 Brickell Ave., Ste. 704-S
Miami, FL 33131
tel. 305/871-7487
or 305/871-7485
after-hours emergencies:
tel. 305/331-0636
fax 305/871-0860
consulate_fla@costarica
-embassy.org
Attention to the public: Mon.–Fri.
9 A.M.–1 P.M.
Jurisdiction: Florida

New Orleans
Consulate General
World Trade Center Bldg.
2 Canal St., Ste. 2334
New Orleans, LA 70130
tel. 504/581-6800
after-hours emergencies:
tel. 504/256-2027
fax 504/581-6850
consulcrno@aol.com
Attention to the public: Mon.–Fri.
9 A.M.–noon, 1–3 P.M.
Jurisdiction: Alabama, Arkansas,
Kentucky, Louisiana, Mississippi,
Tennessee

New York
Consulate General
80 Wall St., Ste. 718
New York, NY 10005
tel. 787/509-3066
after-hours emergencies:
tel. 908/623-6310
fax 212/509-3068
connycr@cs.com

Attention to the public: Mon.–Fri.
10 A.M.–3 P.M. (summer),
9 A.M.–2 P.M. (winter)
Jurisdiction: Connecticut, Maine,
Massachusetts, New Hampshire,
New Jersey, New York, Pennsylvania, Rhode Island, Vermont

Phoenix
Honorary Consulate
7373 E. Doubletree Ranch Rd.,
Ste. 200
Scottsdale, AZ 85258
tel. 480/951-2264
fax 480/991-6606
burkeap@aol.com
Attention to the public: by
appointment only
Jurisdiction: Arizona

Puerto Rico
Consulate General
Avenida Ponçe de Leon,
Edificio 1510
Oficina P1, Esquina Calle Pelaval
San Juan, Puerto Rico 00909
tel. 787/723-6227
after-hours emergencies:
tel. 787/627-3220
fax 787/723-6226
consuladopr@yunque.net
Attention to the public: Mon.–Fri.
9 A.M.–2 P.M.
Jurisdiction: Puerto Rico

San Antonio
Consulate
6836 San Pedro, Ste. 116
San Antonio, TX 78216
tel. 210/824-8474

after-hours emergencies:
tel. 210/386-6839
fax 210/824-8489
mrojasconsulsa@msn.com
Jurisdiction: Texas

San Francisco
Consulate
P.O. Box 7643
Fremont, CA 94537
tel. 510/790-0785 (9 A.M.–
noon only)
after-hours emergencies (beeper):
800/790-8561
fax 510/792-5249
consulsfo@hotmail.com
Attention to the public: by
appointment only
Jurisdiction: Idaho, Montana,
Northern California, Oregon,
Washington, Wyoming

St. Paul
Honorary Consulate
2424 Territorial Rd.
St. Paul, MN 55114
tel. 651/645-4103
fax 651/645-4684
cr-consulate@2424group.com
Jurisdiction: Minnesota

Canada
**The Embassy of
Costa Rica in Canada**
135 York St., Ste. 208
Ottawa, ON K1N 5T4
tel. 613/562-2855
There are Costa Rican consulates
in Calgary, Montreal, Toronto,
and Vancouver.

Costa Rica

U.S. Embassy
Physical Address:
Calle 120 Avenida 0, Pavas
San José, Costa Rica
Hours: 8 A.M.–4:30 P.M.
tel. 506/220-3939
after-hours tel. 506/220-3127
fax 506/220-2305
or 506/232-7944
http://usembassy.or.cr

Local Mail Address:
Apartado 920-1200 Pavas
San José, Costa Rica

U.S. Mail Address:
U.S. Embassy San José
APO AA 34020

Canadian Embassy
Physical Address:
Officentro Executivo La Sabana,
Sabana Sur
Edificio 5, Piso 3
San José, Costa Rica

Mailing Address:
Apartado Postal 351-1077
Centro Colón
San José, Costa Rica
tel. 506/296-4146
fax 506/296-4270

British Embassy
Apartado 815, Edificio Centro
Colón, Piso 11
San José 1007, Costa Rica
tel. 506/221-5566
fax 506/233-9938

VISAS

Visa/Entry Requirements
www.costarica-embassy.org

U.S. State Department
http://travel.state.gov/passport_services.html

COSTA RICAN GOVERNMENT MINISTRIES

Association of American Chambers of Commerce in Latin America
AACCLA
www.aaccla.org

Banco Central de Costa Rica
Central Bank of Costa Rica
www.bccr.fi.cr

Cámara de Industrias de Costa Rica
Chamber of Industries
www.cicr.com

Cámara de la Construcción
Chamber of Construction
www.construccion.co.cr

Cámara Nacional de Turismo (CANATUR)
The Costa Rica National Chamber of Tourism
www.costarica.tourism.co.cr

Compañía Nacional de Fuerza y Luz, S.A.
National Power Company
www.cnfl.go.cr

Dirección General de Aduanas, Ministerio de Hacienda
Costa Rican Customs Office
www.impuestos.go.cr

Instituto Costarricense de Electricidad (ICE)
National Institute of Electricity
(telecommunications, cell
phones, phone lines)
www.ice.go.cr

Instituto Nacional de Seguros (INS)
National Institute of Insurance
www.ins.go.cr

Ministerio de Agricultura y Ganadería
Ministry of Agriculture
www.mag.go.cr

Ministerio de Ciencia y Tecnología
Ministry of Science
and Technology
www.micit.go.cr

Ministerio de Educación Pública
Ministry of Public Education
www.mep.go.cr

Ministerio del Ambiente y Energía
Ministry of Environment
and Energy
www.minae.go.cr

RACSA
Radiográfica Costarricense

(telecommunications, Internet)
www.racsa.co.cr

MAKING THE MOVE

Association of Residents of Costa Rica (ARCR)
Invaluable help in relocating or
even just thinking about it.
tel. 506/221-2053
fax 506/255-0061
www.casacanada.net/arcr

Live in Costa Rica Tours
Author and longtime Costa Rica
resident Christopher Howard offers relocation/retirement tours for
those considering moving to Costa
Rica. There are tours around the
Central Valley, to the mid-Pacific
coast (Jacó, Quepos, and Dominical), and to Guanacaste coast
(Flamingo, Tamarindo, Samara,
and Carrillo). Custom tours are also
available.
tel. 506/222-1090
crbooks@racsa.co.cr
www.liveincostarica.com

Costa Rican Tourism Offices
In Costa Rica
There are four official tourist offices:
Peñas Blancas (at the border with
Nicaragua, open 8 A.M.–8 P.M.); Paso
Canoas (at the Panama border, open
6 A.M.–10 A.M.); at the Juan Santamaría Airport (near San José, open
Mon.–Fri., 9 A.M.–5 P.M.); and in
downtown San José (open Mon.–Fri.,
9 A.M.–1 P.M., 2 P.M.–5 P.M.)

The San José office is right behind the Teatro Central, in the Plaza de la Cultura, Calle 5, Avenida Central y Segunda. You could call 506/222-1090, but it's better to go in person, since the staff rarely answers the phone. Or try the website, www .tourism-costa-rica.com.

Apart from the official tourist offices, cities and towns bristle with signs advertising "Tourist Information." Mostly these are private agencies trying to sell specific tours, but the people there are usually friendly and will give you information even if you don't want to go on their tour.

United States
Costa Rica Tourist Office
1100 Brickell Ave., Ste. 801
Miami, FL 33131
tel. 800/343-6332

Canada
Costa Rica Tourist Office
135 York St., Ste. 208
Ottawa, Ontario K1N 5T4
tel. 613/562-2855

United Kingdom
Costa Rica Tourist Office
14 Lancaster Gate
London W2 3LH
tel. 0171/706-8844
fax 0171/706-8655

Time
www.hilink.com.au/times
(time in Costa Rica is the same as U.S. Central Standard Time: GMT - 6 hours)

Weather
www.weather.com
www.intellicast.com
www.usatoday.com/weather/ forecast/wglobe.htm

Maps
http://centralamerica.com/cr/ maps/mapcosta.htm
www.zurqui.holowww.com/ crinfocus/crmap/crmap .html (complete road map of Costa Rica)
www.pathfinder.com
www.omnimap.com/
www.photo.net/cr/overall -map.html

HEALTH
General Health Information
The Centers for Disease Control
This Atlanta, Georgia, institution is an invaluable resource for the health issues you may confront when traveling or living in countries all over the world.
traveler's health hotline:
tel. 877/394-8747
www.cdc.gov/travel

The World Health Organization
The Geneva, Switzerland–based WHO has a special section devoted to traveler's health on their website.
www.who.int/ith

www.tripprep.com
Vaccination requirements and
health issues in more than 200
countries.

Emergencies and Reporting Crime

Dial 911 in an emergency.

Crimes discovered after the fact
should be reported to the nearest
Organization of Judicial Investigation (OIJ) Office. The OIJ is the
equivalent of the FBI but is under
the authority of the judicial branch
of the Costa Rican government.
The OIJ is responsible for investi-
gating major crimes. Call 506/222-
1365 or 506/221-5337.

If you have a traffic accident,
leave the vehicles where they are,
and call both the Transito (Traffic
Police, at 506/222-9330 or 506/222-
9245) and the Insurance Investiga-
tor (800/800-8000). Both of these
officials will come, eventually, to
the accident scene upon notifica-
tion and file their reports. Only
after they do so can you legally
move your vehicle.

Hospitals and Clinics

Red Cross ambulance: 128 or 911
or tel. 506/221-5818

Public Hospitals in San José

San Juan de Dios:
tel. 506/257-6282
Hospital México:
tel. 506/232-6122
Children's Hospital:
tel. 506/222-0122

Calderon Guardia:
tel. 506/257-7299
Blanco Cervantes:
tel. 506/257-8122
Women's Hospital:
tel. 506/257-9111
Poison Center: tel. 506/223-1028
Burn Unit: tel. 506/257-0180

Private Clinics/ Hospitals in San José

Clínica Santa Rita:
tel. 506/221-6433
Clínica Biblica: tel. 506/257-0466
(emergency number)
or 506/257-5252
Clínica Católica: tel. 506/283-6171
or 506/283-6616
Hospital CIMA (in Escazú):
tel. 506/208-1143
(emergency number)

Alajuela

San Rafael: tel. 506/441-5011
Valverde Vega: tel. 506/445-5388
San Francisco de Asís:
tel. 506/444-5045
Upala: tel. 506/447-0181
Los Chiles: tel. 506/447-1045
Monte Sinaí, Ciudad Quesada:
tel. 506/460-1080
San Carlos: tel. 506/460-1176
or 506/460-0553
CCSS (Caja) Clinics in San Carlos:
tel. 506/479-9142 (La Fortuna),
506/473-3089 (Pital), 506/477-
7075 (Santa Rosa), 506/472-2044
(Venecia)

Puntarenas

Monseñor Sanabria:
tel. 506/663-0033

Max Terán: tel. 506/777-0922
Golfito: tel. 506/775-0011
Ciudad Neily: tel. 506/783-4111
San Vito de Coto Brus:
tel. 506/773-3103
Ciudad Cortés: tel. 506/788-8197

Guanacaste
Enrique Baltodano:
tel. 506/666-0011
Anexión de Nicoya:
tel. 506/685-5066

Limón
Tony Facio: tel. 506/758-2222
Guápiles: tel. 506/710-6801

Heredia
San Vicente de Paul:
tel. 506/237-5944

Cartago
Max Peralta: tel. 506/550-1999
Chacón Paut: tel. 506/279-9192
Wílliam Allen: tel. 506/556-4343

Health Insurance in Costa Rica

The government has a monopoly on all forms of insurance, and since 1924 there has been only one provider: the Instituto Nacional de Seguros, tel. 506/223-5800, www .ins-cr.com. But even monopolies need help sometimes, so the INS allows private agents to help you arrange for INS-provided insurance. The INS website lists many agents, and one English-speaking agency you might look into is Garrett & Associates, which boasts "2,500 satis-fied clients, including many foreign residents and several major multi-national corporations." The firm acts as agent for the three main Group Medical policies that are available to foreigners at a discount—those of the Canadian Club, American Legion Post 10, and the Association of Residents of Costa Rica (ARCR).

Garrett & Associates
Apdo 5478 - 1000 Costa Rica
tel. 506/233-2455
fax 506/222-0007
garrins@sol.racsa.co.cr
www.edenia.com/garrett

International Health Insurance

Aetna Inc.
151 Farmington Ave.
Hartford, CT 06156
tel. 860/273-0123
www.aetna.com

Amedex
7001 SW 97th Ave.
Miami, FL 33173
tel. 305/275-1400
www.amedex.com

Blue Cross/Blue Shield
www.bcbs.com

International Citizens
67 Coddington St., Ste. 201
Quincy, MA 02169
tel. 617/328-1565
or 877/328-1565
fax 617/328-0615
www.internationalcitizens.com

USHealthplans.com
1009 Oak Hill Rd., Third Fl.
Lafayette, CA 94549
tel. 800/922-8844
fax 925/299-8010
www.ushealthplans.com

Insurance Brokers

You can buy insurance through these companies; their websites can help you compare prices among insurance providers.

Global Insurance Net
7700 N. Kendall Dr., Ste. 503
Miami, FL 33156
tel. 305/274-0284
fax 305/274-2572
questions@global
insurancenet.com
www.globalinsurancenet.com

**Insurance
Consultants International**
308 Epps St.
Tomball, TX 77375
tel. 281/516-3633
or 800/576-2674
fax 603/843-6662
www.globalhealthinsurance.com

Insurance to Go
500 Professional Center Dr.,
Ste. 515
Novato, CA 94947
tel. 415/898-0584
or 877/598-8646
fax 415/898-0877
info@insurancetogo.com
www.insurancetogo.com

Medibroker
www.medibroker.com

Travel Insurance Providers in North America

Some of these companies also provide longer-term international health insurance.

American Express
tel. 800/234-0375
www.americanexpress.com

International SOS Assistance
tel. 713/521-7611
or 800/523-8930
corpcomm@internationalsos.com
www.internationalsos.com

Multinational Underwriters
tel. 317/262-2132
or 800/605-2282
fax 317/212-2140
insurance@mnui.com
www.mnui.com

Travelers
tel. 203/277-0111
or 800/243-3174
www.travelers.com

**Traveler's
Emergency Network**
tel. 800/471-3695
www.tenweb.com

TravelGuard International
tel. 715/345-0505
or 877/216-4885
www.travelguard.com

Wallach and Company
tel. 703/687-3166
or 800/237-6615
info@wallach.com
www.wallach.com

Travel Insurance Providers in Costa Rica

Costa Rica's INS (Instituto Nacional de Seguros) offers traveler's insurance that covers emergency medical or dental treatment. Buy coverage at travel agencies or call the INS office in San José at 506/223-5800.

Travel Insurance Providers for U.S. Veterans

Health Visions Corporation (HVC)
HVC helps U.S. veterans and military retirees in Costa Rica access their veterans' medical benefits without any out-of-pocket expense.
Agent: James Young
Heredia, Costa Rica
tel. 506/262-2525
or 506/367-3251
jet08442@aol.com
www.hvisions.com/hvc

EMPLOYMENT

Cámara de Exportadores de Costa Rica (CADEXCO) (Chamber of Exporters of Costa Rica)
www.cadexco.or.cr

Cámara de Industrias de Costa Rica (Chamber of Industries)
www.cicr.com

Centro para la Promoción de Exportaciones e Inversiones (PROCOMER) (Export and Investment Promotion Center)
www.procomer.com

Colegio de Abogados (Lawyers' Guild)
tel. 506/253-1947
fax 506/283-0576
www.abogados.or.cr

Costa Rican/American Chamber of Commerce (AMCHAM)
tel. 506/220-2200
fax 506/220-2300
www.amcham.co.cr

Costa Rican Investment and Development Board (CINDE)

CINDE Costa Rica
La Uruca San José, Costa Rica
tel. 506/299-2800
fax 506/299-2869
invest@cinde.org
www.cinde.or.cr

CINDE California
2033 Gateway Pl.
5th and 6th Fl.
San Jose, CA 95110
tel. 408/573-6146
fax 408/988-8090
cindeca@cinde.org

CINDE New York
500 5th Ave., Ste. 925
New York, NY 10110

tel. 212/704-2004
fax 212/997-9839
cindeny@cinde.org

Volunteer Organizations
ANAI Association
Works in bird conservation and to protect leatherback turtles on the Caribbean coast.
tel. 506/224-3570
fax 506/253-7524
anaicr@racswa.co.cr

APREFLOFAS
Works mostly in wildlife protection.
tel. 506/240-6087
fax 506/236-3210
www.preserveplanet.org

ASVO
(Association of Volunteers Working in Protected Areas)
Basic Spanish and one-month commitment required for work in national-park maintenance and turtle conservation.
tel. 506/233-4989
aso89@racsa.co.cr

Construyendo Oportunidades
Needs help with programs for teenaged mothers.
tel./fax 506/253-7841

Damas Voluntarios
Help out in day care/nutrition center for young kids.
tel. 506/228-0279

fax 506/288-0235
aquiros@racsa.co.cr

Dolphin Foundation of Costa Rica
Dolphins and turtles too.
tel. 506/394-2632
fax 506/786-7636
www.divinedolphin.com

EcoTeach
Matches U.S. student volunteers with humanitarian and ecological organizations.
tel. 800/626-8992
www.ecoteach.com

Escuela Universitaria para Niños
Environmental education for kids.
tel./fax 506/237-7086
escuelauniversitaria@hotmail.com

Finca la Flor
Environmental education, including organic farming and medicinal plants.
tel. 506/534-8003
www.la-flor-de-paraiso.org

Fundación Paniamor
You'll need good Spanish to work with this agency dedicated to preventing domestic abuse.
tel. 506/225-5031
fax 506/234-2956

Genesis II Cloud Forest Preserve
Cloud forest preserve needs help

with reforestation and in its experimental nursery. You should be physically fit, able to commit to four weeks, and pay US$150 a week.
tel./fax 506/381-0739
www.genesis-two.com

Habitat for Humanity
The Costa Rican branch of this international organization needs help building simple houses and in its office.
tel. 506/296-8120
fax 506/232-8679
tnelson@hfhlac.org

Humanitarian Foundation
Provides programs for at-risk Ticos.
tel. 506/249-1516
gynstrom@racsa.co.cr

McKee Project
Needs vets and support workers to help spay and neuter street cats and dogs.
tel./fax 506/293-6461
www.mckeeproject.org

Monteverde Butterfly Garden
Tour guides and groundsworkers needed.
tel./fax 506/645-5512
wolfej@racsa.co.cr

National Parks of Costa Rica
Needs help with park maintenance. Within Costa Rica, dial 192
http://centralamerica.com/cr/parks

www.sinac.go.cr (official government site, in Spanish)

Peace Corps
www.peacecorps.gov

Salvation Army
Rehab programs for alcoholics; shelters for abused women and children.
tel. 506/223-4864
fax 506/223-0250
ejesal@racsa.co.cr

Sarapiquí Conservation Learning Center
Teach English and computer skills to locals; good Spanish and a six-month commitment preferred.
tel. 506/766-6482
fax 506/766-6011
lrngcntr@racsa.co.cr

Vecinos
Programs for at-risk kids.
tel./fax 506/227-3868
vecinos@racsa.co.cr

VIDA (Association of Volunteers in Research and Environmental Development)
Matches volunteers with humanitarian and ecological organizations.
tel. 506/221-8367
fax 506/223-5485
www.vida.org

COMMUNICATIONS

The area code for all of Costa Rica is 506. There are no city codes, and most telephone numbers have seven digits.

Major Long-Distance Providers

AT&T
tel. 800/CALL-ATT (800/225-5288)

MCI
tel. 800/888-8000

Sprint
tel. 800/FON-CALL (800/366-2255)

Phone and Internet Service

RACSA
(Radiográfica Costaricennse)
in San José at Avenida 5 and Calle 1 (5th Ave. and 1st St.)
tel. 506/287-0087
www.racsa.co.cr

Private Mail Services

AAA Express Mail
tel. 506/233-4993
fax 506/221-5056

Aerocasillas
Escazú—Trilogia Building 3, across from PriceSmart,
tel. 506/208-4848
La Uruca—300 meters (328 yds.) north of Hotel San José Palacio,
tel. 506/232-6892
www.aerocasillas.com

Daily Mail
tel. 506/233-4993
fax 506/221-5046

Star Box
P.O. Box 405-1000
San José
tel. 506/257-3443
fax 506/233-5624

Trans-Express "Interlink"
P.O. Box 02-5635
Miami, FL 33102
tel. 506/296-3973
or 506/296-3974
fax 506/232-3979
www.transexpress.com.gt/

TRAVEL AND TRANSPORTATION

Daniel Oduber International Airport

Located in Liberia, Guanacaste, less than an hour from many northern Guanacaste beaches.

Juan Santamaría International Airport (SJO)

Has international and domestic terminals and is located just north of San José.

Tobias Bolaños Airport

For smaller domestic and charter flights; located in Pavas, a bit closer to San José than the larger international airport.

Airlines That Fly to Costa Rica

Air Canada
tel. 888/247-2262
www.aircanada.com

American Airlines
tel. 800/433-7300
www.aa.com

America West
tel. 800/235-9292
www.americawest.com

Continental
tel. 800/231-0856
www.continental.com

Delta
tel. 800/241-4141
www.delta.com

Iberia
www.iberia.com

Lacsa/Taca
www.grupotaca.com

MartinAir
tel. 800/777-7401
www.martinair.com

Mexicana
www.mexicana.com

Northwest
www.nwa.com

United
tel. 800/864-8331
www.united.com

Airlines That Fly Within Costa Rica

Aero Bell
tel. 506/290-0000
aerobell@racsa.co.cr

Aero Coastal Sol
tel. 506/440-1444
fax 506/441-2671
flyacs@racsa.co.cr

Helicópteros Turísticos Tropicales
tel. 506/296-0460

NatureAir
toll-free from U.S. or Canada
tel. 800/235-9272
Costa Rica tel. 506/220-3054
info@natureair.com
www.natureair.com

Paradise Air
tel. 506/231-0938
fax 506/296-1429
www.flywithparadise.com

Pitts Aviation
tel. 506/296-3600

Sansa Airlines
tel. 506/221-9414
or 506/255-2176
fax 506/255-2176
www.flysansa.com

Travelair
www.get2-costarica.com/
travelair.htm

Car Rental

Alamo
www.alamocostarica.com

Budget
www.budget.co.cr

Elegante
www.eleganterentacar.com

Europcar
www.europcar.co.cr

Hertz
www.hertzcostarica.com

Hola
www.hola.net

Mapache
www.mapache.com

Tropical
www.tropicalcarrental.com

Bus Companies

Fantasy Bus
(shuttle vans)
tel. 506/220-2126
fax 506/220-2393
www.graylinecostarica.com

Interbus
(shuttle vans)
tel. 506/283-5573
fax 506/283-7655
www.costaricapass.com

Tica Bus
(big buses)
tel. 506/221-8954

fax 506/223-8158
www.ticabus.com

For more bus information, check out www.costaricabybus.com.

Taxis

Coopeguaria
(San José)
tel. 506/226-1366

Coopeirazú
(San José)
tel. 506/254-3211

Coopetaxi
(San José)
tel. 506/235-9966

Coopetico
(San José)
tel. 506/224-7979 or 224-1313

Radio Taxi Liberia
(Liberia)
tel. 506/666-0574

Sarchí
(Sarchí)
tel. 506/454-4028

Taxis Yuli
(Heredia)
tel. 506/362-1409

Unidos
(San José)
tel. 506/221-6865

REAL ESTATE

See the Prime Living Locations chapters for names of specific real estate agents.

Costa Rican Real Estate Agents Chamber
Lobbies for mandatory licensing of real estate agents.
tel. 506/283-0191
fax 506/283-0347
www.camaracbr.or.cr

Guanacaste Association of Realtors
Approximately 50 members with knowledge of local beach and rural properties.
tel. 506/670-0472
fax 506/670-0807
www.gar.or.cr

Stewart Title
Provides title searches and title guarantees.
tel. 506/258-5600
fax 506/221-5320
www.stewarttitlelatinamerica.com

CULTURAL DIRECTORY

The Julia and David White Arts Colony
Ex–Los Angeleno Bill White started this lovely retreat after both of his children tragically took their own lives. Both were artistically inclined, and Bill decided he would create a gorgeous, peaceful place where artists could come and do nothing but pursue their work. At any given time there are two writers, two visual artists, and two composers lucky enough to be in residence at Bill's lush spread half an hour outside San José in Ciudad Colón.
tel. 506/249-1414
www.forjuliaanddavid.org

Museums in San José
Museo de Arte Costarricense (Costa Rican Art Museum)
East end of Sabana Park
tel. 506/222-7175
www.cr/arte/musearte/
musearte.htm

Museo de Arte y Diseño Contemporáneo (Art and Design Museum)
In the old prison building (Antigua Fanal) on 3rd Ave btwn. 13th and 15th Aves.
tel. 506/257-7202
www.madc.ac.cr

Museo de Insectos (Insect Museum)
On the UCR campus (San Pedro), in the Music Bldg.
tel. 506/207-5318

Museo de Jade (Jade Museum)
On the 11th floor of the INS Building, btwn. 5th and 7th Aves., and 11th and 13th Sts.
tel. 506/223-5800
www.cr/arte/jade/musejade.htm

**Museo de los Niños
(Children's Museum)**
Central Ave., at 17th St.
tel. 506/258-4929

**Museo de Oro
(Gold Museum)**
Plaza de la Cultura, 5th St.
at 2nd Ave.
tel. 506/243-4202
www.museosdelbancocentral.org/
eng/gold/index.htm

**Museo Nacional
(National Museum)**
17th St. at 2nd Ave.
tel. 506/257-1433
www.cr/arte/museonac/
museonac.htm

Theaters in San José
**Teatro Melico Salazar
(Melico Salazar Theater)**
On 2nd Ave., diagonal from
the Cathedral
tel. 506/221-4952
www.intnet.co.cr/culture/melico/
melico.html

**Teatro Nacional (National
Theater)**
Plaza de la Cultura, 5th St.
at 2nd Ave.
tel. 506/221-1329
www.guiascostarica.com/
teatro.htm

Cultural Centers
in San José
Alliance Française
7th Ave. at 5th St., 200 meters (219
yds.) west of the INS bldg.
tel. 506/222-2283
fax 506/233-5819
alcultfr@sol.racsa.co.cr
www.alianzafr.ac.cr

Casa Italia
200 meters (219 yds.) south of KFC
in Barrio La California
tel. 506/224-6049

Mexican Cultural Center
250 meters (273 yds.) south of Sub-
aru dealership in Los Yoses
tel. 506/283-2333

**North American
Cultural Center**
100 meters (109 yds.) north of the
Automercado Los Yoses, in Barrio
Dent, San José
tel. 506/207-7500
fax 506/224-1480
mercadeo@cccncr.com
www.cccncr.com

Spanish Cultural Center
Next to the Farolito in
Barrio Escalante
tel. 506/257-2919
ccultucr@racas.co.cr

TOURISM AND
RECREATION
General Tourism
www.ahcostarica.com

www.arweb.com/cr
www.centralamerica.com
www.clickoncostarica.com
www.costaricaoutdoors.com
www.costarica.tourism.co.cr
www.ecotour.org
www.gatewaycostarica.com
www.incostarica.net
www.lovecostarica.com
www.online.co.cr
www.planeta.com
www.travel.state.gov
www.visitcostarica.com

National Parks
http://centralamerica.com/
    cr/parks/
www.sinac.go.cr (official government site, in Spanish)

Regional Information
Monteverde
www.monteverdeinfo.com

Nosara
www.nosara.com

Puntarenas
www.puntarenas.com

Sarapiqui
www.sarapiquirainforest.com

Southern Costa Rica
www.exploringcostarica.com
www.ecotourism.co.cr

Tamarindo
www.tamarindo.com

Conservation Organizations and Wildlife Information
Amigos de las Aves/ Friends of the Birds
http://hatchedtoflyfree.home
stead.com

Birds of Costa Rica
www.interlog.com/~rainfrst/
birds.html

Butterflies of Costa Rica
www.centralamerica.com/cr/
butterfly/index.htm

Caribbean Conservation Corp.
www.cccturtle.org

Earthwatch
www.earthwatch.org

Guanacaste Conservation Areas
www.acguanacaste.ac.cr

Monteverde Conservation League
www.monteverdeinfo.com/mon
teverde_conservation_league.htm

Nature Conservancy
www.tnc.or

Organization of Tropical Studies
www.ots.ac.cr
www.ots.duke.edu

Tropical River Foundation
www.riostro.com

Recreation
Ballooning
www.serendipityadventures.com

Biking
www.bikingincostarica.com

Birding
Organization for Tropical Studies'
birding trips: http://www.ots.ac
.cr/es/biocursos/
Richard Garrigues's list
of Costa Rica birds: www
.angelfire.com/bc/gonebirding

Bungee Jumping
www.bungee.co.cr

Canopy Tours (ziplines)
www.arenal.net/canopy-tour
-costa-rica/
www.canopytour.com
www.monteverdeinfo.com/
canopy/tour.htm
http://samarabeach.com/
ps32.html

Diving
www.diversalertnetwork.com
www.isladelcoco.com
www.naui.org
www.padi.com
www.underseahunter.com

Fishing
http://centralamerica.com/cr/fish
www.excitementsportfishing.com
www.fishcostarica.com

www.flyfishcostarica.com

Golf
www.amrita-it.com/golf/
courses.htm
www.centralamerica.com/cr/
golf/index.htm
www.golfbytes.com
www.golfcr.com
www.traveling.com/golf
www.worldgolf.com/courses

Horseback Riding
www.horsebackridecostarica.com
www.lacarana.com

Rafting and Kayaking
www.costaricaexpeditions.com
www.costaricarios.com
www.costasolrafting.com
www.escondidotrex.com
www.igaunatours.com
www.riostropicales.com
www.sarapiqui.com
www.toenjoynature.com

Surfing
www.alacransurf.com
www.centralamerica.com/cr/surf
www.crsurf.com
www.latinsurf.com
www.surfcostarica.com
www.surfex.com
www.surfoutfitters.com

Windsurfing and Kitesurfing
www.hotel-tilawa.com
www.3cornersbolanosbay.com
www.ticowind.com
www.suntoursandfun.com

Spanish Phrasebook

PRONUNCIATION GUIDE

Spanish pronunciation is much more regular than that of English, but there are still occasional variations.

Consonants

c — before 'a,' 'o,' or 'u,' like 'c' in "cat"; before 'e' or 'i,' like 's'

g — before 'e' or 'i,' like 'ch' in Scottish "loch"; elsewhere like 'g' in "get"

h — always silent

j — like 'h' in "hotel," but stronger

ll — like 'y' in "yellow"

ñ — like 'ni' in "onion"

r — always pronounced as strong 'r'

rr — trilled 'r'

v — similar to 'b' in "boy" (not as English 'v')

y — similar to English, but with a slight 'j' sound. When standing alone, pronounced like the 'e' in "me."

z — like 's' in "same"

b, d, f, k, l, m, n, p, q, s, t, w, x — as in English

Vowels

a — as in "father," but shorter

e — as in "hen"

i — as in "machine"

o — as in "phone"

u — usually as in "rule"; when it follows a 'q,' the 'u' is silent; when it follows an 'h' or 'g,' it's pronounced like 'w'—except when

it comes between 'g' and 'e' or 'i,' in which case it's also silent (unless it has an umlaut, when it's again pronounced as English 'w')

Stress and Accent Marks

Words in Spanish follow a few basic rules as to which syllable is stressed (emphasized).

1. Words ending in a vowel, -n, or -s are stressed on the next to the last (penultimate) syllable, as in *nada* (NA-da), *origen* (o-RI-hen), or *esto* (ES-to).

2. Words ending in any consonant except -n or -s are stressed on the last syllable, as in *doctor* (doc-TOR), *ciudad* (see-u-DAHD), or *comer* (co-MAIR).

3. When a word does not follow rules #1 or #2 above, a written accent is used to show where the emphasis should be placed, as in *rápido* (RAP-ee-do), *compró* (cohm-PRO), or *limón* (lee-MOHN).

4. Written accents are also used to differentiate between words that are pronounced the same but have different meanings:

si — if

sí — yes

el — the

él — he

5. Remember that emphasizing the wrong syllable of a word can make

it into another word entirely. Consider the word *animo*. With stress on the first syllable (AH-ni-mo), we have the noun *ánimo,* meaning "spirit, intention, or courage." With stress on the second syllable (animo, pronounced ah-NEE-mo), we have the first person present tense form of the verb *animar,* meaning 'to encourage.' Finally, with stress on the final syllable (animó), we have the third person preterite form of the same verb.

NUMBERS

0 — *cero*
1 — *uno* (masculine)
1 — *una* (feminine)
2 — *dos*
3 — *tres*
4 — *cuatro*
5 — *cinco*
6 — *seis*
7 — *siete*
8 — *ocho*
9 — *nueve*
10 — *diez*
11 — *once*
12 — *doce*
13 — *trece*
14 — *catorce*
15 — *quince*
16 — *dieciseis*
17 — *diecisiete*
18 — *dieciocho*
19 — *diecinueve*
20 — *veinte*
21 — *veintiuno*
30 — *treinta*
40 — *cuarenta*

50 — *cincuenta*
60 — *sesenta*
70 — *setenta*
80 — *ochenta*
90 — *noventa*
100 — *cien*
101 — *ciento y uno*
200 — *doscientos*
1,000 — *mil*
10,000 — *diez mil*
1,000,000 — *un millón*

DAYS OF THE WEEK

Sunday — *domingo*
Monday — *lunes*
Tuesday — *martes*
Wednesday — *miércoles*
Thursday — *jueves*
Friday — *viernes*
Saturday — *sábado*

TIME

Latin Americans mostly use the 12-hour clock, but in some instances—usually associated with plane or bus schedules—they may use the 24-hour military clock. Under the 24-hour clock, for example, *las nueve de la noche* (9 P.M.) would be *las 21 horas* (2100 hours).

What time is it? — *¿Qué hora es?*
It's one o'clock. — *Es la una.*
It's two o'clock. — *Son las dos.*
At two o'clock. — *A las dos.*
It's ten to three. — *Son tres menos diez.*
It's ten past three. — *Son tres y diez.*

It's three fifteen.— *Son las tres y cuarto.*

It's two forty-five. — *Son tres menos cuarto.*

It's two thirty. — *Son las dos y media,* or *Son las dos y trienta.*

It's six A.M. — *Son las seis de la mañana.*

It's six P.M. — *Son las seis de la tarde.*

It's ten P.M. — *Son las diez de la noche.*

Today — *hoy*

Tomorrow — *mañana*

Morning — *la mañana*

Tomorrow morning — *mañana por la mañana*

Yesterday — *ayer*

Week — *la semana*

Month — *mes*

Year — *año*

Last night — *anoche*

The next day — *el día siguiente*

USEFUL WORDS AND PHRASES

Most Spanish-speaking people consider formalities important. When approaching someone for information or any other reason, do not forget the appropriate salutation—good morning, good evening, etc. Standing alone, the greeting *hola* (hello) may sound brusque.

Hello. — *Hola.*

Good morning. — *Buenos días.*

Good afternoon. — *Buenas tardes.*

Good evening. — *Buenas noches.*

How are you? — *¿Cómo está?*

Fine. — *Muy bien.*

And you? — *¿Y usted?*

So-so. — *Más o menos.*

Thank you. — *Gracias.*

Thank you very much. — *Muchas gracias.*

You're very kind. — *Muy amable.*

You're welcome — *De nada* (literally, "It's nothing.")

Yes — *sí*

No — *no*

I don't know. — *No sé.*

It's fine; okay — *Está bien.*

Good; okay — *Bueno.*

Please — *por favor*

Pleased to meet you. — *Mucho gusto.*

Excuse me (physical) — *Perdóneme.*

Excuse me (speech) — *Discúlpeme.*

I'm sorry. — *Lo siento.*

Goodbye. — *adiós*

See you later. — *hasta luego* (literally, "until later")

More — *más*

Less — *menos*

Better — *mejor*

Much; a lot — *mucho*

A little — *un poco*

Large — *grande*

Small — *pequeño; chico*

Quick; fast — *rápido*

Slowly — *despacio*

Bad — *malo*

Difficult — *difícil*

Easy — *fácil*

He/She/It is gone; as in, "she left" or "he's gone." — *Ya se fue.*

I don't speak Spanish well. — *No hablo bien el español.*

I don't understand. — *No entiendo.*

How do you say. . . in Spanish? — *¿Cómo se dice. . . en español?*

Do you understand English? —*¿Entiende el inglés?*

Is English spoken here? (Does anyone here speak English?) — *¿Se habla inglés aquí?*

TERMS OF ADDRESS

When in doubt, use the formal *usted* (you) as a form of address. If you wish to dispense with formality and feel that the desire is mutual, you can say, *Me puedes tutear* (you can call me *"tú"*). Also see below for a special note on *vos,* an alternative for *tú* that's common in Costa Rica but rarely taught in Western classrooms.

I — *yo*
You (formal) — *usted*
You (familiar) — *tú* or *vos*
He/him — *él*
She/her — *ella*
We/us — *nosotros*
You (plural) — *ustedes*
They/them (all males or mixed gender) — *ellos*
They/them (all females) — *ellas*
Mr.; sir — *señor*
Mrs.; madam — *señora*
Miss; young lady — *señorita*
Wife — *esposa*
Husband — *marido; esposo*
Friend — *amigo* (male); *amiga* (female)
Sweetheart — *novio* (male); *novia* (female)
Son; daughter — *hijo; hija*
Brother; sister — *hermano; hermana*
Father; mother — *padre; madre*

Grandfather; grandmother — *abuelo; abuela*

GETTING AROUND

Where is. . . ? — *¿Dónde está. . . ?*
How far is it to. . . ? — *¿A Cuanto está. . . ?*
from. . . to. . . — *de. . . a. . .*
Highway — *la carretera*
Road — *el camino*
Street — *la calle*
Block — *la cuadra*
Kilometer — *kilómetro*
North — *norte*
South — *sur*
West — *oeste; poniente*
East — *este; oriente*
Straight ahead — *al derecho; adelante*
To the right — *a la derecha*
To the left — *a la izquierda*

ACCOMMODATIONS

Is there a room? — *¿Hay cuarto?*
May I (we) see it? — *¿Puedo (podemos) verlo?*
What is the rate? — *¿Cuál es el precio?*
Is that your best rate? — *¿Es su mejor precio?*
Is there something cheaper? — *¿Hay algo más económico?*
Single room — *un sencillo*
Double room — *un doble*
Room for a couple — *matrimonial*
Key — *llave*
With private bath — *con baño*
With shared bath — *con baño general; con baño compartido*

Hot water — *agua caliente*
Cold water — *agua fría*
Shower — *ducha*
Electric shower— *ducha eléctrica*
Towel — *toalla*
Soap — *jabón*
Toilet paper — *papel higiénico*
Air conditioning — *aire acondicionado*
Fan — *abanico; ventilador*
Blanket — *frazada; manta*
Sheets — *sábanas*

PUBLIC TRANSPORT

Bus stop — *la parada*
Bus terminal — *terminal de buses*
Airport — *el aeropuerto*
Launch — *lancha; tiburonera*
Dock — *muelle*
I want a ticket to. . . — *Quiero un pasaje a. . .*
I want to get off at. . . — *Quiero bajar en. . .*
Here, please. — *Aquí, por favor.*
Where is this bus going? — *¿Adónde va este autobús?*
Round-trip — *ida y vuelta*
What do I owe? — *¿Cuánto le debo?*

FOOD

Menu — *la carta; el menú*
Glass — *taza*
Fork — *tenedor*
Knife — *cuchillo*
Spoon — *cuchara*
Napkin — *servilleta*
Soft drink — *refesco*
Coffee — *café*
Cream — *crema*

Tea — *té*
Sugar — *azúcar*
Drinking water — *agua pura; agua potable*
Bottled water — *agua en botella*
Beer — *cerveza*
Wine — *vino*
Milk — *leche*
Juice — *jugo*
Eggs — *huevos*
Bread — *pan*
Watermelon — *sandía*
Banana — *banano*
Plantain — *plátano*
Apple — *manzana*
Orange — *naranja*
(without) Meat — *(sin) carne*
Beef — *carne de res*
Chicken — *pollo; gallina*
Fish — *pescado*
Shellfish — *mariscos*
Shrimp — *camarones*
Fried — *frito*
Roasted — *asado*
Barbecued/Grilled — *a la parrilla*
Breakfast — *desayuno*
Lunch — *almuerzo*
Dinner (often eaten in late afternoon) — *comida*
Dinner; late-night snack — *cena*
The check; the bill — *la cuenta*

MAKING PURCHASES

I need. . . — *Necesito. . .*
I want. . . — *Deseo. . . or Quiero. . .*
I would like. . . (more polite) — *Quisiera. . .*
How much does it cost? — *¿Cuánto cuesta?*

What's the exchange rate? — *¿Cuál es el tipo de cambio?*
May I see. . . ? — *¿Puedo ver. . . ?*
This one — *ésta/ésto*
Expensive — *caro*
Cheap — *barato*
Cheaper — *más barato*
Too much — *demasiado*

HEALTH

Help me, please. — *Ayúdeme, por favor.*

I am ill. — *Estoy enfermo.*
Pain — *dolor*
Fever — *fiebre*
Stomachache — *dolor de estómago*
Vomiting — *vomitar*
Diarrhea — *diarrea*
Drugstore — *farmacia*
Medicine — *medicina*
Pill; tablet — *pastilla*
Birth control pills — *pastillas anti-conceptivas*
Condom — *condón; preservativo*

SPECIAL NOTE: *VOS*

In Costa Rica, as well as in several other Central and South American countries, the pronoun *"tú"* is not frequently heard. More commonly used, and rarely taught to Westerners in their Spanish classes, is *vos*.

Essentially, *vos* is used in the same instances as *tú,* that is, between two people who have a certain degree of casual familiarity or friendliness, in place of the more formal *usted.* The *vos* form is derived from *vosotros,* the second person plural (you all) still used in Spain. However, *vosotros* is not used in Latin America, even in places where *vos* is common.

For all tenses other than the present indicative, present subjunctive, and command forms, the *vos* form of the verb is exactly the same as *tú.* Hence: *tú andaste/vos andaste* (past tense), *tú andabas/vos andabas* (past imperfect), *tú andarás/vos andarás*(future), *tú andarías/vos andarías* (conditional).

In the present indicative, the conjugation is the same as with *tú,* but the last syllable is stressed with an accent. The exception is with -ir verbs, in which the final "i" is retained, instead of changing to an "e." Hence: *tú andas/vos andás, tú comes/vos comés, tú escribes/vos escribís.*

In the present subjunctive, the same construction is followed as with the normal subjunctive, except the *vos* "á" accent is retained. Hence: *tú andes/vos andés, tú comas/vos comás, tú escribas/vos escribás.*

In radical changing verbs like tener, *poder,* or *dormir,* the *vos* form does not change from vowel to dipthong *(tienes, puedes, duermes)* in the present subjunctive form. Hence: *vos tengás, vos podás, vos durmás.*

Vos commands are formed by simply dropping the final "r" on the infinitive and adding an accent over the last vowel. Hence: *vos andá, vos comé, vos escribí.* When using object pronouns with *vos, te* is still used. Hence: *Yo te lo escribí a vos.*

One common irregular *vos* form is *sos,* for *ser* (to be). Also, because the conjugation would be bizarre,the verb *"ir"* is not used in the *vos* form. Instead, use *andar: vos andás.*

Glossary

aguacates: avocados
aguacero: downpour
aguinaldo: Christmas bonus
ballena: whale
boticas: pharmacies
buzón: mailbox
chapulín: tractor
chicha: corn liquor
cochino: "piggy", dirty
colón: Costa Rican currency
correos: post office
estranjero: stranger
farmacias: pharmacies
fútbol: soccer
grano de oro: coffee ("grain of gold")
impuesto de ventas: sales tax
lluvia: rain

mayor: main
menudo: loose change
pensionado: pensioner/retiree
personas de la tercera edad:
    senior citizens
polacos: roving vendors
polideportiva: sports center
precaristas: squatters
presupuesto: cost estimate
pueblo: town
pulpería: general store
puro Tico: pure Costa Rican
quebradas: creeks
residenciales: gated communities
sabanero: cowboy
soda: café/restaurant
trucha: trout

Suggested Reading

GUIDEBOOKS AND NATURAL HISTORY

Alvarado, Guillermo. *Costa Rica: Land of Volcanoes*. Cartago, Costa Rica: Editorial Tecnología de Costa Rica, 1993. A detailed and fascinating look at the fiery mountains that are still shaping Costa Rica. With maps and color photos.

Baker, Christopher. *Moon Handbooks Costa Rica*. Emeryville, California: Avalon Travel Publishing, 2004. One of the most comprehensive guidebooks on the market. Lots of good background information, and a lively writing style.

Bernhardt, Ed. *The Costa Rican Organic Home Gardening Guide*. New Dawn Center, 2003. The founder of the New Dawn organic farm and education center gives practical and comprehensive advice about starting an organic garden in Costa Rica. www.newdawn center.org.

Carr, Archie. *The Windward Road*. Gainesville, Florida: University of Florida Press, 1955. A book about sea turtles in Central America by the man who not only pioneered the study of the creatures but also founded the Caribbean Conservation Corp.

Cole-Christenson, Darryl. *A Place in the Rain Forest: Settling the Costa Rican Frontier*. Austin, Texas: University of Texas Press, 1997. A remarkable account of pioneering in the southern region now known as Coto Brus. Stick with it and you'll find out a lot about farming, squatters, and how very remote this area was just fifty years ago.

Del Sol, Alexander. *The Southern Costa Rica Handbook*. Self-published by author, 2002. Covers the southern Pacific coast from Dominical down to Pavones. The advantage of focusing on a limited area is that the author (a resident of Puerto Jiménez, on the Osa Peninsula) is able to describe hotels and restaurants in great detail. With rudimentary maps, no photos, and an easygoing, conversational writing style. Order from author: fax 506/735-5045, alexdelsol@yahoo.com.

De Vries, Phillip. *Butterflies of Costa Rica and Their Natural History (Volumes 1 and 2)*. Princeton, New Jersey: Princeton University Press, 2000. The real deal for butterfly fanatics. Lots of color plates.

Evans, Sterling. *The Green Republic: A Conservation History of Costa Rica*.

Amarillo, Texas: University of Texas Press, 1999. Detailed account of the history of the national park system and the rise of ecological awareness in Costa Rica.

Mayfield, Michael and Rafael Gallo. *The Rivers of Costa Rica: A Canoeing, Kayaking, and Rafting Guide.* Birmingham, Alabama: Menasha Ridge Press, 1992. Takes on Costa Rica's major navigable rivers.

Parise, Mike. *The Surfer's Guide to Costa Rica.* Los Angeles, California: Surfpress Publishing, 1999. *The* guide for surfers traveling to Costa Rica. Information on 70 breaks on both coasts and more than 100 hotels nearest the breaks. Tips on what to pack, how to pack surfboards, and how to get to remote places.

Stiles, Gary and Alexander Skutch. *A Guide to the Birds of Costa Rica.* Ithaca, New York: Cornell University Press, 1989. The birder's bible, with color plates.

Wainwright, Mark. *The Natural History of Costa Rican Mammals.* Distribuidores Zona Tropical, S.A., 2003. There are many books on Costa Rican mammals, but this one really stands out. Compact enough to be a field guide, it is nevertheless quite comprehensive, with color plates of not only the animals, but also drawings of scat and tracks. Wainwright provides details of dens, range, vocalizations, derivations of common and scientific names, evolutionary history, even local folklore and mythology. The book has 400 illustrations and is written in a very clear and sometimes witty style. A joy!

Wallace, David R. *The Quetzal and the Macaw: The Story of Costa Rica's National Parks.* San Francisco: Sierra Club Books, 1992. A very readable history of the formation of the country's park system.

HISTORY, POLITICS, AND CULTURE

Biesanz, Mavis, Richard Biesanz, and Karen Biesanz. *The Ticos: Culture and Social Change in Costa Rica.* Boulder, Colorado: Lynne Rienner Publishers, 1999. An excellent book for those who want to understand Costa Rica and its people. The authors take on everything from history to "marital relations and gender roles."

Coates, Anthony G., ed. *Central America: A Natural and Cultural History.* New Haven, Connecticut: Yale University Press, 1999. Chapters by different authors, most authorities in their fields, take on geological origins, differences between the surrounding oceans, the importance of natural corridors, the history of native people and colonizers from pre-

Columbian to modern times, and current conservation issues.

Edelman, Marc and Joanne Kenen, eds. *The Costa Rican Reader.* New York: Grove Weidenfeld, 1989. A collection of articles by diverse authors, covering many aspects of Costa Rican history and politics. Includes the text of former president Oscar Arias Sanchez's 1987 peace plan, for which he won the Nobel Peace Prize.

Helmuth, Charlene. *Culture and Customs of Costa Rica.* Westport, Connecticut: Greenwood Press, 2000. A useful and very readable introduction to Tican culture, including chapters on visual arts, performing arts, and literature.

Honey, Martha. *Hostile Acts: U.S. Policy in Costa Rica in the 1980s.* Gainesville, Florida: University of Florida Press, 1994. Account of U.S. influence in the isthmus during the tumultuous 1980s. The author lived in Costa Rica from 1983 to 1991 and brings an insider's view to the subject. Arguing that Costa Rica should be the best example of the type of country the U.S. government says it is trying to foster, Honey shows how U.S. actions actually undermined the country until Costa Rican president Arias stood up to U.S. pressure, providing a regional solution with his Central American Peace Plan.

Lefever, Harry G. *Turtle Bogue: Afro-Caribbean Life in a Costa Rican Village.* Selinsgrove, Pennsylvania: Susquehanna University Press, 1992. A professor records the folk history of the Caribbean coast town of Tortuguero.

Molina, Iván and Steven Palmer. *The History of Costa Rica.* San José, Costa Rica: Editorial de la Universidad de Costa Rica, 2002. A short and readable introduction to the country's history.

Paige, Jeffery M. *Coffee and Power: Revolution and the Rise of Democracy in Central America.* Cambridge, Massachusetts: Harvard University Press. 1998. Central American politics and development, as seen through the lens of the all-important coffee business.

Palmer, Paula. *What Happen: A Folk History of Costa Rica's Talamanca Coast.* Publications in English S.A., 1993. The author, a North American sociologist, has collected fascinating oral histories from the Afro-Caribbean people who settled the towns of Cahuita, Puerto Viejo, and Manzanillo on Costa Rica's Atlantic coast. Out of print, but not impossible to find.

Palmer, Paula, Juanita Sánchez, and Gloria Mayorga. *Taking Care of Sibö's Gifts.* San José, Costa Rica: Editorama S.A.,

1993. One of the few books on indigenous Costa Rican culture by indigenous authors.

FICTION AND TRAVELOGUE

Benz, Stephen. *Green Dreams: Travels in Central America*. Oakland, California: Lonely Planet, 1998. The section on Costa Rica explores the gap between the country's ecological aspirations and its need for economic development.

Henry de Tessan, Christina, ed. *Expat: Women's True Tales of Life Abroad*. New York: Seal Press, 2002. These 21 accounts of living abroad all over the world give interesting perspectives on the expat experience.

Ras, Barbara, ed. *Costa Rica: A Traveler's Literary Companion*. Berkeley, California: Whereabouts Press, 1994. Short stories and novel excerpts by Costa Rican authors, organized by geographical zone.

Weisbecker, Allan C. *In Search of Captain Zero: A Surfer's Road Trip Beyond the End of the Road*. Los Angeles: JP Tarcher, 2002. Chronicles the author's trip through Mexico and Central America in search of good waves and an old friend who has disappeared. The "end of the road" turns out to be on the Caribbean coast of Costa Rica, and there are some nice descriptions of the famed Salsa Brava, a wave near Puerto Viejo that draws highly skilled and adventurous surfers.

Young, Allen. *Sarapiquí Chronicle: A Naturalist in Costa Rica*. Washington, D.C.: Smithsonian Institution Press, 1991. Travelogue of northern Costa Rica.

For more books by Costa Rican authors, see the Literature section of the People and Culture chapter.

KID'S BOOKS

Baden, Robert. *And Sunday Makes Seven*. Morton Grove, Illinois: Albert Whitman & Co., 1990. Folk tales for kids 4–8.

Forsyth, Adrian. *Journey Through a Tropical Jungle*. Englewood Cliffs, New Jersey: Silver Burdett Press, 1996. A lighthearted romp through a Costa Rican forest.

Henderson, Aileen. *The Monkey Thief*. Minneapolis, Minnesota: Milkweed Editions, 1998. A 12-year-old boy visits his uncle in Costa Rica, and learns about monkeys, smugglers, and the rain forest.

DRIVING TO COSTA RICA

Nelson, Mike. *Central America by Car*. Wanderlust Publications,

1997. "Mexico Mike" gives advice on how to navigate the isthmus from behind the wheel of your car.

Pritchard, Raymond. *Driving the Pan-American Highway,* 6th edition. San José, Costa Rica: Costa Rica Books, 1997. An old classic (now edited by Chris Howard) that needs updating, but offers tips on border crossing and sightseeing. Available from Costa Rica books, 800/365-2342 or at www.drivetocentralamerica.com.

Wessler, Dawna Rae. *You Can Drive to Costa Rica in 8 Days.* Harmony Gardens Publishing, 1998. Tales and advice from two non–Spanish speaking surfer gringos who made the trip in their 22-year-old VW van.

MISCELLANEOUS

Hasbrouck, Edward. *The Practical Nomad.* Emeryville, California: Avalon Travel Publishing, 2003. A cult classic and deservedly so, this book helps you think about the world and how to best move through it. Great practical information (on airfares, for example) and even better philosophy (just what do we mean when we talk about first, second, and third worlds?).

Kohls, L. Robert. *Survival Kit for Overseas Living, Fourth Edition.* Yarmouth, Maine: Nicholas Brealey/Intercultural Press, 2001. Offering up a fascinating look at culture shock and cultural bias, this book helps readers take inventory of their own cultural "baggage" before venturing abroad. Short on practical detail about individual countries but long on strategies for developing intercultural communication skills, no matter where you plan to go.

Peterson, Roger A. *The Legal Guide to Costa Rica.* San José, Costa Rica: Amerilatin Consultares, 2002. Covers everything from property rights to extradition. You can order a copy at www.costa ricalaw.com.

Index

Acknowledgments

Many thanks to Andres Zamora and Alvaro Porras of Remax Lider in San José; William Aspinall Murray of Arenal Obervatory Lodge; Chris Simmonds, Jim Main, and Brigette O'Shaughnessy of Remax/Ocean Surf Realty in Tamarindo; Linda Koss of the Residents Association in Nosara; Wendy Rockwell of Monteverde; Robert Stowell of Nosara Real Estate in Nosara; Brenda Burnside in Nosara; Heather Ellis of Chica Surf in Tamarindo; Alberto Lizárraga of Hotel Liberia in Liberia; Joy Rothke and Bill Linnemeier of La Fortuna; Bill White of the Julia and David White Arts Colony in Ciudad Colón; Aldo y Coco y Aldito of Playa Negra; Edward Hasbrouck; Christopher Baker; Maarten Oosterhoff, Laure Maillard, Caroline Sauriol, and Gert-Jan van't Hag for picking me up after I fell at the waterfall outside Montezuma; Iris Maillox of Remax in Playas del Coco; Allan Templeton of Costa Verde in Manuel Antonio; Ray Beise of Pura Jungla in Playa Negra; Alejandra Vega and Grayline Tours/Fantasy Bus; John McCuen of 7th Street Books in San José; Michael Kaye of Costa Rica Expeditions; Kirt Wackford and Ana Munoz; Peggy Windle; Victoria Schwarz; and Mary Ann Jackson, a.k.a. Ruby Babaloa, of Brooklyn, New York. Thanks to everyone at Avalon Travel Publishing, especially editor Amy Scott, copy editor Emily McManus, graphics coordinator Susan Snyder, production coordinator Darren Alessi, designer Amber Pirker, map editor Olivia Solís, publicist Erik Riesenberg, series manager Mia Lipman, Ellen Cavalli for her level head, and surfmistress Jane Musser for getting me back in the water. A special thanks to Houman Pirdavari for his excellent photographs and for knowing how to talk to me in a riptide. To everyone else who lent me a hand and helped me see how varied a country Costa Rica is, *un abrazo, y mil gracias.*

U.S.~Metric Conversion

1 inch	=	2.54 centimeters (cm)
1 foot	=	.304 meters (m)
1 yard	=	0.914 meters
1 mile	=	1.6093 kilometers (km)
1 km	=	.6214 miles
1 fathom	=	1.8288 m
1 chain	=	20.1168 m
1 furlong	=	201.168 m
1 acre	=	.4047 hectares
1 sq km	=	100 hectares
1 sq mile	=	2.59 square km
1 ounce	=	28.35 grams
1 pound	=	.4536 kilograms
1 short ton	=	.90718 metric ton
1 short ton	=	2000 pounds
1 long ton	=	1.016 metric tons
1 long ton	=	2240 pounds
1 metric ton	=	1000 kilograms
1 quart	=	.94635 liters
1 US gallon	=	3.7854 liters
1 Imperial gallon	=	4.5459 liters
1 nautical mile	=	1.852 km

To compute Celsius temperatures, subtract 32 from Fahrenheit and divide by 1.8. To go the other way, multiply Celsius by 1.8 and add 32.

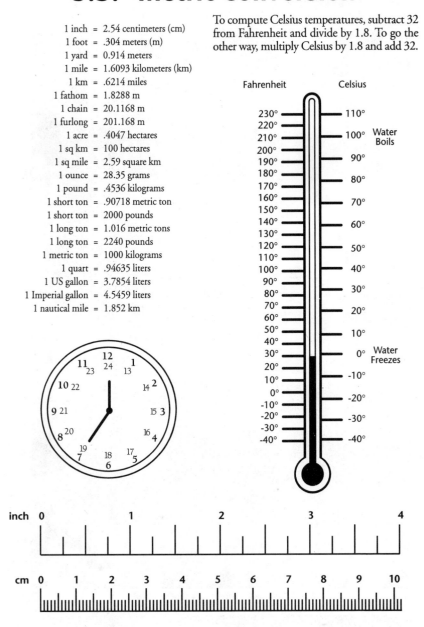

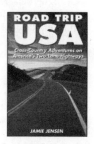

Living Abroad in Costa Rica
Avalon Travel Publishing
1400 65th Street, Suite 250
Emeryville, CA 94608, USA
www.travelmatters.com

Editor: Amy Scott
Series Managers: Mia Lipman, Erin Raber
Copy Editor: Emily McManus
Designers: Amber Pirker, Justin Marler
Graphics Coordinator: Susan Snyder
Production Coordinator: Darren Alessi
Map Editor: Olivia Solís
Cartographers: Kat Kalamaras,
    Mike Morgenfeld
Indexer: Rachel Kuhn

ISBN: 1-56691-652-6
ISSN: 1549-1412

Printing History
1st edition—September 2004
5 4 3 2

Text © 2004 by Erin Van Rheenen.
Maps © 2004 by
Avalon Travel Publishing, Inc.
All rights reserved.

Avalon Travel Publishing
An Imprint of
Avalon Publishing Group, Inc.

AVALON
publishing group incorporated

Keeping Current

Although we strive to produce the most up-to-date book that we possibly can,
change is unavoidable. Between the time this book goes to print and the time
you read it, the cost of goods and services may have increased, and a handful of the
businesses noted in these pages will undoubtedly move, alter their prices, or close
their doors forever. Exchange rates fluctuate—sometimes dramatically—on a daily
basis. Federal and local legal requirements and restrictions are also subject to
change, so be sure to check with the appropriate authorities before making the
move. If you see anything in this book that needs updating, clarification, or cor-
rection, please drop us a line. Send your comments via email to atpfeedback@
avalonpub.com, or write to the address above.